Warring with Words

Scholars in many of the disciplines surrounding politics explicitly utilize either a narrative perspective or a metaphor perspective (though rarely the two in combination) to analyze issues—theoretical and practical, domestic and international—in the broad field of politics. Among the topics they have studied are:

- competing metaphors for the state or nation which have been coined over the centuries in diverse cultures;
- the frequency with which communal and international conflicts are generated, at least in part, by the clashing religious and historical narratives held by opposing groups;
- the cognitive short-cuts employing metaphor by which citizens make sense of politics;
- the need for political candidates to project a convincing self-narrative;
- the extent to which the metaphors used to formulate social issues determine the policies which will be developed to resolve them;
- the failure of narratives around the security of the nation to take account of the individual experiences of women and children.

This volume is the first in which eminent scholars from disciplines as diverse as social psychology, anthropology, political theory, international relations, feminist political science, and media studies, have sought to integrate the narrative and the metaphor perspectives on politics.

It will appeal to any scholar interested in the many ways in which narrative and metaphor function in combination as cognitive and rhetorical instruments in discourse around politics.

Michael Hanne is Associate Professor of Comparative Literature at the University of Auckland, New Zealand. His research interests include literature of cross-cultural encounter, narrative, and metaphor across the disciplines, folktales, and reworking stories. In 2010, he convened a symposium at the University of California, Berkeley, entitled "Binocular Vision: Narrative and Metaphor in Medicine." The papers from which he edited for a special issue (volume 44, issue 3) of the journal *Genre: Forms of Discourse and Culture* in 2011.

William D. Crano is a Professor of Psychology at Claremont Graduate University. His basic research is concerned with social influence, especially the impact of minorities on the beliefs and actions of the majority, and on the effects of self-interest on attitudes and actions. His applied research is concerned with the development of persuasive and instructional information to prevent the spread of HIV/AIDS, and to prevent drug abuse, in children and adolescents. He is a fellow of the APA and APS, has been a NATO Senior Scientist, a Fulbright Fellow to Brazil, and a liaison scientist in the behavioral sciences for the Office of Naval Research, London. He also has served as the Chair of the Executive Committee for the Society of Experimental Social Psychology, and as Director of the Program in Social Psychology at NSF.

Jeffery Scott Mio is Professor in the Psychology and Sociology Department at California State Polytechnic University, having earned his PhD in clinical psychology at the University of Illinois in 1984. He specializes in three lines of research: metaphors, and their use in political persuasion; multicultural issues; and how to develop allies. He teaches multicultural issues at both the undergraduate and graduate levels in addition to social psychology, cognitive psychology, and psychopathology. Mio has published numerous articles and books and has received an Emmy award for his role as a consultant in a public television educational series.

Warring with Words

Narrative and Metaphor in Politics

**Edited by Michael Hanne,
William D. Crano, and
Jeffery Scott Mio**

Psychology Press
Taylor & Francis Group

NEW YORK AND LONDON

First published 2015
by Psychology Press
711 Third Avenue, New York, NY 10017

and by Psychology Press
27 Church Road, Hove, East Sussex BN3 2FA

Psychology Press is an imprint of the Taylor & Francis Group, an informa business

Library of Congress Cataloging-in-Publication Data

Warring with Words: Narrative and Metaphor in Politics / edited by
   Michael Hanne, William D. Crano, and Jeffery S. Mio.
      pages cm
  1. Politics.   2. Metaphor.   3. Social Psychology.   I. Hanne,
Michael.   II. Crano, William D.   III. Mio, Jeffery S.
BF575.P9N48   2014
155.9'2—dc23
2012048031

ISBN: 978-1-84872-567-6 (hbk)
ISBN: 978-1-84872-568-3 (pbk)
ISBN: 978-1-315-77601-9 (ebk)

Typeset in Times
by Apex CoVantage, LLC

Printed and bound in the United States of America by Publishers Graphics, LLC on sustainably sourced paper.

Contents

Contributors

Chiara Bottici, The New School for Social Research, USA

Lori D. Bougher, Princeton University, USA

William D. Crano, Claremont Graduate University, USA

Mark Danner, University of California at Berkeley, USA

Michael Hanne, University of Auckland, New Zealand

Phillip L. Hammack, University of California at Santa Cruz, USA

Sammyh S. Khan, University of Exeter, UK

James H. Liu, Victoria University of Wellington, New Zealand

Michael P. Marks, Stanford University, USA

Jeffery Scott Mio, California State Polytechnic University, Pomona, USA

Cris Shore, University of Auckland, New Zealand

Michael Sinding, Vrije Universiteit, Amsterdam

Annick T. R. Wibben, University of San Francisco, USA

Susan Wright, Aarhus University, Denmark

Preface

William D. Crano

When Michael Hanne, Jeff Mio, and I began planning this conference, we singly and in concert recognized the generative potential of a symposium devoted to the topic of narrative and metaphor in politics. This symposium, owing to the subject matter chosen for Claremont's Symposium on Applied Social Psychology, brought together leading intellectuals from a host of allied but distinct and independent disciplines, whose insights, understanding, and wit promised, as Horace would have it, to inform and to delight. I am happy to be able to report that the consensus of those who attended the meeting and read various chapters we have collected here was that the authors of this volume took full advantage of the opportunity. Their presentations are not just instructive, but without exception of impressive quality. Perhaps even more remarkable, the various and diverse presentations seemed to speak each to the others, to add depth and value to the other authors' views and visions. Although far from reaching paradigmatic agreement on the modes and means of understanding the forces at play in narrative and metaphor in political behavior, the creative possibilities sparked by the authors' presentations are more than impressive, especially given the diversity of their disciplines and consequent worldviews (Kuhn, 1996). Despite the range of views they expressed, their distinct visions and axiomatic presuppositions, the speakers clearly breached disciplinary boundaries, creating dialogues that both enlightened and excited. There was very little evidence of Kuhn's (1996) incommensurability in this varied group, and if you ever are in need of a good example of inter- or transdisciplinary scholarship, this conference in its totality provides all that is needed. In honesty, the editors—Mike Hanne, Jeff Mio, and I—cannot take credit for much of this, other than to claim, with no small degree of pride, that it is we who organized this meeting in the first place.

It would be next to impossible to summarize all that was said at this year's edition of the Claremont Symposium on Applied Social Psychology, or that has been written in this volume's pages, and I will not try to do so. The diversity of views, much anticipated though possibly even broader than expected, clearly may stimulate impressive and important reconsideration for many readers in the ways the substantive issues of this meeting relate to their own research.

I believe the symposium's participants and the chapters that summarize their contributions will have as stimulating an effect on its readers as they did on the live audience's thinking about narrative, metaphor, and their role in domestic and international politics.

As always, it is our happy duty to tip our collective hats to the founder and long-time director of the Claremont Symposium on Applied Social Psychology, Professor Stuart Oskamp, whose guidance and dedication was instrumental in nurturing this wonderful collection of spoken and written insights for the first quarter century of its existence. To say that the symposium would not have been possible without Stuart's devotion and strong intellectual guidance would be to state the obvious. More important is the visionary perspective that Professor Oskamp displayed in his choice of topics and speakers over the years. His work pointed the way to a truly *applied* social psychology, a movement in the field in full-throated advance. This series played an important role in bringing the field back to its roots, to research that matters, not just to the lone scientists toiling in their collective laboratories, but to the society that fosters their work. Campbell (1969) made a similar call to the field in his classic *Reforms as Experiments*, in which he argued explicitly that the scientific method be brought to bear on issues of societal importance, and implicitly that, if we were to ignore this call, the society might well find us unworthy of their further consideration. In my opinion, the current volume has gone a great distance in satisfying the requirements of both Oskamp and Campbell.

References

Campbell, D. T. (1969). Reforms as experiments. *American Psychologist, 24*, 409–429.
Kuhn, T. S. (1996). *The structure of scientific revolutions* (3rd ed.). Chicago: University of Chicago Press.

1 An Introduction to the "Warring with Words" Project

Michael Hanne

Introduction

"When a surgeon . . . cuts and cleans and amputates, and the wound bleeds, do we say to him your hands are stained with blood? Or do we thank him for saving the patient?" were the rhetorical questions posed in early June 2012 by Syrian president Bashar al-Assad, to justify the actions of his security forces, accused by international observers of torture and mass murder (Borger, 2012a). Grotesquely inappropriate though these questions will seem to most readers, Assad is, of course, far from unique among modern political leaders in using a medical metaphor to frame a questionable military or political intervention as not merely defensible but professional and praiseworthy. Terms such as "surgical strike" (Bissett, 2002), "shock treatment" (De Leonardis, 2008), and "ethnic cleansing" (Ahmed, 2010), have become all too familiar medical euphemisms over the last 20 years for state and communal violence. Global antiterrorist raids are regularly justified on the basis that "terrorism is a cancer that has long since metastasized" (Heiler, 2001). (There is an especially sick irony in the fact that Assad, himself, was trained as a doctor and embarked on advanced medical training in London, before being recalled to Syria in 1994, on the accidental death of his brother, to be groomed to take over from his father as president.)

The metaphor employed by Assad entails an implied narrative: of infection introduced from outside and/or of a carcinoma that has formed within the body politic, of exceptional measures being taken at the direction of "the doctor" to deal with these threats, of pain to be experienced by the citizen cells populating the body, and of a promise of eventual restoration of health. With such a metaphor and its associated narrative, the speaker offers a frame, or cognitive lens, through which the audience is invited to view the topic. Much of the power of the metaphor lies in its capacity to evoke an analogical narrative, without making that narrative so explicit that its aptness can easily be challenged. ("How many more amputations before the patient dies?")

The "Warring with Words" project, of which this volume is the culmination, sprang from the recognition that over the last 10 years or so researchers have increasingly focused on the key role played by narrative and by metaphor in every aspect of political theory and practice. The aspiration of this volume, and of the symposium at Claremont Graduate University in March 2012 of which it is the fruit, has been to bring together a team of eminent scholars to document more or less comprehensively current thinking on the many ways in which narrative and metaphor function as cognitive and rhetorical instruments in discourse around politics, both domestic and international. In addition to revised versions of the papers presented at the symposium, this volume includes chapters specially written on topics not covered at the symposium itself. We are above all seeking to integrate the narrative and the metaphor perspectives, which have previously been studied separately.

In this chapter I aim to identify the many strands of work on narrative and metaphor in politics, to identify the sources for each strand in the wider fields of narrative studies and metaphor studies of the last 30 years, and to illustrate some of the ways in which the two perspectives may be effectively integrated, to achieve what I have previously called "binocular vision," that is, looking equally at a subject area through both a narrative lens and a metaphor lens (Hanne, 2011). In the early part of the chapter, I shall continually return to medical metaphors and narratives, which probably constitute the most prominent and durable strand, to illustrate their extreme polyvalence.

Medical Metaphors and Narratives

Medical metaphors are regularly employed by political leaders, not only to justify their own actions, but to denigrate others and, more generally, to shape political discourse in their favor. So, for instance, British prime minister Margaret Thatcher referred to her Labour Party opponents as quack doctors whose supposed remedies would only exacerbate the country's sickness: "Labour's real prescription for Britain is the disease half the world is struggling to cure" (October 1989, quoted in Charteris-Black, 2005, p. 102). In the words of Michael Orsini and Paul Saurette (2011),

> The use of medical metaphors in politics is a well-honed rhetorical strategy. We talk of "diagnosing" political and social ills; of government having to "prescribe tough medicine"; and of politicians "sugar-coating" policies the public doesn't want to swallow. Sometimes these metaphors help clarify the political world. Other times the rhetorical comparison hides more truth than it reveals. (p. 125)

Whereas much use of narrative and metaphor by political actors is consciously emotive and so manipulative (Dunbar, 2001), certain metaphors are in general circulation, and politicians themselves may, to a considerable extent, be entangled in a web of narratives and metaphors of which they are not wholly conscious. Medical metaphors, especially, circulate widely in political discussion in the media and become part of general political discourse. A fine article on Haiti for the *New York Times* by journalist and political commentator Mark Danner is headlined, "To *heal* Haiti, look to history not nature" (2010, *New York Times*, my emphasis).[1] And, in an article for the *Guardian* on the implications of the Dayton Accord for the recovery of Bosnia after the wars in former Yugoslavia, Julian Borger (2012b) uses an extraordinarily vivid and effective medical simile: "Like a hastily applied plaster cast, it healed the wounds at the expense of setting Bosnia's bones at distorted, disfiguring angles" (p. 1).

More generally, the phrases "a healthy society" (usually, to be aspired to), or "a sick society" (referring to an existing situation in need of treatment) are in widespread circulation. A striking example is to be found in the famous Long Telegram sent to the US administration in Washington in 1946 by George Kennan, when he was American chargé d'affaires in Moscow. He first outlined the official Soviet view of capitalism in the West—that it bore "within itself germs of creeping disease" and was destined to collapse from internal convulsions and the rising power of socialism. Kennan's (1946) recommendation for future US policy towards the USSR was that "Much depends on health and vigor of our own society. World communism is like a malignant parasite which feeds only on diseased tissue. This is point at which domestic and foreign policy meet." (In these statements, he slips easily, as we all do, between metaphor and simile and, for that reason, in this chapter when discussing metaphor, I shall also be referring to the other tropes, including simile, metonymy, and synecdoche, which involve thinking by analogy in a political context.) Today, in retrospect, after the eventual collapse of communism, it is especially remarkable that Kennan had no sense that Soviet communism itself might be mortally ill.

Grand Claims for Metaphor and Narrative in Politics

Political discourse in the modern era is saturated with medical and other metaphors. In fact, it has been suggested by some scholars of politics that metaphors are the prime means by which politicians and citizens alike conceptualize, and act in, political situations. In their outstanding work *Metaphorical World Politics*, Francis A. Beer and Christ'l De Landtsheer (2004) assert that "[w]orld politics are metaphorically imagined and articulated. . . . Metaphors are significant condensation symbols of similarity and difference, inside-outside, self-other. Metaphors prime audiences and frame issues; they organize communities and cooperation; they stimulate division and conflict; they mobilize support and opposition. Domestic and international leadership and power are the subjects and the stakes in the struggle for meaning embedded in metaphorical world politics" (p. x). More specifically, Lori D. Bougher, a contributor to this volume, argues that citizens employ "metaphorical reasoning" to make sense of the abstractions and condense the complexities of the political world (Bougher, 2012). "The more abstract, complex, or unfamiliar the topic, the more likely metaphorical reasoning will be employed" (Bougher, 2012, p. 148). And, in the words of Edward Slingerland and colleagues, "metaphors guide reasoning, focus normative reactions, and create or dissipate motivations" (Slingerland, Blanchard, & Boyd-Judson, 2007). Moreover, according to anthropologist Cris Shore (1997), the influence of metaphors "is greatest when they appear natural and normal, thereby escaping our attention" (p. 150). (See also Thompson, 1996). Metaphors feature in the "struggle for meaning" in politics among political leaders, citizens, and the media.

Equally grand claims have been made for the role of narrative in politics by scholars such as Phillip L. Hammack (a contributor to this volume) and Andrew Pilecki (2012), who assert that "our political existence is fundamentally storied" (p. 97) and that political psychology is best understood in terms of a narrative framework. They highlight the role of narrative in constructing our political identity, both individual and collective, in the development of group solidarity through shared stories, and in the emergence of movements of resistance against oppressive power. They introduce the concept of "narrative engagement—that members of society engage with collective stories of what it means to inhabit a particular political entity, be it a nation-state, a resistance movement, or a political party" (Hammack & Pilecki, 2012, p. 77). They follow Bakhtin in asserting that we "navigate a polyphonic context in which multiple storylines circulate and compete for dominance and primacy in individual appropriation" (Hammack & Pilecki, 2012, p. 79). They underline the way in which leaders weave narratives relating to their personal political development into the larger narratives they construct "to frame particular political issues and to motivate adherence to a particular political agenda." (Hammack & Pilecki, 2012, p. 80). Political narratives, like political metaphors, are passed around the triangle: political protagonists, citizens, and the media.

The grand claims of Beer and De Landtshheer on the metaphor side and Hammack and Pilecki on the narrative side were, it should be said, to a considerable extent foreshadowed by Murray Edelman as early as 1971 in his *Politics as symbolic action*, where he explicitly linked metaphor and narrative. He wrote, "Metaphors and myths are devices for simplifying and giving meaning to complex and bewildering sets of observations that evoke concern. Political events and trends are typically complex and ambiguous, and they become foci of anxiety" (Edelman, 1971, p. 65).

How Narrative and Metaphor Frame
Thinking in Political Contexts

Interlinked though I suggest they are, narrative and metaphor frame our political thinking in somewhat different ways. Narrative is an interpretive device, which directs our attention to events (past, present, and future), agents, sequence, spatial and social context, and causality, in the form of a more or less unified plot. Metaphor offers a way of viewing, of seeing one item (often an abstract concept) in terms of another (often concrete). Metaphor is, on the surface at least, intuitive and atemporal and, in the words of Philip Wheelwright (1962), offers "an angle of vision, a perspective, through which reality can be held in a certain way, a unique way, not entirely commensurate with any other way" (p. 170).[2] Nevertheless, it will be argued that, in political discourse, narrative and metaphor both have cognitive and emotive dimensions, that we regularly slip backwards and forwards between the two, and that this oscillation has generally been neglected by researchers.

Modern Narrative and Metaphor Studies in Wider Context

Attention to narrative and metaphor in politics stems originally, of course, from the broad claims over the last thirty years that narrative and metaphor are "primary cognitive instruments" (Mink, 1978, p. 131) by which we interpret experience. On the narrative side, we have assertions concerning the crucial role of narrative by such thinkers as Alasdair MacIntyre (1981), Jerome Bruner (1986, 1987, 2003), and Theodore Sarbin (1986). Sarbin sums up their conclusions in stating that "human beings think, perceive, imagine and make moral choices according to narrative structure" (1986, p. 8). On the other side, we have the assertions concerning the importance of metaphor by philosophers from Aristotle to Nietzsche, Stephen Pepper, and Kenneth Burke and in the last 50 years by philosophers, psychologists and linguists, such as Paul Ricoeur (1977), Andrew Ortony (1979), and George Lakoff and Mark Johnson (1980), culminating in the latter's assertion that "[O]ur ordinary conceptual thinking, in terms of which we both think and act, is fundamentally metaphorical in nature" (Lakoff & Johnson, 1980, p. 3).

These parallel grand claims for narrative and for metaphor might be seen as complementing each other. Nevertheless, narrative studies and metaphor studies have evolved rather separately over the last 30 years and there have been few attempts to integrate them. Just a handful of thinkers have considered the two together and insisted that there is a strong connection between these devices. So Dan Cohen (1998) makes the nicely simple claim that metaphors are compressed narratives and that narratives are extended metaphors. Paul Ricoeur (1983–1985), who wrote major separate works on narrative and on metaphor, makes the more sophisticated assertion that "the meaning-effects produced by each of them belong to the same basic phenomenon of semantic innovation" (vol. 1, p. ix). Whereas metaphor "grasps together" items from different domains, narrative "grasps together" events into a newly invented plot (Ricoeur, 1983–1985, vol. 1, p. x). Both, then, are connective devices, and Deirdre (formerly Donald) McCloskey (1990) makes the intriguing suggestion that the relationship between them is "antiphonal" in the sense that, in any given situation, metaphor answers the questions that narrative cannot answer and narrative answers the questions that metaphor cannot answer. (See my article "Getting to Know the Neighbours: When Plot Meets Knot," Hanne, 1999, for further exploration of this connection.)[3] In this chapter, I aim to demonstrate the multiplicity of relationships between narrative and metaphor in the political context, in which examples may be found to illustrate the validity of all three claims.

Medical Metaphors and Narratives in 20th-Century Politics

Medical metaphors and narratives had a generally disreputable history in the 20th century, noted most particularly in Nazi speeches and documents, where undesirable groups were defined as "bugs" and there was discussion of how to "burn down to the raw flesh the ulcers of our internal well-poisoning" and "to root out all symptoms of disease and germs of destruction that threatened the political health of the state" (Szasz, 2001, p. 145). The fact that the Nazis undertook actual medical experimentation and torture on groups they regarded as undesirable illustrates a point I shall be making regularly in this chapter about the ease with which metaphors may become literalized in practice (see the United States Holocaust Memorial Museum, www.ushmm.org/wlc/en/article.php?ModuleId=10005168). Sadly, as Ilan Pappé (2004) points out, such metaphors have continued to be found in speeches and documents since 1945, including, ironically, documents written in modern Israel, one of which defined the Palestinian Arab population of Galilee as "a cancer in the Jewish body that had to be curbed and contained" (p. 227).

Nevertheless, it is also true that distinguished political leaders such as Martin Luther King, Jr. and Nelson Mandela have made regular and skillful use of medical metaphors in their speeches and writings. So, early in his campaigning, Martin Luther King, Jr. projected this vivid mini-narrative: "old man segregation is on his deathbed. But history has shown that social systems have a great last-minute breathing power and the guardians of the *status quo* are always on hand with their oxygen tents to keep the old order alive" (10 April, 1957, quoted in Charteris-Black, 2005, p. 78). On other occasions, he used a more conventional metaphor and narrative scenario: "Segregation is a cancer in the body politic, which must be removed before our democratic health can be realized" (23 June, 1963, quoted in Charteris-Black, 2005, p. 78). Nelson Mandela, in his inaugural speech as president of South Africa and, many times since, has referred to the "healing of the wounds" caused by apartheid. On a more theoretical level, Orsini and Saurette (2011) ask whether the notion of "the political placebo effect" is useful for understanding "important and observable effects other than those that would be predicted by" dominant theories (p. 125). On a rather lighter note, it is intriguing to find peace and conflict studies specialist John Paul Lederach (2005) arguing that peace agreements at the end of a conflict are "social and political antacids, temporary acid reducers that create an exit for symptomatic problems and an opportunity to create a way to work on repeated patterns and cycles of destructive relationships" (p. 48; quoted by Min, 2005). Much more dramatically, in the field of environmental politics, some activists have made the emotive claim that human beings as a whole are a "cancer on the planet." One of the strongest proponents of this metaphor unpacks its narrative implications in detail, concluding that "[a] cancerous tumor continues to grow even as its expropriation of nutrients and disruption of vital functions causes its host to waste away. Similarly, human societies undermine their own long-term viability by depleting and fouling the environment. With civilization as with cancer, initial success begets self-defeating excess" (MacDougall, 1996, p. 82). The emotive power of the metaphor in this instance derives largely from the fact that it is employed to refer to all of us, rather than to some group of Others.

It should be evident that there is great diversity of application of the medical metaphor-and-narrative combination. Sometimes, it arises on a theoretical level, sometimes in the realm of practical politics. Sometimes the emphasis is on "disease," sometimes on "treatment." Sometimes the sickness is represented as originating from outside, sometimes from within.

Opposing Sets of Narratives and Metaphors

There is, I suggest, a constant competition in progress among contrasting narratives and metaphors, employed to frame political issues. Although this has long been obvious in relation to narrative, in the context, for instance, of competing narratives advanced by political candidates about what they have achieved and aim to achieve, the point was first made in relation to metaphors, I believe, in 1971 by Murray Edelman, who wrote "alternative metaphors compete to define particular political issues; but the metaphor that is officially disseminated usually enjoys a significant advantage. It is the first definition of the issue most people receive" (pp. 71–72).[4] Any new narrative-metaphor formulation initiated by a politician may be adopted or repudiated by the media and by political commentators. Inducing commentators to adopt such metaphors must be a major achievement for any political leader. I shall refer later to the extraordinary success that George W. Bush had in selling the phrase "War on Terror" to the media and the general public. Again, in the words of Edelman (1971), "Political opposition frequently rallies around a competing metaphorical definition, of course. For those who accept it, this definition similarly becomes a continuing bulwark of conformity to the position of the group in question" (Edelman, 1971, p. 72). So, in relation to systems of healthcare, George Annas (1995) has pointed out that the "market" metaphors offered by commentators on the right (with the keywords "choice," "freedom," "competition") are increasingly countered on the left by metaphors of "ecology" (with keywords "community," "sustainability," "quality," etc.).

It is worth noting that antagonistic groups will often select a metaphorical description or slogan for themselves whose antithesis is self-condemnatory— and not the description actually chosen by those who oppose them. So, for instance, those who are "pro-life" imply that their opponents are "pro-death," whereas those opponents describe themselves as "pro-choice," thereby suggesting that those on the other side are "anti-choice."

One of the most successful rhetorical tactics in politics is to formulate a metaphor for the opposing group, which can be readily ridiculed. A fine example of such a metaphor is "trickle-down economics," a term brandished by politicians on the left to ridicule right-wing economics which those on the right have almost never embraced in relation to domestic politics (Sowell, 2012), although it was regularly used in a positive sense in relation to the economies of developing countries (Aghion & Bolton, 1997). Mitt Romney, in the first debate with Barack Obama in the 2012 presidential campaign, turned this metaphorical weapon back against those who had used it to attack his economic policies, when he accused Obama and the Democrats of favoring "trickle-down *government*" (emphasis added; Jensen & Talev, 2012). John Kenneth Galbraith (1982) made "trickle-down economics" sound even less feasible by employing the late-19th-century term, the "horse and sparrow" theory, whereby "If you feed the horse enough oats, some will pass through to the road for the sparrows."

Strong Metaphors Generate Strong Narratives

Unconventional or "strong" metaphors, and metaphors used in surprising ways, such as the "old man segregation" and the "humanity as cancer" metaphors quoted earlier, may enable creativity, provide novel insights, generate new knowledge, or, of course, provoke a hostile reaction. Donald Schön (1979) points to the use of the disease metaphor of "urban blight" in town planning, and shows that it necessarily tends to entail the policy narrative of "radical surgery," rather than a more moderate intervention. Indeed, it has been suggested that striking new metaphors actually change the schema through which we gain new knowledge (Petrie & Oshlag, 1993). It is also true that any single cluster of narratives and metaphors (such as the medical cluster) may be employed, as we have seen, to contrary purposes by opposing groups. Moreover, as Kenneth Burke (1953) was one of the first to point out in his *Rhetoric of Motives*, while a metaphor shines light on one feature of a situation, it may obscure or distort the perception of other features. In the words of Murray Edelman (1971), again, "[p]olitical metaphors . . . create and filter out value premises. They highlight the benefits that flow from a course of action and erase its unfortunate concomitants, helping speaker and listeners to conceal disturbing implications from themselves" (p. 70). So, with his metaphor of military action as surgery, Assad invites his audience to share his perspective on the actions of his military, thereby ignoring their brutality. Nevertheless, it seems highly unlikely that anyone who did not already share his view would be persuaded by this metaphor.

The "Body Politic" in the History of Political Theory

Up to this point, I have referred especially to metaphors and narratives derived from medicine, because they are employed in modern practical politics and its reporting. But these metaphors and narratives clearly grew out of political theory representing the state as a human body, going back to the Middle Ages and earlier. The notion of the body politic was first fully developed by 12th-century theologian John of Salisbury (Guilfoy, 2008; Musolff, 2009). For John, the state was best regarded as a body, with the prince as its "head," the senate being the heart, and the church being the soul. Every social group corresponded to one or another part of the body, right down to the peasants and craftsmen, who were the feet. The body metaphor not only captures notions of structure and hierarchy but also has narrative implications for the health of the society. As Andreas Musolff (2009) points out, John cited the Biblical "if your eye or your foot offend you, root it out and cast it away from you" (Matthew 18:9) to justify "*amputation* and elimination" of anyone who rebels against the divinely directed monarchical state (p. 241), a grim precedent, we may now see, for Assad's description of his policies.

Over the following centuries, the "body politic" metaphor came to be interpreted and reworked with different emphases, by thinkers from Jean Gerson to Christine de Pizane, and from Thomas Hobbes to Thomas Paine. So, whereas Gerson emphasized the authority of the princely head over the rest of the body politic, de Pizane underlined the organic dependence of all parts on each other. Such theorization evolved, and was taken up for practical purposes by rulers and political thinkers in different ways over the following centuries (Nederman, 2007; Nederman & Shogimen, 2011). In a fascinating recent essay, Kathryn Banks (2009) illustrates the extraordinary adaptability of the "body" metaphor in late-16th- and 17th-century European thought, with political unrest being sometimes represented as a disease resulting from a failure of coordination of the body's limbs or organs and sometimes from a lack of the required balance among the Galenic "humors" making up the body. (See also Musolff, 2010). At a certain moment, it was even suggested that the health of the French nation could only be assured by its being "bled" with the murder of the king (Banks, 2009, p. 209). In the early 17th century in Britain, the metaphor of the body politic was used by King James I to emphasize the complete dependence of the body on its "head" (the monarch), but when the (literal) head of King Charles was removed by execution, the metaphor of the body politic survived in modified form, with parliament being referred to as "the soul" of the new Commonwealth (Anon note, 1997, p. 1841). Thomas Hobbes, writing *Leviathan* in the context of the English Civil War, depicts the Commonwealth as a kind of artificial "body," visually represented in the famous frontispiece, whose "head" (which, in Hobbes's view should still be a monarch) will prevent warfare among the humans who make it up. (See also Skinner & Squillacote, 2010.)

Moving on another century and more, with the founding of the US, it has been suggested by several thinkers that the metaphor of the machine, designed by humans, with its "checks and balances" and "levers" took over from the metaphor of the divinely designed body that prevailed in Britain. More thorough research has shown, however, that the two metaphors coexisted in both

Britain and the US during the 18th century (Anon note, 1997). This overlap occurred, in part, because, in the 18th century, the body itself came to be represented increasingly in terms of a machine, made up of "pumps," circulating blood and other fluids through the system. As we shall see repeatedly in the discussion that follows, key metaphors in politics are almost always polyvalent, in that they are capable of being adopted and adapted for a great variety of purposes. Michael Sinding, in his chapter for this volume, takes up the complex question of images of the body politic in the 18th century.

While some commentators suggest that the metaphor of the body politic has, in large part, faded from common use, others have argued that it is still very much alive and pernicious. It seems that the medieval and Renaissance "body politic" metaphor has become blended with Pasteur's metaphor of the body as "under attack" from infectious and other diseases. Skinner and Squillacote (2010), developing the ideas of Hannah Arendt and Emily Martin, argue that this blended metaphor has generated rigid binaries of "healthy/sick" and "clean/dirty," which encourage Western states to see themselves as constantly under threat from, and by implication in a defensive war with, societies which live by other values.

Operating at a tangent with these conceptions of the modern state are the metaphors that represent the state as a named, idealized, sometimes eroticized, female body. In her chapter for this volume, Chiara Bottici refers to the mythical figure of Marianne, symbolizing the French Republic (supposedly threatened by Islamic conceptions of women in society) and, in their chapter, James H. Liu and Sammyh S. Khan discuss the utilization by Indian nationalists of the image of India as a maternal body. (See also McKean 1998.)[5] Critique amongst feminist scholars of the instrumental use of the image of the nation as female body is well summed up by Jan Jindy Pettman (1996): "Eroticizing the nation/country as a loved woman's body leads to associating sexual danger with boundary transgression" (p. 188). The woman-nation does not desire; rather she is an object of desire, which can "materialize in competition between different men for control . . . a triangle, a love story, a fairy tale is often constructed, necessitating a villain, a victim, and a hero" (Pettman, 1996, p. 188). Krista Scott (1999) adds the crucial point: "Rape as a very real and horrible act of war, formerly regarded as an insult to the men of the nation, is now beginning to be recognized as a human rights violation of a very specifically gendered nature." And, returning to the specific case of India, journalist Charukesi Ramadurai (2004) writes, "there has always been a celebration of the nation's female body—and of her citizens' male gaze—beneath the seeming veneration is the need for possession and dominance."[6]

Proliferation of Medical Metaphors in Modern Politics

The proliferation of metaphors in the modern era portraying the national leader as a doctor, charged with prescribing medicine that is unpleasant but necessary, or employing surgery, to keep the political body healthy has run in step with scientific advances in biomedicine, and specifically with the proliferation of war metaphors in the discourse of western medicine, first in reference to infectious diseases, but then in reference to cancer (Fuks, 2009). (See also my paper on narrative and metaphor in medicine; Hanne, 2011).

This is only one example of the fact, little recognized by linguists, that the transmission of meaning in metaphor is not always unidirectional. That is, the source analog can be used as a target, but the target too can act as source. Indeed, when two-way transmission occurs, there often arises a feedback effect, raising the intensity of the metaphorical effect in both directions. Deborah Tannen (1998) and others have argued that the everyday language and culture of the US, in particular, have become saturated with war metaphors—with "war on poverty," " war on drugs" being some of the best-known early examples—and that this, in turn, has tended to normalize war (in the literal sense) in our minds.

I have focused, up to this point, primarily on metaphors and narratives derived from medicine, which, as I have said, make up only one of the many seams of metaphor and narrative in political discourse (although probably the richest) to have been studied in recent years. I have sought to demonstrate, through intensive discussion of this one combination of metaphors and narratives, not only their ubiquity in political practice, theory, and comment but also the extraordinary range of political purposes for which, and rhetorical operations in which, they feature. Among the many other metaphors employed by politicians, by citizens, by political theorists and in reporting and comment on politics with which we are familiar are those of means of transport,[7] theater, sport, family relations, mechanics, accounting, music, and so forth, all of which receive appropriate mention in the pages that follow.

Scope of This Project

On several grounds, the task we have set ourselves in "Warring with Words" is very challenging. In the first place, even from this brief foray into medical metaphors and narratives, it will be evident that work on narrative and metaphor in politics has been undertaken from a range of disciplinary perspectives and on a range of specific areas and topics, by political philosophers (e.g., Guilfoy), anthropologists (e.g., Shore), international relations specialists (e.g., Beer), linguists (e.g., Charteris-Black), communication scholars (e.g., Feldman & De Landtsheer), feminist commentators (e.g., Pettman), policy specialists (e.g., Schön), and political psychologists (e.g., Hammack). They, in turn, have drawn their inspiration from work in wider narrative studies and metaphor studies by a great range of thinkers in different disciplines. Equally, it will be clear that, while some researchers focus on domestic politics, others concentrate on international relations, and while some take a primarily theoretical perspective, others pursue practical objectives, such as peacemaking. Moreover, as should be evident from the examples of research just referred to, scholars tend, with few exceptions, to follow either the narrative path or the metaphor path—rarely both.

The aim of the "Warring with Words" project is to bring this diverse array of scholars into conversation with each other—a face-to-face conversation in the context of the Claremont symposium, and a virtual conversation in the context of this volume. Given the extreme diversity of the material to be incorporated into this chapter, deciding on its organization posed a major challenge. It seemed to make sense to arrange it in three sections:

- First, there is discussion of the grand narrative schemata and grand metaphor frames at work in public debate around politics.
- Second, it focuses on some of the explanatory narratives and conceptual metaphors employed by scholars and commentators for interpreting and theorizing about domestic and international politics.
- Third, there is a survey of the many ways in which politicians, activists, journalists and citizens, seek to "do things with narrative and metaphor," the multiple narratives and metaphors in circulation, and their dynamic interaction, the use of narrative and metaphor in predicting, planning, reasoning, persuading, campaigning, and, more generally, capturing the discursive space in politics.

Inevitably there will turn out to be considerable interchange of ideas among the three levels, facilitated by those working in the media. So, for instance, politicians, who operate on what is identified here as the third, everyday practical level, are constantly mining the grand narratives and grand metaphors of the first level, as well as the explanatory narratives and metaphors envisaged by scholars on the second level, for the purpose of arguing their case, both domestically and internationally.

Because of the extreme range of topics discussed, in this chapter I inevitably skim over the depth and detail of theory in each area, seeking to illustrate the broad topography of the field with a variety of concrete examples. I leave it to my colleagues, in the specialist essays that follow, to contribute the theoretical substance on each topic. Similarly, this chapter does not aim to be encyclopedic in its bibliographical reference, preferring to list key current works, which will, in turn, lead the reader to additional bibliographical sources.

Grand Narrative Schemata and Grand Metaphor Frames

"Political Myths" and Their Associated Metaphors

As a number of political philosophers have emphasized over the last 40 years, political events on both the domestic and the international level are in large part shaped by the grand ideological narratives, taken for reality and shared by members of a society or group, which serve as "cognitive lenses" in terms of which citizens view the (political) world (Bennett, 1980; Bottici, 2007; Edelman, 1967, 1971, 1975; Flood, 2002; Hammack, 2011). These have come to be called "political myths," not in the simple sense of silly stories that are widely shared (e.g. "Barack Obama wasn't born in the US"), but in the sense of grand narratives which serve to frame a people's understanding of its own history and character. They vary by country, culture, period, and community, but some have proved remarkably durable. Examples offered by Bottici (2007) include the American myth of the Founding Fathers, the myth of the French Revolution, and the Italian myth of the "Resistance" against Nazi-Fascism. This use of the term "grand narratives" is not to be confused with Lyotard's (1984) use of the same term to refer to philosophical theories in narrative form, such as "historical progress," "the knowability of everything in science," and so on, which he sees as having lost credibility in the postmodern period.

Although "political myths" do embody some historical events, they are distinguished primarily by the perspective and emplotment given to those events. In this respect, theorists of political myth are drawing on the findings of researchers on narrative in a more general sense, who have long asserted that the prime characteristic of narrative is that it offers a perspective on the events it recounts (Gee, 1991) and that those events have been arranged into a plot (Brooks, 1984). Bottici (2007), a contributor to this volume, has highlighted the fact that political myths are not singular entities that have been definitively stated at one point in time, but are interrelational and constantly undergoing reproduction, reinterpretation, and retransmission for application to new circumstances.

A nation is likely to maintain several such myths, which operate alongside each other, and political leaders will, in different circumstances, draw on one or another of them and, when possible, lock them together. Among the myths that have held sway in the US over the last 200 years, some of the most significant have been those of American Exceptionalism, Manifest Destiny, and Civilization versus Barbarism. The concept of Manifest Destiny was first elaborated by influential journalist John L. O'Sullivan (1845) in the 1840s to justify American claims for the territories of Oregon and Texas in such declarations as "[a]nd that claim is by the right of our manifest destiny to overspread and to possess the whole of the continent which Providence has given us for the development of the great experiment of liberty and federated self-government entrusted to us" (O'Sullivan, 1845). Historian William E. Weeks has shown that the concept has built into it a bundle of claims about the virtue of the American people, its mission to spread its institutions, and its destiny under God to do so (Weeks, 1996, p. 61). It not only referred back to stories of the religious inspiration of the first European settlers and the Declaration of Independence, but also forward to American expansion across the whole North American landmass. As has been pointed out by many commentators, the concept has since then been utilized instrumentally to define the US's ideal image of itself and so frame and legitimate many of its (foreign) policies for a great variety of political purposes, right up to the justifications of the invasions of Iraq and Afghanistan by both Presidents Bush, father and son (see, e.g., Esch, 2010). A cluster of narratives has been condensed into the phrase "Manifest Destiny," which now has a great range of possible applications. Obviously, the peoples who have been subjected to the military and political actions legitimated by this grand narrative and metaphor, in the first instance, Native Americans, have their own sets of very different political myths and metaphors, concerning the same events, which will often be invisible to the dominant population.

Indigenous peoples, who have experienced invasion and colonization, strive to maintain political myths and metaphors, which will link accounts of their ancient origins and metaphors of identity with their experiences of more recent traumatic events. In my country, New Zealand, the indigenous Maori people suffered dispossession of much of their land, language, and culture in the 19th century and early 20th century at the hands of European settlers. Each tribe has its own history of the processes, including fraud, trickery, and war, by which their land was appropriated. But, in their claims for restitution over the last 30 years, a driving concept, with both narrative and metaphorical force, is that they are *tangata whenua*, meaning "people of the land." The term *whenua*, which they use for "land," also refers to the "placenta" or "afterbirth." This usage recalls the traditional narratives recounting the birth of humans from mother earth, which is ritually commemorated in the tradition of burying the placenta of a newborn baby in the soil from which its family comes (see www. maoridictionary.co.nz/index.cfm?dictionaryKeywords=tangata+whenua&sea rch.x=36&search.y=11&search=search&n=1&idiom=&phrase=&proverb=&l oan=). Similarly, a key concept in Maori culture is *whakapapa*, usually translated as "genealogy" and so often thought of by Europeans as identical with their notion of "family tree." But the term actually refers to the layers of rock or (mother) earth on which a person's identity is based. It is hard to imagine more vital images of linkage to the land that was stolen from them. Many indigenous peoples see themselves as having this kind of connection to the land on which they and their ancestors have lived, and similar metaphors are built into the political myths with which they face those who have colonized them.

Narratives and Metaphors of Identity

Understanding of the nature of political myths has been greatly enabled by the work of cognitive and social psychologists around the narrative component in our sense of personal identity (Bruner 1987; Damasio 1999; and others) and the work of sociologists and political psychologists on the national and communal stories with which people identify ("imagined communities" in the words of Benedict Anderson, 1991) and within which they imagine themselves (Anderson, 1991; Connerton 1989). Such shared stories serve to define not only national identity, but also communal identity on a much smaller scale. So, Ernest Renan (1990), in an 1882 essay, "What Is a Nation?", pointed out that under Turkish rule, in a single city, such as Salonika or Smyrna, you might find "five or six communities each of which has its own memories and which have almost nothing in common" (p. 11). Much the same was true of many Indian cities under the British Raj. Such communal narratives or collective memories are mediated by forces including family and personal experience, social class, media, culture, and religious institutions. They play a major role in fostering international and communal conflicts.

Nations and groups in antagonistic relations generally hold to contrary and competing grand political narratives and metaphors of identity, which interpret situations and events in ways that justify their own position. Examples that may be cited are almost endless. Liu and Khan, in their chapter for this collection, examine the narratives and metaphors for Indian identity offered by those struggling for independence in the first half of the 20th century. Western politicians and Islamist groups hold to contrary myths to express their understanding of Middle Eastern issues (Bottici & Challand 2006), and parties to the civil war in Yugoslavia have done the same. So, for instance, a crucial component of modern Serbian nationalism has been the myth of continuous Serb resistance to Ottoman rule since the Battle of Kosovo in 1389. I was personally confronted by the emergence of another political myth when I visited Croatia, another of the states into which Yugoslavia disintegrated, shortly after the breakup, where I was presented with a new school history book, which declared that the Croats, who had previously been referred to as an indistinguishable portion of the South Slav migrant tribes that arrived in the region in the late 6th century, were now described as a distinct people who had originally come from Persia. This amendment to the previously accepted history tends, of course, to offer greater legitimacy to the recently completed move to the independence of Croatia.

Phillip L. Hammack (2011) illustrates vividly the way in which the grand narrative of identity that any group tells of itself blends personal experience with shared narratives. So, he shows how the collective narrative shared by many young Israelis today is an amalgam of fragments derived from Biblical stories of the Jewish people, from the narrative of the diaspora, the Holocaust, and family experience in the state of Israel, whereas the collective narrative of most young Palestinians is an amalgam of fragments derived from strands of political Islam and from their experience of successive occupations, Turkish, British, and now Jewish. Whereas young Israelis "narrate redemptive stories," the "Palestinian life stories assume a tragic form that appropriates the national narrative of collective loss and continued failure to achieve independence" (Hammack, 2011; Hammack & Pilecki, 2012, p. 9). Molly Andrews (2007) is another scholar who has worked extensively on the intersection of personal and communal narratives of political experience.

Associated with the grand narratives of identity are a series of metaphors, often culturally specific, relating to fundamental beliefs about human existence, and social structure and organization. Two of the most durable such metaphors are found in Chinese culture, in which the metaphor of the state as patriarchal family, deriving from Confucius and of society as musical harmony pervade the political history of East Asia to this day. It is noteworthy that the term "harmonious society" was still a central concept in the policies of Hu Jintao (Perris, 1983; Ringmar, 2008). Martin Gannon and others have sought to identify single metaphors that, to some degree, encapsulate the attitudes and political ideas of each country. So, Gannon (2001) identifies the "Dance of Shiva" as offering a key image of circularity in biological, family, and social existence for Indian culture. Ireland is epitomized by the metaphor of "Conversation" and Britain by the metaphor of the typical, self-contained British house. In the West, the body metaphors and the machine metaphors, already discussed, have been augmented by numerous secondary metaphors—usually binary—relating to gender, religion, ethnicity, and so on. Metaphors of purity and contamination (often associated with the image of the nation as woman) are to be found in the political and religious discourse of many cultures. These metaphors are susceptible to being adapted to present conflict with another community or nation in narrative terms as an epic battle between good and evil, purity and impurity, true religion and the infidel, and/or freedom and enslavement (Charteris-Black, 2005). Such culture-specific narratives and associated metaphors come to serve as reference items that may be utilized by communal and national leaders for their own purposes. Indeed, they do not function as stable entities, but are constantly renegotiated.

Although more work has been done on the narratives and metaphors associated with conflict between ethnic and religious communities, much the same phenomenon is in operation in debate between antagonistic political parties or groups. In many cases, it is a matter of one party or faction embracing a particular narrative–metaphor formulation and the other embracing a contrasting formulation. So, for instance, on the domestic level, it is clear that, in many settler nations, notably the US, those advocating assimilation of all migrants have long maintained the "melting pot" metaphor, whereas those advocating multiculturalism have opted for metaphors such as "mosaic," "salad bowl," or "patchwork quilt" (Halstead 2007).

Reservoirs of Narratives and Metaphors on Which Opposing Sides Can Draw

However, as Robert Reich, political economist and labor secretary in Bill Clinton's first administration, explained 25 years ago, some nations or communities formulate and hold on to a set of narrative schemata (with associated metaphors) which representatives of competing parties can draw on equally. In his *Tales of a new America* (1987), he outlined four "morality tales" to which Americans of all political persuasions intuitively refer: "the mob at the gates," "the triumphant individual," "the benevolent community," and "the rot at the top." The notion that the same basic stories serve as a common reservoir on which opposing groups may draw for very different political purposes is especially important. So the tale of "the benevolent community" may be told by Democrats to highlight the desirability of a comprehensive health and social welfare program, which will serve those who encounter misfortune, whereas the same tale may be told by Republicans to show that, because we all look after our neighbors on an individual basis, there is no need for a socialized system. Crucial in the context of the present discussion is the way in which these tales come to be distilled down to phrases that are essentially *metaphorical*, for example, "the mob at the gates" and "the rot at the top," and it is this fact that makes them so open to multiple interpretations (Reich, 1987). The "rot at the top" metaphor has most recently been utilized especially to refer to bankers! The intersection of narrative and metaphor occurs at many points, including metaphors occurring as "lexical triggers," often in metaphorical form (e.g., light vs. dark) which set off one of the repository of narratives (Esch, 2010, p. 376).

It has been argued by Chiara Bottici and Benoit Challand (2010) that the "clash of civilizations" hypothesis proposed by Samuel Huntington in the mid-1990s is less a valid description of the nature of conflicts in the current period than a political myth to which, like Reich's (1987) four tales, opposing groups subscribe, but in contrasting ways. On the Western side, Islam is widely represented in the media as fanatical, opposed to modernity, and barbaric, whereas, influential Muslim sources represent the West as idolatrous, materialistic, and imperialistic (Bottici, in this volume).

Research Programs on Narrative and Metaphor by American Intelligence Agencies

The importance of narrative and metaphor in politics has been affirmed in a startling manner recently through initiatives by two American intelligence research agencies. Early in 2011, the Defense Advanced Research Projects Agency (DARPA) launched a project titled "Narrative Networks" to explore the relevance of narrative to national security. Meanwhile, a second intelligence research agency, the Intelligence Advanced Research Projects Activity (IARPA), announced a multimillion-dollar Metaphor Program to develop software for "recognizing, defining and categorizing" metaphor patterns in key languages (including Iranian Farsi and Russian) which might offer insight into the cultural beliefs and worldview of their speakers (IARPA, 2011). The two agencies have invited the collaboration of researchers from disciplines as diverse as political science, cognitive linguistics, narrative analysis, neuroscience, language research, cultural anthropology, and computational linguistics in developing instruments that might be of practical utility to the intelligence agencies.

The DARPA narrative project starts from the recognition that "[n]arratives exert a powerful influence on human thoughts and behavior. They consolidate memory, shape emotions, cue heuristics and biases in judgment, influence in-group/out-group distinctions, and may affect the fundamental contents of personal identity" (DARPA, 2011). So it is claimed that "stories are important in security contexts: for example, they change the course of insurgencies, frame negotiations, play a role in political radicalization, influence the methods and goals of violent social movements, and are likely play a role in clinical conditions important to the military such as post-traumatic stress disorder" (ibid.). It is not easy to tell how aware the originators of the project are of current work on political myth or how likely it is that the researchers will engage with the concept. Researchers are expected to "revolutionize the study of narratives and narrative influence by advancing narrative analysis and neuroscience so as to create new narrative influence sensors, doubling status quo capacity to forecast narrative influence" (DARPA, 2011). Given the technological bias of this invitation to researchers, it is unclear how much they are likely to explore the potentially very fruitful area of political myth, not only the myths propounded in countries seen as hostile to the US but also, at least as important, the myths that are so frequently embodied in the international attitudes and policy of the US itself.

The IARPA (2011) project "will exploit the fact that metaphors are pervasive in everyday talk and reveal the underlying beliefs and worldviews of members of a culture." It aims to "develop automated tools and techniques for recognizing, defining and categorizing linguistic metaphors associated with target concepts and found in large amounts of native-language text." It will then seek to "characterize differing cultural perspectives associated with case studies of the types of interest to the Intelligence Community" (IARPA, 2011). Commentators suggest it will especially examine the part played by metaphors in fostering terrorism and insurgency (Madrigal, 2011). The grand cultural–political metaphors held by people in other cultures and nations, which I have referred to earlier, should be of the greatest possible interest to the originators of the project. Yet here, too, it seems that the agency, in emphasizing technological analysis of "large amounts of text" in key languages has missed several crucial points. The push to automization, assuming, as it does, that language is static and that human beings work as simple stimulus-response machines, ignores some of the fundamental findings of cognitive science.[8] Insight into the constantly shifting grand metaphors through which politicians and citizens of other countries frame their political thinking and behavior is almost certainly more readily gained from specialists in the culture, language, history, and politics of the countries concerned. Moreover, it appears that they, too, are missing the point that it is just as important and illuminating to analyze and evaluate the grand metaphors of their own culture and country.

Explanatory Narratives and Conceptual Metaphors Used by Scholars of Politics

Only quite recently have scholars working in the various subfields of political studies come to examine critically the narratives and the metaphors that they themselves employ in theorizing about politics and interpreting political situations and events. Here, too, studies on metaphor have generally been conducted separately from studies on narrative.

Narrative in the Writing of Political History

Work on the narrative side stems from the fundamental challenge faced by political historians and commentators of explaining how a major event, whether in a domestic or international context, occurred—let alone of predicting how a situation might develop in the future. How did the transition from the apartheid regime to a multiracial democracy occur in South Africa? How did the collapse of the communist regimes in the USSR and Eastern Europe occur? How precisely did the Global Financial Crisis (GFC) come about, and why was it predicted by so few economists? And, looking to the future, when and how will the world emerge from the GFC? When and how will the terrible conflict in Syria end? According to Suganami (2008), the importance and problematic nature of narrative as explanation is often neglected in international relations, but much the same may be said of domestic politics. (See also Fasolt, 2004; Roberts, 2008.)

While historians long asserted that their profession involved reconstructing the past as it actually was, it has increasingly been acknowledged (Dray, 1971; White, 1984; Fasolt, 2004; etc.) that story forms are largely imposed on inherently shapeless and shifting events by narrators who must select from an infinite number of events and shape them in the light of a specific ideological framework (Miller, 1995; Suganami, 2008). In the words of philosopher of history Robert Anchor (1987), the function of narrative is to make "meaningful totalities out of scattered events by means of a plot or storyline" (pp. 133–134). It follows that radically different narrative interpretations may be imposed by commentators on a single cluster of events. As Suganami points out, conflicting narratives of "the same event" are likely to start from different points and to respond to different questions "and this is largely an issue of politics and ethics" (Suganami, 2008, p. 342). Nevertheless, an historical narrative will generally be presented as "coherent, meaningful, and relevant for the theoretical purposes the author specifies" (Wolfgram & Stevens, 2007). Suganami (2008) asserts that the three components of narrative explanation of political events are "chance coincidences, mechanistic processes and human acts" (p. 334). In assessing the validity of any particular account of events, we need to examine not only which data the commentator has included, and which excluded in that account, but the narrative devices, especially perspective, employed in its construction. One of the most vivid illustrations of multiple narratives that have been constructed around "the same event" is to be found in the numerous books written in the 1990s purporting to explain the origins of the war in Bosnia, each of which selects and recounts events differently. David Campbell (1998) offers a brilliant review of ten such books in his article "Metabosnia: Narratives of

the Bosnian War." He concludes that, while it makes sense to "give greater cre-
dence to those accounts which are more comprehensive, or more self-reflexive
about their own presuppositions" (Campbell, 1998, p. 279), no single narrative will emerge as the only plausible one. He therefore follows Nietzsche in
advocating that "only through the clash of competing narratives are we likely
to assemble justifiable knowledge" (Campbell, 1998, p. 281).

To take up another of the cases referred to earlier, there has been much
debate around how large a role Western powers, and especially the US under
the presidency of Ronald Reagan, played in the fall of the Berlin Wall and the
collapse of the Soviet Union, and how much that collapse was due rather to
internal economic and social factors and the personal intervention of Mikhail
Gorbachev. Behind such narratives lie broader theoretical debates over the
attribution of agency, causality, and motivation versus structure in such narratives (Zashin & Chapman, 1974). As I wrote this section, in the weeks preceding the 2012 presidential election, there was ongoing debate in the US about
whether the slowness of the American economic recovery since 2008 was the
consequence primarily of inadequate policies on the part of President Obama,
obstructionism by the Republicans in Congress, or of economic and political
factors mainly outside the control of American politicians.

Metaphors in Political Theory and Analysis and the Narratives They Entail

Research on metaphors employed by political analysts and theorists has probably been even more wide-ranging than research on the narrative side. Major
recent works are Michael P. Marks's (2011) *Metaphors in international relations theory* and Terrell Carver and Jernej Pikalo's (2008) edited volume
Political language and metaphor: Interpreting and changing the world, the
latter dipping into areas of both international and domestic politics. (See also
Okulska & Cap, 2010, *Perspectives in politics and discourse*.) Central to their
discussions is the assertion that metaphors are employed not merely for adorn-
ment or persuasion, but as constitutive elements in the theory itself. In the
words of Carver and Pikalo, "[m]etaphors . . . inform and structure thinking
on discourses and contexts" (2008, p. 4). These two works sketch considerable
portions of the history of political theory in terms of the metaphors which have
dominated in different periods. See, for instance, Pikalo's (2008) account of
the shifts in European theory in the eighteenth century between organic and
mechanical metaphors. And indeed, they point out that the names of many
theories related to politics take the form of metaphors: "game" theory, "chaos"
theory, "constructivist" theory, and so on. (On chaos theory in political science, see Font & Régis, 2006.)

In addition, they show how each of the schools of political theory in the
modern period tends to adhere to a different set of key conceptual metaphors.
So, for instance, the Realist school of international relations adheres to the

metaphor, coined by Hobbes in *Leviathan*, of states as "billiard balls" which collide with each other from time to time (Marks, 2011, p. 6). According to this metaphor, there are no good or bad states and "[o]nly the hard exteriors touch, and heavier or faster moving ones push others out of the way" (Burton, 1972, p. 28). (The "domino theory" of the Cold War period was, in a sense, an adaptation of this metaphor.) By contrast, the Liberal school sees international relations as a "web" or "cobweb" in which relations among states are in the form of intertwined threads (Marks, 2011, p. 6). The Constructivist School of international relations, which rejects the materialist theory (and metaphors) of both the Realists and the Liberals, appreciates, indeed encourages, the proliferation of metaphors, insisting that each metaphor takes its part in "constructing" the world it purports to describe: whether they are metaphors of the state as "container," "motion," "leverage," "balance of power," "sphere of influence" (and other mechanical metaphors); "the body," "family," "evolution" (and other biological and social metaphors); politics as a stage, with actors, and "theatres of war"; politics in terms of "profit and loss"; and so forth. Moreover, any single metaphor or metaphor cluster in the realm of political theory may generate a great variety of interpretations and narrative implications. Richard Little (2007), for instance, has shown that the notion of "balance of power" between nations, far from being an unambiguous reality, is a metaphor, which has been understood and applied in a wide range of different ways over the last 500 years.

Metaphors in Economics and the Narratives They Entail

Much interesting work on the metaphors employed in economics has been undertaken by economists with a background in the study of rhetoric. The key figures in this research are Deirdre McCloskey (1985, 1990, 1994, 2006, 2010), Philip Mirowski (1989), and Arjo Klamer (Klamer & Leonard 1994; Klamer 2009; Klamer & McCloskey 1991). It was McCloskey, in the early 1980s, who initiated discussion of "the rhetoric of economics." In the late 1980s, Mirowski argued that neoclassical economics was founded on (archaic) metaphors deriving from 19th-century physics. Klamer has surveyed the wide range of metaphors employed in economics. With Thomas C. Leonard, he has written a fascinating overview of the field, entitled "So what's an economic metaphor?" (Klamer & Leonard, 1994). They assert that metaphors function in economic discourse in four main ways: as heuristic devices we all, economists and laypeople, employ to conceptualize fresh ideas; as constitutive devices directly employed in theorizing; as pedagogical devices for communicating abstract concepts to laypeople; and as devices for persuading the general public of the desirability of this or that policy.

It would be both inappropriate and impossible to attempt to catalogue and analyze their rich findings here, and I shall limit myself rather to a brief summary of the reservoir of metaphors and narratives (some, but not all, originally generated by economists) on which politicians draw in discussing their policies and records, and on which activists and the general public draw in discussion of economic matters.

We find three major clusters of metaphors in traditional discourse around economics: metaphors of engineering/physics, organic/body metaphors, and social metaphors. So, in the engineering/physics dimension, we talk of "price mechanisms," "equilibrium," "elasticities," "inflation," "policy instruments," "accelerators," "rise and fall in GNP," "pump priming," "overheating," and so on and so on. In the "organic" dimension, we speak of the economy being "sick," "healthy" or "unhealthy," "suffering," "in recovery," and of "economic prescriptions," among others. Of course, the metaphor of "the market" is neither mechanical nor organic; it is social, evoking, as it does, a vision of growers bringing to a town center the fruit and vegetables they have produced and making them available to willing consumers who will buy them on the basis of quality and price. So, "production and consumption," "supply and demand," "rational choice," "consumer satisfaction," and so forth are the buzzwords. Another key social metaphor, that of the journey, with its "ups and downs," "deviations," and "crossroads," more than any of the other clusters perhaps, obviously entails a range of possible narratives. Of course, many common notions in economics may be read as deriving from two clusters. So the concepts of "consumption" and "overheating" may be thought of as both mechanical and organic, whereas "social engineering" explicitly combines two clusters.

I shall leave further discussion of economic metaphors and narratives to the next major section of this chapter, where I shall seek to describe the main ways in which politicians, activists, and the public employ instrumentally the metaphors and narratives for the economy coined by economists.

Contesting Conventional Narratives and Metaphors

Some of the most interesting work on narrative and metaphor in political theory has been undertaken by scholars in indigenous and third-world studies, gender studies, and peace and conflict studies. They not only critique the metaphors and narratives conventionally employed in economics and international relations but also offer alternative metaphors and alternative narratives to represent more adequately the situation and experience of poor nations and marginalized groups. So Amartya Sen (1999) highlights the way in which the metaphor "development" has been identified exclusively with growth in GDP, industrialization, and social modernization, omitting reference to the freedoms (political freedoms, economic facilities, social opportunities, transparency guarantees, and protective security) which he sees as the goals to which development should aspire. In addition, he draws attention to the narrative and metaphorical inadequacy of most explanations of the incidence of hunger globally: "For the elimination of hunger in the modern world, it is crucial to understand the causations of famines in an adequately broad way, and not just in terms of some mechanical balance of food and population" (Sen, 1999, p. 161).

Similarly, feminist international relations specialists, such as Cynthia Enloe (1990), J. Ann Tickner (2001), Christine Sylvester (2013), and Annick T. R. Wibben (2011; a contributor to this project), underline the way in which conventional security studies narratives, focused as they are on high diplomacy, neglect the involvement of women and children as victims of state violence, ignore the possibility that women might influence state policies, and, more generally, fail to ask how the "security" of women, physical and psychological, might be better assured (Chisem, 2011). A number of scholars, especially feminist political scientists, have stressed the need to look behind the grand narratives of international politics and security, to seek out and record the complex and highly differentiated stories of personal experience, which frequently contradict, or at least complicate, the grand narratives (e.g., Chilton, 1996; Andrews, 2007; Wibben, 2011). Others have explored the implications of the use of terminology derived from drama in international relations (e.g., Sylvester, 2003). Scholars working in peace and conflict studies direct attention to the ways in which nations are drawn into conflict situations by the adoption of irreconcilable narratives of history and identity, spurred on by politicians and military leaders using inflammatory metaphors and narrative scenarios, and may be assisted to mend their relations likewise by mediators making skilful use of narrative and metaphor.

I shall detail and explore these kinds of critical and creative work by scholars in the following, final section of this chapter.

How Politicians, Activists, Journalists, and Citizens Seek to "Do Things With Narrative and Metaphor"

Making Sense of Politics With Narratives and Metaphors

Citizens need narrative to make sense of the political world. The narratives they create, or which are supplied to them respond to the questions, "What has happened? What is happening? How do I fit into this story? What might/should happen?" But they also need to fit those narratives into the grander narratives with which their social lives are framed. In the words of J. Hillis Miller (1995), "[t]he human capacity to tell stories is one way men and women collectively build a significant and orderly world around them" (p. 67). Equally, they need metaphors, to answer the questions, "What is this situation like? What model can I apply to this situation to think about how it might be resolved?" And, again, such metaphors will derive from, or need to be reconciled with, the grand metaphors through which they perceive their lives. In the words of Seth Thompson (1986), "Politics without metaphors is like a fish without water" (p. 185). In her chapter for this volume, Lori D. Bougher develops a comprehensive argument about the heuristic role of both narrative and metaphor in what she calls "civic cognition" and its implications for the education of citizens.

Although politicians exploit the need of citizens for political narratives and for metaphors, sometimes, but not always, effectively, and sometimes, but not always unscrupulously, they also need narratives and metaphors themselves to make sense of the political world. Unlikely though it may seem, politicians sometimes actually subscribe to the narratives and metaphors they utter.

Narrative, Metaphor, and Persuasion

The relevance of both narrative and metaphor to political persuasion is strong. Just as Ted Cohen (1979) represents metaphor as inviting the addressee to "intimacy," so Ross Chambers (1984) refers to the "seductive" power of narrative. While narrative draws the audience into understanding a situation in terms of the characters, agency, motivation, and causal connections proposed by the author, so metaphor draws the audience into viewing the situation through the conceptual lens proposed by the person who utters it. Politicians and activists seek to frame public thinking and discourse in relation to their actions and policies (past, present, and future) by the selection of narratives and metaphors, which will crystallize, often in simplified form, the situations in which they are embroiled. More generally, they compete with their rivals to capture the discursive space in politics. So, linguistics scholar George Lakoff and coauthor Elisabeth Wehling (2012) have recently published *The Little Blue Book: The Essential Guide to Thinking and Talking Democratic*, in which they assert that Democrats need to rework the language (especially the metaphors) of politics on their own terms: "They (conservatives) frame public debate in their own language over the whole range of issues. . . . And once they get the public thinking their way, they can control the media, elect their candidates, pass their legislation, and create a new status quo" (p. 62).

On the international level, too, governments interact with each other, whether in collaborative or antagonistic fashion largely by means of narrative and metaphor. Any pronouncement by a leader on international issues has both a domestic audience, in his or her own country, and an audience, of both politicians and citizens, in other countries. There have been comprehensive studies of the repertoire of metaphors employed by leading politicians and political activists in their speeches and writings, most notably *Politicians and rhetoric: The persuasive power of metaphor* by Jonathan Charteris-Black (2005), in which he examines the utterances of figures from Winston Churchill to Tony Blair, and from Martin Luther King, Jr. to George W. Bush, as they have sought to establish their ethical integrity, heighten the emotional impact of their message, and communicate their policies. Charteris-Black treats the stories told by each political figure as secondary to the metaphors they use, focusing especially on the way in which the use of a metaphor by a politician (e.g., of a country being "swamped" by immigrants) may trigger a political myth (that immigrants will come to outnumber natives; 2005, p. 23).

There have also been studies of narrative and metaphor in terms of their relevance to the psychology (including psychopathology) of political leaders. Ralph Pettman (2011), in his *Psychopathology and world politics*, explores the role of deluded narratives and metaphors in maintaining not only the self-belief of unhinged national leaders, but also the hold they have over their followers. (Perhaps Bashar Al-Assad really *does* believe that he is the "surgeon" fighting to save the life of his people? See also Robins & Post, 1997.)

Metaphor and Narrative in Public Debate About Economics

Returning to the clusters of metaphors for the economy generated by economists, it has been suggested by some commentators that politicians and activists on the left adhere primarily to the "engineering" metaphors (favoring, as they generally do, government interventions in such areas as regulation and taxation), whereas those on the right prefer the organic metaphors (as they expect a "sick" economy to recover if only the "fresh air" of deregulation is assured). See, for instance, a blog by P. Rosenberg (2011), titled "The Economy Is a Machine, Not a Body: The Unseen Power of Metaphors in Guiding How We Think Could Be Key to Escaping from a Prolonged Economic Crisis." Illuminating usage on the other side, John Papola and Russ Roberts (2011) produced a wonderful rap spoof "Fight of the Century," in which their caricature of F. A. Hayek, chants, "The economy's us, we don't need a mechanic/Put away the wrenches, the economy's organic" (see http://econstories.tv/2011/04/28/fight-of-the-century-music-video/). Nevertheless, a glance at public discussions about the economy, such as the policy statements of the Republican and Democrat candidates in the 2012 US presidential election reveals a more confused picture. While Mitt Romney's team certainly spoke of the economy as being "weak" and "anemic," of government spending as "bloated," of the need for "a budget framework that does not threaten our fiscal health" and for "a healthy financial system," it also referred to "the wrenches that the Obama administration has thrown into the economy," its tendency to "ratchet up permanently the size of government," and the need to "reignite the job-creating engine of the United States" and "repair the nation's tax code." It also regularly employed metaphors from the "journey" cluster, referring to the need to get the economy "back on the rails," to the way in which, under previous Republican administrations, "[a]fter we hit bad patches, as in the early years of Ronald Reagan's presidency, the economy came roaring back," and to the Republican candidate having an economic "road map" for the future.

Interestingly, the Democrats employed all of the same metaphor clusters—mechanical, organic and social—but with a different weighting and effect. The social metaphors were particularly prominent. In some of his speeches about the domestic economy, Barack Obama wove rich tapestries of narrative and metaphor, which drew on domains outside those to which economists themselves refer. At the start of a major speech in Osawatomie, Kansas, in late 2011, Barack Obama, began by asserting "I have roots here" and went on to weave together story elements from the lives of his maternal grandparents in World War II ("He was a soldier in Patton's army; she was a worker on a bomber assembly line"), their belief "in an America where hard work paid off, and responsibility was rewarded, and anyone could make it if they tried" and the rise of "the largest middle class and the strongest economy that the world has ever known." Then he sought to tell the story of the decline of the American middle class:

> the basic bargain that made this country great has eroded. Long before the recession hit, hard work stopped paying off for too many people. Fewer and fewer of the folks who contributed to the success of our economy actually benefited from that success. Those at the very top grew wealthier from their incomes and investments—wealthier than before. But everyone else struggled with costs that were growing and paychecks that weren't . . . (Obama, 2011)

So the current crisis did not come out of the blue and, in his account of its origins, he inserted a host of homely metaphors: "for many years, credit cards and home equity loans *papered over* this harsh reality. But in 2008, *the house of cards collapsed* . . . innocent, hardworking Americans who had met their responsibilities . . . were still *left holding the bag*" (Obama, 2011, my italics). The Republicans, he said, "want to go back to the same policies that *stacked the deck* against middle-class Americans for way too many years. Their philosophy is simple: We are better off when everybody is left to fend for themselves and play by their own rules" (Obama, 2011). Although Obama was directly addressing the middle-class citizens of Kansas, he was actually seeking to communicate with those who see themselves as middle class, all over the country, including those with jobs and those who have become unemployed, those who have retained their houses, and those who have lost their homes. Through both the narrative fragments and the metaphors, he was seeking to build both a collective memory and a collective vision for the future with a large portion of the American population. (In their chapter for this volume, Cris Shore and Susan Wright highlight the contrasting narratives and metaphors employed by George W. Bush and Barack Obama in international affairs.)

One of the most striking specific contrasts in the use of a single metaphor between the utterances of Romney and Obama relates to the term *family*. Romney and the Republicans (and especially the Tea Party movement) have used the term to refer to their mandatory ideal of a heterosexual married (Christian) couple and their children and make a quite misleading analogy between the economics of a government and the economics of running a household. Obama, by contrast, regularly employs the term in a strongly metaphorical sense to encompass the American population as a whole, in all its ethnic, political, social, and sexual diversity.

A dramatic metaphor from the social (journeying) cluster which recurred regularly in the economic discourse of both major parties towards that of the "fiscal cliff" which the US faced at the end of 2012 (resulting in tax increases, spending cuts, and a corresponding reduction in the budget deficit) if new legislation was not agreed. George Lakoff, 2012, wrote a wonderful little blog, titled "Why It's Hard to Replace the Metaphor of the 'Fiscal Cliff,'" discussing

Paul Krugman's suggestion that the real danger of the present situation is the Republicans' proposal for an "austerity bomb" and Robert Reich's recommendation that "bungee-jumping over the fiscal cliff" would be a better strategy (Lakoff, 2012). Another, homely, typically American, metaphor on which the two parties have diametrically opposed views is that of the economic "pie." For those on the right, the priority is to "grow the pie" (on the assumption that all will benefit from that growth), whereas those on the left focus more on the fairness of the distribution of the pie, whether it is growing or shrinking.

Within western economies, there is wide agreement that "the market" is a key factor in economic prosperity. The major disagreement concerns the extent to which the functioning of the market should be regulated by legislation and be counterbalanced by social considerations. For those on the right, the term "market" is used as if it denoted a literal (indeed unquestionable) reality. A major objection from those on the left is the way in which, by a further metaphorical leap, it is applied (again often unquestioningly) to fields such as healthcare and education. So the hospital patient and the school or university student are now "customers" or "clients" who are offered "consumer choice" among competing institutions, which should be obliged to lay out their wares in front of them. This process has reached the point where the concept of "the citizen" has been split into the very different concepts of "stakeholder" and "consumer" (Patterson, 1998; Yeager, 2011). Political and economic theorists should doubtless take some responsibility for the tendency to employ metaphor in such reductive and literalizing ways. It is noticeable that economists who seek to debunk neoclassical economics regularly deploy analogies with the history of other disciplines to illustrate how backward their opponents are. So economist Steve Keen (2011), for instance, asserts, "The reason they continue with this delusion [free market economics] is for the same reason that astronomers stuck with the Ptolemaic version of the solar system long after anomalies were discovered between the theory's predictions and observation: it's all they know, and their whole world is organized around it" (Pilkington, 2011).[9] I look forward eagerly to the undergraduate economics textbook long promised by Deirdre McCloskey, Arjo Klamer, and others titled *The Economic Conversation*, now projected to be published by Palgrave/Macmillan in 2014.

Environmental and third-world activists have developed their own traditions of metaphor (and narrative) usage in relation to economic and associated issues (Luks, 1998). I have already referred to Amartya Sen's (1999) critique of the terms "growth" and "development" as they have been conventionally used, without reference to human rights and fair distribution of wealth. By and large, the metaphors they employ link the organic and the social domains, to assert that human beings should see themselves as members of a fragile ecological system which encompasses all of humanity and the physical world—and the term *system* is used in an organic, rather than mechanical sense. The terms *renewable, sustainable, interdependence, depletion or degradation of natural resources*, and *species extinction* recur (United Nations Environment Program, 2011).

Politicians Employ Narrative and Metaphor in Relation to International Conflicts

When politicians speak on international topics, they are generally addressing both a domestic and a foreign audience, and the latter may be divided between the specialists (politicians, diplomats or businesspeople) and a more general foreign audience. One of the difficulties of such speeches is that a narrative or a cluster of metaphors may work well with one of those audiences and badly with another. One of the most striking modern examples of a metaphor that hit the wrong note for a large part of the foreign audience (as well as many in the domestic audience) was that chosen by President George W. Bush in announcing the first retaliatory action after the attacks of September 11 2001, "[t]his *crusade*," which was understood, not surprisingly, by many Muslims who may have had no sympathy for Al-Qaeda, as foreshadowing a general attack on Islam.

By contrast, President Obama used a speech in Cairo in May 2009 to try to set the relationship between the US and the countries of the Middle East on a new and more positive footing. As with the Osawatomie speech, he wove together narrative fragments of several different kinds to remarkable effect. He spoke of the 1,000-year history of the Islamic institutions of learning that hosted him; centuries of coexistence and cooperation between Middle Eastern countries and the West, but also the history of conflict and religious wars; the regrettable reality of Western colonialism in the Middle East in the 20th century; the growing sense among Muslims that the West is hostile to Islam; the attacks on US soil of 9/11; his own early personal positive familiarity with Islam, growing up in Indonesia; the curious fact that Morocco was the first nation in 1796 to recognize the newly established US. With this composite narrative he sought to evoke a context in which a positive relationship between the US and the countries of the Middle East might seem feasible. The initial response from political leaders in the region (with the exception of the leadership in Iran) was very positive. How it was received in Kansas, I do not know.

Political actors may seek to build a relatively sustained narrative (as Obama did in his Cairo speech) or they may make a series of brief narrative utterances, whether in statement or question form, which do not constitute a complete narrative. This was the tactic of Iranian President Mahmoud Ahmadinejad when he made his notorious speech attacking the US and the West to the United Nations on September 22, 2011. Cleverly, he mixes statements; for example, "Approximately, three billion people of the world live on less than 2.5 dollars a day, and over a billion people live without having even one sufficient meal on a daily basis" and questions, for example, "Who abducted forcefully tens of millions of people from their homes in Africa and other regions of the world during the dark period of slavery, making them a victim of their materialistic greed?" and a reference to the assistance the US and Britain had previously given to Saddam Hussein in the war between Iraq and Iran, all of which it was difficult for anyone to contradict, with statements, which few could accept, doubting the reality of the Holocaust and alluding to "the mysterious September 11 incident," in such a way as to suggest that the latter was orchestrated by the US administration to offer a pretext for attacking Afghanistan and Iraq.

On occasions, a metaphorical term will come to circulate widely in one part of the world in relation to events in another part, with those who use it assuming wrongly that the protagonists in those events have used it about themselves. A prime current example is the term *Arab Spring*, which was apparently coined by American commentator Marc Lynch in the journal *Foreign Policy* in January 2011 and was taken up generally in the West. As Arab politics scholar Joseph Massad has pointed out, the term used by activists in the various states of North Africa and the Middle East is rather "the Arab Revolution" (Massad, 2012). Moreover, Massad asserts that "[t]he dubbing of the uprisings in the Arab world by western governments and media as 'Arab Spring' . . . was not simply an arbitrary or even seasonal choice of nomenclature, but rather a US strategy of controlling their aims and goals." The West was illegitimately seeking to associate itself with, and even take some credit for, uprisings against regimes that had actually "served US interests faithfully for a long time" (Massad, 2012).

It has been pointed out that political leaders will often construct metaphor clusters in an international context, whose ambiguity they exploit in the defense of their actions and policies. One of the most vivid examples of this is detailed by Dalia Gavriely-Nuri (2010), who catalogues the many ways in which successive Israeli leaders have employed the phrase "extend the hand of peace" to justify their policies towards the Palestinians and Lebanon. From its first articulation in "The Declaration of the Establishment of the State of Israel" (1948), "it has been repeated endlessly in speeches made by Israeli political leaders . . . While expressing the sincere will to make peace, use of the metaphor simultaneously demonstrates moral superiority, feelings of deprivation, latent threats, and recognition of its handiness for creating a positive image abroad" (Gavriely-Nuri, 2010, p. 449). The extreme elasticity of its use by different Israeli leaders is best illustrated in the words of Moshe Dayan and Yitzchak Rabin. Following Israel's victory in the 1967 Six-Day War, Dayan made the essentially self-contradictory declaration: "We have returned to the most sacred of our holy places. We have returned in order never to be separated again . . . To our Arab neighbors, we extend, even at this hour—and especially at this hour—our hand in peace" (quoted in Gavriely-Nuri, 2008, p. 458). Rabin used "a creative and picturesque version of the metaphor" (Gavriely-Nuri's words) in response to a Palestinian terror attack just a year after signing the Oslo Accords in 1993: "Our hand is always extended in peace but its fingers are always on the trigger" (quoted in Gavriely-Nuri, 2008, p. 458). The phrase "extend our hand in peace" has, she asserts, become a public relations phrase, which will be picked up by Israel's supporters internationally as a sign of their good faith. She goes on to point out that, by 2002, Yasser Arafat "had learned to use the metaphor's connotations to turn the tables on the Israelis" (Gavriely-Nuri, 2008, p. 461). Leaders on both sides were asserting that their sincere offers of peace were meeting with no response.

One of the moments that most fully challenge politicians' rhetorical powers is when they take a nation into war—or into a form of military intervention that they choose not to call war. In recent times, examples of the former would include the first President Bush taking the US into the First War in Iraq, and the second President Bush and British prime minister Tony Blair taking their countries into wars in both Afghanistan and Iraq, and an example of the latter is the US intervention in Haiti after the earthquake. The narratives they constructed and the metaphors, old or new, which they employed played crucial roles in their attempts to legitimate their actions and persuade the leaders of other countries and their own citizens. In the case of the First Iraq War, George Lakoff (2003) was one of the first to highlight the role of metaphor in the president's justification of the war. "Metaphors can kill. The discourse over whether to go to war in the Gulf was a panorama of metaphor" (Lakoff, 2003). He drew attention to the reliance on the "widespread, relatively fixed set of metaphors" of cost-benefit and the implicit underlying metaphors of politics as business and morality as accounting (ibid.). In addition, there was the process of personification, by which Iraq was identified with Saddam Hussein and the war was represented as a form of hand-to-hand combat. "Thus, the US sought to 'push Iraq back out of Kuwait' or 'deal the enemy a heavy blow,' or 'deliver a knockout punch'" (ibid.). (As Charteris-Black, 2005, indicates, the identification of the whole population of Iraq with its government actually involves a process of depersonification, which tends to make the killing of non-military citizens more acceptable.) Lakoff also pointed out that elements from the typical fairy tale were applied to the war. In referring to the Iraqi invasion of Kuwait as "rape," Bush evoked the stock figures of narratology: Saddam Hussein as villain, Kuwait as victim, the United States and its partners as heroic rescuers, Saudi Arabia as benevolent helper etc., though many of us had difficulty in seeing the corrupt royal family in Kuwait as a damsel in distress (Lakoff, 2003). In the case of the Second Iraq War, there has been much criticism of the lack of truthfulness of the narrative by which the second President Bush justified the invasion, especially the claims that Saddam Hussein was building up new weapons of mass destruction and that Al-Qaeda was active in Iraq and of the amnesia shown by the American and British leadership about their earlier support for Saddam Hussein, now judged villainous, during the Iran–Iraq war. In addition, Bush's confidence that the "liberation" of Iraq would be achieved quickly and (relatively) painlessly proved misplaced.

In initiating military intervention, US administrations have often combined narrative and metaphor in formulae by which they deny that the present case will follow the pattern of some earlier (disastrous) intervention; for example, "this will not be another Vietnam," and intervening in Haiti after the earthquake "will not be like Somalia" (Freeman, 2009). It is likewise regularly argued that the failure to intervene at an early point in a conflict situation would involve Munich-like appeasement (Thompson, 1996, p. 192).

The rhetorical strategy of reductive identification of a country with its leader or even with a faction within its government, for example, Iran with President Ahmadinejad or Palestinians with the Hamas leadership, is particularly common (Wendt, 1992). It is found in the extraordinary statement by presidential candidate Romney that "the Palestinians have no interest whatsoever in establishing peace" (Stein, 2012).

A key metaphorical formula that has circulated over the last 11 years has been "the War on Terror." Its acceptance by most of the media and, consequently, by a high proportion of ordinary citizens is, to say the least, alarming. There has, in fact, been little recognition that the phrase is indeed a metaphor—the tendency is rather to understand it literally. There have, even so, been several significant attempts at deconstruction of the metaphor. Stuart Croft, for instance, sees the phrase as embodying a meta-narrative with four main elements: (1) the construction of the enemy as a bunch of evil-doers who attacked innocent U.S. citizens because they hate freedom and democracy; (2) the idea that no one within the federal government should be blamed for what happened on September 11, 2001; (3) the claim that the United States has the sacred mission to fight for freedom and justice; (4) the belief this fight should take a global form, under the leadership of the United States but with strong international support (Croft, 2006).

More specifically, and currently, there is much discussion of the implications for counter-terrorist activity of the various metaphors chosen to represent terrorism (Kruglanski, Crenshaw, Post, & Victoroff, 2007). One of the most interesting examples is the paper by Kruglanski et al. (2007) who analyze the very different metaphors for describing the phenomenon of terrorism itself: as "war," as "disease," as "crime," as "product of prejudice." They argue that each of these four main metaphors generates a corresponding metaphor for counter-terrorism: "defensive war," "containment of social epidemic," "law enforcement," "process of prejudice reduction," each with its own narrative entailment and its own strengths and weaknesses (Kruglanski et al., 2007). Consequently, they argue that, rather than seizing on any one of them as the single appropriate metaphor, it is desirable to move between them in a critical and analytical way.

Another demanding situation is maintaining antagonism or rivalry towards another country, where a frozen metaphor and/or competing analogical narratives are often employed. So, for instance, the terms *Cold War* and *arms race* were employed on both sides to refer to the more than 40-year period of tension between the countries of the North Atlantic Treaty Organization (NATO) and the Soviet Union and its allies. As Edelman (1971) explains, each side held to a myth that "revolves around hostile plotters and benevolent leaders, and both factions carefully plan the future and can shape it according to their plans" (p. 77). President Ronald Reagan significantly altered this relationship when, in 1983, he first used the term *Evil Empire* for the USSR. The characterization demeaned the Soviet Union and angered Soviet leaders. For his American audience, the phrase evoked equally science fiction and biblical associations—it is significant that his very first recorded use of it was in a speech on March 8, 1983 to the National Association of Evangelicals in Orlando, Florida. Reagan said,

> They preach the supremacy of the state, declare its omnipotence over individual man and predict its eventual domination of all peoples on the Earth. They are the focus of evil in the modern world. . . . So, in your discussions of the nuclear freeze proposals, I urge you to beware the temptation of pride, the temptation of blithely declaring yourselves above it all and label both sides equally at fault, to ignore the facts of history and the aggressive impulses of an evil empire, to simply call the arms race a giant misunderstanding and thereby remove yourself from the struggle between right and wrong and good and evil. (Reagan, 1983)

The Soviet Union, for its part, alleged that the United States was an imperialist superpower seeking to dominate the entire world, and that it was fighting against the US in the name of humanity. (On occasions, Soviet leaders referred to their relationship with the West in less grand and more colloquial metaphorical terms. So, Nikita Khruschchev declared in a speech in Yugoslavia on August 24 1963, "Berlin is the testicle of the West. When I want the West to scream, I squeeze on Berlin.")

One of the most interesting pairs of narrative/metaphorical formulations relating to situations of long-term international antagonism is to be found in the way in which Castro's administration in Cuba and successive administrations in the US have represented their relationship. It has been pointed out that

> Cuban leaders often characterize the relationship with the metaphor of David and Goliath, which conveys the image of a small, valiant defender facing an enormous aggressor. American leaders invoke images of Gulliver and the Lilliputians, in which the giant is benign and honorable. He chooses to suffer the pinpricks that the little people occasionally inflict on him rather than destroy the attackers, which he could do easily, because the giant's intention is to help them not kill them. (Brenner & Castro, 2000, p. 236)

One of the more bizarre metaphorical characterizations of a group of nations is George W. Bush's representation in his 2002 State of the Nation speech of N. Korea, Iran and Iraq as an "Axis of Evil" of nations which contributed to terrorism and sought weapons of mass destruction. The phrase suggested a parallel with the alliance among the Axis powers of the Second World War and also (like Reagan's "Evil Empire") a biblical reference. Matt Bonham has studied this phrase in detail. He and his coauthor highlight the oddness of suggesting that there was some kind of alliance between the governments of Iran and Iraq, which had long been at war with each other and a third, very distant nation, North Korea, with which neither had strong relations (Heradtsveit & Bonham, 2007). They underline the fact that Bush's wish was to present to the American public the case in a very few words for the war to dislodge Saddam Hussein, which he would initiate the following year (Heradtsveit & Bonham, 2007).

The Iranian leadership was particularly offended by the associations of this phrase, seeing it as indicating the US administration's preoccupation with glossing over its true motivations, especially its religious and economic inspirations, for involvement in the Middle East. Other commentators have drawn attention to the tendency for the Chinese and American governments to misunderstand metaphors used by the other. L. Su (2004) writes of the challenge for Westerners in understanding Chinese metaphorical idioms that derive from a specific historical or mythical event, whereas Edward Slingerland and others (2007) look at the specific case of diplomatic communications over the collision in 2001 of an American and a Chinese plane over international waters. They points to a mismatch between the Chinese metaphors, which depicted them as "victims" and the American metaphors which depicted the situation as involving a "game" requiring "a technical fix" (Slingerland et al., 2007). In Slingerland et al.'s (2007) words, "[a]s long as neither side acknowledged the contingent nature of their own framing, nor the competing metaphorical frame of the other, then consequently, each counterpart's attitudes and behavior must only have seemed irrationally hysterical or brutally insensitive to the other" (p. 73).

Narratives and Metaphors of Collaboration, Solidarity, and Negotiation

There are other situations of interaction and negotiation, in which national leaders employ narrative and metaphor in collaborative enterprises. Research on this topic mostly focuses on the conceptual metaphors involved in international collaboration. The chapter by one of the contributors to this volume, Michael P. Marks, concerns the conceptual metaphors involved in international collaboration in the broad sense (see also Docherty, 2004). Work has also been done on the role of metaphor in shaping the identity of the United Nations. Researcher Lisa J. McEntee-Atalianis (2011), who examined speeches by the secretary-general of one of its agencies, found that metaphors were basically organized in binary, polarized form to represent the organization as seeking to promote a series of positive objectives and to protect its members against the negative forces threatening it. The agency itself is anthropomorphized through metaphors associated with personhood, caring and responsibility, natural life cycle, and family. Its activities are depicted using image schemas implying a range of narratives of journey, construction, and war (against global threats of illegal and disruptive activities).

One of the richest areas for research has been that of the metaphors that have been employed by politicians and officials in the various countries of the European Union to describe the processes of development and integration in the organization. So, Paul Chilton and Mikhail Ilyin (1993) have pointed out that, when representatives of different countries use the term "common European house" to refer to the EU, each will tend to be referring back to the shape which houses typically take in their own country, which varies from the apartment block to the single family home.[10] Cris Shore (1997) catalogues the metaphors employed within the EU to refer to integration under the headings "journeying" (in some cases by road, in others by rail—which allows for countries to be derailed—even by bicycle, sometimes with a predetermined destination, sometimes with the destination still to be determined); "engineering" (with one or more countries serving as the "dynamo"); "container" (with countries being included or excluded); and "organic" (where the union grows and evolves). "Far from being simply window-dressing, used to embellish the political process with colorful imagery," writes Shore, "I suggest that these metaphors are central to the process of imagining and conceptualizing Europe. . . they are also key weapons in a struggle to direct and control the European agenda" (1997, p. 127). He poses a series of important questions, including "Whose interests are served by these metaphors of Europe? To what extent do they work as instruments of power? How do they lend legitimacy and authority to particular conceptions of Europe, while imposing silence or closure on other conceptions?"

Iseult Honohan (2008) explores the range of metaphors used to refer to solidarity, both within a nation and among nations. She points out that metaphors of "family" and "kinship" tend to suggest a bounded, unitary image and that the "friendship" and "team" metaphors imply the existence of an enemy, or at least an opposing group. She looks for alternative metaphors which take better account of diversity within and between nations. She sees the "archipelago" metaphor proposed by C. Kukathas as having some positive features, but still as suggesting that the individual islands of the archipelago are bounded. Her preference is for "social capital," partly because it recasts social connection in the terms of the dominant field of economics, but also because it underlines the value of multiple voluntary associations for building generalized trust. And, as she says, "[p]art of the success of 'social capital' may lie in the implicit ambiguity as to whether it is a kind of capital that belongs to society or an individual social resource" (Honohan, p. 78; see also Bartkus & Davis, 2009).

Aboriginal Australian lawyer Noel Pearson (2007) takes up the specific issue of identity in a multicultural society: "We need a better metaphor for popular comprehension of how people with varied identities come together to form a united nation," proposing "*layers* of identity." Unlike most commentators, in his proposal he explicitly shows how this metaphor entails (or is entailed by) a narrative: "The merging of unity and diversity in any nation requires a narrative that explains how assimilation into a national community, based on values and institutions that have their basis in a particular history, is consistent with respect and tolerance for many layers of bridging and bonding identities within the nation" (Pearson, 2007; see also Halstead, 2007).

We are very familiar with the use of metaphors for different sorts of relations between countries. Alliances between countries are often referred to in terms of "friendship," "partnership," "commonwealth," and so on. Colonizers regularly referred to themselves as playing a "parental," "educational" or "guardian" role towards subject peoples, over whose land they sometimes established "protectorates." Governments may have good or bad relations with their "neighbors," among others.

Changing relations between governments are often expressed and, indeed, negotiated in metaphorical terms. In his chapter for this volume, Jeffery Scott Mio identifies three possible options when a negotiator is faced with a powerful metaphor in debate: ignore the metaphor, defeat the metaphor by means of another, or extend the metaphor, to turn it back against the speaker (p. 239). He argues, that "metaphor extension" may be the most effective tactic.

Narrative and Metaphor in Policy Making

A number of specialists in policy studies have focused on the role of metaphor in policy-making, drawing attention to the fact that the metaphor selected to define any problem tends to determine the policy options that will be investigated to resolve it (e.g. Schön, 1979; Thibodeau and Boroditsky, 2011; Yanow, 2000). Such options usually expand into narrative scenarios. As will be clear from cases already cited, this will be equally evident in the context of domestic problem solving (e.g., dealing with crime [Thibodeau & Boroditsky, 2011] or urban decay [Schön, 1979]), and in the context of international problem solving (e.g. the US dealing with terrorism.) This is not to say that policy makers should abandon the use of metaphors. In the words of Seth Thompson (1996), "the simplifying and clarifying function of metaphors makes policy decisions possible . . . metaphor is necessary to link tangible means to intangible ends" (p. 194). In addition to metaphors that positively frame a policy, however, there are metaphors employed, often to devastating effect, to undermine the policy of an opponent. In attacking the original healthcare reform proposal of the Clinton administration, those opposed to the plan on the grounds that some features of it would be overly bureaucratic came up with a pair of metaphors which dominated and quickly ended discussion of it. It was, they said, a system "with the compassion of the IRS and the efficiency of the Post Office" (Thompson, 1996, p. 195). From the perspective of an outsider such as myself, a curious feature of American debate around policy making in relation to such fields as health care and gun control is the unwillingness of politicians, voters, and the media to register and learn lessons from the narratives of nations whose policies in that field have been more successful.

Narrative and Metaphor in Peacemaking

There has been major interest, too, among peace activists and scholars of international relations in exploring the relevance of metaphor and narrative not only, as we have seen, to fomenting discord resulting in war, but also to making and maintaining peace. Most striking have been the initiatives to bring together scholars and citizens from countries and communities, which have formerly been at war, to see if they can rework the mutually exclusive narratives held by the various parties to the conflict into a single, multifaceted narrative comprehensible and acceptable to all. Charles Ingrao of Purdue University, for instance, has sought to contribute to future peace among the states of former Yugoslavia by bringing together more than 250 scholars from the Balkans, Europe and the United States for this purpose (Ingrao & Emmett, 2012; see also Bajraktari & Serwer, 2006). Phillip L. Hammack (2011) has studied initiatives for peacemaking in Israel/Palestine that have brought young Jewish Israelis and young Palestinians together to exchange narratives. Funk and Said (2004) explore the broader issue of whether it may be possible for mediators to assist representatives of Islam and of the West, if not to agree on a common narrative, at least to come to see the complementarity of the narratives to which they hold. "Islam and the West are truly between stories—between the stories of the past, and the story they must create. All who identify with Islam and with the West can become coauthors of this new story" (Funk & Said, 2004, p. 26).

Meanwhile, specialists in peace and conflict studies have also come to underline the utility of metaphor in peacemaking and in negotiation between parties in conflict (in political and other contexts). They emphasize the value of studying the metaphors employed by the various parties and by mediators, of seeking to replace the metaphors of war and violence with more neutral metaphors (e.g., conflict as game), and positive metaphors (e.g., conflict as tide, or dance, or continental divide, peace building as web weaving, peace builders as yeast, etc.; Min, 2004). (See www.beyondintractability.org for a valuable list of resources on the role of narrative and metaphor in conflict studies and resolution.) Martin Luther King, Jr. in his "I have a dream" speech of 1963 looked forward to being able "to transform the jangling discords of our world [often misquoted as "nation"] into a beautiful symphony of brotherhood." Jayne Seminare Docherty (2004) is one of very few writers on conflict studies to underline the role of both narrative and metaphor in war making and peacemaking.

Most attempts at peacemaking on the official level have used less creative metaphors, such as the "Roadmap for Peace" in the Israel–Palestine conflict, proposed in 2002–2003 by the US, the European Union, Russia, and the United Nations. The eventual goal of the plan was to achieve the vision of two states, a secure state of Israel and an independent, peaceful, democratic Palestinian state. The road map had the merit of proposing a staged series of actions on both sides, which would take the opposing parties along the "road" to eventual peace. As is well known, the first phase, which was supposed to include the end to Palestinian violence, Palestinian political reform, Israeli withdrawal from Palestinian cities and freeze on settlement expansion, and Palestinian elections, was never fully implemented. The reasons for this included a refusal on the part of Ariel Sharon to implement the freeze on expansion of Israeli settlement in the Occupied Territories and the refusal of Hamas to implement a ceasefire. Over the following months and years, the plan collapsed. This, it may be said, reveals a weakness in the linear image of a road map: if the first stage of the journey is not completed, then there is no possibility of the remaining stages being accomplished.

Narrative and Metaphor in Election Campaigns

In election campaigns, especially presidential campaigns, the candidates, with the assistance of their speechwriters and backers, seek to construct images of themselves by means of narrative and metaphor, which will display them to best advantage, not only in terms of their political record and policies for the future but also in terms of their personal lives. Meanwhile, they strive, again largely by means of narrative and metaphor, to construct images of their opponent which suggest unreliability, mendacity, privilege, and so on. I am writing just a few weeks after the 2012 US presidential election, and it has been fascinating to see the two main candidates spinning narratives and fashioning metaphors for these purposes.

In mid-2010, in the run-up to the congressional elections, the website Global Language Monitor, which monitors news, blogs, and social networks, announced that the number one political buzzword was *narrative*. Although it may no longer hold quite so strong a position, it certainly continues to be a key term and concept in the political media. Its significance in the campaign context consists largely in the need for candidates and parties to build relatively simple narratives about their respective records and policies for the future that will, at as many points as possible, touch the self-narratives, including economic, moral and religious narratives, of a large proportion of voters. Two years later, in the run-up to the 2012 elections, the site's president Paul J. J. Payack wrote that it had observed profound differences between the actual concerns of the public and the political narratives of both parties. Interestingly, he notes that both candidates failed to respond to one of the top current buzzwords, the metaphorical expression "toxic politics" (Payack, 2012).[11]

Mitt Romney's speech accepting the Republican candidacy (which can be found at www.npr.org/2012/08/30/160357612/transcript-mitt-romneys-acceptance-speech) was designed "to convince Americans that his values were the same as theirs—that they could trust him just as much as trust where he wants to take the country." As a sympathetic commentator described it,

> he didn't so much give a speech but instead unveiled stories that allowed
> his listeners to see greater depth to the fabric of the man that Romney

is—versus the man of which they may have read. Less a titan than a family man, Romney spoke of a life with children not unlike the lives of voters he seeks. Just as importantly, he addressed the economic conditions of viewers, not of a faceless economy. From their unemployment to their children's education, Romney spoke of people, not numbers. (Del Beccaro, 2012)

Obama's 2012 acceptance speech was organized around the metaphor of the two candidates offering divergent paths. Obama presented his record as demonstrating his endeavors to stimulate the economy, to save major industries, to ensure educational opportunities and adequate health care for all, and his opponent's record and program as failing on all those issues. He ended by declaring, almost in the gospel mode of Martin Luther King, Jr.

America, I never said this journey would be easy, and I won't promise that now. Yes, our path is harder—but it leads to a better place. Yes our road is longer—but we travel it together. We don't turn back. We leave no one behind. We pull each other up. We draw strength from our victories, and we learn from our mistakes, but we keep our eyes fixed on that distant horizon, knowing that providence is with us, and that we are surely blessed to be citizens of the greatest nation on earth. (Obama, 2012)

In the first debate between Obama and Romney, it was interesting to find that Romney had appropriated the "two paths" metaphor. One of the contributors to this volume, Jeffery Scott Mio, has undertaken a piece of research, with other scholars, which suggests that candidates who use metaphor liberally are consistently seen as having more charisma than those who employ metaphor less (Mio, Riggio, Levin, & Reese, 2005). Given Obama's much greater propensity to use metaphor, it was interesting to see the 2012 election result bearing out that claim.

Narrative, Metaphor, and the Media

A rich store of metaphors is employed to describe the ideal role of the media in a democracy. I found the following descriptors in a single article by a respected commentator for the United Nations: "watchdog," "guardian of public interest," "conduit between governors and governed," serving to "inform, educate and engage the public," and "provide a culture of community conversation by activating inquiry on serious public issues," "buttressing and deepening democracy," and giving "voice to all sides of a conflict." The media may, however, "fan the flames of discord," be "manipulated," and "hobbled by stringent laws, monopolistic ownership and sometimes brute force" (Coronel, 2004).

Then there is the question of how journalists themselves employ narrative and metaphor in their own work and, as importantly, record and critique the narratives and metaphors utilized by politicians. The challenge of providing an adequate narrative in relation to political events or situations is faced not only by historians writing of the past but by journalists and political commentators writing of ongoing situations. Crucial factors in determining the adequacy of a narrative report of a political situation are the energy and rigor with which information is collected, the extent to which views on all sides have been canvassed, the chronological starting point chosen, and the overall shape given to the story. In a conversation later in this volume, journalist and media professor Mark Danner talks of the way in which he, as a journalist, often thinks he knows "the true story" about a conflict situation before he visits the country concerned, but usually finds he must abandon that story once he has arrived there, and construct a fresh narrative which takes account of all he sees and hears there. To take a single instance, he explains how, in attempting to understand the miserable situation of Haitians in modern times, he felt he had to go back 250 years and retrace the history of external interventions (especially by the US) over successive years. Among the many temptations faced by those who work in the media are to repeat and recycle uncritically the partial or misleading narratives passed to them by politicians and the military (for instance, narratives around Saddam Hussein's retention of weapons of mass destruction), and Danner insists on the need for journalists to constantly question and critique the narratives offered them by governments and corporations. There has been a good deal of discussion, for instance, of the pros and cons of having journalists "embedded" with the troops in Iraq and Afghanistan, especially the difficulty they experience in gaining a broader perspective on the military and political situation in the country. (See, for instance, the blog for *The New York Times* of journalist Stephen Farrell, 2010, titled "Embedistan.")

Early in this chapter, I cited several examples of striking metaphors coined by journalists to illuminate a political situation. A specialist on the former Yugoslavia told me the other day (2013) that he could not imagine a more accurate image of the peace settlement which came out of the Dayton Accord than Julian Borger's: "Like a hastily applied plaster cast, it healed the wounds at the expense of setting Bosnia's bones at distorted, disfiguring angles" (Borger, 2012b). Only too often, however, journalists rely on banal, clichéd metaphors in their reporting and comment (for instance, of the "presidential race," "arm wrestle," etc.). There is, I have suggested, a specific responsibility on journalists to critique the often overly simple, sometimes downright deceptive, metaphors propagated by politicians and officials (for instance, that of the War on Terror). Mark Danner, in our conversation in this volume, explains the way in which he both critiques official or conventional narratives and metaphors and creates fresh narratives and fresh metaphors to capture the essence of a situation.

Conclusion

The broad message of this chapter concerns the need to be alert to the power of both narrative and metaphor in every form of political discourse. In the first place, we need to be aware of their manipulation by politicians. Roy Peter Clark (2012), an American writer, editor, teacher of writing and president of the Poynter Institute for Media Studies, claims that we need "a professional Narrative Watcher" to "reveal how political parties and others seeking power use verifiable facts, half-truths, and misinformation to tell stories designed to promote their own interests." At the same time, we should scrutinize the political narratives and metaphors to which we ourselves subscribe. Australian aboriginal lawyer Noel Pearson (2007) asserted, "We often become prisoners of our own metaphors. Humans need metaphors to communicate and when metaphors work to capture complexity, they are wonderful. When they are inadequate they are worse than useless: they hold our collective imaginations captive and constrained." (See also Skinner & Squillacote, 2010).

The great American philosopher Martha Nussbaum (1997) has argued that, if we are all to participate fully in a democratic society, we must, first, develop the capacity for critical examination of our own ideas and traditions and, second see ourselves as human beings bound to all other human beings by ties of recognition and concern. Behind these two requirements she insists lies a third: the need for us all to develop "narrative imagination"—the capacity both to generate and to comprehend complex narrative (Nussbum, 1997). In the light of the "Warring with Words" project, I would like to add a fourth requirement: the ability to critique simplistic and dishonest metaphors employed by politicians and the media and to generate, and acknowledge the value of, multiple metaphors for any situation, so as to facilitate creative thinking about the issue in hand. (See also Baumer, Sinclair, & Tomlinson, 2010). Beyond that, I suggest the importance for us all to be constantly aware of the dynamic and varied relationship between narrative and metaphor in the political context.

Notes

1 Danner makes the point, in the conversation recorded for this book, that the title was almost certainly chosen by a *New York Times* subeditor, rather than himself.
2 For a sound introduction to narrative and narrative studies, see H. Porter Abbott (2002). For comprehensive coverage of most subfields within narrative studies, see Herman, Jahn, and Ryan (2010). For an introduction to metaphor, see Kövecses (2003). The nearest we have to an encyclopedic work on metaphor studies is Gibbs (2008).
3 In that article, I mistakenly asserted that Ricoeur made no explicit links between narrative and metaphor.
4 See also H. M. Drucker (1970).
5 For a discussion of the figure of Wonder Woman and the representation of the US, see Mitra Emad (2006).
6 Similarly, see Nussbaum (2004).
7 The second most durable political metaphor is almost certainly that of 'the ship of state', first outlined by Plato in Book 6 of the *Republic*. It, too, has been employed over the centuries to a host of different political purposes, with one of the most interesting recent examples being the claim that the role of government should be 'steering, rather than rowing' (Osborne and Gaebler, 1993).

8 I owe this observation to Phillip L. Hammack.
9 He makes a second analogy with physicists who resisted Planck's quantum theory.
10 The "European house" metaphor has taken on another dimension with the current economic crisis. So, for instance, British prime minister David Cameron countered the demands of Conservative colleagues who pressed for the UK to leave the EU at the start of the Eurocrisis, by saying that he found it "utterly indecent, threatening to move out of a street, just at the moment when your neighbor's house is on fire. Instead, you must help extinguishing the fire" (Cuperus, 2011).
11 The adjective *toxic* came to prominence in recent politics when "toxic debt" was seen to be a major contributing factors in the in the Global Financial Crisis.

References

Aghion, P., & Bolton, P. (1997, April). A theory of trickle-down growth and development. *The Review of Economic Studies, 64* (2), 151–172

Ahmadinejad, M. (2011, September 23). Address by H. E. Dr. Mahmoud Ahmadinejad President of the Islamic Republic of Iran Before the 66th Session of the United Nations General Assembly. Retrieved at http://publicintelligence.net/mahmoud-ahmadinejad-speech-to-un-general-assembly-transcript-september-22–2011/

Ahmed, A. S. (1995). "Ethnic cleansing": A metaphor for our time? *Ethnic and Racial Studies, 18* (1), 1–25.

Anchor, R. (1987). Narrativity and the transformation of historical consciousness. *Clio 16* (2), 121–137.

Anderson, B. O'G. (1991). *Imagined communities: reflections on the origin and spread of nationalism* (Rev. and extended ed.). London: Verso.

Andrews, M. (2007). *Shaping history: Narratives of political change.* Cambridge: Cambridge University Press.

Annas, G. (1995, March 16). Reframing the debate on health care reform by replacing our metaphors. *The New England Journal of Medicine, 332* (11), 744–747.

Anon note. (1997). Organic and mechanical metaphors in late eighteenth-century American political thought. *Harvard Law Review 110* (8), 1832–1849.

Bajraktari, Y., & Serwer, D. (2006). Explaining the Yugoslav catastrophe: The quest for a common narrative (United States Institute for Peace). Retrieved from: www.usip.org/publications/explaining-yugoslav-catastrophe-quest-common-narrative

Banks, K. (2009). Interpretations of the body politic and of natural bodies in late sixteenth-century France. In A. Musolff & Jörg Zinken (Eds.), *Metaphor and Discourse* (pp. 233–247). London: Palgrave Macmillan.

Bartkus, V. O., & Davis, J. H. (2009). *Social capital: Reaching out, reaching in.* Cheltenham: Edward Elgar.

Baumer, E. P. S., Sinclair, J., & Tomlinson, B. (2010). "America is like Metamucil": Fostering critical thinking and creative thinking about metaphor in political blogs. In *Proceedings of the 28th international conference on human factors in computing systems (CHI 2010)* (pp. 1437–1446). Atlanta: ACM Press.

Beer, F. A., & De Landtsheer, C. (2004). Metaphorical war and peace. In F. A. Beer & C. De Landtsheer (Eds.), *Metaphorical world politics* (pp. 111–120). East Lansing: Michigan University Press.

Bennett, W. L. (1980, December). Myth, ritual, and political control, *Journal of Communication, 30* (4), 166–179.

Bissett, A. (2002, November). *Surgical strikes: Ideological weaponry.* Paper presented at the sixth ETHICOMP international conference on the social and ethical impacts of information and communication technologies, Universidade Lusiada, Lisbon, Portugal. Retrieved from www.ccsr.cse.dmu.ac.uk/conferences/ethicomp/ethicomp2002/abstracts/8.html

Borger, J. (2012a, June 8). Assad compares army's role to surgeon saving a patient. *The Guardian Weekly*, p. 5.

Borger, J. (2012b, April 4). Bosnian war 20 years on: Peace holds but conflict continues to haunt. *The Guardian Weekly*, pp. 1 and 5.

Bottici, C. (2007). *A philosophy of political myth.* Cambridge: Cambridge University Press.

Bottici, C., & Challand, B. (2010). *The myth of the clash of civilizations.* New York: Routledge.

Bougher, L. D. (2012). The case for metaphor in political reasoning and cognition. *Political Psychology*, *33* (1), 145–163.

Brenner, P., & Castro, S. (2009). David and Gulliver: Fifty years of competing metaphors in the Cuban-United States relationship. *Diplomacy & Statecraft*, *20* (2), 236–257.

Brooks, P. (1984). *Reading for the plot: Design and intention in narrative.* Cambridge, MA: Harvard University Press.

Bruner J. (1986). *Actual minds, possible worlds*, Cambridge, MA: Harvard University Press.

Bruner, J. (1987). Life as narrative. *Social Research*, *54*, 11–32.

Bruner, J. (2003). *Making stories: Law, literature, life.* Cambridge MA: Harvard University Press.

Burke, K. (1953). *A rhetoric of motives.* New York: Prentice-Hall.

Burton, J. W. (1972). *World society.* Cambridge: Cambridge University Press.

Campbell, D. (1998). Metabosnia: Narratives of the Bosnian War. *Review of International Studies*, *24*, 261–281.

Carver, T., & Pikalo, J. (Eds). (2008). *Political language and metaphor: Interpreting and changing the world.* London and New York: Routledge.

Chambers, R. (1984). *Narrative seduction and the power of fiction.* Minneapolis: University of Minnesota Press.

Charteris-Black, J. (2005). *Politicians and rhetoric: The persuasive power of metaphor.* Basingstoke and New York: Palgrave Macmillan.

Chilton, P. (1996). *Security metaphor: Cold War discourse from containment to common house.* New York: Peter Lang.

Chilton, P., & Ilyin, M. (1993). Metaphor in political discourse: The case of the "common European house." *Discourse and Society*, *4* (1), 7–31.

Chisem, J. (2011, May 14). Security studies and the marginalization of women and gender structures. Retrieved at www.e-ir.info/2011/05/14/security-studies-and-the-marginalisation-of-women-and-gender-structures/

Clark, R. P. (2012, February 21). How "narrative" moved from literature to politics and what this means for covering candidates. *Poynter*. Retrieved at www.poynter.org/how-tos/newsgathering-storytelling/writing-tools/162834/how-narrative-moved-from-literature-to-politics-what-this-means-for-covering-candidates/

Cohen, D. H. (1998). Schoolhouses, jailhouses and the house of being: The tragedy of philosophy's metaphors, *Metaphilosophy*, 29, 6–19.

Cohen, T. (1979) Metaphor and the cultivation of intimacy. In S. Sacks (Ed.), *On metaphor* (pp. 1–10). Chicago: University of Chicago Press.

Connerton, P. (1989). *How societies remember.* Cambridge: Cambridge University Press.

Coronel, S. S. (2004). The role of the media in deepening democracy. United Nations Online Network in Public Administration and Finance, 28 December, 2007. Retrieved at http://unpan1.un.org/intradoc/groups/public/documents/un/unpan010194.pdf

Croft, S. (2006). *Culture, crisis and America's war on terror.* Cambridge: Cambridge University Press.

Cuperus, R. (2011, 8 November). Europe's burning house. Column in *Social Europe Journal.* Retrieved at www.social-europe.eu/2011/11/europes-burning-house/

Damasio, A. (1999). *The feeling of what happens: Body and emotion in the making of consciousness.* New York: Harcourt Brace.

Danner, M. (2009). *Stripping bare the body: politics, violence, war.* New York: Nation Books.

Danner, M. (2010, January 21). To heal Haiti, look to history, not nature. *New York Times.* Retrieved at www.nytimes.com/2010/01/22/opinion/22danner.html?pagewanted=all

DARPA (2011, October 7). *Broad Agency announcement. Narrative networks* (DSO DARPA-BAA-12–03). Retrieved from http://darpa.mil/opportunities/solicitations/dso_solicitations.aspx

Del Beccaro, T. (2012, September 3). The essential value connection in Romney's acceptance speech. Retrieved from www.forbes.com/sites/realspin/2012/09/03/the-essential-value-connection-in-romneys-acceptance-speech/

De Leonardis, F. (2008). War as a medicine: the medical metaphor in contemporary Italian political language. *Social Semiotics, 18* (1), 33–45

Docherty, J. S. (2004). Narratives, metaphors and negotiation. *Marquette Law Review, 87* (4), 847–851.

Dray, W. H. (1971). On the nature and role of narrative in historiography, *History and Theory, 10,* 153–171.

Drucker, H. M. (1970). Just analogies?: The place of analogies in political thinking, *Political Studies, 18* (4), 448–460.

Dunbar, K. (2001). The analogical paradox: Why analogy is so easy in naturalistic settings, yet so difficult in the psychological laboratory. In D. Gentner, K. Holyoak, & B. Kokinov (Eds.), *The analogical mind: Perspectives from cognitive science* (pp. 313–334). Cambridge, MA: MIT Press.

Edelman, M. (1967). Myth, metaphors and political conformity. *Psychiatry, 30*(3), 217–228.

Edelman, M. (1975) Language, myths, and rhetoric. *Trans-Action, 12,* 14–21.

Edelman, M. (1971). *Politics as symbolic action.* New York: Academic Press.

Emad, M. (2006). Reading WonderWoman's body: Mythologies of gender and nation. *Journal of Popular Culture, 39,* 954–984. Retrieved from www.d.umn.edu/~memad/EmadWonderWomanJrnlPopCulture06.pdf

Enloe, C. (1990). *Bananas, beaches and bases: Making feminist sense of international politics.* Berkeley: University of California Press.

Esch, J. (2010). Legitimizing the "War on Terror": Political myth in official-level rhetoric. *Political Psychology, 311* (3), 357–391.

Farrell, S. (2010, June 25). Embedistan. *New York Times.* Retrieved from http://atwar.blogs.nytimes.com/2010/06/25/embedistan-2/

Fasolt, C. (2004). *The limits of history.* Chicago: University of Chicago Press.

Feldman, O., & De Landtsheer, O. (1998). *Politically speaking: a worldwide examination of language used in the public sphere.* Westport, CT: Greenwood.

Flood, C. (2002). *Political myth: A theoretical introduction.* New York: Garland.

Font, J. P. P., & Régis, D. (2006, July). *Chaos theory and its application in political science.* Paper delivered at IPSA—AISP Congress Fukuoka, Japan. Retrieved from http://dev.ulb.ac.be/sciencespo/dossiers_membres/dandoy-regis/fichiers/dandoy-regis-publication18.pdf

Freeman, R. (2009, April, 19). Is Iraq another Vietnam? Actually, it may become much worse. Retrieved January 23, 2014, from www.commondreams.org/views04/0419-11.htm.

Fuks, A. (2009, July). *The military metaphors of modern medicine.* Paper presented at the conference on Health, Illness, and Disease, Oxford, UK. Retrieved from www.inter-disciplinary.net/wp-content/uploads/2009/06/hid_fuks.pdf

Funk, N. C., & Said, A. Z. (2004). Islam and the West: Narratives of conflict and conflict transformation. *International Journal of Peace Studies, 9* (1), 1–26.

Galbraith, J. K. (1982, February 4). Recession economics. *New York Review of Books 29* (1). Retrieved from www.nybooks.com/articles/archives/1982/feb/04/recession-economics/?pagination=false

Gannon, M. J. (2001). *Working across cultures: Applications and exercises.* Thousand Oaks, CA: Sage.

Gavriely-Nuri, D. (2008). If both opponents "extend hands in peace"—Why don't they meet? Mythic metaphors and cultural codes in the Israeli peace discourse. *Journal of Language and Politics, 9* (3), 449–468.

Gee, J. P. (1991), Memory and myth: A perspective on narrative. In A. McCabe & Carole C. Peterson (Eds.), *Developing narrative structure* (pp. 1–25). Hillsdale, NJ: Erlbaum.

Gibbs, R. (Ed., 2008). *The Cambridge handbook of metaphor and thought.* Cambridge: Cambridge University Press.

Global Language Monitor. Retrieved from www.languagemonitor.com/category/politics/

Guilfoy, K. (2008). John of Salisbury. In E. N. Zalta (Ed.), *The Stanford encyclopedia of philosophy.* Retrieved from http://plato.stanford.edu/archives/fall2008/entries/john-salisbury/

Halstead, J. M. (2007). Multicultural metaphors. In K. Roth & I. Gur-Ze'ev (Eds.), *Education in the era of globalization* (pp. 146–160). Dordrecht: Springer.

Hammack, P. L. (2011). *Narrative and the politics of identity: The cultural psychology of Israeli and Palestinian youth.* Oxford: Oxford University Press.

Hammack, P. L., & Pilecki, A. (2012). Narrative as a root metaphor for political psychology. *Political Psychology,* 33 (1), 75–103.

Hanne, M. (1999). Getting to know the neighbours: When plot meets knot. *Canadian Review of Comparative Literature, 26* (1), 36–50.

Hanne, M. (2011, Fall). The binocular vision project: An introduction. *Genre, 44* (3), 223–237.

Heiler, R. (2001, September 20). On metaphors and the importance of being thorough. The news behind the news. Institute for Advanced Strategic and Political Studies, Israel. Retrieved from www.israeleconomy.org/nbn/nbn422sp.htm

Heradstveit, D., & Bonham, G. M. (2007). What the Axis of Evil metaphor did to Iran. *Middle East Journal, 61* (3), 421–440.

Herman, D., Jahn, M., & Ryan, M.-L. (Eds.). (2010), *Routledge encyclopedia of narrative theory*. London and New York: Routledge.

Honohan, I. (2008). Metaphors of solidarity. In T. Carver & J. Pikalo (Eds.), *Political language and metaphor: Interpreting and changing the world* (pp. 69–82). London and New York: Routledge.

Intelligence Advanced Research Projects Activity. (2011, May 20). *Broad agency announcement, IARPA-BAA-11–04, Metaphor program, incisive analysis.* Retrieved from www.iarpa.gov/Programs/ia/Metaphor/solicitation_metaphor.html

Ingrao, C. & Emmett, T. A. (Eds.) (2012). *Confronting the Yugoslav controversies: A scholars' initiative* (2nd ed.). West Lafayette, Indiana: Purdue University Press.

Jensen, K., & Talev, M. (2012, October 4). Romney in debate says Obama favors "trickle-down" government. *Bloomberg.* Retrieved from www.bloomberg.com/news/2012–10–03/romney-gets-chance-to-shift-race-in-debate-tonight-with-obama.html

Kennan, G. F. (1946, February). The long telegram. Retrieved from http://wps.prenhall.com/wps/media/objects/108/110880/ch26_a1_d1.pdf

King, M. L., Jr. (1963, August 28). "I have a dream" speech. Retrieved from www.americanrhetoric.com/speeches/mlkihaveadream.htm

Klamer, A., & Leonard, T.C. (1994). So what's an economic metaphor? In P. Mirowski (Ed.), *Natural images in economics* (pp. 20–51). Cambridge: Cambridge University Press.

Klamer, A., & McCloskey, D. M. (1991). Accounting as the master metaphor of economics. *European Accounting Review*, *1*, 146-160.

Klamer, A. (2009). Rhetoric. In J. Peil & I. V. Staverin (Eds.), *Handbook of economics and ethics.* (pp. 449–454). Northampton, MA: Edward Elgar.

Kövecses, Z. (2003). *Metaphor: A practical introduction.* Oxford: Oxford University Press.

Kruglanski, A. W., Crenshaw, M., Post, J. M. & Victoroff, J. (2008). What should this fight be called? Metaphors of counterterrorism and their implications, *Psychological Science in the Public Interest*, 8 (3), 97–133.

Khrushchev, N. (1963, August 24). Nikita Khruschev. Retrieved from http://en.wikiquote.org/wiki/Nikita_Khrushchev

La Ferla, R. (2005, 20 October) Families confront a perilous world. *New York Times.* Retrieved from www.nytimes.com/2005/10/20/fashion/thursdaystyles/20TEENS.html?pagewanted=print

Lakoff, G. (2003, March 18). Metaphor and war: The metaphor system used to justify war in the gulf (1991) and Metaphor and war, again. *AlterNet.* Retrieved from www.alternet.org/story/15414/

Lakoff, G. (2012, December 3). Why it's hard to replace the metaphor of the "fiscal cliff." *Huffington Post.* Retrieved from www.huffingtonpost.com/george-lakoff/why-its-hard-to-replace-t_b_2230577.html

Lakoff, G., & Johnson, M. (1980). *Metaphors we live by.* Chicago and London: Chicago University Press.

Lakoff, G. & Wehling, E. (2012). *The little blue book: The essential guide to thinking and talking democratic.* New York: Simon and Schuster.

Lederach, J. P. (2005). *The moral imagination: The art and soul of building peace.* New York: Oxford University Press.

Little, R. (2007). *The balance of power in international relations: Metaphors, myths and models.* Cambridge and New York: Cambridge University Press.

Luks, F. (1998). The rhetorics of ecological economics. *Ecological Economics*, *26* (2), 139–149.

Lyotard, J-F. (1984). *The postmodern condition: A report on knowledge* (G. Bennington & B. Massumi, Trans.). Minneapolios: University of Minnesota Press.

MacDougall, A. K. (1996 Fall). Humans as cancer. *Wild Earth*, pp. 81–88.

MacIntyre, A. (1981). *After virtue: A study in moral theory*. London: Duckworth.

Madrigal, A. (2011, May 25). Why are spy researchers building a "metaphor program"? *The Atlantic*. Retrieved from www.theatlantic.com/technology/archive/2011/05/why-are-spy-researchers-building-a-metaphor-program/239402/

Marks, M. P. (2011). *Metaphors in international relations theory*. New York: Palgrave/Macmillan.

Massad, J. (2012, August 29). The "Arab Spring" and other American seasons. *Aljazeera*. Retrieved from www.aljazeera.com/indepth/opinion/2012/08/201282972539153865.html

McCloskey, D. (1985). *The rhetoric of economics*. Madison: University of Wisconsin Press.

McCloskey, D. (1990). Storytelling in economics. In C. Nash (Ed.), *Narrative in culture: The uses of storytelling in the sciences, philosophy and literature* (pp. 5–22). London and New York: Routledge.

McCloskey, D. (1994). *Knowledge and persuasion in economics*. Cambridge: Cambridge University Press.

McCloskey, D. (2006). *The bourgeois virtues: Ethics for an age of commerce*. Chicago: University of Chicago Press.

McCloskey, D. (2010). *Bourgeois dignity: Why economics can't explain the modern world*. Chicago: University of Chicago Press.

McEntee-Atalianis, J. L. (2011). The role of metaphor in shaping the identity and agenda of the United Nations: The imagining of an international community and international threat. *Discourse and Communication*, *5* (4), 393–412.

McKean, L. (1996). Bharat Mata: Mother India and her militant matriots. In: J.S. Hawley & D. M. Wulff (Eds.), *Devi: goddesses of India* (pp. 250–280). Berkeley: University of California Press.

Miller, J. H. (1995). Narrative. In F. Lentricchia & T.McCaughlin (Eds.), *Critical terms for literary study* (2nd ed., pp. 66–79). Chicago: Chicago University Press.

Min, X. (2005, July). Metaphors. In G. Burgess & H. Burgess (Eds.), *Beyond intractability*. Conflict Information Consortium, University of Colorado, Boulder. Retrieved from www.beyondintractability.org/bi-essay/metaphors

Mink, L. O. (1978). Narrative form as a cognitive instrument. In R. H. Canary & H. Kozicki (Eds.), *The writing of history: Literary form and historical understanding* (pp. 129–149). Madison: University of Wisconsin Press.

Mio, J. S. (1996). Metaphor, politics, and persuasion. In J. S. Mio & A. N. Katz, *Metaphor: implications and applications* (pp. 127–146). Mahwah, NJ: Lawrence Erlbaum Associates.

Mio, J. S., Riggio, R. E., Levin, S., & Reese, R. (2005). Presidential leadership and charisma: The effects of metaphor, *The Leadership Quarterly*, *16*, 287–294.

Mirowski, P. (1989). *More heat than light: Economics as social physics: Physics as nature's economics*. Cambridge: Cambridge University Press.

Moyers, B. (1993) Why are the media important? In S. Biagi (Ed.), *Media reader: Perspectives on mass media industries, effects, and issues* (2nd ed., pp. 3–5). Belmont, CA: Wadsworth.

Musolff, A. (2009). Metaphor in the history of ideas and discourses: How can we inter-pret a medieval version of the *body-state* analogy. In A. Musolff & Jörg Zinken (Eds.), *Metaphor and discourse* (pp. 233–247). London: Palgrave Macmillan.

Musolff, A. (2010). Political metaphor and *bodies politic*. In U. Okulska & P. Cap (Eds.), *Perspectives in politics and discourse* (pp. 23–41). Amsterdam and Philadel-phia: John Benjamins.

Nederman, C. J. (2007, October). Christine de Pizan and Jean Gerson on the body poli-tic: The limits of intellectual influence. Paper given at the Medieval Studies Working Group, France-Chicago Center, and Department of Political Science, University of Chicago, Chicago. Retrieved from http://ptw.uchicago.edu/Nederman07.pdf

Nederman, C. J., & Shogimen, T. (2011). Best medicine? Medical education, practice and metaphor in John of Salisbury's *Policraticus and Metalogicon*. *Viator, 42* (1), 55–74.

Nussbaum, M. (1997). Narrative imagination. In *Cultivating humanity* (pp. 85–112). Cambridge, MA: Harvard University Press.

Nussbaum, M. (2004). Body of the nation: Why women were mutilated in Gujarat. *Boston Review, 29* (3), 33–38.

Obama, B. (2011). Full text of President Obama's economic speech in Osawatomie, Kans. Retrieved at http://articles.washingtonpost.com/2011–12–06/politics/35285189_1_hard-work-strongest-economy-osawatomie-high

Obama, B. (2012, September 6). Transcript: President Obama's convention speech. Retrieved from www.npr.org/2012/09/06/160713941/transcript-president-obamas-convention-speech

Okulska, U., & Cap, P. (2010). *Perspectives in politics and discourse*. Amsterdam: John Benjamins.

Orsini, M., & Saurette, P. (2011). "Take two and vote in the morning": Reflections on the political placebo effect. *The Journal of Mind-Body Regulation, 1* (3), 125–137. Retrieved from http://mbr.synergiesprairies.ca/mbr/index.php/mbr/article/view/478

Ortony, A. (Ed.). (1979). *Metaphor and thought.* Cambridge: Cambridge University Press.

Osborne, D., & Gaebler, T. (1993) *Reinventing government: How the entrepreneurial spirit is transforming the public sector.* New York: Plume.

O'Sullivan, J. (1845). Annexation. *United States Magazine and Democratic Review 17* (1), 5–10. Retrieved from http://web.grinnell.edu/courses/HIS/f01/HIS202–01/Documents/OSullivan.html

Papola, J., & Roberts, R. (2011). *Fight of the century*. Retrieved from http://econstories.tv/2011/04/28/fight-of-the-century-music-video/

Pappé, I. (2004). *A history of modern Palestine: One land, two peoples*. Cambridge and New York: Cambridge University Press.

Patterson, P. M. (1998). Market metaphors and political vocabularies: The case of the marginalized citizen. *Public Productivity & Management Review, 22* (2), 220–231.

Payack, P. J. J. (2012, July). Campaign narratives at odds with voters' concerns. Retrieved from http://thehill.com/blogs/congress-blog/presidential-campaign/237529-campaign-narratives-at-odds-with-voters-concerns

Pearson, N. (2007, September 29). Identity on parade, *The Australian*. Retrieved from www.theaustralian.com.au/news/opinion/identity-on-parade/story-e6frg786–1111114527117

Perris, A. (1983). Music as propaganda: Art at the command of doctrine in the People's Republic of China. *Ethnomusicology*, *27* (1), 1–28.

Petrie, H. G., & Oshlag, R. S. (1993). Metaphor and learning. In A. Ortony (Eds.), *Metaphor and thought* (pp. 579–609). Cambridge: Cambridge University Press.

Pettman, J. J. (1996). *Worlding women: a feminist international politics*. London and New York: Routledge.

Pettman, R. (2011). *Psychopathology and world politics*. London: Imperial College Press.

Pikalo, J. (2008). Mechanical metaphors in politics. In T. Carver & J. Pikalo (Eds.), *Political language and metaphor: Interpreting and changing the world* (pp. 41–54). London and New York: Routledge.

Pilkington, P. (2011). Debunking economics: An interview with Steve Keen: Part 1. Retrieved January 5, 2014, from www.nakedcapitalism.com/2011/11/philip-pilking ton-debunking-economics-%E2%80%93-an-interview-with-steve-keen-%E2%80%93-part.html

Porter Abbott, H. (2002). *The Cambridge introduction to narrative*. Cambridge, UK, and New York: Cambridge University Press.

Ramadurai, C. (2004). Life and times of Bharat Mata. Retrieved from http://charukesi. com/blog/2004/09/07/life-and-times-of-bharat-mata/

Reagan, R. (1983, March 8). President Reagan's speech before the National Association of Evangelicals. Retrieved from www.reagan.utexas.edu/archives/speeches/1983/30883b.htm

Reich, R. (1987). *Tales of a new America*. New York: Times Books.

Renan, E. (1990). "What is a nation?" In Bhabha, H. (Ed.), *Nation and narration* (pp. 8–22). London: Routledge.

Ricoeur, P. (1977). *The rule of metaphor: Multi-disciplinary studies of the creation of meaning in language* (R. Czerny, Trans., with Kathleen McLaughlin and John Costello). Toronto and Buffalo: University of Toronto Press.

Ricoeur, P. (1983–85). *Time and narrative*. 3 vol. (Kathleen McLaughlin & David Pellauer, Trans.). Chicago: Chicago University Press.

Ringmar, E. (2008). Metaphors of social order. In T. Carver & J. Pikalo (Eds.), *Political language and metaphor: Interpreting and changing the world* (pp. 57–68). London and New York: Routledge.

Robins, R. S., & Post, J. (1997). *Political paranoia: the psychopolitics of hatred*. New Haven, CT: Yale University Press.

Roberts, G. (2006). History, theory and the narrative turn in IR. *Review of International Studies*, *32*, 703–714.

Rosenberg, P. (2011, 24 August). The economy is a machine, not a body: The unseen power of metaphors in guiding how we think could be key to escaping from a prolonged economic crisis. *Aljazeera*. Retrieved from www.aljazeera.com/indepth/opinion/2011/08/2011821102242384922.html

Sarbin, T. R. (1986). The narrative as a root metaphor for psychology. In T. R. Sarbin (Ed.), *Narrative psychology: The storied nature of human conduct* (pp. 3–21). New York: Praeger.

Schön, D. (1979). Generative metaphor: A perspective on problem-setting in social policy. In A. Ortony (Ed.), *Metaphor and thought* (pp. 254–83). Cambridge: Cambridge University Press.

Scott, K. (1999). Imagined bodies, imagined communities: Feminism, nationalism, and body metaphors Retrieved from www.feministezine.com/feminist/modern/Imagined-Bodies-Imagined-Communities.html

Sen, A. (1999). *Development as freedom.* Oxford: Oxford University Press.

Shore, C. (1997). Metaphors of Europe: Integration and the politics of language. In C. Shore & S. Nugent, *Anthropology and cultural studies* (pp. 126–159). London and Chicago: Pluto Press.

Skinner, D., & Squillacote, R. (2010). New bodies: Beyond illness, dirt, vermin and other metaphors of terror. In U. Okulska & P. Cap (Eds.), *Perspectives in politics and discourse* (pp. 43–60). Amsterdam and Philadelphia: John Benjamins.

Slingerland, E., Blanchard, E. M., & Boyd-Judson, L. (2007). Collision with China: Conceptual metaphor analysis, somatic marking, and the EP-3 Incident. *International Studies Quarterly, 51* (1), 53–77.

Sowell, T. (2012). "Trickle down" theory and "tax cuts for the rich." Stanford, CA: Hoover Institution Press. Retrieved from www.webcitation.org/6AvD7JHEC

Stein, S. (2012, September 18). Mitt Romney video: "Palestinians Have No Interest Whatsoever In Establishing Peace." *The Huffington Post.* Retrieved from www. huffingtonpost.com/2012/09/18/mitt-romney-palestine-video_n_1892862.html

Su, L. (2004), Cultural effects as seen in Chinese metaphors, *Intercultural communication Studies, 13* (3), 61–66.

Suganami, H. (2008). Narrative explanation and international relations: Back to basics. *Millennium—Journal of International Studies, 37* (2), 327–356.

Sylvester, C. (2003). Dramaturgies of violence in international relations [Editorial]. *Borderlands,* 2 (2). Retrieved from www.borderlands.net.au/vol2no2_2003/sylvester_editorial.htm

Sylvester, C. (2013). *War as experience: Contributions from international relations and feminist analysis.* London: Routledge.

Szasz, T. (2001). *Pharmacracy: Medicine and politics in America.* Westport CT: Praeger Publishers.

Tannen, D. (1998). *The argument culture: Moving from debate to dialogue.* New York: Random House.

Thibodeau, P. H., & Boroditsky, L. (2011). Metaphors we think with: The role of metaphor in reasoning. *PLoS ONE, 6* (2), e16782. doi:10.1371/journal.pone.0016782

Thompson, S. (1996). Politics without metaphors is like a fish without water. In J. S. Mio & A. N. Katz (Eds.), *Metaphor: Implications and applications* (pp. 185–201). Mahwah, NJ: Lawrence Erlbaum.

Tickner, J. A. (2001). *Gendering world politics: Issues and approaches in the post-cold war era.* New York: Columbia University Press.

UNEP (2011). Towards a green economy: Pathways to sustainable development and poverty eradication: A synthesis for policy makers. Retrieved January 4, 2014, from www.unep.org/greeneconomy

Weeks, W. E. (1996). *Building the continental empire: American expansion from the Revolution to the Civil War.* Chicago: Ivan R. Dee.

Wendt, A. (1992). The state as person in international theory, *Review of International Studies, 31,* 289–316.

Wheelwright, P. (1962). *Metaphor and reality.* Bloomington: Indiana University Press.

White, H. (1984). The question of narrative in contemporary historical thought. *History and Theory, 23,* 1–33.

Wibben, A. (2011). *Feminist security studies: A narrative approach.* Abingdon: Routledge.

Wolfgram, W. C. & Stevens, C. (2007, February). *The uses of historical narrative: Events and non-events in the field of international relations.* Paper presented at the annual

50 *Michael Hanne*

meeting of the International Studies Association 48th Annual Convention, Hilton Chicago, Chicago. Retrieved from www.allacademic.com/meta/p179116_index.html

Yanow, D. (2000). *Conducting interpretive policy analysis.* Newbury Park, CA: Sage.

Yeager, L. B. (2011). *Is the market a test of truth and beauty? Essays in political economy.* Auburn, AL: Ludwig von Mises Institute.

Zashin, E., & Chapman, P. C. (1974). The uses of metaphor and analogy: Toward a renewal of political language. *The Journal of Politics, 36,* 290–326.

2 Mind, Story, and Society

The Political Psychology of Narrative

Phillip L. Hammack

He is the son of immigrants and the grandson of a coal miner. A devout Catholic with consistently conservative views on topics like abortion and homosexuality, he lost a son born prematurely, solidifying the connection to his faith and values. For him, it takes a *family*, not a village, and the culture has shifted too far from recognition of this simple fact. He is a culture warrior, committed to securing that the institutions of yesteryear do not erode into the slippery slope of moral relativism and new ideas. He is a defender of the past, a steward of what is safe, secure, and comforting.

He is the son of a white, educated woman from Kansas and a bright Kenyan studying in the United States at the time of his conception. On one side, his grandparents confronted the shifting cultural and economic tides of a society in rapid development. On another, his extended family confronted the painful cultural and economic consequences of colonialism and its aftermath. He immersed himself in culture after culture, both at home and abroad, he was seeking a sense of identity, longing for a place in which he and his name might not be classified as exotic, a place of comfort and security.

For a moment in the US primary election of 2012, it looked as though these two men might compete on the global stage for leader of the world's most powerful nation. Yet the arc shifted, and another personal narrative emerged to capture the sentiment of an anxious populace, confronted with the possibility of continuing cultural and economic decline. The son of a self-made man, the descendant of a group persecuted for its beliefs and practices, emerged as the Republican nominee for president of the United States.

The personal narratives of these three men—Rick Santorum, Barack Obama, and Mitt Romney—reveal the contours of identity possibility in a complex world of cultural and historical change, characterized by the movement of people and ideas more fluidly across borders than ever before (Nesbitt-Larking & Kinnvall, 2012). They are redemptive stories of men who faced distinct challenges in life—the loss of a mother to cancer at a young age (Obama), the loss of a child at birth (Santorum), and experience with religious persecution (Romney). Yet their stories diverge in the narrative positions with which they would seek to guide political behavior. If one identifies with the devout Catholic and his emphasis on the protection of the heterosexual family as the central institution of social life, one is more likely to oppose social policy that might redefine that institution (e.g., same-sex marriage legislation). If one identifies with the son of a multicultural union, one is more likely to be sensitive to oppression and marginalization of some groups, for his is a story of the negotiation and management of stigma and subordination (Hammack, 2010b). Those who identify with his personal narrative might be more supportive of a view of institutions as always potentially oppressing some groups over others, thus viewing same-sex marriage as a necessary corrective to cultural heterosexism or heterosexual privilege and, consequently, supporting political attempts to achieve marriage equality.

The stories of these well-known politicians illustrate one of the functions of narrative I argue is central to political psychology. A primary role of narrative in political life is *to motivate the political behavior of individuals to align their actions*. Through a process of identification with personal narratives of leaders, collective political behavior is achieved—whether that behavior involves voting, protesting, or other forms of cultural participation of a political nature. As we come to identify with the leader's life story, we see a mirror for our own stories, and this identification serves as a powerful motivational force as individuals coordinate, either explicitly or implicitly, their behavior. In coordinating activity through cultural practice, individual subjectivity is constructed, and a status quo of power and intergroup relations is reproduced, challenged, or repudiated.

Narrative does not simply play a defining role in political life via the personal narratives of leaders, however. To limit the significance of narrative to this role would be to suggest that the link from mind to society is extremely self-centered—that it relies exclusively on the psychological connection between two individuals (the leader and the ordinary citizen). To limit the significance of narrative to this role would also ignore decades of psychological theory and research and hold only to popular views of early social psychology and crowd behavior that ascribed almost all power to the influence of a leader (e.g., Freud, 1921/1959). Such views were popular in the era of totalitarianism, when all that was thought necessary to motivate atrocity was a leader with a charismatic, authoritarian personality (e.g., Adorno, Frenkel-Brunswik, Levinson, & Sanford, 1950).

In this chapter, I argue that narrative is a powerful rhetorical tool used far beyond the life stories of particular political candidates. Rather, consistent with growing arguments in social, cultural, and developmental psychology (e.g., Bamberg, 2011; Bhatia, 2011; Freeman, 2011; Hammack, 2008; McLean, Pasupathi, & Pals, 2007; Pasupathi, Mansour, & Brubaker, 2007; Syed & Azmitia, 2008), I suggest that we comprehend the social world through narrative—by clustering concepts, ideas, categories, characters, and events into a running dramatized storyline—provided to us through various forms of cultural construction, including the news media, entertainment industry, literature, law, and, of course, political discourse and rhetoric. In other words, our understanding of the social world is shaped by the meaning accorded people, places, events, and ideas and transmitted through the vehicles of culture—not a "neutral" culture but one understood as always serving the interests of some groups over others, a concept of culture informed by a recognition of power and domination (see Gjerde, 2004).

Although political rhetoric is typically framed as a set of truth claims, it is not the "accuracy" of narratives that is relevant to scientific analysis but rather the political positions they construct and the political actions they seek to motivate. The central premise of narrative is that it is fundamentally concerned with sense-making (Bruner, 1990, 1991, 2001). Narratives provide order, coherence, sensibility, and meaning to the world, and individuals call on narrative to bring a sense of coherence to their own life course (Cohler, 1982; McAdams, 1990, 1997). Political actors exploit this fundamental psychological premise to motivate sets of actions that will contribute to the larger jockeying for power of some groups over others. Narrative is thus not neutral but is always deployed to serve some interest for the maintenance or attainment of status, power, and dominance.

Narrative represents the ideal "root metaphor" for political psychology, similar to social psychologist Ted Sarbin's (1986) prescient call for narrative as the root metaphor for the discipline of psychology at large. Sarbin (1986) argued for a "narratory principle" in psychology: "that human beings think, perceive, imagine, and make moral choices according to narrative structures" (p. 8). Sarbin, along with other major figures in the discipline around the same time (e.g., Bruner, 1986, 1990; Cohler, 1982), saw the science of mind and behavior as firmly grounded in an engagement with language and metaphor. It has taken some time for the discipline to fully realize the seismic implications for this insight into our theories and research practices, but that day has clearly now arrived in political psychology (Hammack & Pilecki, 2012). This chapter seeks to provide a further anchor for scholars engaged in the interdisciplinary quest to link politics and the mind through rigorous theorizing and empirical inquiry.

A brief further note on the history of the narrative concept and its intrinsic interdisciplinary appeal is in order. One of the remarkable benefits of the narrative concept is its appeal to a wide range of scholars. Attention to narrative emerged with the invention of the novel as a particular cultural form (McAdams, 2012). Thus, scholars in the humanities have been at the forefront of theorizing the narrative concept (e.g., Dray, 1971; White, 1987). By the 1980s, it had become clear that narratives were not just for novels, and psychologists increasingly turned to the narrative concept to theorize psychotherapy (Schafer, 1980), human development across the life course (Cohler, 1982), cultural participation (Bruner, 1986, 1990), and the formation of personality and identity (McAdams, 1988). Narrative was seen as a vital humanistic corrective in the psychological literature to the cold, computer metaphor of cognitive science and as a way to restore the idea of human beings as meaning-makers actively engaged in intentional acts (Bruner, 1990). Not surprisingly, when scholars from fields like sociology, politics, and history began to fully engage with the narrative concept, they found this psychological approach of relatively limited value, for its (over)emphasis on human agency and its neglect of a direct statement on the relative power of particular narratives. In other words, true to psychology's disciplinary biases, early narrative psychologists initially saw narrative as a kind of universal process, with the "absent standard" of its elaboration being the actor at the center of global power—the European American heterosexual male (see Sampson, 1993).

The political psychology of narrative offers a corrective to the psychologist's penchant for directing his or her conceptual gaze in this hegemonic, universalizing direction and to the non-psychologist's penchant for neglecting the significance of the individual mind in social and political action. In the remainder of this chapter, I posit three premises of the political psychology of narrative and three psycho-political functions of narrative, expanding upon my argument for the centrality of narrative in both political and psychological life. My intent is to integrate perspectives on narrative and discourse that have emerged somewhat separately in psychological and political science (and related fields such as sociology) and to make the assumptions underlying this integration explicit. I offer examples of methodological approaches to narrative research in political psychology, including some that fuse levels of analysis and are inherently interdisciplinary or "transdisciplinary" in their efforts to be problem centered, rather than discipline centered. Finally, I conclude with a statement on the need for social scientists of narrative, psychology, and politics to offer practical knowledge that will advance interests of global social justice and the repudiation of violence as a means of silencing some narratives in the interest of domination.

Narrative, Politics, and Mind: Three Premises, Three Functions

The underlying assumption of a narrative approach in political psychology is that language, broadly conceived, represents the mechanism through which self and society are mutually constituted (Hammack & Pilecki, 2012). This assumption is rooted in classic and contemporary social science theory that emphasizes the content of mind as socially constructed through interaction and engagement with a system of meaning and signification apparent in language (e.g., Bakhtin, 1981; G. Mead, 1934; Vygotsky, 1934/1962). Narrative explains how concepts long theorized as central to political life—including interests, identities, ideologies, and mentalities—are consolidated in both individual and collective cognition and mobilized to achieve political ends.

Premise 1: Interests and Identities as Narratives

In the 2012 Republican presidential primary, former House Speaker Newt Gingrich was solidly defeated by former Massachusetts Governor Mitt Romney, but Gingrich received considerable support from those who identified as "White Evangelicals" in states such as South Carolina and Florida (CNN, 2012). What is it about Newt Gingrich that might have motivated individuals who identify as Evangelical to enter a voting booth and mark the box next to his name? His demonstrated infidelity in the realm of that most sacred institution to Evangelicals—heterosexual marriage—was not likely a consideration. Rather, Gingrich appeared to deploy a particular political rhetoric that appealed to those who identify as Evangelical (Edsall, 2012). Those who identify as Evangelical also appear to be among the Republican Party's most enraged at the state of US national decline (Edsall, 2012). To the extent that Gingrich was able to successfully capture the affect of anger and rage in his rhetorical performances, he facilitated an identification process between the Evangelical and himself—an identification which motivated a particular political act on behalf of the Evangelical (i.e., a vote cast for Newt).

My point is that identity politics is not simply a popular term in the academy; it is a behavioral phenomenon. Our identities guide our political behavior, whether that behavior is situated at the level of a private voting booth in South Carolina or Florida, a mass protest against a hegemonic government in Egypt or Syria, or the actions of a coordinated social movement like the US "Occupy" movement of 2012. The link between identities and interests has been a topic of great concern for scholars of politics, economics, and sociology, but psychology provides the conceptual bridge to make sense of this link through the concept of narrative. We interpret our interests in material or symbolic terms by using narrative—by crafting a story of who we are and why engaging in some political action (e.g., casting a vote for a particular candidate, joining a social movement, engaging in a protest, etc.) is consistent with our interests. This narrative *is* our identity, and it provides the lens through which we justify our actions, to both ourselves and others (McAdams, 1993, 1996).

Two of psychology's great theorists—William James and Erik Erikson—spoke of identity in terms of a consciousness of self-sameness, by which they meant a sense that one is the same person from one day to the next (e.g., Erikson, 1959, 1968; James, 1890). In other words, identity confers coherence and continuity in the psychological experience of everyday life. Erikson (1959, 1968) importantly extended this view by fusing it with a more explicit concern with *social* identity—the idea that identity is not just about our sense of self but also about our sense of belonging to a group and a set of ideological commitments. In one of his most famous books, Erikson (1958) provided an analysis of Martin Luther not simply as an interesting character in religious history but as a political actor motivated by a passionate ideology in conflict with the dominant ideology of the day (i.e., corrupt Catholicism).

But what is the relationship between the psychological concept of *identity* and the economic or political concept of *interest*? In social psychology, interest became supplanted by the identity concept with the history of experimental social psychology. Muzafer Sherif's (Sherif, 1956, 1958; Sherif, Harvey,

White, Hood, & Sherif, 1961) famous Robbers Cave experiment assumed that conflict between groups was driven by a real competition of material interests. Although Sherif and colleagues did demonstrate that conflict could be reduced when groups were compelled to cooperate to achieve "superordinate" goals related to common material interests (e.g., securing a common water supply), a key finding of the experiment was that constructing a symbolic difference between groups—giving them distinct names (or, in the jargon of social psychology, activating a categorization process)—was enough to instill and maintain intergroup hostility. Although Sherif himself preferred to emphasize the finding related to superordinate goals, this study offered a tipping point for other social psychologists to place identity at the forefront of their studies (e.g., Tajfel & Turner, 1979, 1986). It suggested that, over and above material interests, the symbolic nature of categorization into discrete social units (i.e., identities) could prove determinative of behavior.

In the 1970s, social identity theory—a perspective that has been of great interest in political psychology (e.g., Brewer, 2001; Huddy, 2001; Reicher, 2004)—affirmed in highly controlled laboratory experiments that mere categorization into arbitrary social groups was sufficient to activate in-group bias (Tajfel & Turner, 1979, 1986). Tajfel and Turner (1986) argued that in-group bias in the lab was the analogue to ethnocentrism in the real world, but in-group bias likely speaks to an even broader phenomenon in which individuals psychologically align their actions to vie for status and power (e.g., Sidanius & Pratto, 1999).

Identity, then, is not a neutral feature of individual psychological experience or development. Rather, it is a tool for collective action, a mechanism through which configurations of power are constructed, maintained, or resisted (see Polletta & Jasper, 2001). To the extent that we have an identity, we act upon the world in such a way as to coordinate with others so identified to advance our interests. In this frame, the theory of the rational actor in political behavior diminishes and is supplanted by a view of persons as pawns in the game of identity politics. This helps us to see why many vote against their individual economic interest—their narrative of identity compels them to act in a way that favors alignment with the group's interest (communicated itself through rhetoric) to compete for status and power.

A concern with identity has grown all the more central to psychology as the identity concept has increased in cultural and political relevance (and discourse) since the peak of Erikson's theorizing in the 1960s or Tajfel's initial theoretical and experimental work in the 1970s (Hammack, 2008). But only relatively recently has a clear and compelling paradigm to empirically access what James and Erikson meant when they spoke of a "sense" of identity or what the interpretation of social identity in Tajfel and Turner's (1986) theory might look like at the level of individual social cognition. That paradigm is narrative (Hammack & Pilecki, 2012; Pilecki & Hammack, in press).

The central premise of narrative identity development is that we construct life stories that provide a sense of meaning, coherence, and purpose across the life course (McAdams, 2008, 2011; Singer, 2004). These life stories assume a particular form, integrate thematic content, and are situated in an ideological setting—all of which guide our interpretation of the world and, as a consequence, behavior. McAdams (2006) has shown that highly generative adults in the US tend to narrate redemptive life stories which likely contribute to their ability to be generative (i.e., engaged in activity associated with care for the next generation; see Erikson & Erikson, 1981; McAdams & de St. Aubin, 1992). My research suggests that Jewish Israeli and Palestinian youth narrate radically divergent life stories (Hammack, 2011a). In the case of Jewish Israeli youth, a redemptive form and thematic content related to historic persecution, existential insecurity, and exceptionalism appear to provide important sources of psychological resilience to war and conflict, even as this narrative legitimizes their continued subordination of the Palestinians (Hammack, 2009b, 2011a). Palestinian youth, by contrast, narrate life stories "contaminated" (McAdams & Bowman, 2001) or "spoiled" (Goffman, 1963) by their subordinate and perpetually unrecognized national identity status (Hammack, 2010a, 2011a). This contaminated form is maintained through thematic content that emphasizes loss and dispossession, existential insecurity, and the legitimacy of resistance—the latter of which legitimizes the use of violence against Jewish Israelis.

Our identities are thus not merely categorical labels that organize the world of social relations. Rather, we live our identities by constructing personal narratives that provide a vocabulary to the experience of inhabiting a particular social category. As we internalize the master narrative of belonging to a particular category—man, woman, gay, straight, Black, White, Israeli, Palestinian, Catholic, Protestant, to name a few in the realm of probably inappropriate binaries—we construct an identity anchored in our rhetorical engagement with the world (Hammack, 2011b). Hence, to the extent that the politics of identity drives political behavior, motivating particular forms of political action, narrative is the vehicle through which individual actors come to identify with leaders and movements (Polletta, 2006).

Premise 2: Ideologies and Mentalities as Narratives

Narrative identity development does not occur in a political or cultural vacuum. Rather, the stories with which we engage as we develop coherent identities are normative scripts about not only how the world *is* but also how it *might be*. In other words, narratives are not just *descriptive*; they are *prescriptive*. These normative scripts represent ideologies in the neutral sense of that term—as broad systems of beliefs that cohere and form a particular worldview (van Dijk, 1998). They characterize a particular "mentality" about the world and its presumed ideal order. Just as my personal narrative of identity leads me to act a certain way in the political world because of the social category I inhabit, my mentality about the world and how it "ought" to be provides further narrative content that guides my political action.

Narrative, then, is not a concept relegated to individual psychological processes of identity formation or meaning making. Rather, group life operates through collective processes of storytelling that construct a coherent account of group mentality or ideology. This idea can be linked to Durkheim's (1893/1984) notion of collective consciousness: "The totality of beliefs and sentiments common to the average members of a society forms a determinate system with a life of its own. It can be termed the collective or common consciousness" (pp. 38–39). Durkheim's student Maurice Halbwachs (1992) later emphasized the concept of collective memory in the study of groups and society, and a whole field of knowledge has flourished in this area in sociology, anthropology, and politics (e.g., Wertsch & Roediger, 2008).

Concepts assumed to occur at the collective level—such as ideology, mentality, or collective memory—can be subsumed just as easily under the rubric of narrative as the personal narratives of identity psychologists have increasingly come to study. Thinking of these phenomena as narratives is useful because it specifies their location and a clear method for empirical study. Ideologies, mentalities, and collective memories are embodied in narratives that proliferate in societies—in anchoring texts, speeches of political leaders, media representations, and other cultural artifacts. Narrative is thus an empirical umbrella for a host of phenomena that scholars who emphasize collective or societal levels of analysis can call upon.

Social psychologists have increasingly directed their attention toward these ideas of collective cognition, through concepts such as group beliefs (Bar-Tal, 1990, 2000) and master narratives (Hammack, 2011a, 2011b). In contrast to the original notion of a "group mind" (McDougall, 1921) or "crowd" psychology (Le Bon, 1895), these more contemporary approaches view individuals and settings as co-constituted. In other words, consistent with the central axiom of cultural psychology (Shweder, 1990), persons and contexts "make one another up" as actors appropriate some narratives they encounter but repudiate others (Hammack, 2011b).

Narratives are anchored in *beliefs*, which are "basic knowledge categories such as ideology, values, norms, decisions, inferences, goals, expectations, religious dogmas, or justifications" (Bar-Tal, 2000, p. xii). When beliefs form a coherent cluster in the form of a larger group or *master* narrative (Fivush, 2010; Hammack, 2011b), they invoke a shared sociopsychological repertoire which provides a heuristic for individuals to interpret reality (Bar-Tal, 2000, 2007). Social reproduction depends upon cultural participants appropriating these shared beliefs by invoking master narratives to motivate their behavior and coordinate their activity, itself then providing a common "consciousness" rooted in experience of the material and practical world.

In other words, master narratives compel individuals to appropriate a particular "mentality" or worldview that will then guide collective behavior toward some political end. They contain within them an ideological setting intended to offer what Isaiah Berlin (1976) refers to as "views, goals, and pictures of the world" and provide us with an interpretive anchor for what we consider "true, beautiful, and efficient" (Shweder, 2003). Master narratives construct a form of reality as it "ought" to be, rather than what it may in fact be on the ground. In this way, narratives become tools to guide collective sentiment and action toward some imagined end.

The clearest examples of the role of shared beliefs or master narratives have emerged from research on intractable conflict. In the Israeli context, Bar-Tal and colleagues have illustrated how Jewish Israeli society relies upon shared beliefs related to patriotism (Bar-Tal, 1993), security (Bar-Tal, Jacobson, & Freund, 1995), siege (Bar-Tal & Antebi, 1992), victimization (Bar-Tal, Chernyak-Hai, Schori, & Gundar, 2009), and delegitimization (Bar-Tal, 1989; Bar-Tal & Hammack, 2012) (for an overview, see Bar-Tal, 1998). Bar-Tal (2000) argues that these beliefs construct an *ethos* of conflict which frames the psychological experience of all citizens in a conflict setting (Bar-Tal, Sharvit, Halperin, & Zafran, 2012), influencing how Jewish Israelis interpret encounters with Palestinians (Bar-Tal, Raviv, Raviv, & Dgani-Hirsch, 2009). The point here is that individuals interpret reality using clusters of beliefs that can be considered widely "distributed" among a populace to fulfill basic needs related to security and identity, and these are particularly evident in settings in which groups feel insecure (Pettigrew, 2003).

The emphasis on beliefs as central components of narrative somewhat de-emphasizes the role of affect in securing individual appropriation of the beliefs that comprise a master narrative. An overemphasis on rational cognition obscures the provocative nature of narrative. That is, the evaluative and prescriptive dimension of narrative is anchored in affect, and response to narratives is not always rational. Thus, there has been greater attention in recent literature in social and political psychology on the critical role of emotion in guiding actions. For example, studies have shown how emotions such as anger (e.g., Zarowsky, 2000, 2004), humiliation (e.g., Fattah & Fierke, 2009), and hatred (e.g., Halperin, 2008) are fundamental to the collective narratives that intend to motivate individuals to either maintain or challenge the status quo.

Master narratives do not proliferate solely in settings of active intractable conflict, though. Narratives are constructed in stable liberal democracies in the same way to persuade members of a populace to engage in political acts. In the 2012 US presidential election, both Obama and Romney called on narratives of national identity intended to respond to the wide-scale perception of national decline. They called on distinct tropes, but their goal was identical: to construct a storyline that would evoke a sentimental identification and a sense of command over the direction the national storyline might ultimately take. Whereas Romney (2012a, 2012b) anchored his narrative in the notion that Americans are "eternal optimists" whose values are rooted in the freedom of individual choice, Obama's (2012a, 2012b, 2012c) rhetoric emphasized ordinary Americans as intelligent, hardworking, and perseverant.

Whether in settings of conflict, war, or stable liberal democracy, master narratives represent rhetorical devices by which groups vie for power, status, and legitimacy. In war and conflict, these master narratives are often perceived as compulsory for identification, particularly when the group perceives existential insecurity (Hammack, 2011a, 2011b). Master narratives represent ideologies about the nature of truth, beauty, goodness, and efficiency (Shweder, 2003). They provide interpretive anchors on which individuals become motivated to engage in the intentional acts that form a "culture" (Bruner, 1990). In this way, narrative provides a window into the collective mentality of a group—its understanding of the nature of reality and the contours of imagined possibility.

Premise 3: Narratives as Performances

The third premise which underlies a political psychology of narrative is that narratives are neither solely "out there" in the material world of cultural products or historical artifacts (e.g., textbooks, films, political speeches) or "in there" in the inner reaches of the human mind. Rather, narratives are performed and lived in social practice. Autobiographies are constructed through performance, as individuals engage in "acts of meaning" (Bruner, 1990). In this performance, a status quo of politics is either reproduced or repudiated.

The case of Israeli and Palestinian social practices in which ordinary citizens participate provides an example. While Jewish Israelis celebrate their Independence Day commemorating their victory in the 1948 Arab–Israeli War, Palestinians engage in collective protest the same day to commemorate what they call the *Nakba* (Catastrophe). Jewish Israelis perform their narrative of resilience, redemption (from the tragedy of the diaspora and European anti-Semitism), and exceptionalism through participation in rituals commemorating Independence (Kook, 2005; Zerubavel, 1995). By contrast, Palestinians perform their narrative of loss, dispossession, and tragedy through acts of collective protest on the same occasion (Sa'di & Abu-Lughod, 2007). Social psychologists and political scientists converge on the central tenet that these polarized narratives maintain and exacerbate the conflict between Palestinians and Israelis, mobilizing and justifying acts of political violence (e.g., Bar-Tal & Salomon, 2006; Kaufman, 2009; Rouhana & Bar-Tal, 1998). For Israelis and Palestinians, narratives guide and coordinate their activities, but participation in these activities also shifts the narratives from their location in texts, artifacts, or individual minds to a performative space in which they are lived and embodied.

The performative aspect of narrative is not relevant only to contexts of intractable conflict. Two recent political movements in the US illustrate the role of narrative in social practice intended to achieve some political end. In the 2010 US midterm elections, the Tea Party movement constructed a narrative of "impending tyranny" to motivate individuals disaffected and discontent with the economic state of affairs to organize and protest for a radical right-wing agenda (Barstow, 2010). The Tea Party movement effectively used affect, namely, anger and fear, to instill its narrative of doom (Rasmussen & Schoen, 2010; Zernike, 2010). If one considers the outcome of that election, the narrative and its performance in widely covered protests achieved at least some of its political ends, claiming several winning candidates.

At the other end of the US political spectrum, the Occupy Wall Street movement relied upon a narrative of economic injustice to mobilize individuals to engage in collective protest (e.g., Hardt & Negri, 2011). Although it is less clear that these actions achieved concrete political ends, they were nevertheless the subject of much attention in the general public and a considerable amount of discussion. The story of Wall Street executives hoarding and growing their wealth amidst formidable economic hardship for the majority of Americans provided the impetus for a left-wing push to reconsider how capitalism is practiced in the US.

The point is that narratives are not static storylines about groups or individuals but rather are political acts in themselves. We embody narratives through our own set of practices, and these practices themselves make our identities. In other words, consistent with cultural psychology's thesis of "mutual constitution" (Shweder, 1990), minds and acts are co-constituted: How and what we think is shaped by what we do, but we act in ways that cohere with existing thoughts and sentiments.

The Psycho-Political Functions of Narrative

To summarize the premises of a narrative approach to linking politics and mind, it is useful to articulate the psycho-political functions of narrative. By "psycho-political" functions, I mean the role narrative assumes in both mental experience—cognition, emotion, and behavior—and in influencing the power configuration of a society. Narrative, I argue, links mind and politics as it provides a "leading activity" in both the mental and political spheres. Here I am indebted to the cultural psychological approach of Vygotsky (1978), who emphasized the role of activity in securing the appropriation of linguistic tools that guide human development, and to the symbolic interactionist approach of George Herbert Mead (1934), who emphasized mind, self, and society as co-constructed in social acts.

The three premises outlined above speak to three concrete functions of narrative. First, narratives *provide individuals with a vocabulary* to interpret the sensory world. They specify a path to meaning. They allow us to make sense of what we see, hear, feel, and touch by going beyond mere description to both explanation and prescription. Narratives confer meaning, sensibility, and order to an otherwise chaotic and often troubling series of events. The Holocaust is a story of totalitarian madness and power gone deeply awry. Yet its inability to succeed in its eugenics-inspired end, coupled with the triumph of Israel and the demise (although by no means eradication) of global master narratives of ethnic hierarchy, constructs a redemptive story through which good defeats evil, light rises over dark. Thus, the Holocaust narrative, as it is deployed in most of the world as a story of ultimate evil (it is noteworthy that the terms *Nazi* and *Hitler* immediately evoke the sinister in English language rhetoric; see Jackson, 2005), describes and explains historical events but also *prescribes* a moral order in which genocide becomes an ultimate evil of humanity (Staub, 2011). For Jewish Israelis, the darkness of Diaspora anti-Semitism, culminating in the Holocaust, offers a foil to the narrative of modern Israeli identity (Zerubavel, 1995, 2002), and particularly the identity of the native-born or *Sabra* Israeli as a force with which to be reckoned (Almog, 2000). In other words, contemporary Jewish Israelis understand their own subjectivity in light of the Holocaust narrative, among many other narratives intended to provide them with a collective sense of purpose and coherence. Their experience of the material world—including the violence of continued conflict with the Palestinians or impending conflict with Iran—is mediated through these narratives.

According to Foucault (1982), subjectivity is not simply a state of identity *consciousness* or self-awareness. Rather, subjectivity ties us to our identities through *conscience* and results in our subjugation to others through "control and dependence" (p. 781). Thus narrative, by constructing subjectivity, motivates particular sets of actions on the world that we perceive as compulsory if we are to be "faithful" to our identities. These actions fundamentally concern acts of power and domination, or the quest thereof. The second psycho-political function of narrative is thus *to motivate coordinated activity* among a collective that will enhance the power of the group and, in the process, affirm, construct, or reconstruct a narrative in which the group achieves elevated power or value in the larger matrix of social categories.

Here Foucauldian notions of power and language intersect with social identity theory, providing a bridge from a theoretical position rarely invoked in psychology to one that has come to dominate the discipline (or at least the subdiscipline of social psychology). Both perspectives are concerned with how individuals come to conceive their membership in arbitrarily constructed social categories and how that conception then influences behavior. At the core of both perspectives is the idea of power and social value. In Tajfel and Turner's (1979) "minimal group" experimental paradigm, the categories constructed may be rather meaningless, but they are sufficiently *meaningful* to activate in-group bias, manifest behaviorally in acts of favoritism toward in-group members. In the real world of social categorization in which membership in a group confers, or fails to confer, all sorts of rights, privileges, and opportunities, identity is an even more central tool to guide our actions (Reicher, 2004). But until we bridge these theoretical perspectives—one which emphasizes how discourse constructs subjectivity (Foucault, 1978, 1982), and one which emphasizes how social categorization influences behavior (Tajfel & Turner, 1979, 1986)—through *narrative*, we are missing the mechanism through which the larger process of social relations and continued cycles of domination, liberation, or resistance occur. Narrative allows us to directly probe this process while it is underway, rather than to simply speculate on it historically, as some might claim Foucault to have done, or to do no more than simply continue to demonstrate the phenomenon in rarefied laboratory conditions, as many social psychologists might be accused of doing today.

In motivating action, narrative comes to achieve its third psycho-political function: *to clearly play a role in politics.* That is, by constructing subjectivity in such a way as to motivate action, be it casting a vote for Mitt Romney or joining a massive assembly in Tahrir Square, narrative becomes the vehicle for acquiring or exercising power, status, or authority. In this frame, narratives are not simply tools we as individuals use to make meaning, or documents of collective memory that enhance our solidarity and security in a group. Rather, narratives are the means through which politics unfolds in human communities on a universal scale. To the extent that all human communities use language as a form of communication, they use narratives as a form of motivation, domination, and liberation—as tools in the universal competition for status and power.

Interrogating Narrative

One of the gems of narrative is that it anchors concepts often viewed as abstract—ideology, identity, collective memory, social practice—in an empirically accessible product: *the story.* Stories have beginnings, middles, and ends. They have characters. They have themes or tropes. They have motifs intended to educate, motivate, and explain. They represent the most rudimentary form of our cognitive engagement with the social world, when one considers storytelling at the crib (Nelson, 2006).

Stories pervade our lives, and the task of the narrativist is to access, document, interrogate narratives—to witness them and to represent them to a broader audience, but also to make sense of the particularity of their psychopolitical functions in a given sociopolitical context. The narrativist is thus a problem-centered social scientist, concerned with how individuals and groups construct, deconstruct, and reconstruct their worlds through the linguistic practice of narration. The methodological toolkit of the narrativist includes, at minimum, ethnography, experimentation, life-story analysis, and discourse analysis, and I detail examples of empirical work that calls upon these approaches below.

At the core of a narrative approach is the central premise of a hermeneutic philosophy of science—namely, the assumption that *interpretation* is axiomatic to human life, development, and social organization (e.g., Dilthey, 1923/1988; Ricoeur, 1981; Tappan, 1997). The individual is a thinking, acting, intuiting subject of a social order he or she must navigate and, in his or her interpretive engagement with the existing sensory world, either reproduce or repudiate through his or her own actions. Any empirical approach to stories in the social world hence assumes that they are intrinsically interpretations of reality, and it is the *interpretations* that concern that narrativist, not whether or not the story may be considered "accurate" according to some material property of the empirical world.

The hermeneutic philosophy of science, originating especially in the work of nineteenth-century psychologist Wilhelm Dilthey (e.g., 1894/1977), is anchored in the idea that the scientist seeks to *understand* human and historical life. This early view of psychology as integrative of historical and cultural analysis was largely discarded in favor of a psychology more aligned with the natural sciences and the delineation of lawful regularities of mind and behavior (Gergen, 1976). The "descriptive" and "historical" psychology of Dilthey was largely eclipsed by the ahistoric empiricism of William James and Wilhelm Wundt (although Wundt later emphasized two distinct branches of psychology—one dealing with physiology and one dealing with "culture" or "folk psychology"; see Wundt, 1916).

The narrative approach advocated here is thus not necessarily novel in its emphasis on meaning and interpretation; it is linked to a philosophical stance that was present at the birth of psychological science. The ascendance of narrative in contemporary psychology reveals a renaissance of integrative and holistic perspectives of the person as historically situated and history as at least in part psychologically determined through the meaning persons make of their situated lives (e.g., Erikson, 1958). The hermeneutic philosophy guides the narrative empiricist toward multiple levels of analysis (e.g., the individual, the cultural, the historical, the economic, the political), but it does so in a way that is focused on psychological *engagement* with the material world through acts of interpretation (e.g., Bruner, 1990; Hammack, 2011b; Tappan, 1997).

The anchoring point for a hermeneutic science focused on meanings and interpretations, fusing levels of analysis, is that the world is fundamentally and universal *textual*, by which I mean that material conditions and experiences command the construction of a coherent storyline which explains why they are, how they could be different (if so desired), and how one might achieve some change toward this end. The pothole in a street has an origin story; it evokes emotion when one encounters it; it has a solution story that requires human action. This may seem a trivial example, but it reveals the universality with which narrative operates in the mind and on the world. When narratives clash in their fundamental meaning, conflicts occur. The suicide bombing at an Israeli checkpoint in the occupied West Bank has two radically divergent interpretations for Israelis and Palestinians—and the result is that violence endures and even escalates, as the two interpretations fail to meet (Hammack, 2011a; Rotberg, 2006; Rouhana & Bar-Tal, 1998).

The point is that a narrative approach conceives of human experience and action as a text (e.g., Ricoeur, 1984). The aim, then, is to identify the storylines individuals and groups use to make sense of the social world. At the smallest level of analysis, one can collect the individual's own personal narrative or his response to a constructed narrative. In the social sciences, the former approach is represented in life-story narrative analysis (e.g., Lieblich, Tuval-Mashiach, & Zilber, 1998), whereas the latter is represented in experimental studies in which subjects respond to a narrative account presented by the researcher (either constructed or a real-life stimulus such as a film or newspaper article). Life-story narrative analysis requires a text—the product of a life-story interview (e.g., McAdams, 1993). For those interested in narrative, identity, and politics, the interesting point of analysis in these texts centers on one's political position or viewpoint, or one's experience of a particular social category (e.g., oppressed minority; e.g., Ephrem & White, 2011; Hammack & Cohler, 2011). Psychologists who study life-story narratives have illustrated how "conservatives" and "liberals" in the US (McAdams et al., 2008) or Israelis and Palestinians narrate divergent life stories (Hammack, 2011a)—how their forms, thematic content, or ideological settings reveal the salience of their political positions or self-understandings.

In studies of individual *response* to political narratives, the goal is to understand how stories influence thought, judgment, affect, or behavior at the individual level (although typically reported in aggregate using statistical methods). For example, Bullock and Fernald (2005) examined responses to the way in which George W. Bush's proposed elimination of the dividend tax was framed. They found that the framing of the meaning of wealth and how it was acquired (e.g., product of personal initiative) affected individuals' support for the policy. Gross (2008) illustrated how opinion on policy issues such as mandatory minimum sentencing is shaped by the affective content of the narrative constructed to frame an event. Baird and Gangl (2006) found that the framing of the US Supreme Court as rendering "political" decisions rather than following legal guidelines increases citizens' negative perceptions of the Court. Eibach and Keegan (2006) examined how Blacks and Whites respond differently to social change related to racial equality depending on whether the change is constructed as a "loss" or a "gain." Although these types of studies are not typically situated within the larger literature on narrative in social psychology, they detail how individuals respond to narratives about politics in ways that inform how leaders and policy makers might use rhetoric to mobilize individuals and groups to support policy or to take action.

Psychology is often criticized for its analysis of the self-contained individual as its primary unit of analysis (e.g., Sampson, 1989). Although both life-story narrative analyses and narrative response studies take context seriously, they study texts primarily in static form—as constructed by the individual storyteller or as responded to by an individual. Discourse analysis takes a different approach by considering how narratives are deployed in widely disseminated texts (e.g., political speeches or manifestos) or in conversation (see Woofitt, 2005). Thus, the narrativist who takes a discourse analytic approach does not study individuals but rather *units of text*, such as utterances in a conversation or lines in a speech.

Most notably, discourse analysis has been used to examine the content and form of political rhetoric, typically in speeches or formal settings of political discourse. For example, Gibson (2012) analyzed the content of a British television program in which audience members could question authorities such as politicians, journalists, or commentators during the build-up to the 2003 invasion of Iraq. By relying upon this interactive source of textual data—conversations between audience members and authorities with particular political positions toward the war—he was able to illustrate how attitudes toward war are dialogically constructed. In the case of his analysis, the story for or against war was not a static text but a dynamic one in the midst of being coauthored between the British public and authorities.

A more common approach to discourse analytic research is to analyze the content of political speeches directly for their rhetorical aims. For example, Gholizadeh and Hook (2012) analyzed the speeches of Ayatolla Khomeini during the 1978–1979 Iranian revolution. They illustrated how Khomeini used the narrative of the Battle of Karbala and the idea of a "dangerous foreign other" to mobilize an anxious populace. Similar types of analyses have been conducted in speeches or official statements of political leaders in the UK about immigration and asylum (Capdevelia & Callaghan, 2008) or about the left-right political spectrum (Weltman & Billig, 2001), Hamas leaders in Palestine about the role of religion in society (McVittie, McKinlay, & Sambaraju, 2011), and George W. Bush and his administration officials in the US about the "war on terror" (Esch, 2010). The emphasis in this methodological approach is more concretely on the semantic and hermeneutic functions of language and its intended target for individual or collective perception.

Of all options in the methodological toolkit of the narrativist, the most comprehensive, but exhausting, of methods is ethnography. Long considered the ideal way to access the customs, practices, and ideologies of a group (e.g., Malinowksi, 1927; M. Mead, 1928), ethnography relies upon participant observation and immersion into a group of study, thus providing a window into how stories may serve to construct meaning of political configurations and political violence. The ethnographer seeks to capture narratives in action through analysis of cultural artifacts in various textual forms (e.g., media representations, educational textbooks), but unlike other methods, the ethnographer embeds him- or herself within the community for some period to allow for an intimate analysis. He or she uses methods of field research common in anthropology and sociology involving the collection of a large corpus of qualitative data to understand how narratives shape meaning in a broad array of contexts.

Ethnographic practices and the nature of ethnographic writing have shifted considerably since the origin of this method in cultural anthropology (e.g., Clifford & Marcus, 1986; Denzin, 1997; Hammersley, 1992). For the would-be ethnographer of narrative, politics, and the mind, the goal is not to conduct the "detached" analysis of phenomena from a distance that once dominated the core practices of participant observation. Rather, the goal is to shift the lens toward what Tedlock (1991) calls "the observation of participation" (p. 69). In this frame, which Tedlock (1991) actually calls *narrative ethnography*, analysis of "self" (i.e., ethnographer and his positionality vis-à-vis the group of study) and "other" are intertwined in a single narrative account of the *dialogue* that characterizes ethnographic practice.

Because of its holistic, immersive approach, ethnography affords a much wider corpus of data for the narrativist to interrogate. Ethnographers have examined such topics as how historical narratives are represented and engaged with in educational settings in Israel (Dalsheim, 2007), how displaced Bosnian mothers constructed coherent narratives of war trauma (Robertson & Duckett, 2007), how Somali refugee narratives challenge dominant psychiatric conceptions of trauma (Zarowsky, 2000, 2004), and how intergroup contact efforts between Israeli and Palestinian youth fail in their attempt to indoctrinate superordinate identity narratives (Hammack, 2009a, 2011a). Increasingly, ethnographers integrate levels of analysis to understand how individual narratives and collective narratives intersect and are co-constitutive. In these approaches, life-story narrative analysis is often embedded within a larger set of ethnographic practices, and life-story texts are considered *in relation to* master narratives or dominant discourses. For example, Zenker's (2010) analysis of interviews with a West Belfast Catholic over the course of extended fieldwork illustrated how he challenged local hegemonic narratives of conflict trauma. My work with Palestinian and Israeli youth reveals the way in which they appropriate some aspects of group master narratives while actively challenging others, using both life-story narrative analysis and hermeneutic analysis of historical documents and political speeches (Hammack, 2011a).

In sum, interrogating narrative involves a commitment to a hermeneutic philosophy of science in which the aim is to understand the phenomenon of human interpretation in context. Experience of the world is textually mediated and embodied in the narratives individuals either construct or respond to in their actions. These narratives are accessible through methods that require individuals to directly provide them (e.g., life-story interviews) or to offer their interpretation or response (e.g., surveys administered or observations obtained in the context of an experiment). But they are also accessible through political speeches and other formal texts to which individuals are exposed en masse and through conversations (e.g., discourse analysis). And in the most comprehensive manner possible (i.e., ethnography), narratives are examined as sets of interconnected "webs of significance" (Geertz, 1973) with which individuals engage. In these types of studies, stories can be located at every level and are examined as part of a larger system of meaning, signification, and interpretation.

Narrative and Political Change

The purpose of this chapter has been to offer an integrative statement about mind, politics, and stories by outlining three fundamental premises and three functions of narrative, as well as a broad and inclusive methodological statement about how narrative might be empirically interrogated at multiple levels of analysis. To conclude, I stake the position that an emphasis on human interpretation in political context requires a normative commitment for the narrativist to "do good," by which I mean that the product of narrative study is itself a narrative which can play a role in the very social system it seeks to describe and explain. In other words, the knowledge produced through narrative inquiry stands to evoke a response to a political configuration or a status quo of domination and subordination. In this way, the product of narrative inquiry is itself a text that may support or challenge a status quo of intergroup relations.

The "interpretive turn" in social science research in general (Rabinow & Sullivan, 1987), and political psychology research in particular (Hammack & Pilecki, 2012), does not simply represent an epistemological or philosophical shift from positivism or postpositivism to constructionism. Rather, I suggest that the turn toward language, meaning, and interpretation in political perspective pivots political psychology toward a normative, critical position in which the ends of justice and social change toward equality are explicit. In other words, a narrative approach recognizes the narrativist him- or herself and the analysis he or she produces as part of the cycle of social stasis and change. Hence, his or her analysis may work explicitly for ends conceived as contributing to the betterment of human communities, rather than as supporting a status quo of domination or inequality.

In this frame, all knowledge is considered inherently political, and the narrativist's task is to offer a critical interrogation of the role of stories in social and psychological life. He or she constructs a story, or series of stories, about this role at a particular historical moment—a time of anxiety about national decline among Americans, or a time of political and cultural transition in parts of the Arab Middle East, or a time of economic anxiety in Europe. The point is to play a role in the discourse itself, toward positive ends that benefit a greater number of individuals and communities.

Here I do not actually stake a radical claim for narrative inquiry. I merely suggest that the normative ideology implicit in most social science research in political psychology becomes explicit and always frames the questions that guide the work. Thus, the problems the narrativist addresses might more clearly focus on how narratives promote violence and align themselves with social movements which seek to advance the interest of social justice on a global scale. In this way, narrative science—as a normative science—prescribes a set of ideals for peace and positive intergroup relations that emphasizes checks on the human inclination toward social dominance and hierarchy apparent in the history of wars, genocides, and mass atrocities (Staub, 2011).

Just as a film of the continued struggle of Native Americans on the Pine Ridge Reservation in the US presents a text to motivate political concern or action (Becker & Everett, 2012), the product of narrative inquiry might use a story *of stories* to work for some political end. Although the challenge to construct an accessible academic text in the context of increasingly isolated

language communities is formidable, there are examples of attempts to produce what Sampson (1993) calls "transformative knowledge." Cohler's (2007)
work on the changing historical context in which gay men constructed autobiographies in the US over the course of the 20th century reflects a concern
with describing and explaining the shift in vocabulary and social practices
increasingly available to same-sex attracted men during this era, but he also
aims to provide a document that could liberate contemporary youth from the
confines of narrow visions of categorical sexual identity labels. Lykes's extensive research among the Maya in Guatemala explicitly seeks to use narrative
to contribute to greater social justice for the indigenous community (e.g.,
Lykes, Blanche, & Hamber, 2003). Her work has gone beyond that of engaged
researcher to social advocate seeking to secure resources for the community
(Lykes, 2012). Of course, much work in conflict settings seeks to produce
knowledge that will expose the injustice of hegemonic narratives that oppress
an out-group and their impact on the mind of the oppressor (e.g., Rosler, Bar-
Tal, Sharvit, Halperin, & Raviv, 2009), or inform the kinds of peace-building
and reconciliation practices in which we engage (e.g., Andrews, 2003, 2007;
Hammack, 2011a).

The idea of narrative is rooted in the assumptions of a socially constructed
world, always in a dynamic state of mutual constitution through cognitive
processes, linguistic practices, and mediated social activity and interaction.
The narrative concept links the stuff of thought and feeling with documents
of life—life stories, speeches, media representations, cultural artifacts accessible on paper or online, and the like. Stories surround us and offer us access
to the intersection of cognition, emotion, and intentional action on the world.
Transcending disciplinary boundaries, we can interrogate stories as individuals engage with them, in conversation or in response to some storied stimulus, and we can map how stories "out there" converge with stories "in there"
by viewing the entirety of social life as interconnected storylines always in
process. Finally, investigators of narrative themselves construct narratives
that are not neutral vis-à-vis the political behavior, dynamics, or configuration they describe and explain. The political psychology of narrative is thus
an integrative science which sees persons and settings as mutually constituted in relation to received matrices of power and the relative meaning
and value of social categories, and the products of narrative science themselves may alter the very historical reality they seek to describe (Gergen,
1973). The task, then, of the narrativist of politics and psychology is to
produce knowledge that, to paraphrase Marx, goes beyond understanding
toward change itself.

References

Adorno, T. W., Frenkel-Brunswik, E., Levinson, D. J., & Sanford, R. N. (1950). *The
    authoritarian personality*. New York: Harper & Brothers.
Almog, O. (2000). *The Sabra: The creation of the new Jew* (H. Watzman, Trans.).
    Berkeley: University of California Press.

70   *Phillip L. Hammack*

Andrews, M. (2003). Grand national narratives and the project of truth commissions: A comparative analysis. *Media, Culture & Society*, *25*(1), 45–65.

Andrews, M. (2007). *Shaping history: Narratives of political change*. New York: Cambridge University Press.

Baird, V. A., & Gangl, A. (2006). Shattering the myth of legality: The impact of the media's framing of Supreme Court procedures on perceptions of fairness. *Political Psychology*, *27*(4), 597–614.

Bakhtin, M. M. (1981). *The dialogic imagination* (C. Emerson & M. Holquist, Trans.). Austin: University of Texas Press.

Bamberg, M. (2011). Who am I? Narration and its contribution to self and identity. *Theory & Psychology, 21*(1), 3–24.

Bar-Tal, D. (1989). Delegitimization: The extreme case of stereotyping and prejudice. In D. Bar-Tal, C. Graumann, A. W. Kruglanski, & W. Stroebe (Eds.), *Stereotyping and prejudice: Changing conceptions* (pp. 169–188). New York: Springer-Verlag.

Bar-Tal, D. (1990). *Group beliefs: A conception for analyzing group structure, processes, and behavior*. New York: Springer.

Bar-Tal, D. (1993). Patriotism as fundamental beliefs of group members. *Politics and the Individual, 3*(2), 45–62.

Bar-Tal, D. (1998). Societal beliefs in times of intractable conflict: The Israeli case. *International Journal of Conflict Management, 9*(1), 22–50.

Bar-Tal, D. (2000). *Shared beliefs in a society: Social psychological analysis*. Thousand Oaks, CA: Sage.

Bar-Tal, D. (2007). Sociopsychological foundations of intractable conflicts. *American Behavioral Scientist, 50*(11), 1430–1453.

Bar-Tal, D., & Antebi, D. (1992). Siege mentality in Israel. *International Journal of Intercultural Relations, 16*(3), 251–275.

Bar-Tal, D., Chernyak-Hai, L., Schori, N., & Gundar, A. (2009). A sense of self-perceived collective victimhood in intractable conflicts. *International Review of the Red Cross, 91*, 229–258.

Bar-Tal, D., & Hammack, P. L. (2012). Conflict, delegitimization, and violence. In L. Tropp (Ed.), *Oxford handbook of intergroup conflict* (pp. 29–52). New York: Oxford University Press.

Bar-Tal, D., Jacobson, D., & Freund, T. (1995). Security feelings among Jewish settlers in the occupied territories: A study of communal and personal antecedents. *Journal of Conflict Resolution, 39*(2), 353–377.

Bar-Tal, D., Raviv, A., Raviv, A., & Dgani-Hirsh, A. (2009). The influence of the ethos of conflict on Israeli Jews' interpretation of Jewish-Palestinian encounters. *Journal of Conflict Resolution, 53*(1), 94–118.

Bar-Tal, D., & Salomon, G. (2006). Israeli-Jewish narratives of the Israeli-Palestinian conflict: Evolution, contents, functions, and consequences. In R. I. Rotberg (Ed.), *Israeli and Palestinian narratives of conflict: History's double helix* (pp. 19–46). Bloomington: Indiana University Press.

Bar-Tal, D., Sharvit, K., Halperin, E., & Zafran, A. (2012). Ethos of conflict: The concept and its measurement. *Peace and Conflict: Journal of Peace Psychology, 18*(1), 40–61.

Barstow, D. (2010, February 15). Tea Party lights fuse for rebellion on right. *New York Times*. Retrieved August 17, 2012 from www.nytimes.com/2010/02/16/us/politics/16teaparty.html?_r=1&pagewanted=all

Becker, E. (Director), & Everett, S. (Producer). (2012). *Honor the treatise* [Film]. Retrieved August 15, 2012 from http://vimeo.com/41673110

Berlin, I. (1976). *Vico and Herder: Two studies in the history of ideas*. London: Hogarth.

Bhatia, S. (2011). Narrative inquiry as cultural psychology: Meaning-making in a contested global world. *Narrative Inquiry, 21*(2), 345–352.

Brewer, M. B. (2001). The many faces of social identity: Implications for political psychology. *Political Psychology, 22*(1), 115–125.

Bruner, J. (1986). *Actual minds, possible worlds*. Cambridge, MA: Harvard University Press.

Bruner, J. (1990). *Acts of meaning*. Cambridge, MA: Harvard University Press.

Bruner, J. (1991). The narrative construction of reality. *Critical Inquiry, 18*, 1–21.

Bruner, J. (2001). Self-making and world-making. In J. Brockmeier & D. Carbaugh (Eds.), *Narrative and identity: Studies in autobiography, self and culture* (pp. 25–37). Philadelphia: Johns Benjamin.

Bullock, H. E., & Fernald, J. L. (2005). Predicting support for eliminating the dividend tax: The role of framing and attributions for wealth. *Analyses of Social Issues and Public Policy, 5*, 49–66.

Capdevila, R., & Callaghan, J. E. M. (2008). "It's not racist. It's common sense." A critical analysis of political discourse around asylum and immigration in the UK. *Journal of Community & Applied Social Psychology, 18*(1), 1–16.

Clifford, J., & Marcus, G. E. (Eds.). (1986). *Writing culture: The poetics and politics of ethnography*. Berkeley: University of California Press.

CNN (2012). Exit polls: South Carolina. Retrieved August 15, 2012 from www.cnn. com/election/2012/primaries/epolls/sc

Cohler, B. J. (1982). Personal narrative and the life course. In P. Baltes & O.G. Brim (Eds.), *Life span development and behavior* (Vol. 4, pp. 205–241). New York: Academic Press.

Cohler, B. J. (2007). *Writing desire: Sixty years of gay autobiography*. Madison: University of Wisconsin Press.

Denzin, N. K. (1997). *Interpretive ethnography: Ethnographic practices for the 21st century*. Thousand Oaks, CA: Sage.

Dalsheim, J. (2007). Deconstructing national myths, reconstituting morality: Modernity, hegemony and the Israeli national past. *Journal of Historical Sociology, 20*(4), 521–554.

Dilthey, W. (1977). *Descriptive psychology and historical understanding* (R. M. Zaner & K. L. Heiges, Trans.). The Hague: Martinus Nijhoff. (Original work published 1894)

Dilthey, W. (1988). *Introduction to the human sciences: An attempt to lay a foundation for the study of society and history* (R. J. Betanzos, Trans.). Detroit, MI: Wayne State University Press. (Original work published 1923)

Dray, W. H. (1971). On the nature and role of narrative in historiography. *History and Theory, 10*(2), 153–171.

Durkheim, E. (1984). *The division of labor in society* (W. D. Halls, Trans.). New York: Free Press. (Original work published 1893)

Edsall, T. D. (2012). Newt Gingrich and the future of the right. Retrieved August 15, 2012 from http://campaignstops.blogs.nytimes.com/2012/01/29/newt-gingrich-and-the-future-of-the-right/

Eibach, R. P., & Keegan, T. (2006). Free at last? Social dominance, loss aversion, and White and Black Americans' differing assessments of racial progress. *Journal of Personality and Social Psychology, 90*(3), 453–467.

Ephrem, B., & White, A. M. (2011). Agency and expression despite repression: A comparative study of five Ethiopian lesbians. *Journal of Lesbian Studies, 15*(2), 226–246.

Erikson, E. H. (1958). *Young man Luther: A study in psychoanalysis and history*. New York: Norton.

Erikson, E. H. (1959). *Identity and the life cycle*. New York: Norton.

Erikson, E. H. (1968). *Identity: Youth and crisis*. New York: Norton.

Erikson, E., & Erikson, J. (1981). On generativity and identity: From a conversation with Erik and Joan Erikson. *Harvard Educational Review, 51*(2), 249–269.

Esch, J. (2010). Legitimizing the "War on Terror": Political myth in official-level rhetoric. *Political Psychology, 31*(3), 357–391.

Fattah, K., & Fierke, K. M. (2009). A clash of emotions: The politics of humiliation and political violence in the Middle East. *European Journal of International Relations, 15*(1), 67–93.

Fivush, R. (2010). Speaking silence: The social construction of silence in autobiographical and cultural narratives. *Memory, 18*(2), 88–98.

Foucault, M. (1978). *The History of Sexuality, Vol. 1. An introduction* (R. Hurley, Trans.). New York: Pantheon.

Foucault, M. (1982). The subject and power. *Critical Inquiry, 8*, 777–795.

Freeman, M. (2011). Stories, big and small: Toward a synthesis. *Theory & Psychology, 21*(1), 114–121.

Freud, S. (1959). *Group psychology and the analysis of the ego* (J. Strachey, Trans.). New York: Norton. (Original work published 1921)

Geertz, C. (1973). *The interpretation of cultures*. New York: Basic Books.

Gergen, K. J. (1973). Social psychology as history. *Journal of Personality and Social Psychology, 26*(2), 309–320.

Gergen, K. J. (1976). Social psychology, science and history. *Personality and Social Psychology Bulletin, 2*, 373–383.

Gholizadeh, S., & Hook, D. W. (2012). The discursive construction of the 1978–1979 Iranian revolution in the speeches of Ayatollah Khomeini. *Journal of Community & Applied Social Psychology, 22*(2), 174–186.

Gibson, S. (2012). "I'm not a war monger but . . .": Discourse analysis and social psychological peace research. *Journal of Community & Applied Social Psychology, 22*(2), 159–173.

Gjerde, P. F. (2004). Culture, power, and experience: Toward a person-centered cultural psychology. *Human Development, 47*, 138–157.

Goffman, E. (1963). *Stigma: Notes on the management of spoiled identity*. New York: Simon & Schuster.

Gross, K. (2008). Framing persuasive appeals: Episodic and thematic framing, emotional response, and policy opinion. *Political Psychology, 29*(2), 169–192.

Halbwachs, M. (1992). *On collective memory* (L. Coser, Trans.). Chicago: University of Chicago Press.

Halperin, E. (2008). Group-based hatred in intractable conflict in Israel. *Journal of Conflict Resolution, 52*(5), 713–736.

Hammack, P. L. (2008). Narrative and the cultural psychology of identity. *Personality and Social Psychology Review, 12*(3), 222–247.

Hammack, P. L. (2009a). The cultural psychology of American-based coexistence programs for Israeli and Palestinian youth. In C. McGlynn, M. Zembylas, Z. Bekerman, & T. Gallagher (Eds.), *Peace education in conflict and post-conflict societies: Comparative perspectives* (pp. 127–144). New York: Palgrave Macmillan.

Hammack, P. L. (2009b). Exploring the reproduction of conflict through narrative: Israeli youth motivated to participate in a coexistence program. *Peace and Conflict: Journal of Peace Psychology, 15*(1), 49–74.

Hammack, P. L. (2010a). The cultural psychology of Palestinian youth: A narrative approach. *Culture & Psychology, 16*(4), 507–537.

Hammack, P. L. (2010b). The political psychology of personal narrative: The case of Barack Obama. *Analyses of Social Issues and Public Policy, 10,* 182–206.

Hammack, P. L. (2011a). *Narrative and the politics of identity: The cultural psychology of Israeli and Palestinian youth.* New York: Oxford University Press.

Hammack, P. L. (2011b). Narrative and the politics of meaning. *Narrative Inquiry, 21*(2), 311–318.

Hammack, P. L., & Cohler, B. J. (2011). Narrative, identity, and the politics of exclusion: Social change and the gay and lesbian life course. *Sexuality Research and Social Policy, 8,* 162–182.

Hammack, P. L., & Pilecki, A. (2012). Narrative as a root metaphor for political psychology. *Political Psychology, 33*(1), 75–103.

Hammersley, M. (1992). *What's wrong with ethnography? Methodological explorations.* New York: Routledge.

Hardt, M., & Negri, A. (2011, October 11). The fight for "real democracy" at the heart of Occupy Wall Street. Retrieved July 15, 2012 from www.foreignaffairs.com/articles/136399/michael-hardt-and-antonio-negri/the-fight-for-real-democracy-at-the-heart-of-occupy-wall-street

Huddy, L. (2001). From social to political identity: A critical examination of social identity theory. *Political Psychology, 22*(1), 127–156.

Jackson, R. (2005). *Writing the war on terrorism: Language, politics and counterterrorism.* Manchester, England: Manchester University Press.

James, W. (1890). *The principles of psychology.* New York: Henry Holt.

Kaufman, S. J. (2009). Narratives and symbols in violent mobilization: The Palestinian-Israeli case. *Security Studies, 18*(3), 400–434.

Kook, R. (2005). Changing representations of national identity and political legitimacy: Independence Day celebrations in Israel, 1952–1998. *National Identities, 7*(2), 151–171.

Le Bon, G. (1969). *The crowd: A study of the popular mind.* New York: Ballantine. (Original work published 1895)

Lieblich, A., Tuval-Mashiach, R., & Zilber, T. (1998). *Narrative research: Reading, analysis, and interpretation.* Thousand Oaks, CA: Sage.

Lykes, M. B. (2012). One legacy among many: The Ignacio Martín-Baró Fund for mental health and human rights at 21. *Peace and Conflict: Journal of Peace Psychology, 18*(1), 88–95.

Lykes, M. B., Blanche, M. T., & Hamber, B. (2003). Narrating survival and change in Guatemala and South Africa: The politics of representation and a liberatory community psychology. *American Journal of Community Psychology, 31*(1/2), 79–90.

Malinowski, B. (1927). *Sex and repression in savage society.* London: Kegan Paul, Trench, Trubner & Co.

McAdams, D. P. (1988). *Power, intimacy, and the life story: Personological inquiries into identity.* New York: Guilford.

McAdams, D. P. (1990). Unity and purpose in human lives: The emergence of identity as a life story. In A. I. Rabin, R. A. Zucker, R. A. Emmons, & S. Frank (Eds.), *Studying persons and lives* (pp. 148–200). New York: Springer.

McAdams, D. P. (1993). *The stories we live by: Personal myths and the making of the self.* New York: Guilford.

McAdams, D. P. (1996). Personality, modernity, and the storied self: A contemporary framework for studying persons. *Psychological Inquiry, 7*(4), 295–321.

McAdams, D. P. (1997). The case for unity in the (post)modern self: A modest proposal. In R. D. Ashmore & L. Jussim (Eds.), *Self and identity: Fundamental issues* (pp. 46–80). New York: Oxford University Press.

McAdams, D. P. (2006). *The redemptive self: Stories Americans live by.* New York: Oxford University Press.

McAdams, D. P. (2008). Personal narratives and the life story. In O. P. John, R.W. Robins, & L.A. Pervin (Eds.), *Handbook of personality: Theory and research* (3rd ed., pp. 242–262). New York: Guilford.

McAdams, D. P. (2011). Narrative identity. In S. J. Schwartz, K. Luyckx, & V. L. Vignoles (Eds.), *Handbook of identity theory and research* (Vols. 1 & 2, pp. 99–115). New York: Springer.

McAdams, D. P. (2012). *The psychological self as actor, agent, and author.* Manuscript submitted for publication.

McAdams, D. P., Albaugh, M., Farber, E., Daniels, J., Logan, R. L., & Olson, B. (2008). Family metaphors and moral intuitions: How conservatives and liberals narrate their lives. *Journal of Personality and Social Psychology, 95*(4), 978–990.

McAdams, D. P., & Bowman, P. J. (2001). Narrating life's turning points: Redemption and contamination. In D. P. McAdams, R. Josselson, & A. Lieblich (Eds.), *Turns in the road: Narrative studies of lives in transition* (pp. 3–34). Washington, DC: American Psychological Association Press.

McAdams, D. P., & de St. Aubin, E. (1992). A theory of generativity and its assessment through self-report, behavioral acts, and narrative themes in autobiography. *Journal of Personality and Social Psychology, 62,* 1003–1015.

McDougall, W. (1921). *The group mind.* London: Cambridge University Press.

McLean, K. C., Pasupathi, M., & Pals, J. L. (2007). Selves creating stories creating selves: A process model of self-development. *Personality and Social Psychology Review, 11*(3), 262–278.

McVittie, C., McKinlay, A., & Sambaraju, R. (2011). Social psychology, religion and inter-group relations: Hamas leaders' media talk about their vision for the future. *Journal of Community & Applied Social Psychology, 21*(6), 515–527.

Mead, G. H. (1934). *Mind, self and society.* Chicago: University of Chicago Press.

Mead, M. (1928). *Coming of age in Samoa.* New York: Morrow.

Nelson, K. (Ed.). (2006). *Narratives from the crib.* Cambridge, MA: Harvard University Press.

Nesbitt-Larking, P., & Kinnvall, C. (2012). The discursive frames of political psychology. *Political Psychology, 33*(1), 45–59.

Obama, B. H. (2012a). Remarks by the President at a campaign event (July 27). Retrieved August 1, 2012, from www.whitehouse.gov/the-press-office/2012/07/27/remarks-president-campaign-event

Obama, B. H. (2012b). Remarks by the President at a campaign event (August 1). Retrieved August 1, 2012, from www.whitehouse.gov/the-press-office/2012/08/01/remarks-president-campaign-event

Obama, B. H. (2012c). Remarks by the President at the National Urban League Convention. Retrieved August 1, 2012 from www.whitehouse.gov/the-press-office/2012/07/25/remarks-president-national-urban-league-convention

Pasupathi, M., Mansour, E., & Brubaker, J. R. (2007). Developing a life story: Constructing relations between self and experience in autobiographical narratives. *Human Development, 50*, 85–110.

Pettigrew, T. F. (2003). Peoples under threat: Americans, Arabs, and Israelis. *Peace and Conflict: Journal of Peace Psychology, 9*(1), 69–90.

Pilecki, A., & Hammack, P. L. (in press,). "Victims" versus "righteous victims": The rhetorical construction of social categories in historical dialogue among Israeli and Palestinian youth. *Political Psychology.*

Polletta, F. (2006). *It was like a fever: Storytelling in protest and politics.* Chicago: University of Chicago Press.

Polletta, F., & Jasper, J. M. (2001). Collective identity and social movements. *Annual Review of Sociology, 27*, 283–305.

Rabinow, P., & Sullivan, W.M. (1987). The interpretive turn: A second look. In P. Rabinow & W. M. Sullivan (Eds.), *Interpretive social science: A second look* (pp. 1–30). Berkeley: University of California Press.

Rasmussen, S., & Schoen, D. (2010). *Mad as hell: How the Tea Party movement is fundamentally remaking our two-party system.* New York: Harper.

Reicher, S. (2004). The context of social identity: Domination, resistance, and change. *Political Psychology, 25*(6), 921–945.

Ricoeur, P. (1981). *Hermeneutics and the human sciences: Essays on language, action, and interpretation* (J. B. Thompson, Trans.). New York: Cambridge University Press.

Ricoeur, P. (1984). The model of the text: Meaningful action considered as a text. *Social Research, 51*, 185–218.

Robertson, C. L., & Duckett, L. (2007). Mothering during war and postwar in Bosnia. *Journal of Family Nursing, 13*(4), 461–483.

Romney, M. (2012a, April 24). A better America begins tonight. Retrieved August 1, 2012 from http://foxnewsinsider.com/2012/04/24/transcript-of-mitt-romneys-speech-a-better-america-begins-tonight/

Romney, M. (2012b, June 28). Response to Supreme Court's heath care ruling. Retrieved August 1, 2012 from http://foxnewsinsider.com/2012/06/28/full-transcript-read-mitt-romneys-response-to-supreme-courts-health-care-ruling/

Rosler, N., Bar-Tal, D., Sharvit, K., Halperin, E., & Raviv, A. (2009). Moral aspects of prolonged occupation: Implications for an occupying society. In S. Scuzzarello, C. Kinnvall, & K. R. Monroe (Eds.), *On behalf of others: The psychology of care in a global world* (pp. 211–232). New York: Oxford University Press.

Rotberg, R. I. (2006). Building legitimacy through narrative. In R. I. Rotberg (Ed.), *Israeli and Palestinian narratives of conflict: History's double helix* (pp. 1–18). Bloomington: Indiana University Press.

Rouhana, N. N., & Bar-Tal, D. (1998). Psychological dynamics of intractable ethnonational conflicts: The Israeli-Palestinian case. *American Psychologist, 53*, 761–770.

Sa'di, A. H., & Abu-Lughod, L. (Eds.). (2007). *Nakba: Palestine, 1948, and the claims of memory.* New York: Columbia University Press.

Sampson, E. E. (1989). The challenge of social change for psychology: Globalization and psychology's theory of the person. *American Psychologist, 44*(6), 914–921.

Sampson, E. E. (1993). Identity politics: Challenges to psychology's understanding. *American Psychologist, 48*(12), 1219–1230.

Sarbin, T. R. (1986). The narrative as a root metaphor for psychology. In T. R. Sarbin (Ed.), *Narrative psychology: The storied nature of human conduct* (pp. 3–21). New York: Praeger.

Schafer, R. (1980). Narration in the psychoanalytic dialogue. *Critical Inquiry*, *7*, 29–54.

Sherif, M. (1956). Experiments in group conflict. *Scientific American*, *195*, 54–58.

Sherif, M. (1958). Superordinate goals in the reduction of intergroup conflict. *American Journal of Sociology*, *63*(4), 349–356.

Sherif, M., Harvey, O. J., White, B. J., Hood, W. R., & Sherif, C. (1961). *Intergroup conflict and cooperation: The Robbers Cave experiment*. Norman: Oklahoma Book Exchange.

Shweder, R. A. (1990). Cultural psychology—What is it? In J. W. Stigler, R. A. Shweder, & G. Herdt (Eds.), *Cultural psychology: Essays on comparative human development* (pp. 1–46). New York: Cambridge University Press.

Shweder, R. A. (2003). *Why do men barbecue? Recipes for cultural psychology*. Cambridge, MA: Harvard University Press.

Sidanius, J., & Pratto, F. (1999). *Social dominance: An intergroup theory of social hierarchy and oppression*. New York: Cambridge University Press.

Singer, J. A. (2004). Narrative identity and meaning making across the adult lifespan: An introduction. *Journal of Personality*, *72*(3), 437–459.

Staub, E. (2011). *Overcoming evil: Genocide, violent conflict, and terrorism*. New York: Oxford University Press.

Syed, M., & Azmitia, M. (2008). A narrative approach to ethnic identity in emerging adulthood: Bringing life to the identity status model. *Developmental Psychology*, *44*(4), 1012–1027.

Tajfel, H., & Turner, J. (1979). An integrative theory of intergroup conflict. In W. G. Austin & S. Worchel (Eds.), *The social psychology of intergroup relations* (pp. 33–47). Monterey, CA: Brooks/Cole.

Tajfel, H., & Turner, J. (1986). The social identity theory of intergroup behavior. In S. Worchel & W. Austin (Eds.), *Psychology of intergroup relations* (pp. 7–24). Chicago: Nelson-Hall.

Tappan, M. B. (1997). Interpretive psychology: Stories, circles, and understanding lived experience. *Journal of Social Issues*, *53*(4), 645–656.

Tedlock, B. (1991). From participant observation to the observation of participation: The emergence of narrative ethnography. *Journal of Anthropological Research*, *47*(1), 69–94.

van Dijk, T. A. (1998). *Ideology: A multidisciplinary approach*. Thousand Oaks, CA: Sage.

Vygotsky, L. S. (1962). *Thought and language* (E. Hanfmann & G. Vakar, Trans.). Cambridge, MA: MIT Press. (Original work published 1934)

Vygotsky, L. S. (1978). *Mind in society: The development of higher psychological processes*. Cambridge, MA: Harvard University Press.

Weltman, D., & Billig, M. (2001). The political psychology of contemporary anti-politics: A discursive approach to the end-of-ideology era. *Political Psychology*, *22*(2), 367–382.

Wertsch, J. V., & Roediger, H. L. (2008). Collective memory: Conceptual foundations and theoretical approaches. *Memory*, *16*(3), 318–326.

White, H. (1987). *The content of the form: Narrative discourse and historical representation*. Baltimore, MD: Johns Hopkins University Press.

Wooffitt, R. (2005). *Conversation analysis and discourse analysis: A comparative and critical introduction*. Thousand Oaks, CA: Sage.

Wundt, W. M. (1916). *Elements of folk psychology: Outlines of a psychological history of the development of mankind* (E. L. Schaub, Trans.). New York: Macmillan.

Zaraowsky, C. H. A. (2000). Trauma stories: Violence, emotion and politics in Somali Ethiopia. *Transcultural Psychiatry, 37*(3), 383–402.

Zaraowsky, C. H. A. (2004). Writing trauma: Emotion, ethnography, and the politics of suffering among Somali returnees in Ethiopia. *Culture, Medicine and Psychiatry, 28*(2), 189–209.

Zenker, O. (2010). Between the lines: Republicanism, dissenters and the politics of meta-trauma in the Northern Irish conflict. *Social Science & Medicine, 71*(2), 236–243.

Zernike, K. (2010). *Boiling mad: Inside Tea Party America.* New York: Henry Holt.

Zerubavel, Y. (1995). *Recovered roots: Collective memory and the making of Israeli national tradition.* Chicago: University of Chicago Press.

Zerubavel, Y. (2002). The "mythological Sabra" and Jewish past: Trauma, memory, and contested identities. *Israel Studies, 7*(2), 115–144.

3   Governing Spirits

Body Politic Scenarios and Schemas in the French Revolution Debate

Michael Sinding

Introduction: Orientation by Turns

The French Revolution Debate in the Linguistic and Cultural Turns

The "pamphlet wars" over the meaning of the French Revolution in 1790s Britain constitute one of the most important political debates in Western history. The debate is considered the crucible in which modern liberalism and conservatism were forged, with Burke's defense of traditional religion and hierarchy as bulwarks against anarchy in *Reflections on the Revolution in France* an inspiration to modern conservatism, and Paine's defense of a natural right to rational self-government in *Rights of Man* inspiring both radical and liberal views of democracy and the welfare state (Claeys, 2007). The debate was sparked by Burke's fierce attack on the Revolution's events, participants, and philosophy. The series of responses and counterresponses that followed comprise in total more than 100 pamphlets. Burke and Paine were by far the most important participants; their texts became extremely popular and were celebrated by their allies and reviled by their opponents. We might describe the outcome by saying that Burke's side won the battle, but Paine's side won the war: England retained its system of government that balanced monarchy against parliament, revolutionary thought was suppressed as England went to war with France, but today royalty has generally lost effective power, and democracy is our default political ideal. The cultural importance of the debate, its period, and its language have been increasingly recognized in the past 50 years—intellectual and cultural aspects since E. P. Thompson's (1963/1984) *Making of the English Working Class*, and linguistic aspects since James Boulton's (1963) *Language of Politics in the Age of Wilkes and Burke* (for selections with commentary see Butler, 1984, and Hampsher-Monk, 2005; for commentary see Clemit, 2011). But studies of language and rhetoric in the debate have not yet drawn on the tools of cognitive linguistics to model its conceptual patterns.

My particular interest is in characterizing how patterns of metaphor and narrative in these texts construct some basic building blocks of conservative and liberal commonsense worldviews. Such conceptual-rhetorical patterns could offer a key to one of the major psychological and cultural divisions of the modern world.

Metaphor and Narrative in the Linguistic, Cultural and Cognitive Turns

The topic of metaphor and narrative in politics can be seen as developing from broad turns in the humanities toward emphasizing linguistic and cultural factors in experience and writing (since the 1960s, accelerating in the 1980s), and, within those turns, more specific turns to metaphor and to narrative as basic devices of linguistic and cultural expression. I approach the topic from the perspective of the more recent cognitive turn within the humanities, which draws on cognitive science to explore the role of mental factors in language, behavior and culture (since the 1980s, accelerating in the 1990s; see Zunshine, 2010, for an overview). I seek to weave together two major strands within that turn, conceptual metaphor theory (CMT) and cognitive narratology, whose vibrancy stems from their pursuit of the insight that metaphor and narrative are fundamental structures of human thought. As with the general turns to metaphor and narrative over the past 30 to 40 years (as Hanne, 1999, 2011, shows), the parallel surges in cognitive analyses of metaphor and of narrative have not had much to say to one another.[1] That should change, because the two structures certainly interact often and powerfully in discourse. If they are both fundamental to thought, we will not be able to understand thought without understanding how they relate to one another.

Given these almost-converging trends in research, I try to throw light on the general question of the nature of metaphor–narrative interaction by examining how they interact in constructing worldview in political arguments involving body politic metaphors. I take the notion of the schema as the main type of conceptual structure that links cognitive research on metaphor and on narrative. I propose to examine the role of schemas in several "metaphor scenarios" that are central in the debate—that is, conventional metaphors played out in the form of mini-narratives using rich experiential knowledge of source domains to create rich conceptualization and evaluation of target domains. I consider how, in these scenarios, the interplay between the specific and abstract levels of schema structure contributes to framing concepts and worldviews.

Background

Conceptual Metaphor Theory

Until 1980, so the story goes, metaphor was thought of as primarily linguistic, a use of expression X to substitute for expression Y. For example, "the head of the country" substitutes "head" for "ruler," and the incongruous expression achieves some rhetorical effect unavailable to the expected expression. In 1980, George Lakoff and Mark Johnson's *Metaphors We Live By* (2003 [1980]) replaced this Aristotelian picture with CMT, according to which metaphor is primarily a matter of thought and only secondarily a matter of language. A metaphor on this view is a mapping of conceptual structure from one conceptual domain to another, typically from the more concrete to the more abstract or subjective, and the mapping carries with it language, inference, imagery and emotion. So the Body Politic implies a mapping from the elements of a conceptual schema for the human body to the elements of a conceptual schema for a social group. At a minimum,

> Body → Social group
> Head → Group leader
> Body parts → Group members

The main inference is that the leader guides the people as the head guides the body. CMT soon expanded this approach to metaphor in everyday language into a far-reaching program of analyzing fundamental theoretical concepts in reason and philosophy, literature and the other arts, politics, law, economics, even mathematics—for an overview, see Lakoff and Johnson (1999); for CMT studies of political discourse, see Carver and Pikalo (2008), Charteris-Black (2005), Chilton (1996), Lakoff (2002, 2004, 2006, 2008) and Lakoff and the Rockridge Institute (2006).

Cognitive Narratology

Slightly later than CMT, a cognitive narratology (CN) took shape, inspired by research on narrative-like structures (frames, scripts, schemata, story grammars) in human intelligence in fields such as psychology, sociology, linguistics and artificial intelligence (for reviews, see Herman, 2003, especially Herman's introduction and chapter; and Herman, 2010). CN flowered into exceptionally rich and sophisticated models of narrative processing in Monika Fludernik's (1996) *Toward a "Natural" Narratology* and David Herman's (2002) *Story Logic*. It now addresses the full slate of narratological topics, including character, plot, narration, genre, rhetoric, style, emotion and functions such as entertainment, persuasion, therapy, explanation and problem solving.

Unlike CMT, however, CN is an approach rather than a theory and is too diverse to have typical ways to approach its materials, such that we could say, "CN says narrative is this; narrative uses these conceptual structures and does that with them; here's an example." I take from CN that narrative is a way of globally structuring (small or large chunks of) experience, concepts and discourse. Metaphors can structure parts of these things, but a text, experience or story can have overall narrative structure. The following few points about the role of narrative in structuring concepts are salient for purposes of examining how metaphor scenarios construct worldviews in texts.

Fine narrative structure in the sense of discourse elements sequenced in storytelling form (Herman's "micro-designs") provides the platform for playing out conventional metaphors into detailed scenarios. We can make a political argument by telling a brief story about the Body Politic in words.

Coarse narrative structure in the sense of whole texts that cohere globally as "narratives" (Herman's "macro-designs") provides a basis for linking multiple uses of metaphor, including multiple metaphor scenarios. That is, metaphors in discourse may be linked via a shared narrative backbone, and metaphor patterning in narratives may be explicable in terms of narrative structures and functions. A political theory of revolution would include scattered narrations of events, and might repeat certain metaphors to "spin" those events.

Nonnarrative texts, such as the ones we consider in the following, lack overall narrative coherence but often use narrative opportunistically, presenting their topics using multiple metaphor scenarios that are partly coherent—running in parallel, overlapping, blending or clashing. Highly rhetorical passages often use a number of metaphors for the same topic.

Because the flow of discourse in such texts shifts between argument and narrative, their flow of schematic conceptualization has a structure that is both narrative and logical. Abstract theories, however loose or rigorous, have logical connections among the concepts, and the metaphors used to represent concepts and conceptual connections in theories often reflect or create the logical structure in their schematic-imagery structure. Metaphors used for a certain person are often related by imagistic logic to metaphors used for their actions, their ideas, their rivals, etc.

As I aim to reconstruct some central spatial and force schemas defining major concepts in these arguments and their scenarios, we need to digress briefly into the nature of the conceptual structures underlying the forms of metaphor–narrative interaction.

Conceptual Structures of Metaphor and Narrative: Schemas, Image Schemas and Force Dynamics

Schemas are organized structures of elements and relations representing typified knowledge of things, situations and events. They enable us to fill in the gaps of the information we encounter in order to construct coherent and logical mental representations of that to which the information refers. We use schemas to parse the noisy welter of experience and discourse (including narrative) into meaningful forms. Momentarily seeing a woman with a backpack staring at a chart on a train station wall, I can draw on my *journey* schema (and other schemas) to make plausible inferences about a larger context of action, her present point in her action trajectory, with its likely past and future actions, her mental and emotional state, and more. I use the same schemas to make sense of a story that opens with "She listened to the screech of brakes on rails, checked her watch, and wondered if she had time for a coffee before the departure whistle." CMT argued that metaphors prompt us to map schemas from "source" to "target" concepts. An expression such as "I'm on track for a promotion" maps our schema for train travel onto our schema for professional progress, such that the train is the professional, its destination is the promotion, and the track is the sequence of actions that will result in the promotion. If we hear that a relationship has "gone off the rails," we map the train to people in a relationship, its movement along the track to relationship progress, and its crash to relationship failure. For CMT these are instances of the more general conceptual metaphor Life is a Journey, which systematically maps the *journey* schema onto our knowledge of life, such that the person living their life is a traveler, purposes are destinations, means to achieve purposes are routes, difficulties are impediments, choices are crossroads, counselors are guides, and so on (Lakoff & Turner, pp. 3–4).

CMT sought general principles of metaphoric mapping: Exactly what kinds of conceptual structure were mapped in metaphors, and how? One important answer was that metaphor typically mapped "image schema" structure from source to target. Image schemas are skeletal spatial relations concepts with a small number of parts and relations, which we experience as "recurring, dynamic pattern[s] of our perceptual interactions and motor programs" (Johnson, 1987, p. xiv), as they "structure indefinitely many perceptions, images, and events" (p. 29). For example, a *container* is a "bounded space with an interior and an exterior," which we may map onto other images such as a house, or a country on a map. We also use image schemas metaphorically, to structure non-imagistic "abstract target domains . . . such as wakefulness, alertness, and living": we may go "in" or "out" of houses and countries, and also pass out, tune out, or snuff out a candle (Lakoff & Turner, 1989, p. 97). Other image schemas include *path*, *contact*, and human orientations such as *up/down* and *center/periphery*.

Multiple metaphors can cohere in virtue of shared image-schematic structure (Lakoff & Johnson, 2003 [1980], chaps. 9, 15–17). Literary studies have explored how such structure underpins textual coherence at a level deeper than the linguistic or imagistic surface. Lakoff and Turner (1989) show various kinds of coherence across metaphors within individual poems. Metaphors for the same target may cohere if their source domains are subcategories of a more general category (LIFE AS JOURNEY in the form of sea voyage, road trip, uphill struggle, etc.). Metaphors may also cohere through sharing more complex structure. For example, LIFETIME AS DAY and YEAR and LIFE AS FLAME and FIRE can all be seen as *cycles*, and more complexly as instances of the more general composite metaphor of "life as a waxing and waning cycle of heat and light" (Lakoff & Turner, 1989, p. 88).

Image schemas are also fundamental to structuring narratives, as narratives prototypically chart out experience-level events into spatialized storyworlds (Herman, 2002), and stories frequently connect and blend with other stories in virtue of shared schematic structure (Turner, 1996). Image schemas in sentences and narratives commonly involve a force structure, and around the same time that image schemas appeared, Leonard Talmy (1988) developed a comparable notion of "force dynamics." For my purposes, the key point is that image schemas typically have force-structure and that scenarios involve configurations of image schemas whose forces interact in changing patterns. For convenience, I refer to both spatial and force schemas as "schematic imagery."[2] I use these concepts somewhat loosely, because the present chapter is a prelude to a larger study of how my two texts construct contrasting worldviews.[3]

Metaphor in Discourse and Metaphor Scenarios

The 1990s saw increasing emphasis on studying how metaphors appear and function in actual language use, to test strong claims that metaphors are stable conceptual mappings that actively structure all thought and language (e.g., Cameron & Maslen, 2010; Goatly, 1997; Musolff & Zinken, 2009; Semino, 2008). Musolff's (2006) notion of "metaphor scenarios" is an instance of this direction. Musolff analyzes how discourse about the European Union often elaborates metaphors of *courtship, marriage* and *family-building* into "mini-narratives." These are not just a matter of one or two words in random sentences being borrowed from a simple and general source domain, but rather richly detailed specifications of whole little scenes at the "subdomain" levels of structure. Elena Semino (2008, p. 10) describes scenarios as "mental representations of particular situations, and the settings, entities, goals and actions that are associated with them" (p. 10); for example, a BATTLE scenario is finer-grained than the WAR conceptual domain. Scenarios configure source elements into narrative structures, which help language users apply the elements to complex target domains. Such narratives can also "spin out" into emergent discourse traditions within communities. Musolff's notion is useful for analyzing metaphor in discourse because scenarios are "smaller and less complex than conceptual domains, but richer in content than image schemata" (ibid), yet they also contain image-schematic structure, which provides a basis for linking them with other similarly structured scenarios.

We now turn to a review of a certain tradition of conceptualizing the Body Politic, in order to set a context for Burke's and Paine's particular uses of the metaphor.

The Body Politic and the Governing Spirit: Typical Mappings and Variations

The idea of a society as a single human body is an extremely venerable and widespread conventional metaphor, and can be very powerful. We still use the language of "head" and "members" (as well as "heart," "soul," "voice," "healthy" vs. "sick" and more) to talk about groups as if they were individual bodies, but not all groups are political groups. Personification is also an extremely general category of metaphor, by which any kind of entity may be understood as a person, allowing us to talk about the mental and physical activity of states (France is trying to export its revolutionary principles; England is watching events in France warily) and other political entities (the Revolution announces a new age of reason, the Whig Party hopes to win the election), as well as other concrete and abstract entities.[4]

The Body Politic is also extremely various in conceptualization, expression and application.[5] The dynamics of the body can be described in many different ways to emphasize any number of different visions of political systems, policies and actions, such as egalitarianism/ hierarchy, moderate/ extreme and religious/ secular. Hale's (1971) history of the Body Politic emphasizes two traditions for the metaphor. One tradition considers the body's balance of elements and hence its diseases and health; another considers the "structure and interrelation" of the body's parts (Hale, 1971, p. 7) and hence their harmonious and/ or hierarchical organization.

I am most interested in uses that focus on a folk model of how an internal "spirit" governs the body. This implies an incorporeal substance that can inhabit the body, hold it together, animate it and control its movements. Such uses of the Body Politic elaborate on our intuitive sense of the internal dynamics of our bodies, especially the dynamics of relations of muscular force among the parts and with objects and forces "out there." This variant of the Body Politic is effective for specifying psychosocial causation because it can represent how mental forces flow through mental faculties and bodily structures into action scenarios. It often represents how action derives from an inner world in which passionate drives confront a reason controlling and directing a will interacting with an outer world of attractive and repelling objects and people. It is therefore a powerful model for conceptualizing moral-political ideals and evaluations.

Versions of this variant of the metaphor are frequent and significant throughout history, and a few major examples can reveal the main lines of mappings and uses. Isocrates's *Areopagiticus* (BCE 355) sees the polity as the soul or mind of the state's body (Hale, 1971, p. 19). In Plato's *Timaeus*, "body, soul, city, and universe all exhibit a similar hierarchic pattern": just as a rational intelligence governs the body, philosopher-kings should govern the city-state (Zavadil, 2009, p. 222). For Aristotle, constitutions of animals resemble well-governed city-states. The soul is the "central organ of authority" over animal bodies, and the parts live and function naturally by their "structural attachment" to it. In the state, once order is established, individual members perform their natural useful functions as ordered, not needing a ruler for each activity (Hale, 1971, pp. 23–24). Cicero treats natural law in terms of Plato's cosmology: A single mind rules the universe rationally, giving it law, just as the single intelligence in the head governs the body, and man-made law governs the republic (Zavadil, 2009, pp. 224–225). (For this reason, Zavadil, 2009, suggests that "the 'natural law' tradition has a body metaphor at its root"; p. 225.) Seneca stresses how the mind's control of the body maps to a need for a single ruler to control the tumultuous multitude surrounding him (Zavadil, 2009, p. 225). The Christian Bible treats unity in Christ as the unity of bodily members that share each other's experience, destiny, dependence and care, despite different locations and functions, with love as the unifying force (I Corinthians 6:15–16; Hale, 1971, p. 28). Medieval writers saw all levels of being (universe, world, church, state, individual) as "permeated with a life or soul of their own" that created order and meaning (Hale, 1971, p. 47). At the turn of the 16th century, Richard Hooker called law the "soul of a politic body", animating, holding together, and driving its parts (Hale, 1971, p. 84), whereas King James I saw himself as "author and giver of strength" to the law ("often called the unifying sinews or soul of the body politic") and thus above it (Hale, 1971, pp. 111–112). For Milton, the luxury of fleshly delights has seduced the soul of the church away from its original animating spirit of unity and meekness (Hale, 1971, p. 122). The detailed body-state mapping opening Hobbes's *Leviathan* emphasizes that in this "Artificiall Man . . . the *Soveraignty* is an Artificiall *Soul*, as giving life and motion to the whole body" controlling officials as joints, reward and punishment as nerves, wealth as strength and so on (Hobbes, 1968 [1651], p. 81). The vitality of the *governing spirit* in Western social thought provides a clarifying context for Burke's and Paine's articulation of political visions via models of human character and behavior built on metaphors of bodily forces and substances.

The French Revolution Debate as War of Bodies Politic

Burke and Paine both refer to the Body Politic metaphor, and both use terms such as "body," "bodies," "corporate," "corporation" and so on to refer to political groups. However, many of these uses are brief and offhand, and it seems likely that in those cases the source domain of the body is not strongly imagined, and that the metaphor is thus not doing much significant conceptual work. Indeed, one sense of the word *body* is simply "any object." For the most important and interesting uses of the Body Politic metaphor, the use of the body to assert the unity of a social group is only a starting point. I want to consider more extensive arguments that use more richly detailed patterns of bodily dynamics to frame and evaluate patterns of social dynamics.

The principles at issue are very basic ones concerning the rights of the governed to determine their government. Burke's essay takes as his starting-point a recent sermon praising the Revolution by the Dissenting preacher Richard Price. Price claims that the 1688 Glorious Revolution established for the English people three fundamental rights:

1. To choose our own governors.
2. To cashier them for misconduct.
3. To frame a government for ourselves. (quoted in Burke, 1790/2001, p. 162; Paine, 1791–1792/1992, p. 13)

Burke attacks Price's principles and Paine defends them, based on their accounts of the purpose and origin of government and rights. Both preface their political-philosophical analyses with an account of the actual situation in France. Indeed, for both writers, the framing of the Revolution and the framing of their political principles depend on each other. Hence, I focus on how two key passages in each text frame two central subtopics, one actual (the French situation) and one ideal (a normative political situation). In both cases, the evaluative framing of the actual situation serves to justify or reinforce an evaluative framing of ideals of government's relation to society. In Burke's case the current French situation is a damning indictment of democratic politics that serves to reinforce his praise of English hereditary political powers as both natural and moral. In Paine's case the prerevolutionary French situation was a damning indictment of monarchical principles, vindicating the revolutionary struggle and reinforcing his praise of democratic politics as natural and moral.

Burke

Burke's (2001 [1790]) *Reflections* began as a reply to a personal letter from a young gentleman in France asking his opinion of the Revolution. The energy, not to say vehemence, of Burke's reply soon led him to transform his initial epistolary frame into a book-length essay addressing a wide audience on what he considered to be not only the most pressing political issue of the day but the most momentous event in history. Because Price's sermon is evidence that French efforts to export revolution to England are bearing fruit, Burke goes on to excoriate the Revolution very thoroughly.

1. Actual Bodies Politic: Liberty Broken
Loose as Escape, Explosion and Fire

We may begin with the Body Politic introduced on the first page of Burke's (2001 [1790]) *Reflections*, in which he expresses a wish that France's new government will be "animated by a spirit of rational liberty," will gain a "permanent body, in which that spirit may reside, and an effectual organ, by which it may act" (p. 145). Burke's doubts about the prospects soon become clear with his metaphor scenario of the nation as a madman escaped from prison:

> Is it because liberty in the abstract may be classed amongst the blessings of mankind, that I am seriously to felicitate a madman, who has escaped from the protecting restraint and wholesome darkness of his cell, on his restoration to the enjoyment of light and liberty? Am I to congratulate a highwayman and murderer who has broke prison upon the recovery of his natural rights? This would be to act over again the scene of the criminals condemned to the galleys, and their heroic deliverer, the metaphysic Knight of the Sorrowful Countenance.

When I see the spirit of liberty in action, I see a strong principle at work; and this, for a while, is all I can possibly know of it. The wild gas, the fixed air, is plainly broke loose; but we ought to suspend our judgment until the first effervescence is a little subsided, till the liquor is cleared, and until we see something deeper than the agitation of a troubled and frothy surface. I must be tolerably sure, before I venture publicly to congratulate men upon a blessing, that they have really received one. . . . I should, therefore, suspend my congratulations on the new liberty of France until I was informed how it had been combined with government, with public force, with the discipline and obedience of armies, with the collection of an effective and well-distributed revenue, with morality and religion, with the solidity of property, with peace and order, with civil and social manners. . . . The effect of liberty to individuals is that they may do what they please; we ought to see what it will please them to do, before we risk congratulations which may be soon turned into complaints. Prudence would dictate this in the case of separate, insulated, private men, but liberty, when men act in bodies, is power. Considerate people, before they declare themselves, will observe the use which is made of power and particularly of so trying a thing as new power in new persons of whose principles, tempers, and dispositions they have little or no experience, and in situations where those who appear the most stirring in the scene may possibly not be the real movers. . . .

. . . The beginnings of confusion with us in England are at present feeble enough, but, with you, we have seen an infancy still more feeble growing by moments into a strength to heap mountains upon mountains and to wage war with heaven itself. Whenever our neighbor's house is on fire, it cannot be amiss for the engines to play a little on our own. (pp. 151–154)

The second paragraph develops another metaphor scenario, of the spirit of liberty as a forceful substance ("strong principle" and "wild gas") that has broken loose from the container it normally exists in (a body or other container). The gas creates agitated motion within a liquid and then a "frothy surface" that is difficult to see through, meaning that the excitement of the specifics of recent events makes it difficult to understand their deeper causes and implications. This "gas" metaphor is de-emphasized as Burke goes on to equate liberty in individuals and in groups with a body's power of action, but it is consistent with the later metaphor of a "new power" in persons who are "stirring" and "movers." The third paragraph extends the schematic metaphor of force-overflowing-container in two new specific scenarios: first, a feeble infant growing quickly into a mighty giant acting destructively (with an allusion to Titans attacking Olympus and Miltonic rebel angels attacking heaven); then, an effort to block a house fire from spreading to a neighboring house.

The overall argument, then, criticizes (or at least refuses to praise) French liberty by construing it as (potentially) an escaped criminal madman, then explains that judgment by analyzing the dangers of the spirit of liberty in terms of the dangers of an explosive gas, a fast-growing giant, and a spreading fire. In general, the schematic imagery provides the causal framing in which "liberty" can lead to confusion and destruction; the specific source scenarios of escaped prisoners, aggressive giants and spreading fires provide the evaluative framing of this interpretation of the situation's causality. This schematic imagery is elaborated and extended in numerous other passages, to structure related target concepts in relevant ways.

2. Ideal Bodies Politic: Passing on Liberties as Inheritance, Handover and Offspring

The next key passage rejects the idea of fabricating a new government from scratch (disgusting and horrifying to Burke, 2001 [1790], p. 181) based on an alternative framing of liberties in terms of an "inheritance" metaphor scenario that highlights how they are secured by government (rather than nature):

> from Magna Charta to the Declaration of Right it has been the uniform policy of our constitution to claim and assert our liberties as an entailed inheritance derived to us from our forefathers, and to be transmitted to our posterity—as an estate specially belonging to the people of this kingdom, without any reference whatever to any other more general or prior right. By this means our constitution preserves a unity in so great a diversity of its parts. We have an inheritable crown, an inheritable peerage, and a House of Commons and a people inheriting privileges, franchises, and liberties from a long line of ancestors.
>
> This policy appears to me to be the result of profound reflection, or rather the happy effect of following nature, which is wisdom without reflection, and above it. A spirit of innovation is generally the result of a selfish temper and confined views. People will not look forward to posterity, who never look backward to their ancestors. Besides, the people of England well know that the idea of inheritance furnishes a sure principle of conservation and a sure principle of transmission, without at all excluding a principle of improvement. It leaves acquisition free, but it secures what it acquires. Whatever advantages are obtained by a state proceeding on these maxims are locked fast as in a sort of family settlement, grasped as in a kind of mortmain forever. By a constitutional policy, working after the pattern of nature, we receive, we hold, we transmit our government and our privileges in the same manner in which we enjoy and transmit our property and our lives. The institutions of policy, the goods of fortune, the gifts of providence are handed down to us, and from us, in the same course and order. Our political system is placed in a just correspondence and symmetry with the order of the world and with the mode of existence decreed to a permanent body composed of transitory parts, wherein,

by the disposition of a stupendous wisdom, molding together the great mysterious incorporation of the human race, the whole, at one time, is never old or middle-aged or young, but, in a condition of unchangeable constancy, moves on through the varied tenor of perpetual decay, fall, renovation, and progression. Thus, by preserving the method of nature in the conduct of the state, in what we improve we are never wholly new; in what we retain we are never wholly obsolete. By adhering in this manner and on those principles to our forefathers, we are guided not by the superstition of antiquarians, but by the spirit of philosophic analogy. In this choice of inheritance we have given to our frame of polity the image of a relation in blood, binding up the constitution of our country with our dearest domestic ties, adopting our fundamental laws into the bosom of our family affections, keeping inseparable and cherishing with the warmth of all their combined and mutually reflected charities our state, our hearths, our sepulchres, and our altars. (pp. 183–184)

Burke's scenarios here seem to contrast the idea of a Body Politic with that of a Family Politic, but there is no strict contrast in the "inheritance" and "individual" scenarios, because the former is made up of a sequence of groups of the latter, and even in this passage Burke concentrates on present society as a unit distinct from its past and future forms.

The first paragraph sets out the scenario of legal inheritance of property, highlighting the connection of past, present and future generations within a family. The advantage of this single principle is its unifying many parts of the constitution (i.e., the classes that constitute society). The next paragraph affirms the naturalness of the inheritance principle, contrasting it with a revolutionary "spirit of innovation." Schematic metaphors specify the revolutionary spirit's self-regarding quality: It has "confined views" and looks neither forward nor back; hence, it is atomistic, isolated from sources and offshoots and perhaps contemporaries. The following sentences add to the inheritance scenario two complementary source scenarios of secure bodily transmission that the constitutional policy follows—one of holding an object firmly in one's hand(s) and passing it to another person's hand(s) and the other of transmitting physical being from parents to children. The relations among these scenarios are complex: The "idea of inheritance" (as a source domain for the target of stable political structure) is understood to encompass both legal inheritance of property from parents to children and physical inheritance of biological features from parents to children. This source domain, however, is itself understood metaphorically: Inheritance (in both legal and biological senses) is understood in terms of physical transfer of an object from hand to hand. Thus, the advantages of the system are "grasped as in a kind of mortmain forever" (where *mortmain*, from the French for "dead hand," is a legal term for "the condition of lands or tenements held inalienably by an ecclesiastical or other corporation"; Burke, 2001 [1790], p. 184n140). And political institutions and powers, property and human traits ("the gifts of providence") are "handed down to us, and from us," received and held.

Because we have multiple specific scenarios referring metaphorically to the same target process, it seems plausible that they convey their meaning by evoking a schematic scenario that fits them all—that of substance that can persist over time, can be transferred between owners and can be improved in some abstract sense. The terms *conservation, transmission* and *improvement* refer to abstract "principles" and must evoke a schematic rather than a specific scenario. The schematic structure of the "inheritance" transmission scenario is that of a substance being moved by force from one body to another. In the "handover" version of transmission, the substance is a solid object held forcibly by one hand being moved to and released into the forcible hold of another hand. In the "offspring" version of the scenario, the transmission is more direct: Part of one body's essential substance passes out of it to form (an essential basis of) a new independent substantial body. The handover and offspring scenarios give the schematic causal structure their strongly positive emotional evaluation of close physical and personal ties. The property-giving scenario (and potentially the handover scenario) provides all the strong (mixed) feelings between giver and receiver and among love, sacrifice and obligation.

At this point Burke introduces the Body Politic metaphor that may be his most crucial because upon it hangs the justification of his inheritance model of the state. The inheritance model is perfectly suited to society's "mode of existence" as defined by the kind of "body" that it is. Society is "a permanent body composed of transitory parts" because individuals are mortal but groups persist indefinitely. The physical substance of all present individuals is connected to past and future generations via ongoing reproduction; dying parts are replaced by other parts of the same substance, so the identity of the whole is continuous. The key inference is that the Body Politic includes not just all living people in the state, but all past and future members. Burke draws the boundary of "society" so widely to underpin further inferences about the nature of social ties, obligations and rights.

Conventionally, what is transmitted from parents to children, the substance they have in common, is "blood." The "image of a relation in blood" suggests past–future family relations, but this leads to a stress on "family affections," emphasizing relations among living family members. Such affections are understood in terms of strong close connections of substance ("binding up" the constitution with "domestic ties," "keeping inseparable" our relations both near and far) or of energy (cherishing the "warmth" of "mutually reflected charities," where charities could suggest both charitable feeling and actions of giving).

Burke insists that nature (correspondence with the order of the universe) is the basis of his view, but the logic of the argument depends on schematic metaphor. He frames the causal structures of immediate familial social relations (familial descent and bonds, property inheritance) in terms of bodies linked through time by physical transmission of substances and uses those schematic causal structures to metaphorically frame the larger and more abstract concepts of society (Body Politic/lineal family) and polity constitution (inheritance).

Paine

Burke's attack on the Revolution came as a shock to many, not least Thomas Paine, because Burke had been a strong supporter of the American revolutionaries and a friend of Paine. The friendship was over, and Paine's resounding counterattack (in two parts, 1791/1792) set out to defend the Revolution and its principles and to stoke the fires of revolutionary hope. *Rights of Man* is also an extremely powerful text, and it became even more famous and notorious than Burke's *Reflections*. It was read throughout England and Europe, and was soon banned and burned (along with effigies of Paine) as seditious. The text attacks Burke's version of the events of the Revolution, and Burke's reasons for criticizing Price, then goes on to state his own political philosophy. We now consider two key passages from Paine's text that offer parallel but contrasting scenarios as ways of framing the key topics framed by those passages of Burke examined earlier.

1. Actual Bodies Politic: Liberty Versus Despotism as Battle of Giants

Although the first few pages of *Rights of Man* defend Price's account of the origin and nature of political authority and rights against Burke's attack, Paine soon turns to the affairs of France. He reframes Burke's representation of "the springs and principles of the French revolution" (1992 [1791–1792], p. 19) by presenting an alternative narrative of the revolutionaries and their actions, a narrative that characterizes and evaluates the relevant actors, relations and forces in quite contrary ways. Paine challenges Burke's account of the Revolution as the frenzied assault of a mob on a "mild and lawful Monarch" (qtd. in Paine, 1992 [1791–1792], p. 19) by conceding the "moderation" of Louis XVI and insisting that the real enemy was Monarchy as a deep-rooted principle of despotism (Paine, 1992 [1791–1792], pp. 19–20):

> When despotism has established itself for ages in a country, as in France, it is not in the person of the King only that it resides. It has the appearance of being so in show, and in nominal authority; but it is not so in practice, and in fact. It has its standard every where. Every office and department has its despotism, founded upon custom and usage. Every place has its Bastille, and every Bastille its despot. The original hereditary despotism resident in the person of the King, divides and subdivides itself into a thousand shapes and forms, till at last the whole of it is acted by deputation. This was the case in France; and against this species of despotism, proceeding

on through an endless labyrinth of office till the source of it is scarcely perceptible, there is no mode of redress. It strengthens itself by assuming the appearance of duty, and tyrannises under the pretence of obeying.

. . . There were, if I may so express it, a thousand despotisms to be reformed in France, which had grown up under the hereditary despotism of the monarchy, and became so rooted as to be in a great measure independent of it. (Paine, 1992 [1791–1792], pp. 20–21)

Paine rejects Burke's narrative of the taking of the royals as melodramatic nonsense, and defends the revolutionaries' behavior as moderate in the circumstances. He also raises the issue of narrative perspective, attacking Burke's exclusive identification with the nobles' position and viewpoint, as it results in contempt for the perspective of the rest of the nation: "He pities the plumage, but forgets the dying bird" (Paine, 1992 [1791–1792], p. 24; cf. Paine's criticism of the "mob" schema, p. 30). This explains why Burke ignores the Bastille, the prison that had become a notorious symbol for the abuse of the weak by the powerful. Paine returns to his personification of despotism when he corrects this omission of balancing facts by narrating the "transaction of the Bastille" as the other side of the revolutionary story (1992 [1791–1792], p. 24). He helps the facts to speak by framing the incident in the genre of heroic romance, and taking this framing as an epitome of the Revolution as a whole:

The mind can hardly picture to itself a more tremendous scene than what the city of Paris exhibited at the time of taking the Bastille, and for two days before and after, nor conceive the possibility of its quieting so soon. At a distance this transaction has appeared only as an act of heroism, standing on itself; and the close political connection it had with the Revolution is lost in the brilliancy of the achievement. But we are to consider it as the strength of the parties, brought man to man, and contending for the issue. The Bastille was to be either the prize or the prison of the assailants. The downfall of it included the idea of the downfall of Despotism; and this compounded image was become as figuratively united as Bunyan's Doubting Castle and Giant Despair. (Paine, 1992 [1791–1792], p. 24)[6]

These passages give us something akin to Burke's use of the *governing spirit* to depict France. Paine uses the term *principle* rather than *spirit*, but the terms have similar meanings at the time.[7] If "Despotism" is "resident in the person of the king" but then "divides and subdivides" so that it can spread and "reside" in many places (departments and offices everywhere)—then it is conceived as (a) a bodily substance, in (b) a location, but (c) moving, through (d) a setting, with (e) varying levels of force (it "grows up" and "strengthens itself"), and (f) taking various "shapes and forms" as it goes. The substance seems to be fluid (or perhaps plant-like), as it "proceeds through" a setting of channels, spreading and differentiating without leaving its point of origin. As its movement is partly expansion, it can appear in many locations, with the original location regarded as "source" and "root." This conception is essential to Paine's justification of the Revolution because it allows him to characterize despotism as intrinsic to the political system and pervading all of its parts. Despotism in the usual literal sense is a quality of a monarch's actions or personality. But Paine's metaphor scenario unifies and reifies its qualities as the internal essence of a network of connected entities that are omnipresent, continuous and strongly connected to one another and to their locations, far beyond the monarch's person and actions. It follows that despotism cannot be eliminated by replacing a monarch, nor can it be fixed by gradual reform.

The second passage connects the taking of the Bastille with the broader Revolution by a series of metonymic framings: affirming the taking of the Bastille as an "act of heroism," it recontextualizes it as the general political conflict embodied in single combat ("man to man"). Next, Paine connects the setting of the single combat scene to other elements of the combat script—that is, the setting will be what the assailant gets from the combat, whether the assailant wins or is defeated: The Bastille will be "the prize or the prison." He makes the setting-outcome embody the enemy principle ("the downfall of it included the idea of the downfall of despotism"; Paine, 1992 [1791–1792], pp. 24). Finally, he makes that metonymy allegorical by alluding to Bunyan's *Pilgrim's Progress* to personify despotism as a giant, then intensifies the metonymy into a figuratively united compounded image of giant-in-castle (despotism blends three images: the Bastille, the Giant and the Giant's Castle).

Despotism as a substance is embodied in a specific archetypal scenario of apocalyptic "final battle" for the Bastille, a scenario that heightens the prison's symbolic cultural meaning by fusing it with actual events and novel allegorical symbolism. Paine's focus on the negative principle animating the ancien régime (despotism) and the positive principle animating the revolutionaries (liberty) add up to a reframing of the French situation as an ultimate battle between good and evil principles.[8]

Paine later moves out from these specifics to propose his own political philosophy based on a vision of human psychosocial nature.

2. Ideal Bodies Politic: Society as Natural Creation of Individuals Exchanging, Aggregating and Circulating Powers

Paine explicitly rejects traditional versions of the Body Politic metaphor and proposes a new version: "A nation" he writes, "is not a body, the figure of which is to be represented by the human body; but is like a body contained within a circle, having a common center, in which every radius meets; and that center is formed by representation" (Paine, 1992 [1791–92], p. 143). The comment appears in Part II, where Paine elaborates his democratic version of the social contract myth; that elaboration builds on his democratic myth of the origin of rights in Part I. It allows us to link the "body" source domain to the use of schematic imagery in his foregoing discussion of social structures and forces. But to make sense of this we must reconstruct some preceding steps of the argument.

Part II is largely devoted to attacking government as such, and the hereditary governments of Europe in particular. The attack rejects the Burkean view that societies need governments to maintain order by restraining antisocial passions, with its premise of "the ignorance and fallibility of mankind" (Burke, 2001 [1790], p. 414). The first chapter of Part II, "Of Society and Civilization" (Paine, 1992 [1971–1972], pp. 127–31), argues that governments are largely an "imposition" because societies already do most of what governments claim to. That is, societies naturally develop peaceful order because of natural human sociability, shared interests and exchange of aid and trade.

In Paine's initial version of the social contract story, individuals entering society pool their powers, but retain full access to the pool. Joining society is not giving up rights but securing those that require group strength (e.g. security and protection). Individuals "throw" or "deposit" those rights into a "common stock" and "take the arm of society," become a "proprietor" in it and draw on its capital as a matter of right (Paine, 1992 [1971–1972], p. 39). This account serves to set the stage for Part II's antigovernment metaphor scenario of spontaneously arising social order—a kind of prequel to the social contract:

> Great part of that order which reigns among mankind is not the effect of government. It has its origin in the principles of society and the natural constitution of man. . . . The mutual dependance and reciprocal interest which man has upon man, and all the parts of a civilized community upon each other, create that great chain of connection which holds it together. The landholder, the farmer, the manufacturer, the merchant, the tradesman, and every occupation, prospers by the aid which each receives from the other, and from the whole. Common interest regulates their concerns, and forms their law; and the laws which common usage ordains, have a greater influence than the laws of government. In fine, society performs for itself almost every thing which is ascribed to government.
>
> To understand the nature and quantity of government proper for man, it is necessary to attend to his character. As Nature created him for social life, she fitted him for the station she intended. In all cases she made his natural wants greater than his individual powers. No one man is capable, without the aid of society, of supplying his own wants; and those wants, acting upon every individual, impel the whole of them into society, as naturally as gravitation acts to a center.
>
> But she has gone further. She has not only forced man into society, by a diversity of wants, which the reciprocal aid of each other can supply, but she has implanted in him a system of social affections, which, though not necessary to his existence, are essential to his happiness. There is no period in life when this love for society ceases to act. It begins and ends with our being.

. . . a great part of what is called government is mere imposition. . . .

So far is it from being true, . . . that the abolition of any formal government is the dissolution of society, that it acts by a contrary impulse, and brings the latter the closer together. All that part of its organization which it had committed to its government, devolves again upon itself, and acts through its medium. . . . In short, man is so naturally a creature of society, that it is almost impossible to put him out of it.

. . . It is to the great and fundamental principles of society and civilization—to the common usage, universally consented to, and mutually and reciprocally maintained—to the unceasing circulation of interest, which, passing through its million channels, invigorates the whole mass of civilized man . . . that the safety and prosperity of the individual and the whole depends.

. . . If we consider what the principles are that first condense men into society, and what the motives that regulate their mutual intercourse afterwards, we shall find, by the time we arrive at what is called government, that nearly the whole of the business is performed by the natural operation of the parts upon each other. (Paine, 1992 [1791–1792], pp. 127–129)

Paine integrates force and spatial imagery in the overall image of what we could today call a self-organizing system. A personified Nature creates man for social life. As in the Despotism scenario, Paine concentrates on the location and movement of forceful substances in people, or perhaps a single forceful substance (because it is implanted by Nature) that operates through people. Here, of course, the substance is a positive one. It is fluid and freely moving and shared, rather than solid, binding and oppressive, and deeply rooted. The following chapter returns to develop the "circulating forces" version of the Body Politic to reverse conventional associations of democracy with barbarity and hierarchy with civilization. In democracies, commerce promotes peaceful "civil intercourse of nations, by an exchange of benefits" (Paine, 1992 [1791–1792], p. 172), whereas plundering monarchies reduce both: "Like blood, [commerce] cannot be taken from any of the parts, without being taken from the whole mass in circulation, and all partake of the loss" (Paine, 1992 [1791–1792], p. 173).[9]

The "principles" and "interest" and "wants" and "affections" are somewhat ambiguous as to whether they are forces or substances. They seem to be partly magnet-like forces of attraction, since they draw and hold people together, impelling them toward a common center. Yet they are also partly substances, because they are given as aid and circulate through channels to invigorate, protect and prosper society. In short, Paine seems to be working with a generic force- or energy-substance that blends both concepts.

It now remains to compare summarized schematic forms of the moral-political visions of Burke and Paine. This will allow us to clarify just how and where they use schemas and scenarios to structure their social visions in contrasting ways.

Summary and Conclusion

We may attempt to summarize how conceptual metaphors emerge from Burke's and Paine's texts to structure their opposing worldviews by listing the main schematic mappings (in numbered italics) and their subordinate scenario mappings inferable from these passages. I attempt primarily to capture the logical hierarchical order of mappings (i.e., from general claims and premises through arguments to conclusions) and, secondarily, to arrange them in the order they appear (see Table 3.1). Some compromise between these aims is necessary, as the texts are informal arguments.

Table 3.1 Burke's and Paine's conceptual metaphors (mappings of schematic imagery and scenarios)

1. Liberty

Super-schema	*Liberty is*	*a forceful substance* *-moving out across (internal and external) bodily restraints*		
Schema 1.		-a forceful entity's power of action		
Schema 2.			-an individual body's power	
Scenario 2a.				-a person escaped from cell (dangerous prisoner/ madman)
Scenario 2b.				-a fast-growing person (feeble infant > destructive giant)
Schema 3.			-a natural force	
Scenario 3a.				-strong gaseous "principle" -causing agitated motion of fluid -causing frothy surface difficult to see through
Scenario 3b.				-a fire -spreading from house to house

2. Social Structures

Super-schema	*Social structures are*	*-substances transmitted from body to body*		
Schema 1.	Political institutions are		-inheritances	
Schema 1a.			-inheritance is	-substance transmitted from person to person
Scenario 1a.				-property legally given to descendants

Scenario 1b.			-inherited property is			-objects given from hand to hand
Scenario 1c.					-bodily substance transmitted from parent to child ("blood")	
Schema 2.	Society is		-a body composed of parts			
				-the body's structure is permanent, the parts are transitory		
				-(stable) laws and institutions are the body's structure		
				-(mortal) individuals are the body's parts		
Scenario 2a.				-the body is an object -molded together in the hands of God		
Schema 3.	Society is		-held together by social affections			
Schema 3a.			-social affections are bonds (ties) between parts			
Scenario 3a.				-social affections begin (spatially/ temporally) in family		
Schema 3b.				-family affections are strong bonds between parts		
Scenario 3b.					-strong bonds	-make parts inseparable -keep parts close -convey warmth

Paine's conceptual metaphors (mappings of schematic imagery and scenarios):

1. Despotism

Super-schema	*Despotism is a forceful substance spread throughout space*	
Schema 1.		-despotism is a substance ("principle") originating in body of King
		-spread of despotism through institutions is the substance subdividing and spreading through channels to pervade whole
Scenario 1a.		-the Bastille is the centre of the substance -the Bastille epitomizes despotism (synecdoche)
Scenario 1b.		-pervasive despotism (Bastilles everywhere) is the omnipresence of the substance
Scenario 2a.	-the battle for the Bastille is heroic battle between Despotism-substance and Liberty-substance	
Scenario 2b.		-the downfall of despotism (in the Bastille) is destruction of the substance

(*continued*)

Table 3.1 (Continued)

2. Civilized societies

Super-schema			*Civilized societies are configurations of forces arising from natural force interactions*
	Social order		
Schema 1.	Society is a whole consisting of parts		
Sub-schema 1a.	-mutual dependence, reciprocal interests and aid are forces connecting parts		
Sub-schema 1b.		-all parts act on one another; all get forces from one another and from whole	
Sub-schema 1c.			-exchange of forces connects parts and holds whole together
	Social safety and prosperity		
Schema 2.	Society is a mass		
Sub-schema 2a.	-common usage and interest are forces		
Sub-schema 2a.i.	-social relations are channels		
Sub-schema 2a.ii.	-social interactions and integration are driven and regulated by parts operating on one another		
Sub-schema 2b.	-social interactions are forces passing through channels of mass		
Sub-schema 2c.		-social interaction as a whole is unceasing circulation of forces through channels	
Sub-schema 2d.			-circulation invigorating mass is creation of safety and prosperity
	Suitable amount of government for society		
Schema 3.	Society is a container		
Sub-schema 3a.	-individuals are inside the container		
Sub-schema 3a.i.	-man's natural sociability is strong attachment to container interior ("it is almost impossible to put man out of society")		
Schema 4.	Human character is a configuration of forces		
Sub-schema 4a.	-wants, powers and affections are forces		
Sub-schema 4b.		-wants are greater than individual powers	
Sub-schema 4b.i.		-wants motivating men into society are forces impelling parts toward a centre	
Sub-schema 4c.			-social affections are lifelong forces implanted by nature
Schema 5.	(Hence) society itself does most of what is ascribed to government		
Sub-schema 5a.	-much government is imposition of excess forces from outside		
Sub-schema 5b.	-abolition of government is not dissolution of configuration of forces		
Sub-schema 5c.	-abolition of government brings parts of configuration closer together		

These summaries indicate that both Burke and Paine rely heavily on the *governing spirit* variant of the Body Politic to articulate their accounts of political psychology and political theory, though their stories about that spirit are detailed in quite contrary ways. The linguistic evidence for my claims is not as strong as it could be because I have limited myself to a few selected passages and I have had to reconstruct some of the logic of the metaphor scenarios by inference from what is stated to what is left unstated. In Paine's text especially, expressions relating to action, power, force and control are often not explicitly connected with the body, but rather are used in fairly generic senses. However, by making a few modest leaps to generalize over various uses of metaphor, one may posit conceptual models that help make sense of the overall logic of the texts, and their rhetorical power, and that could then be tested in other texts and corpora to get at the "supra-individual" cultural-historical perspective on metaphoric thought.

The very different but equally familiar configurations of scenarios of bodily, family and social experience I have described help form, in some significant way, the basis of Burke's and Paine's structures of moral and political thought. This analysis may help explain how so many people could side with one of these texts as powerfully true and damn the other as totally incomprehensible. If the pamphlet war is a war of contrasting versions of the same concepts, a war of systems of thought structured by contrasting metaphors and scenarios for the same targets, then conservatives and radicals of the 1790s could not but see the same world in systematically contrasting ways, and there is reason to believe that a similar bifurcation of cognitive vision has descended to the thought and discourse of our own day.

Notes

1 Exceptions in linguistics include Musolff (2006), Ritchie (2006) and Lakoff (2008) and, in literary studies, Pettersson (2005) and a number of the papers in Fludernik (2011). Turner (1996) bridges linguistic and literary studies, seeking to explain linguistic patterns in terms of narrative structure.
2 Talmy's (1988) force-dynamics is a new category of semantic structure. He sketches some implications for conceptual structure beyond sentence-level, and others have studied force dynamics and image schemas in argumentative and narrative discourse (Freeman, 1993, 1995, 1999; Kimmel, 2005, 2011; Oakley, 2005; Sinding, 2011; Turner, 1991). Image schemas continued to be central although controversial in CMT, with recent developments exploring in greater detail how they are embodied in the brain, how they work dynamically in relation to one another and to force dynamics, to contexts of situated action and extended discourse and to culture (see De Mulder, 2007; Hampe & Grady, 2005; Oakley, 2007).
3 In this chapter, I forego the usual practice of presenting names of schematic imagery in small capitals, as this implies a too-rigid distinction between individual schematic images, and between them and other concepts. Text analysis involves us in complex relations among various aspects of concepts in thought and discourse (e.g., concrete concept, abstract concept, image schema, metaphor, event, word, story), and I need to introduce new schematic imagery and compounds. For example, *substance* and *energy* are essential conceptions for the metaphors in my text, as are processes such as *condensation/expansion*, and complex or compound

schematic imagery (e.g., *contained substance expanding*). Lexical items and their associated images, events and image schemas are rudimentary starting points for text analysis, and we must be flexible in adapting notions developed for analyses of words and sentences for analysis of discourse flow. Any scaling-up of sentence-level theoretical structures must consider how those structures interconnect and evolve as sentence leads into sentence in larger meaning structures. I have tried to make the identity of conceptual elements sufficiently clear in context. This account of metaphoric schematic imagery in texts is adapted from Sinding (2011).

4 This has been called the EVENTS ARE ACTIONS metaphor. See, for example, Lakoff and Johnson (1980, pp. 33–34; 1999, p. 212) and Turner (1999, pp. 26–52).

5 Kathryn Banks (2009) argues, on the basis of a flexibility that even accommodates contradictory meanings, that although the Body Politic and other metaphors may "adapt themselves" better to expressing some meanings than others, their meanings are not predetermined (p. 206).

6 The reference is to John Bunyan's influential allegory *The Pilgrim's Progress* (1678/1684), in which the pilgrim Christian makes his way to the Celestial City. Christian is captured by Giant Despair and tormented in the dungeon of Doubting Castle, but later escapes. In Part II, Mr. Great-heart slays the Giant, demolishes his Castle and frees imprisoned pilgrims.

7 *The Oxford English Dictionary* (2007) notes a "substance" sense of "principle" used at this time: "a fundamental source or basis of something," with subsenses "a fundamental quality determining the nature of something" and in chemistry "an active or characteristic constituent of a substance."

8 It is possible that Burke's "escaped prisoner" metaphor for French liberty relates to the liberation of the Bastille, but Burke considered the Bastille a merely symbolic concern.

9 Paine explicitly bases his notion of commerce on synecdoche from a human-scale scenario: "Commerce is no other than the traffic of two individuals, multiplied on a scale of numbers; and by the same rule that nature intended for the intercourse of two, she intended that of all" (1992 [1791–1792], p. 172).

References

Banks, K. (2009). Interpretations of the body politic and of natural bodies in late sixteenth-century France. In A. Musolff and J. Zinken (Eds.), *Metaphor and discourse* (pp. 205–218). Houndmills: Palgrave Macmillan.

Boulton, J. T. (1963). *The language of politics in the age of Wilkes and Burke*. London: Routledge and Kegan Paul.

Burke, E. (2001) [1790]. *Reflections on the revolution in France*. A critical edition. (J. C. D. Clark, Ed.). Stanford, CA: Stanford University Press.

Butler, M. (Ed.) (1984). *Burke, Paine, Godwin, and the revolution controversy*. Cambridge: Cambridge University Press.

Cameron, L., & Maslen, R. (Eds.) (2010). *Metaphor analysis*. London: Equinox.

Carver, T., & Pikalo, J. (Eds.). (2008). *Political language and metaphor*. London: Routledge.

Charteris-Black, J. (2005). *Politicians and rhetoric: The persuasive power of metaphor*. Houndmills: Palgrave Macmillan.

Chilton, P. (1996). *Security metaphors*. New York: Peter Lang.

Claeys, G. (2007). *The French revolution debate in Britain: The origins of modern politics*. British history in perspective. Houndmills: Palgrave Macmillan.

Clemit, P. (Ed.) (2011). *The Cambridge companion to British literature of the French revolution in the 1790s*. Cambridge collections online. Cambridge: Cambridge University Press. doi:10.1017/CCOL9780521516075

De Mulder, W. (2007). Force dynamics. In D. Geeraerts & H. Cuyckens (Eds.), *The Oxford handbook of cognitive linguistics* (pp. 294–317). Oxford: Oxford University Press.

Fludernik, M. (1996). *Towards a "natural" narratology*. London: Routledge.

———. (Ed.). (2011). *Beyond cognitive metaphor theory: Perspectives on literary metaphor*. New York: Routledge.

Freeman, D. (1993). "According to my bond": *King Lear* and re-cognition. *Language and Literature, 2*, 1–18.

———. (1995). "Catch[ing] the nearest way": *Macbeth* and cognitive metaphor. *Journal of Pragmatics, 23*, 689–708.

———. (1999). "The Rack Dislimns": Schema and metaphorical pattern in *Antony and Cleopatra*. *Poetics Today, 20*(3), 443–460.

Goatly, A. (1997). *The language of metaphors*. London: Routledge.

Hale, D. G. (1971). *The body politic: A political metaphor in renaissance English literature*. The Hague: Mouton.

Hampe, B., & Grady, J. (Eds.). (2005). *From perception to meaning: Image schemas in cognitive linguistics*. Cognitive Linguistics Research, 29. Berlin: Mouton de Gruyter.

Hampsher-Monk, I. (Ed.) (2005). *The impact of the French revolution: Texts from Britain in the 1790s*. Cambridge: Cambridge University Press.

Hanne, M. (1999). Getting to know the neighbours: When plot meets knot. *Canadian Review of Comparative Literature, 26*(1), 35–50.

———. (2011). The binocular vision project: An introduction. *Genre, 44*(3), 223–37.

Herman, D. (2002). *Story logic: Problems and possibilities of narrative*. Frontiers of narrative. Lincoln: University of Nebraska Press.

———. (Ed.). (2003). *Narrative theory and the cognitive sciences*. CSLI Lecture Notes, 158. Stanford: CSLI.

———. (2010). Narrative theory after the second cognitive revolution. In L. Zunshine (Ed.), *Introduction to cognitive cultural studies* (pp. 155–175). Baltimore: Johns Hopkins University Press.

Hobbes, T. (1968) [1651]. *Leviathan*. Ed. and introd. C. B. Macpherson. Harmondsworth: Penguin.

Johnson, M. (1987). *The body in the mind: The bodily basis of meaning, imagination, and reason*. Chicago: University of Chicago Press.

Kimmel, M. (2005). From metaphor to the 'mental sketchpad': Literary macrostructure and compound image schemas in *Heart of Darkness*. *Metaphor and Symbol, 20* 199–238.

———. (2011). Metaphor sets in *The Turn of the Screw*: What conceptual metaphors reveal about narrative functions. In M. Fludernik (Ed.), *Beyond cognitive metaphor theory: Perspectives on literary metaphor* (pp. 196–223). New York: Routledge.

Lakoff, G. (2002). *Moral politics: How liberals and conservatives think*. 2nd ed. Chicago: University of Chicago Press.

———. (2004). *Don't think of an elephant! Know your values and frame the debate*. White River Junction, VT: Chelsea Green.

———. (2006). *Whose freedom? The battle over America's most important idea*. New York: Farrar, Strauss and Giroux.

————. (2008). *The political mind: Why you can't understand 21st-century American politics with an 18th-century brain.* New York: Viking.

Lakoff, G., & Johnson, M. (2003) [1980]. *Metaphors we live by.* 2nd ed. Chicago: University of Chicago Press.

————. (1999). *Philosophy in the flesh.* New York: Basic.

Lakoff, G., & the Rockridge Institute (2006). *Thinking points: Communicating our American values and vision.* New York: Farrar, Straus and Giroux.

Lakoff, G. & Turner, M. (1989). *More than cool reason: A field guide to poetic metaphor.* Chicago: University of Chicago Press.

Musolff, A. (2006). Metaphor scenarios in public discourse. *Metaphor & Symbol, 21*(1), 23–38.

Musolff, A., & Zinken, J. (Eds.) (2009). *Metaphor and discourse.* Houndmills: Palgrave Macmillan.

Oakley, T. (2005). Force-dynamic dimensions of rhetorical effect. In B. Hampe & J. Grady (Eds.), *From perception to meaning: image schemas in cognitive linguistics* (pp. 443–473). Berlin: Mouton de Gruyter.

————. (2007). Image schemas. In D. Geeraerts & H. Cuyckens (Eds.), *The Oxford handbook of cognitive linguistics* (pp. 214–235). Oxford: Oxford University Press.

Paine, T. (1992) [1791–92]. *Rights of man.* Ed. Gregory Claeys. Indianapolis: Hackett.

Pettersson, B. (2005). Afterword: Cognitive literary studies: Where to go from here. In H. Veivo, B. Pettersson, & M. Polvinen (Eds.), *Cognition and literary interpretation in practice* (pp. 307–322). Helsinki: Helsinki University Press.

Principle (n.d.). In *Oxford English Dictionary* (3rd ed.). Retrieved January 5, 2014, from www.oed.com.ezproxy.auckland.ac.nz/search?searchType=dictionary&q=principle&_searchBtn=Search

Ritchie, L. D. (2006). *Context and connection in metaphor.* Basingstoke: Palgrave Macmillan.

Semino, E. (2008). *Metaphor in discourse.* Cambridge: Cambridge University Press.

Sinding, M. (2011). Storyworld metaphors in Swift's satire. In M. Fludernik (Ed.), *Beyond cognitive metaphor theory: Perspectives on literary metaphor* (pp. 239–257). New York: Routledge.

Talmy, L. (1988). Force dynamics in language and cognition. *Cognitive Science, 12*(1), 49–100.

Thompson, E. P. (1984) [1963]. *The making of the English working class.* Harmondsworth: Penguin.

Turner, M. (1991). *Reading minds: The study of English in the age of cognitive science.* Princeton: Princeton University Press.

————. (1996). *The literary mind: The origins of thought and language.* New York: Oxford University Press.

Zavadil, J. (2009). Bodies politic and bodies cosmic: The roman stoic theory of the "Two Cities." In A. Musolff & J. Zinken (Eds.), *Metaphor and discourse* (pp. 219–232). Houndmills: Palgrave Macmillan.

Zunshine, L. (Ed.). (2010). *Introduction to cognitive cultural studies.* Baltimore: Johns Hopkins University Press.

4 The Politics of the Past

The Myth of the Clash of Civilizations

Chiara Bottici

This society eliminates geographical distance only to reap distance internally in the form of a spectacular separation.

—Debord, *The Society of the Spectacle* (1994, paragraph 167)

The idea that history could ever be the simple reconstruction of how things have actually happened was abandoned a long time ago.[1] The past has always been at the service of the present. Schlegel pointed to this when he observed that the "historian is a turned-back prophet" (Schlegel & Schlegel, 1992, Fragment 80). But if the past is always subject to the construction of an identity in the present, what is the difference between historical and purely mythical accounts of the past? Even more, if not even professional historians are immune from the temptation to subject the past to their vision of the future, what can we expect from professional politicians who are constantly in search of legitimacy?

The aim of this chapter is to argue that mythical and historical narratives are not necessarily the same thing, but that they tend to converge in contemporary societies. In a global society of the spectacle, references to "traditions" tend to assume mythical connotations. I proceed in three steps: I first explain what, in general, constitutes a mythical narrative and a political myth in particular. I then move on to explain how political myth relates to historical narratives and conclude with an analysis of the recent success of the myth about a clash between Islam and the West.

A myth is not a story that is given once and for all in a definitive form. Take, for example, the myth of Ulysses. Of the many variants of this myth, which is the true one: the one that sees him happily coming back home, or that which sees him swallowed up by the sea?[2] It is implicit in the concept of a myth that there can be many legitimate variants of it. Indeed, properly speaking, a myth consists of the *process* of elaboration of the possible variants of a story. This is what Hans Blumenberg (1985) tried to convey with his concept of *Arbeit am Mythos*, or "work on myth." Following Blumenberg, by "work on myth," we mean here a process of elaboration of a single narrative core that stems from a need for *significance*. This need for significance evolves over time, and hence, myth necessarily expresses itself through variants: in each context the same narrative pattern is reappropriated by and responds to different drives, needs and exigencies. Either a narrative core produces a variant that fulfills this task in the new context or it ceases to be a myth and becomes a simple narrative.

The term *significance*, to which I referred earlier, denotes a space between a "simple meaning" and what we can call an "ultimate meaning." Something can have a meaning and not have significance for us—although that which is significant must also have meaning in order to be named in the first place. Therefore, significance is something more than mere meaning. It operates in between what is consciously said about the world and what is unconsciously felt about it. At the same time, what is significant is not necessarily something that answers the ultimate questions about the sense of life and the existence of an afterlife (hence, myth and religion are not exactly the same thing either).[3]

The human need for significance is derived from the particular position of human beings within the world. Following Arnold Gehlen, we can recover a famous Nietzschean expression and define human beings as the "always not yet determined animals" (Gehlen, 1988). As Gehlen (1998) argues, human beings by contrast with other animals are not adapted to a specific environment and are therefore always "noch nicht festgestellt." That is, whereas other animals have a fixed relationship with their environment in the sense that they are adapted to it, human beings change the environment in which they live, and this puts them in a very peculiar relationship with their living conditions.

In the first place, this fact generates culture. As Blumenberg (1985) observed, when the pre-human creature was induced to avail itself of a bipedal posture and to leave the protection of a hidden way of life in the rainforest for the savannah, it exposed itself for the first time to the risks of a widened horizon of perception. This meant that the human creature was led to face the power of the unknown or "the absolutism of reality" (Blumenberg, 1985, p. 1). Being exposed to an always potentially different environment, human beings are subjected to a greater amount of stimuli from the outside world, from which they must seek relief, or *Entlastung* (Gehlen, 1988). Culture and language are the means through which such relief can be obtained. Second, the fact that human beings change their environment means that they have a problematizing relationship with their conditions of existence. Not only can they change them, but they also raise questions about them. As a consequence, human beings need meaning, in order to master the unknown, and significance, in order to live in a world that is not indifferent to them.

The specific way through which myth fights the indifference of the world is by inserting it into a narrative of events. Myth typically addresses the question, "Whence?" rather than "Why?" As Kerényi and Jung (1963) have also pointed out, the function of myth is neither to provide a name for things nor to explain them, but, more specifically, to "ground" them. As they observed, the German language provided the exact word for this function: *begründen* (Kerényi & Jung, 1963, p. 6). The word *begründen*, which can be translated as "to ground" or "to substantiate," derives from the root *grund*. *Grund* means both the English abstract noun *reason* and the concrete noun *ground*. Thus, myths ground experience by telling stories about the origins of things and, therefore, simultaneously where they are going.

Three elements are therefore central to the concept of myth: narrative, significance, and process. It is sufficient to have an ordered series of events in order to have a narrative, but something more is needed in order to have a myth. A myth is a narrative that must respond to a need for significance that changes over time and it is because it has to provide significance within changing circumstances that a myth is best understood as a process, as a "work on myth," rather than as an object.

What, then, is a specifically political myth? A political myth is the work on a common narrative that grants significance to the political conditions and experiences of a social group. What makes a political myth out of a simple narrative is neither its claim to truth nor its content, as many have maintained.[4] For instance, there is nothing political per se in the idea that the world is about to disappear. Notwithstanding this, the narrative of the millennium, which stems from this idea, worked as a political myth, and as a powerful one in certain contexts.

What makes a political myth out of a narrative is the fact (1) that it coagulates and reproduces significance, (2) that it is shared by a given group, and (3) that it can address the specifically political conditions in which a given group lives. A political myth must respond to a need for significance because otherwise, it would be a mere narrative and not a myth, and it must be shared because it must address the specifically political conditions of a social group. One can define politics in the more general sense of whatever pertains to the polis, to the decisions concerning the fate of a community[5] or, *strictu sensu*, as the specific form of power that is characterized by the threat of recourse to legitimate coercion.[6] In both cases, politics concerns life in common, and this is ultimately why a myth must be shared in order to be *political*.

The first consequence of this definition of political myth is that, to paraphrase Gramsci, political myths are not a "piece of paper" (Gramsci, 1996). The work of a political myth cannot be reduced to the stories that we read in our books and archives. These are only *some* of the products of the work on myth. In order to establish whether a narrative is a political myth, we must look not only at its production but also at its reception, at the way in which it is shared. The whole of production–reception–reproduction constitutes the "work on myth."

The second consequence is that political myths are not learned once and for all but rather apprehended through a more or less conscious cumulative exposure to them. Significance locates itself between what is consciously learned and what is unconsciously felt. This also explains the condensational power of political myths, their capacity to condense into a few images or icons.[7] By means of a synecdoche, any object or gesture—a painting, an image, a song, a film, or an advertisement—can recall the whole work on myth that lies behind it.

As myths are not objects but processes, so too icons are not self-contained objects but rather operations of the mind. Without the latter, they would be mere images. An icon does not exist in itself, but only for a (un)consciousness that associates it with something else. In other words, an icon is a symbol. By symbol I do not simply mean signs, according to the etymology of the term.[8] Symbols are not mere signs, but a special kind of sign: They are signs that refer to a hidden or undetermined reality.

This condensational capacity of myths explains why it is often very difficult to analyze them. The work on a political myth is a process that can take place in the most diverse settings: speeches, arts—both visual and non-visual—rituals, social practices, and so on. Although all of them must be kept separate at the analytical level, in fact, mythical discourses are most of the time intermingled with other kinds of discourse; they tend, so to speak, to get lost within them. This brings us to the crucial issue of the relationship between mythical and historical narratives. In particular, if both are told from the standpoint of the present, should we then conclude that there is no difference between the two and that history is simply another form of mythmaking?

Some people have been tempted to argue so. In Robert Young's (1990) view, for instance, the writing of history always implies a process of organizing events in a narrative plot, in a totality within which these events are conferred with meaning. In his view, this means that it hardly differs from creating a myth.[9] As he put it in the provocative title of his book, "history" is simply a "white mythology." The idea of "history," he claims, always reflects a totalizing mode of structuring events that is not only particularistic—because each society has its own specific way of organizing knowledge—but it is also mythological, because it is based on the exclusion of the Other's perspective. Ultimately, Young concludes that history should be seen as myth, as "the preposterous off-spring of a distorting egocentric illusion to which the children of a western Civilization have succumbed like the children of all other Civilizations and known primitive societies" (1990, pp. 16, 19).

There are two problems with this theory. First, it works with a reductive and misleading concept of myth, used here simply in the polemical sense of "illusion." It does not make sense to speak of myth in general, and of political myths in particular, in terms of truth or falsity simply because, as we have discussed, myths do not aim to describe the world as it is, but rather to create it. Even if they are illusions, they are self-fulfilling.[10] Second, it is a view that conflates myth and narrative. In the second chapter of his book, Young (1990) argues that the use of chronology, the code most often used by historians, creates the illusory impression of a uniform, continuous progression. Dates, he observes, tell us something only insofar as they are members of a class. This class may or may not correspond to other classes, such as periods, millennia, or ages; thus, it always reflects a specific organization of an event (Young, 1990). This narrative of uniform progression is, however, illusory and, in this sense, a myth.

Even if we accept the misleading definition of myth as illusion, the fact remains that myth and historical narrative cannot be unified based on their being both distorting and biased. If a narrative is a simple series of events, then arguing that it is illusory because it superimposes upon "real" events a structure that they would otherwise lack appears pointless. Certainly, a narrative involves selection as well as some form of organization. It presupposes a plot that structures events, conferring on them a meaning as part of a whole. So Young is right in pointing out that a certain organization of events is taking place.

However, the point is that every "event" has always been interpreted. No "pure" event is ever accessible to us. As the very etymology of the word indicates, an event is something that *e-venit,* that comes into being from a background of non-becoming-events, which is, ultimately, the reason why history is based on oblivion as much as on memory (Stråth, 2000). The point is, therefore, not to counterpoise "interpreted" and "non-interpreted" events, but rather to determine the degree to which these events have been organized. As Hayden White (1987) has shown in his *The Content of the Form*, there cannot be content that has not already been organized in some form, but different modes of writing history imply different forms and, therefore, different degrees of organization. Annals and chronicles—even statistics—all talk about events that have been organized in one way or another, yet not all have been organized and, therefore, interpreted in the same way.

Whereas myths in general and political myths in particular are always organized through a dramatic structure, the writing of history does not necessarily stage a drama. One may be part of the production and reception of a historical narrative without necessarily taking part in a play. This is not to say that a historical narrative cannot come to work as political myth. Although mythical and historical narratives often overlap, as in the case of most national *mythologems*, it is not always the case, which is why we should endeavor to differentiate between the two.

It, therefore, comes as no surprise that mythical and historical narratives at times differ in their temporal perspectives. Both are narratives recounted from the standpoint of the present, although a myth may also be located outside historical time (such as most of Greek mythology for us today), whereas a political myth may be projected into a future dimension (such as the myth of prosperity). In other words, both history and myth may work as prophecies, but the fact that historians are "turned-back" prophets, to use Schlegel's expression, places further constraints on them. In the first place—nowadays at least—the historian will be asked to follow a method, whereas the very idea of a "mythical method" is senseless. A method implies that procedures can be followed by anybody with the same results, but no such possibility is offered in the case of myth. To put it bluntly, whereas historians are required to refer to openly accessible and, in principle, verifiable evidence, political myths do not need footnotes. This is because, as we have discussed, the primary task of the work on myth is to provide and coagulate significance for a given group and under given circumstances. Therefore, the work on a political myth is located between the conscious and the unconscious level.

But the contemporary spectacularization and virtualization of politics have further increased what has been called the "primacy effect" of political myth (Flood, 1997). By slipping into the social unconscious in the form of political spectacles, political myths can deeply influence our basic and most fundamental perceptions of the world and thus escape the possibility of critical scrutiny. If political myths have always been difficult to analyze, precisely because the work on significance can take place at a more or less conscious level, then the recent emergence of powerful new technologies has rendered the work on political myth less and less perceivable, and therefore more subtle. Indeed, through a peculiar intersection of the extraordinary and the banal, political myths have become the unperceived lenses through which we experience the world, and for this reason, they tend to remain unquestioned (Bottici, 2007).

All these features are shared by most contemporary political myths. Among them, national political myths, such as the myth of the American Founding Fathers, that of the French Revolution, or that of the Italian "Resistance" against Nazi-Fascism, have been analyzed at length by social theorists.[11] What I want to do here is to illustrate these features of political myth through the analysis of a contemporary example that is particularly relevant for us insofar as it is a potentially global political myth: the myth of the clash between civilizations. Why, then, is the idea of a "clash between civilizations" best analyzed as a political myth?

Surely, the idea of a clash between civilizations is *also* something else, a scientific theory in the first place (Huntington, 1996). But myth and theory can often go together very well, and if we limit ourselves to criticizing it as if it were *only* a scientific theory, then we would miss the point, because we neglect where the power of this narrative actually lies. There is indeed a striking gap between the ways in which this narrative was received as a scientific theory and as a narrative, through which people more or less unconsciously look at the world. When it was first proposed by Huntington in the 1990s, the idea of a clash between civilizations was strongly criticized as too simplistic and scientifically naive to render the complexities of world politics. Yet, particularly after September 11 and the terrorist attacks in Europe, this narrative became one of the most powerful and widespread worldviews.[12]

Different surveys of the ways in which these terrorist attacks have been framed in the US and European media show that the idea of a clash between civilizations played a central role in the way these attacks were framed.[13] After those tragic events, this narrative arose to coagulate the emotional shock that they provoked and to provide significance to the political conditions of very different peoples across the globe. What were the reasons for the success of this narrative? How can a theory that has been so strongly criticized as too naive turn into a successful political myth?

In fact, Huntington provided a name to a political myth that was *already* in the making. To see this, one must not only focus on the production of such a myth, but also on the whole process of production–reception–reproduction.

Only by looking at the whole work on myth can we understand how it is possible to criticize the idea of the clash as a scientific theory and still endorse it as a political myth. The reason it was easy for the media to frame the terrorist attacks as a clash between Islam and the West is that there has been a work on this myth that started long before 2001—work that took place at both the conscious and unconscious levels. As a result of this work, in the face of the terrorist attacks, people were more keen to perceive "civilizations" clashing with each other (whatever one can mean by that) than to perceive individual human beings acting out of a more or less complex set of motivations.

Intellectual discourses have played an important role in conveying pieces of the myth of the clash of civilizations. Even if the narrative of the clash between civilizations has been strongly criticized, pieces of this narrative have been circulating unquestioned in the literature for quite a while. Specialized literature on the Middle East has for a long time tended to portray the Muslim world as a radical "Other." The idea that Islam is a religion more fanatical than any other, or that it is fundamentally hostile to modernity, is part of a long tradition of what Edward Said named "orientalist" discourses (Said, 1978). The result is a Eurocentric and negatively biased representation of the Middle East, within which Islam is portrayed as a fixed blueprint that determines an entire way of life for hundreds of millions of Muslims all over the world.

But the myth of a clash between Islam and the West is not only a "Western" political myth. The myth of the clash of civilizations is fed by an equally misleading representation of the West circulating in many Arab and Middle Eastern sources.[14] This points to the existence of a form of Occidentalism—any reductive representation of the West that takes the East as its starting point. Intellectuals such as the Iranian Ali Shariati, the Sayyid Muhammad Taleqani or the Egyptian Sayyd Qutb, depicted the West as idolatrous, materialist, and imperialist and counterpoised it to a spiritual East that follows the precepts of Islam. A dichotomy is thus established between the culture of Islam, at the service of God, and the culture of a new *jahiliyya*, in the service of bodily needs (such as food, sex, and so on) that degrades human beings to the level of beasts.[15]

But intellectual discourses could never have produced a political myth without the work that took place at the unconscious level. The condensational capacity of a political myth is particularly evident in the power of the icons that are transmitted in the media. Iconic images slip into the social unconscious through a process of socialization that begins very early in life. As I have tried to argue elsewhere, the notion of social unconscious differs from both the individual and the collective unconscious (Bottici & Challand, 2010). Let me illustrate this concept through a specific example of an icon. Consider the *Marianne voilée*, the image of the Marianne, symbol of the French Republic, wearing a Muslim veil, which first appeared on October 26, 1985, in the popular French newspaper *Figaro Magazine*. Marianne is one of the most influential French icons in the myth of the clash of civilizations. When one looks at this image, what appears is only a woman with a naked breast, wearing a hijab. Yet, for a contemporary French person, the image evokes much more. Marianne, the beautiful woman with her breasts uncovered, is a symbol of the French Republic as it came out of the French Revolution; thus, it recalls republican values such as freedom from domination, *laicité*, and antitraditionalism. By contrast, in the contemporary French imaginary, the veil recalls images of female submissiveness (if not direct oppression). There is, therefore, a presentation of tradition and oppression on one hand and modernity and freedom on the other. By looking at this image, sensations (the perception of forms, colors, signs, and so on) are transformed into feelings—feelings of incompatibility between two clashing worlds.

This interpretation is reinforced by the context in which it first appeared. Published on the front page of an influential French magazine, the *Figaro Magazine*, on October 26, 1985, the image accompanied a dossier on Arab immigration in France with the revealing title: "Will We Still Be French in Thirty Years?" The heading gives its accompanying image an apocalyptic tenor, suggesting the disappearance of French identity or its dissolution into Muslim traditions. This is an interesting example of the work of icons in the social imaginary, because it very clearly shows the ambivalence of political myth: The image of the veiled Marianne is revelatory of both the fascination and fear of "the others"—that is, those outsiders from an "incompatible civilization" that are migrating into France—and it illustrates Hopper's (2003) point that, even when the unconscious is brought to consciousness and recognized as problematic, it is not considered with detachment and objectivity. Indeed, almost 30 years later, French identity is still far from disappearing.[16]

It is for this reason that I refer here to the concept of a *social* unconscious. Although Freud's unconscious is individual because it is the product of mechanisms of repression of individual experiences, and whereas Jung's is collective because he sees in it the reservoir of universal archetypes, using the term *social* is a way to distinguish it from both. The social unconscious differs from Freud's individual unconscious, because it is not only the result of mechanisms of removal and repression of parts of the individual experience. Particularly if we adopt a weak version of the social unconscious, we must conclude that it is not only formed through repression but also through the simple exposure to contents of which we are not aware.[17] It can *also* be the result of forms of repression, but it is not *necessarily* so. Indeed, it is now a common experience, well documented in the literature, that the human mind is able to consciously process only a certain amount of information at any given time, while others pieces of information necessarily have to remain in the background (Fromm, 2001).[18] This does not mean that they get lost: They are stored somewhere in the depth of our minds, ready to be mobilized when needed. Against this background myths proliferate.

But, as we have seen, the concept of the social unconscious also differs from Jung's collective unconscious. Although the concept is less contestable than it may prima facie appear in its many vulgarizations, the unconscious we refer to here is not universal because it is not the same for all human beings.[19] In our approach to political myth, we are not interested in looking for invariants in space and time, but rather for what is specific to each society. The example of the *Marianne voilée* is paradigmatic in this respect. One must not only be aware that the woman represented is called Marianne and that she is the symbol of the French Republic, but must also have been exposed, more or less subconsciously, to the work of elaboration of those two symbols (Marianne and the veil) which took place in the specific French context to capture the full significance of the icon.

To sum up this point, images such as the *Marianne voilée* are much more powerful conveyers of the myth of the clash between civilizations than any overt statement about it. Further examples of icons can be taken from the section "A Nation Challenged" that the *New York Times* launched immediately after 9/11.[20] Articles appearing in this section had paranoid titles such as "Yes, This Is About Islam," "Barbarians at the Gates," "The Age of Muslim Wars," and "This Is a Religious War"; they were accompanied by pictures of religiously tainted atrocities, hate, and fanaticism. The last article mentioned earlier, for instance, was illustrated with pictures of atrocities from medieval Europe (Sullivan, 2001).

An icon of the myth of the clash of civilizations that is particularly helpful in illustrating the change in the nature of the imaginal[21] we are dealing with is that of the caricature published on September 30, 2005, in the Danish newspaper *Jyllands-Posten*: of the Prophet Mohammed with a fizzing bomb as a turban. Ostensibly a joke, it is nevertheless a very telling one. As Freud (1989), among others, observed, condensation is a typical mechanism at work in wit. It is their brevity, their capacity to carry in such a condensed form a message that reveals resemblances among things that are different, which gives us the specific pleasure of wit (Freud, 1989). It is in its capacity to be a vehicle for the myth of the clash between Islam and the West that the evocative power of the "prophet-bomb" lies.

The Danish caricatures that mocked the prophet Mohammed and the Muslim faith as violent and prone to fanaticism caused vivid reactions on the side of Muslims all around the world. They did not mainly resent the publication of an image of the prophet, which is forbidden in the Muslim faith, but rather the insulting portrayal. Protests went from death threats, as they appeared in websites that mentioned Denmark as a prime terrorist target, to actual attacks, such as those that took place in Islamabad, where in June 2008, a massive car bomb went off outside the Danish embassy, killing 8 and injuring 32 (Lindekilde, 2008). On the other hand, many western newspapers reproduced the contested caricatures in the name of freedom of speech, engendering a true clash of images. In Italy, Calderoli, then minister for reforms and devolution and an exponent of the Italian xenophobic party Lega Nord, appeared on Italian TV in February 2006 with a T-shirt reproducing the caricatures, provoking outrage and further incidents.[22] Among the 12 contested caricatures, that of the Prophet with a bomb in his turban remains the most contested one and has rightly been defined as "iconic of the controversy" (Lindekilde, 2008, p. 2). One of the main reasons for this is precisely because of its spectacular and virtual nature.

That image was circulated on the web, where it was modified to the point where it became difficult to establish its original author. One of the many versions of this icon, for example, is on a cartoon from a blog created in 2009, which explicitly featured the image at the center of the controversy.[23] The cartoon reproduced the contested icon of the prophet with a bomb as a turban, but by drastically modifying it, inserting the face into the body of a huge monster that eats babies and brings destruction everywhere, while tanks and helicopters are trying to kill him. The caricature, which clearly has a slanderous intent, also proves our general point that myths (and icons) are not given once and for all. They are continuously evolving processes, which express themselves through the proliferation of variants. The wit consists here both in the reversal of the Muslim invocation (*Allahu akbar*) into the tile of the cartoon as "Allah Snackbar," which appears next to exploding buildings and in the association kissing and eating. While eating one, the prophet-monster says, "What's wrong? You never seen a prophet kissing babies before?" thus suggesting that, with the excuse of "kissing" us, Islam is actually phagocytizing us. The caption "Dar al-harb" alludes to the traditional separation in Islam between the *Dar al-Islam*, which refers to the space where Islam is the dominant religion, and *Dar al-Harb*, where Islam is in peril. But here it is Islam that is the threat. The image thus synthesizes many of the icons of the evil Arab that circulate in the global society of the spectacle—the turban-headed, sinister eyes, big-nosed prophet, the essential carrier of a religion that is a bomb in itself. A war is declared on the West, and it is waged by a religion: Islam.

This spectacularization of the past tends to turn all historical narratives into a possible site for mythmaking. For example, references to medieval crusades have recently become very common in both the West and the Middle East. The crusades have become a crucial icon of the clash of civilizations, which is particularly interesting because it works on both sides in exactly the same way. The result is that within a few years, the crusades have transformed from an historical event of interest to only a few specialized historians into a popular object of consumption. In the wake of 9/11, films, exhibitions, and publications devoted to them started to proliferate. The link between the medieval crusades and the terrorist attacks was made patent by both intellectual discourses and politicians. Al-Qaeda material is full of references to a supposed crusade that the Western powers are leading in the Middle East at the service of Zionism (Kepel & Milelli, 2008), On the other side, *Foreign Affairs*, which in the past hosted a long series of critical responses to Huntington, launched a special issue just after 9/11, "Long War in the Making," with a leading article arguing that the real roots of the attacks on the Twin Towers lay in 7th-century Arabia, in the medieval crusades, in the Mongol invasion and the demise of the caliphate (Doran, 2002)

This work did not fail to have an impact on the discourse of politicians. President George W. Bush, for instance, often denied that a clash between civilizations was taking place but still from the very beginning described the "war on terrorism" as a crusade. In this way, he implicitly suggested it was about a clash between Islam and the West. We see here a perfect example of how a rational rejection of the paradigm of the clash between civilizations can go hand in hand with its unconscious endorsement. The result of such a work is that people act *as if* a clash between civilizations was taking place and by doing so, make it real.

As Geisser (2003) also observed in his analysis of the sources of Islamophobia in France, French journalists tend to be very cautious in their statements and sometimes even explicitly deny the paradigm of the clash. The sources of Islamophobia are rather the continual insistence in the media on the need for more security and a parallel demonization of Muslims (Geisser, 2003). The French media (like the American media) have operated a sort of systematization of a general discourse about Islam, which depicts it as an immutable and conflictual block. The "Muslim" is represented in the media in standardized ways—praying believers seen from the back, crying and threatening crowds, veiled women, fanatical bearded men, and so on (Geisser, 2003).

It is precisely for understanding how it is possible to criticize the paradigm of the clash as a theory while still endorsing it at a more or less unconscious level that we need to call in the concept of political myth. All these icons are much more powerful, because they operate within the unconscious without it being possible to perceive, let alone critique them. Growing up in contemporary societies inundated by media stimuli, most people encounter an overwhelming number of myths that gradually slip into their unconscious. Young children are exposed to a battery of more or less unconscious stimuli through comics, cartoons, films, and advertisements. A recent survey of the most popular American children's comics, such as *Superman*, *Spider-Man*, and *Captain America*, has shown that the icon of the "fanatical Muslim" has become one of the most powerful representations of the "threat." After the end of the Cold War, the role of the bad guys in these stories ceased to be played primarily by perfidious Eastern Bloc spies, and assumed the features of Muslims, explicitly depicted as fanatical, mad terrorists (Frazzi, 2004).

But the most inexhaustible and rich Western source of icons of the clash of civilizations is Hollywood films. In his survey of the role of Arabs in Hollywood films, Jack Shaheen (2002) has shown that, out of 1,000 films that have Arab or Muslim characters (1996–2000), 12 were "positive" depictions, 52 were "even-handed," and the rest of more than 900 were "negative." The most popular icons of the myth of the clash of civilizations that abound in such films are those of the barbaric bedouin, of the rich and stupid sheik who wants to rape Western women or, finally, that of the mad terrorist and airplane hijacker. This insistence on their "barbarism" and our "superiority" has the reassuring function of making us feel safe, and preemptively eliminating the need for criticism or critique of Western policies toward primarily Muslim states.

Besides the implicit message of such icons (Arab = barbarism and threat), it is interesting to note their evolution and to examine how they can be understood from a psychoanalytical point of view. Let us take, for instance, the female counterpart of the mad fanatical terrorist, the veiled women that we have seen in the *Marianne voileé*. Traditionally, it was sexually provocative belly dancers that worked as the female counterparts of the male threat (e.g., the mad terrorist, the sheik who wants to rape "our" women.) More recently, Arab females have been depicted not solely as submissive veiled women but also potential terrorists themselves, as is the case in films such as *Black Sunday* (1977), *Death Before Dishonor* (1987), and *Never Say Never Again* (1983). This change reflects the unconscious distress Western men feel toward the changing role of women in Western societies themselves: By projecting the threat into *another*, "barbaric" civilization, Western males are freed from the burden of recognizing their own distress vis-à-vis the emancipation of women in the West itself (Semmerling, 2006).

At this point, it is interesting to explicitly apply the strong version of the social unconscious to explain how different versions of the "Muslim woman" help to produce a social unconscious in the way that we described earlier. In recent years, we have witnessed new and striking alliances between "Western feminists" and conservative men who suddenly agree in the common aim to criticize the subordination of the "Muslim woman." Thus, the icon of the female Muslim terrorist, together with that of the submissive veiled woman, form a strong defense mechanism against facing the conflicts and struggles that still exist between men and women in contemporary Western societies. The myth of the clash thus helps to project gender conflicts onto others and to idealize the collective self-image of belonging to the part of the world where "we" have already reached freedom and equality to a large degree.[24]

In conclusion, an old, but new and insidious, political myth inhabits our global society of the spectacle. People increasingly act *as if* a clash between Islam and the West is taking place, and in so doing, they make it exist. As the passage quoted as epigraph to this article suggests, Debord (1994) already understood that globalization, while geographically unifying the world, would at the same time have divided it again through some new, spectacular division between us and them. The politics of the past has become the geography of our present. Intellectual discourses, Hollywood films, children's comics, social practices, and—last, but not least—politicians' actions have all been the sites for the elaboration of the myth of the clash of civilizations. The success of such a narrative shows that, in our contemporary societies, when politics set out on its search for legitimacy in a more or less distant past, it all too easily turns into a myth. Reference to more or less invented traditions has always influenced the politics of the past. The difference is that today, such politics have become, more than ever, imaginal.

Acknowledgments

This chapter draws from a joint research project that I conducted with Benoit Challand and whose results have been published in the volume *The Myth of the Clash of Civilizations* (Bottici & Challand, 2010). I am also indebted to Angela Kuehner, with whom I coauthored a paper on the clash of civilizations which appeared first in a shorter German version under the title "Der Mythos des 'clash of civilizations' zwischen Politischer Philosophie und Psychoanalyse," (Bottici & Kuehner, 2011) and, subsequently, in a longer English version in *Critical Horizons*,Volume 13, Number 1 (2012).

Notes

1 As White (1973) observes, the passage where the German historian Leopold von Ranke described the historical method in such terms has been canonical for a long time in the profession (p. 163).
2 On the different variants of this myth, see Bottici (2007, pp. 127–128).
3 The need for significance is not the need for religion, because something can be significant for a group without answering the ultimate questions of life and death, as religion does. See Bottici (2007).
4 H. Tudor (1972) maintains that what renders a myth specifically political is precisely its subject matter. This definition, however, contrasts with the example of the myth of the millennium that he himself analyses in his work. See Tudor (1972, p. 17).
5 This is the etymological meaning of the term *politics*, which derives from the ancient Greek term *politikos*, the adjective of *polis*, and the city/state (Bobbio, 1990, p. 800).
6 This is quite a widespread view of politics. Among the most influential supporters, see, for instance, Weber (1978).
7 See Flood (1996).
8 The term *symbol* originally denotes two halves of a broken object—the term derives from the Greek *syn-ballo*, which means "putting together."
9 Young (1990) introduces the concept of mythology by quoting a passage from Derrida's critique of metaphysics as "white mythology." The mythological aspect here consists of the illusion of the universality of metaphysics that calls itself "Reason" but is in fact an "Indo–European Mythology," that is, the *mythos* of a specific idiom (Young, 1990).
10 Indeed, it seems as if the white mythologies denounced in the title of Young's (1990) book are all those theories that, from Marxism onward, strive toward the idea of a unique "world history," that is, of history as a totality.
11 See, for instance, Smith (2000) and Stråth (2000). Even a quasi-supranational polity such as the European Union has its own myths, which at times converge with its founding historical narratives (Bottici, & Challand, 2013).
12 I am here following, see Bottici & Challand. (2010).
13 On this point, see again Bottici et al. (2010).
14 See Bottici et al. (2010).
15 For a discussion of Occidentalism, see Bottici et al. (2010). In this usage of the term, we distance ourselves from Buruma and Margalit (2004), who mainly look at Occidentalism as a form of dehumanisation of the West that began with modernity. See Buruma and Margalit (2004).
16 For an analysis of similar images, see Geisser (2003, p. 23).
17 In this sense, it also differs from Fromm's (2001) view of the social unconscious, which defines primarily areas of repression found among the majority of members of a specific class of society. See Fromm (2001).

18 See also Hopper (2003, p. 127).
19 On the universality of archetypes of the collective unconscious, see Jung (1990, p. 4).
20 See in particular Abrahamian (2003, pp. 529–544).
21 On the notion of imaginal politics, see Bottici (2011b). It should be noted here that by "imaginal" I mean what is made of images, independently of whether they are real (and in this sense, it is different from imaginary which is usually associated with unreality).
22 See, for example, Willey (2006).
23 [Untitled caricature of Allah]. Retrieved January 15, 2009, from:http://photos1.blogger.com/blogger/4765/1487/1600/mostots.0.jpg.
24 On this point, I am strongly indebted to the research that I conducted on icons of the clash of civilisations with Angela Kuehner during my stay in Frankfurt. Among the product of this collaboration, see Bottici & Kuehner (2011).

References

Abrahamian, E. (2003). The US media, Huntington and September 11. *Third World Quarterly, 24*(3), 529–544.

Blumenberg, H. (1985). *Work on myth*. Cambridge, MA: MIT Press.

Bobbio, N. (1990). Politica. In N. Bobbio, N. Matteucci, & G. Pasquino (Eds.), *Dizionario di politica* (pp. 800–809). Torino: UTET.

Bottici, C. (2007). *A philosophy of political myth*, Cambridge: Cambridge University Press.

————. (2011b). Imaginal politics. *Thesis Eleven, 106*, 56–72.

Bottici, C., & Challand, B. (2010). *The myth of the clash of civilizations*. London: Routledge.

Bottici, C., & Challand, B., (2013). *Imagining Europe: Myth, memory and identity*. Cambridge, Cambridge University Press.

Bottici, C., & Kuehner, A. (2011). Der Mythos des "clash of civilizations" zwischen Politischer Philosophie und Psychoanalyse. In R. Haubl & M. Leuzinger-Bohleber (Eds.), *Psychoanalyse–leise Stimme des Unbewussten. Festschrift zum 50 Jährigen Bestehen des Sigmund-Freud-Instituts* (pp. 352–372). Göttingen: Vandenhoeck and Ruprecht Verlag.

Buruma, I., & Margalit, A. (2004). *Occidentalism: The West in the eyes of its enemies*. New York: Penguin.

Debord, G. (1994). *The society of the spectacle*. New York: Zone Books.

Doran, M. S. (2002). Somebody else's civil war. *Foreign Affairs, 81*(1), 22–42.

Flood, C. (1996). *Political myth. A theoretical introduction*. New York: Garland.

Frazzi, F. (2004). *Dai dirottamenti all'11 settembre: terrorismo e supereroi in vent'anni di fumetti*. Bologna: Università di Bologna.

Freud, S. (1989). *Jokes and their relation to the unconscious*. New York: Norton.

Fromm, E. (2001). *Beyond the chains of illusion. My encounter with Marx and Freud*. New York: Continuum.

Gehlen, A. (1988). *Man, his nature and place in the world*. New York: Columbia University Press.

Geisser, V. (2003). *La nouvelle islamophobie*. Paris: La Découverte.

Gramsci, A. (1996). *Prison notebooks*. New York: Columbia University Press.

Hopper, E. (2003). *The social unconscious. Selected papers.* London: Jessica Kingsley Publishers.

Huntington, S. (1996). *The clash of civilizations and the remaking of world order.* New York: Simon and Schuster.

Jung, C. G. (1990). *The archetypes and the collective unconscious.* Princeton, NJ: Princeton University Press.

Kepel, G., & Milelli, J.-P. (Eds.), (2008). *Al Qaeda in its own words.* Cambridge, MA: Belknap Press.

Kerényi, K., & Jung, C. G. (1963). *Essays on a science of mythology,* Princeton: Princeton University Press.

Lindekilde L. E. (2008). *Contested caricatures: Dynamics of Muslim claims-making during the Muhammad caricatures controversy.* Florence: European University Institute.

Said, E. (1978). *Orientalism.* London: Routledge.

Schlegel, F. S., & Schlegel, A. W. (1992). *Athenäum. Eine Zeitschrift von A.W. Schlegel und F.S. Schlegel.* Darmstadt: Wissenschaftliche Buchgesellschaft.

Semmerling, T. J. (2006). *Evil Arabs in American popular films.* Austin: University of Texas Press.

Shaheen, J. (2001). *Reel bad Arabs: How Hollywood vilifies a people.* New York: Olive Branch Press.

Smith, A. D. (2000). *Myths and memories of the nation.* Oxford: Oxford University Press.

Stråth, B. (Ed.). (2000). *Myth and memory in the construction of the community.* Brussels: Peter Lang.

Sullivan, A. (2001, October 7). This is a religious war. *New York Times Magazine.* Retrieved from www.nytimes.com/2001/10/07/magazine/this-is-a-religious-war.html

Tudor, H. (1972). *Political myth.* London: Macmillan.

Weber, M. (1978). *Economy and society.* Berkeley: University of California Press.

White, H. (1973). *Metahistory: The historical imagination in nineteenth-century Europe,* Baltimore: John Hopkins University Press.

———. (1987). *The content of the form: Narrative discourse and historical representation,* Baltimore: Johns Hopkins University Press.

Willey, David (2006, February 15). Italy minister stirs cartoon row. *BBC News.* Retrieved January 24, 2009, from http://news.bbc.co.uk/2/hi/europe/4714548.stm

Young, R. (1990). *White mythologies: Writing history and the West.* London: Routledge.

5   On Narrative, Metaphor and the Politics of Security

Annick T. R. Wibben

> To be secure is to be safe is to be sure.
> —Constantinou, "Poetics of Security" (2000, p. 288)

Narrative and metaphor tend to be ignored in the discipline of International Relations (IR) largely because of the way in which the discipline has been constructed as a science. The construction of IR in this manner draws on a particular, modern notion of science. Here science is imagined to be objective and value-neutral, divorced from politics. This traditional notion of modern science has been contested at many points in history (see, e.g., Wibben, 2011), but here let us begin with Robert Cox's (1981) more recent challenge to IR scholars that "theory is always *for* someone and *for* some purpose" (p. 128). Whereas traditional (modern) science assumes the possibility of ahistorical, universally valid discoveries, critical theory points out that "all theories have a perspective [which] derives from a position in time and space, specifically social and political time and space" (ibid). Unlike the modern scientist, the critical theorist, therefore, "does not take institutions and social and power relations for granted, but calls them into question by concerning [him- or herself] with their origins and how and whether they might be in the process of changing" (ibid, p. 129).

It is not enough, however, to simply restate his claim. Instead, we find that it was precisely at the moment where modern science was constructed in this manner that narrative and metaphor disappear from so-called scientific inquiry. As Paul Chilton (1996) notes, political science and IR too, constituting themselves as science in this particular way, "bear the stamp of the rationalist and empiricist beginnings of science" (p. 1). Although political theorizing is heavily dependent on language, key founding texts of IR saw language and metaphor as a problem to be solved by rendering it rational or scientific:

> From the mid-seventeenth century to the mid-twentieth century, rationalists, empiricists, and positivists tended to view metaphor as extrinsic to reason, and even directly threatening to it. Rationality itself was defined in part, and circularly, in terms of the language used to conduct reasoning. Metaphor was interpreted and presented variously as misleading, irrational, emotional, diseased, primitive and absurd. (Chilton, 1996, pp. 1–2)

This distrust of metaphor specifically, and language (including narrative) more generally, is related to both philosophical and political transformations at the time. According to Sandra Harding (1986), a pervasive idea of the time was that "scientists as scientists were not to meddle in politics; political, economic, and social administrators were not to shape the cognitive direction of scientific inquiry" (p. 223). This division of labor, institutionalized in the establishment of academies of the sciences, it was thought, would allow academics to speak truth to power without the interference of persuasive oration, a notion still invoked to this day. In practice, however, the production of knowledge and its modalities are essential to any particular order and truth cannot be divorced from power. Instead, knowledge and power engender one another: "The exercise of power perpetually creates knowledge and, conversely, knowledge constantly induces effects of power," writes Michel Foucault (1980, p. 52). "It is not possible for power to be exercised without knowledge, it is impossible for knowledge not to engender power" (p. 52). That is, the way in which science and politics interact, shape, and alter what happens in reality.

We might say, "The world is seen from a standpoint definable in terms of nation or social class, of dominance or subordination, of rising or declining power, of a sense of immobility or of present crisis, of past experience, and of hopes and expectations for the future" (Cox, 1981, p. 128). If the starting point of knowledge is always the current order, then "there is, accordingly, no such thing as theory in itself, divorced from a standpoint in time and space" (ibid). The supposed division between knowledge and the current world order cannot be upheld in practice—but it does have consequences of a different kind: When science is depicted and valued as separate from power, its influence is more insidious, and it becomes harder to challenge its political effects. This makes it appear *as though* science has a legitimation that rests on an authority other than that provided by the order within which it arises, its political context.

As noted, the discipline of IR replicates this debate including in more recent and still ongoing attempts by neorealists in particular to render IR "extra-scientific" through the development of mathematical models to calculate behavior and predict futures.[1] In the case of security studies, a main feature has been its support for a particular epistemological position that supports the claim that security studies has "gradually evolved into an objective, scientific discipline in which the 'laws' governing the realm of security are discovered or, at least, the correct method for their discovery has been identified" (Krause & Williams, 1996, p. 231). As Stephen Walt (1991) describes it, the goal of strategic studies, which in the U.S. is often synonymous with security studies, is "*cumulative knowledge* about the role of military force. To obtain it the field must follow the standard canons of scientific research" (p. 222). Such appeals to traditional science by IR scholars can be read as attempts to anchor the legitimacy of their findings to something other than authority in order to escape their own historicity (see, e.g., Krause & Williams, 1997). Yet, as Cox (1981) urges, "when any theory so represents itself, it is more important to examine it as ideology, and to lay bare its concealed perspective" (p. 128).

Paying attention to metaphor and narrative, then, is not only to reject this notion of science and point to its inherent bias, but also to (re)discover issues that are left out of the realm of traditional IR. What is more, using the tools developed to analyze narrative and metaphor, it becomes possible to point not only to the ways in which power generates knowledge, but also how certain knowledge engenders particular politics—and what can be done to challenge them. Drawing inspiration from critical and feminist theory, this chapter pays particular attention to the ways in which the framing of security in narrative produces a politics of security that negatively affects not just women, but marginalized populations more generally.

Narrative, Meaning and Security

Narrative, if only temporarily, arrests meaning. The framing of events in narrative is fundamental to a particular order—whether its political, economic, social, symbolic or cultural aspects. As Donald Polkinghorne (1988) points out in his investigation of *Narrative Knowledge and the Human* Sciences, narratives "are the primary way by which human experience is made meaningful" (p. 1). In other words, narratives are performative, in the Butlerian sense, rather than knowledgeable. They produce meaning, loosely based on experience.

Within positivist modern science, it has been experience as *Erfahrung* (a knowledge or skill gained from practice) that, together with the idea of an experiment, has become the basis of the instrumental notion of experience that informs empiricism. Narratives based on experience as *Erfahrung,* therefore, will support the notion of science favored in IR. On the other hand, experience can be viewed as *Erlebnis*, which denotes a lived experience, a phenomenological event, which is the notion that, more often than not, feminist theorizing is based on. However, *Erlebnis* as pre-reflective and immediate is impossible to capture, so that an account of it will always be an approximation and will fail to represent it in its entirety—*Erlebnis* always exceeds representation. At the same time, representation is what we have to work with and narratives both enable and limit representation; experience is narratively constructed (see also Wibben, 1998).

To think of experience as narratively constructed captures the interpretative aspect inherent in any recollection of experience. As it is impossible to reproduce a lived experience (*Erlebnis*), a characterization that includes the interpretative aspect is crucial for feminists in particular. Feminists derive their insights based on women's everyday experience, and as women long subject to others' interpretations of their lives, they tend to be acutely aware of questions of representation. Thinking of experience as narratively constructed alerts us, on one hand, to the conceptualization of experience itself as narrative and, on the other hand, to the variety of narratives telling us what kind of experiences to expect (Wibben, 1998, p. 78ff). "Experience is an integrated construction, produced by the realm of meaning, which interpretatively links recollections, perceptions, and expectations" (Polkinghorne, 1988, p. 16). If experience can only be grasped through retrospective construction via narratives, these narratives warrant close attention.

Narratives always relate to a particular tradition—in a single text or story, very little is new—but they can reframe how an event is seen and thus have a disruptive quality. Poststructuralist narrative theorists are interested in ways to emphasize the latter by focusing on "process, becoming, play, difference, slippage, and dissemination," writes Marc Currie (1998, p. 3). Here the focus is on the contradictory and complex aspects of narrative that, if they are preserved, can highlight historical and political contingencies. Phrased differently, as every narrative is told in reply to a question, "there is no possible statement that cannot be understood as an answer to a question," Hans-Georg Gadamer notes, going on to propose that "it can only be understood as such" (as cited in Grondin, 1991, p. 154). Narratives both enable and limit representation based on our vantage point in history. They shape how we see the world and what is possible within it—for us, at this moment. By preserving their multiplicity, we can learn about those vantage points and develop richer accounts of people's lives.

If we accept this premise, and are committed to adopting a critical perspective, it becomes necessary to understand how narrative produces meaning—in this case, how the field of IR produces particular narratives of security. This is important, because the way a story is told limits what can be seen, who gets to speak, and whose concerns matter, all of which affect, consequently, the possible responses. In other words, the inquiry into processes in narrative is "directed towards an appraisal of the very framework for action, or problematic, which problem-solving theory [of which traditional IR/security studies is a variant] accepts as its parameters" (Cox, 1981, p. 12). IR generally, and security studies in particular, circulates narratives that police our imagination by taming aspirations and adjusting desires to the status quo.

If one scrutinizes the meaning of any concept, one cannot fail to note that it is only within a certain context or tradition that meaning can be produced. What IR scholars mean when they utter "security" is limited by a particular (truncated) story about the role of the state based on the idea that citizens give up certain rights in exchange for protection by the state. In her discussion of the making of modern European states, Spike Peterson (1992) points to the infrastructural power of modern states that "the capacity of the state to actually penetrate civil society, and to implement logistically political decisions throughout the realm" (p. 38, citing Mann). This "permits the maintenance of centralized rule less through direct violence and more through indirect violence" (Peterson, 1992, p. 38). She goes on, stating, "thus the *legitimization* processes [including security narratives!] become key to maintaining (reproducing) state power—and therefore become pivotal to our understanding of that power and the in/securities it constitutes" (Peterson, 1992, p. 38; material in brackets added).

The modern state emerges as the guarantor of the good life within its border and, so the tale continues, this requires its protection from outside threats. Peterson (1992) argues that the state promises various forms of protection: "protecting citizens from each other, protecting rights to privacy, protecting property rights, and protecting citizens from external threats" (p. 50). When security is equated with protection in this way, most people feel some sense of "having" security—"protection calls up images of the shelter against danger provided by a powerful friend, a large insurance policy, or a sturdy roof," according to Charles Tilly, but it also "evokes that racket in which a local strong man forces merchants to pay tribute in order to avoid damage" (as cited in Peterson, 1992, p. 50).[2]

The problem of imagining the role of the state in this way is that protection is not only a matter of the degree to which the state provides shelter or, conversely, institutes a protection racket, but of the trade-offs involved in "the interaction of systems of in/security [which] renders complexities and contradictions such that apparent gains can mask actual costs" (Peterson, 1992, p. 50).[3] Because the degree of gain or loss is always contextually specific and intimately tied to the identity through which one seeks security, Peterson suggests to engage in comparisons of trade-offs and alternatives because this "forces our attention to situational and system context and to the lenses—for example social identities—through which we make choices" (ibid., p. 53).

Governments frame events and their aftermath through the proliferation of traditional security narratives (for a discussion of 9/11, see Wibben, 2011) and generate extraordinary measures in defense of the state—despite all the difficulties with this notion. Traditional security narratives provide legitimization to this modern state-centric order when they limit how we can think security, whose security matters, and how it might be achieved. These accounts rely on a fairly closed narrative structure that makes it almost impossible to think differently of security.

Traditional Security Narratives

Security narratives have four main elements: threats that locate danger, referents to be secured, agents charged with providing security, and means by which threats are contained, and so the tale is told, security provided. Importantly, traditional security narratives are characterized by the assertion that an identification of these elements in any particular situation would provide the basis for a comprehensive security agenda and the containment of danger (Wibben, 2008, 2011). We might say, "The epistemology of security is based on two elements—(a) everything can in principle be known; and (b) if it is known its truth does not change over time" (Huysmans, 1998, p. 245).

The purpose of traditional security narratives is to identify security threats and to contain them. As Chilton (1996) points out the container metaphor is one of "four schemas, all of which have historically been used, and are still used, as the source domain for the metaphorical conceptualization of international relations, defense and security" (p. 50).[4] The container schema shapes traditional understandings of security in a number of ways. It forms the basis of the inside/outside distinction (both for bodies and for states) and in doing so "involves separation, differentiation, and enclosure, which implies restriction and limitation" (Johnson, as cited in Chilton, 1996, p. 51), also visually. Additionally, it provokes the image of defending or shielding: "it typically involves protection from or resistance to, external forces" (Chilton, 1996, p. 51). At the same time, the object within the container is restricted by it and assumes a relative fixity. Meanings of security proliferated in traditional security narratives draw on the container metaphor; there is no continuum between "our" and "their" security or between "inside" and "outside" of states.

It is not surprising, therefore, that security studies has traditionally (and particularly in its strategic studies iteration) focused on the means that are required to achieve external security in this framework—which are assumed to be a strong military—even though it has been pointed out from the early days of security studies in the U.S. that this is a potentially misguided approach. George Kennan, in his assessment of the situation in 1946, was convinced that "it is not Russian military power that is threatening us; it is Russian political power" (as cited in Campbell, 1998, pp. 25–26). And "if it is not entirely a military threat, I doubt that it can be effectively met by military means," he cautioned (ibid.). The greatest danger, therefore, was considered to be that of an economic collapse, which would provide fertile ground for an ideological invasion—at least until the Soviet Union tested its first nuclear weapon in 1949.

The privileging of military means, hence, is not a necessity, but shaped by historical circumstance and selective forgetting/ remembering. To begin, governments have long regarded the military as an instrument of policy and continue to do so long after the symbolic move from ministries of war to ministries of defense and the introduction of a language of security to replace that of conquest (Klein, 1994). "As distance, oceans and borders became less of a protective barrier to alien identities, and a new international economy required penetration into other worlds, *national interest* became too weak a semantic guide," writes James Der Derian (1995), "we found a stronger one in *national security*" (p. 42).[5] This entails a paradox: Discursively the military is seen as being concerned with security in terms of defense (making a continued focus on the military more acceptable to citizens in liberal democracies), yet it gets theorized in terms of the inherently more aggressive "instrument of policy" by which to pursue the "national interest."[6]

Second, the privileging of military means is also connected to attempts to establish security studies as a distinct field of inquiry where the parameters of security became defined in an increasingly narrow fashion. This, combined with the loss of the U.S. nuclear monopoly in the late 1940s, produced a shift from a concern with domestic and nonmilitary threats to the threat of global nuclear war. Given the superpower rivalry between the USSR and the U.S., the central question became, "How could states use weapons of mass-destruction as an instrument of policy, given the risk of nuclear exchange?" (Walt, as cited in Baldwin, 1995). The field's narrowing, then, was also shaped by the focus on the requirements of policy makers. It follows that security studies, at least in its mainstream iteration as strategic studies, has had an (almost exclusive) focus on "the military means that actors in the international system employ to gain their political objectives or ends" (Snyder, 1999, pp. 3–4). Generalists who would explore other aspects of security or possibly even rethink security, were marginalized. A wealth of relevant concepts (and metaphors) "including power, security, war, peace, alliance, terrorism and crisis" (Buzan, 1987, p. 8) were no longer considered worth exploring.[7]

The traditional security narrative (as identified here; see Wibben, 2008, 2011) has never been uncontested, however. From the outset, opposition has drawn "on the contention that it would help little to make national core values secure, if in the process the liberties and the social welfare of the people had been sacrificed" (Wolfers, 1962, p. 157).[8] There often is a direct conflict between providing security for the population and achieving security for the state, not least because the latter has traditionally involved large investments in military infrastructure, hardware and personnel. Those resources are then not available to provide services for the population within a state. This situation is exacerbated when the population that is most affected by the lack of services—from public education, to health care, to social services—does not have a voice in decision making. The question, then, is one of the value of survival for those contained within the state.

What would security look like if one were to shift one's perspective so that the starting point for theory is a different standpoint? What kind of shifts would have to take place, not just in the way IR thinks security (structured both by narrative and metaphor) but also in how policy gets made as resources get allocated according to one or another understanding of what security can mean? These are the kind of questions that critical scholars generally, and feminist scholars in particular, are asking.

Critical Security Narratives

It is important to note here that the aim of my research has never been to find the "real" meaning of security because, indeed, that is not possible or even useful.[9] Instead, I am interested in exploring how the processes of narrating security function and how they produce particular effects. As noted, the framing of events as security issues, via the formulation of particular narratives and the use of metaphors, has important implications for action. If one disagrees with the actions taken to secure us, and the effects thereof, as feminists tend to, one should not only pay attention to the content of these narratives, but also to the framing in narrative that imposes a particular form. It is particularly important to examine how the framing takes place, what it excludes and includes, what it allows us to say and where it imposes silences.

This has been a concern of critical security studies scholars: Ole Wæver (1995) has suggested that "taking security seriously" should imply discussing actual conceptual issues, and Jef Huysmans (1998) has claimed that "the exploration of the meaning of security is the security studies agenda itself" (p. 233). Meanwhile, most of the disagreements that have preoccupied security studies can "be seen as empirical or political questions where people actually agree about the concept of security but differ in their interpretation of what actual threats qualify as security issues" (Wæver, 1999, p. 339). What these critical scholars suggest, and the argument presented here supports, is that interrogating security should not be limited to working solely within the parameters of traditional narratives of security since this would limit the scope of analysis to what is possible within that particular narrative tradition.[10] What is more, attention also needs to be paid to the way in which metaphorical schemas, like that of the container, limit how security can be imagined. As Chilton notes (1996), "the effect of the container schema would certainly explain the perseverance [of] the cognitively satisfying proposals for 'containers', 'canisters', 'hardened shells', 'shelters', and 'shields'" (p. 235).

In the mid-1990s, Keith Krause and Michael Williams (1996) suggested two trends that characterize the post–Cold War re-visioning of the security agenda: *deepening*, "by moving either down to the level of individual or human security or up to the level of national or global security," and *broadening*, "to include a wider range of potential threats" (p. 230). I would suggest, however, that taking security seriously requires more than a simple broadening or deepening. Given the preceding discussion of narrative and metaphor, it is necessary to produce an *opening*—to acknowledge the polysemy of security and show how security narratives already function differently depending on context. Such an opening would garner insights from narrative theory about the importance of framing an event (and pay attention to cognitive schemas provided by metaphor) to apply them in inquiries into the production and impact of security narratives. Such an approach, then, also challenges the frame provided by the container metaphor, opening the container to make it possible to identify points at which narrative coherence breaks down and at which alternative interpretations can be inserted.

Crucial for such an approach is the formulation of security as practice, as a process of securitization, which emerges out of poststructuralist scholarship (e.g., Campbell, 1998; Der Derian, 1992, 1995; Der Derian & Shapiro, 1989; Dillon, 1990, 1996; Shapiro, 1992). Using the term *securitization* to describe a process, rather than a noun or an object, was popularized in the Copenhagen School's *New Framework for Analysis* (Buzan, Wæver, & de Wilde, 1998), which maintains that what is or is not a security issue can only be identified in practice:

> In this approach the meaning of a concept lies in its usage and is not something we can define analytically or philosophically according to what would be "best" . . . "Security" is thus a self-referential practice, because it is in this practice that the issue becomes a security issue—not necessarily because a real existential threat exists but because the issue is presented as

such a threat. . . . The exact *definition* and *criteria* of securitization is constituted by the intersubjective establishment of an existential threat with a
saliency sufficient to have political effects. (pp. 24–25)[11]

This theoretical innovation derives mainly from Wæver's (1997) work for his dissertation, in which he applies speech act theory to the problem of "security." Drawing on this work, he coined the terms securitization (referring to the processes
involved in producing a situation in which a particular event becomes framed in
terms of "security" via the utterance of a speech act) and desecuritization (signify-
ing the attempt to move an issue out of the realm of emergency back into the realm
of 'normal' politics; Wæver, 1995). Taking a closer look at how security concerns
are traditionally presented in the international Buzan et al. (1998) observe the following pattern: (a) Security is evoked whenever an issue is presented as an existential threat to a specific referent object (whether the threat is real or perceived is
irrelevant); (b) by declaring an emergency, the issue is removed from the political
agenda into the realm of security; (c) if, and only when, this move is accepted by
the audience, the securitizing move has been successful.

It is only when security is analyzed as an ongoing process where the parameters of security are formed/generated, that the grip of traditional security narratives on what security means/can mean can be challenged (see, e.g., Edkins,
2002). As Michael Dillon (1990) notes, " 'security' is a process of subjecti-
fication and not the end of an unproblematical subject. Securing something
requires its differentiation, classification and definition. It has, in short, to be
identified" (p. 114). David Campbell's (1998) *Writing Security*, a classic on the
security/identity nexus, illustrates this approach: He discusses how the proliferation of U.S. foreign policy narratives is "central to the constitution, production, and maintenance of American political identity" (p. 8). Campbell notes
that "just as Foreign Policy works to constitute the identity in whose name it
operates, security functions to instantiate the subjectivity it purports to serve.
Indeed, security . . . is first and foremost a performative discourse, constitutive
of political order" (ibid., p. 199).[12] This insight about the relationship between
identity and security is crucial if we are to begin opening security studies—and
narrative approaches, which can help in understanding identity formation, can
bridge different fields as they can be applied to "narrative wherever they can be
found, which is everywhere" (Currie, 1998, p. 1).

Maria Stern (2001, 2005) provides a feminist version of this approach in her
exploration of the life stories of poor Mayan women at the end of the Guatemalan civil war. She points out that their experiences of in security are shaped
by complex intersections between their location in relation to their own community, the dominant *Ladino* community, and the Guatemalan state. Paying
close attention to the construction of identity in personal narratives, she points
out, "Violence that is poorly understood through the lenses of state-centered
security thinking could perhaps be better understood if we began asking questions around the injury that can occur at the confluence of competing identity

claims and the effort at securing subject positions" (Stern, 2001, p. 3). She also proposes that telling their story as security narrative, in the process both naming and eliminating dangers, provides a way for Mayan women to establish "a political identity from which to make claims of protection, for security" (Stern, 2005, p. 116). That is, she provides evidence for the claim that opening the structure of security narratives to allow for different, personal security narratives to be told can challenge what security means—and indeed the very experience of security can be reshaped.

Toward Security Politics

Notwithstanding the important insights discussed earlier, critical approaches, including feminist revisions of security, have had limited success in their appeals to security and remain at the margins. This is the case because a security story that is not set up in this accepted and therefore recognizable form of traditional security narratives is not read as a security narrative. In other words, security narratives that do not conform to the previously discussed structure, and that might challenge its epistemological and ontological assumptions, are not recognized as security talk (Wibben, 2011). This is not surprising because in security studies epistemological, ontological, and political questions tend to be "ignored, subordinated, or displaced by the technically biased, narrowly framed question of *what* it takes to achieve security" (Der Derian, 1995, p. 24; see also. Bobrow, 2001). It is a crucial observation, however, because the security narratives that do not fit these confines, and consequently are not recognized as security talk, do not generate the kind of extraordinary measures that are associated with the utterance of security in IR.

Via narratives we not only *investigate* but also *invent* an order for the world. Security narratives too are *performative* in this way: They constitute a particular order and its corresponding subjects, but they never do so perfectly. "Production is partial and is, indeed, perpetually haunted by its ontologically uncertain double" (Butler, 2009, p. 7). To imagine alternative security narratives then, it is necessary to provide a space where different narratives can exist alongside each other, where their intersections and contradictions can be seen as enriching rather than as problems to be transcended. This requires calling into question not just the form of security narratives themselves, but also the larger frame within which they attain meaning—the field of IR as a modern science. Calling "the frame into question," Judith Butler (2009) suggests, "is to show that the frame never quite contained the scene it was meant to limit, that something was already outside which made the very sense of the inside possible, recognizable" (p. 9).

In IR, poststructuralists such as Rob Walker (e.g., in his 1993 book *Inside/Outside: International Relations as Political Theory*) have made this claim for a while now—as have feminist scholars such as Cynthia Enloe, who tirelessly points to politics happening in places beyond the vision of IR. Enloe

(2004) urges IR scholars to be curious and open to surprise because this allows one to push the limits of the discipline and to see that "the frame never quite determined precisely what it is we see, think, recognize, apprehend" (Butler, 2009, p. 9). If we look hard enough, we find that "something exceeds the frame that troubles our sense of reality; in other words, something occurs that does not conform to our established understanding of things" (Butler, 2009, p. 9). The task for a critical security studies scholar, then, is to continually point to the leakage in the construction of meaning and the excess of life beyond the frame.

For security this means "to understand the discursive power of the concept, to remember its forgotten meanings, to assess its economy of use in the present, to reinterpret—and possibly construct through the reinterpretation—a late modern security comfortable with a plurality of centers, multiple meanings, and fluid identities" (Der Derian, 1995, p. 26). This entails, as Butler (2009) points out, an epistemological problem: "The frames through which we apprehend or, indeed, fail to apprehend the lives of others as lost or injured (loseable or injurable) are politically saturated. They are themselves operations of power" (p. 1). What is more, the ontological implications of framing are also not outside operations of power and "we must make more precise the specific mechanisms through which life is produced" (Butler, 2009, p. 1).

In the case of security, this means that those scholars pointing to the identity/security nexus make crucially important points—security narratives function as " 'frames' that work to differentiate the lives we can apprehend from those that we cannot [and] generate specific ontologies of the subject" (Butler, 2009, p. 3). The subjects of security (more often referred to as its referent objects and even its agents) "are constituted through norms which, in their reiteration, produce and shift the terms through which subjects are recognized" (Butler, 2009, p. 3). And this recognition is both facilitated and limited by a historically contingent ontology that is constantly (re)produced in security narratives making them self-referential.

Fortunately, as Butler (2009) also points out, the operation of norms in this sense is not deterministic: "normative schemes are interrupted by one another, they emerge and fade depending on broader operations of power, and very often come up against spectral versions of what it is they claim to know" (p. 4). This, then, is a plea to move away from security theorizing to doing studies that, in their specificity, explode the neat configurations of security studies. This is how feminists have challenged various disciplines to include (formerly) marginalized voices. María Lugones and Elizabeth Spelman (1983) note that "our visions of what is better are always informed by our perception of what is bad about our present situation" (p. 579). No standpoint outside of history and politics would save us from partiality—instead, it might be better to embrace it in all its specificity to show that the container is overflowing, leaking, and breaking apart. There is no single security narrative, and to insist on one is a form of epistemic violence.

One way of opening space for alternative conceptualizations is by showing that there already are multiple meanings of security. This can be done by referencing the etymology of security as well as by noting connotations of the noun in various contexts. The Latin noun *securitas*, from which the modern "security" derives, "referred, in its primary classical use, to a condition of individuals, of a particular inner sort. It denoted composure, tranquility of spirit, freedom from care" (Rothschild, 1995, p. 61). *Securitas* derives from *sine cura*, "to be without care, free from cares and untroubled" (Neocleous, 2000, p. 9). It thus entails both a condition without danger, that is a condition of safety, as well as being "without care" or negligent. Security, then, has not always been, and probably should not be, unquestioningly considered a good thing (see Constantinou, 2000; Der Derian, 1995; Dillon, 1996; Neocleous, 2000; Rothschild, 1995; Wæver, 1995). Ultimately, as Dillon (1996) points out, being completely secure would be pointless:

> If the human were not free, in the condition of having its being as a possibility to be, there would be—no actions to take, no decisions to make, no dilemmas to face, no relations to relate, no loves to love, no fears to fear, no laws to make, no laws to break. There would be, in short, no politics. (p. 1)

Drawing on Greek readings of security, Costas Constantinou develops several versions of security. To begin, the ancient Greek word for security—*asphaleia*—entails "(a) rightness, not to err (*sphallo*) and (b) to remain standing and firm, not to fall (*sphallo*)" (Constantinou, 2000, p. 291). Here security implies certitude and firmness, whereas in a version drawing on Archilochus, security becomes a struggle to live with one's enemy. Rather than trying to eliminate the danger, one faces danger and tries "to reach a mental state where one is secure in danger, where one can dwell (*katatheis*) next to one's enemy, without surrendering, or dominating, or making friend of foe" (Constantinou, 2000, p. 290). In this version of security, one learns to live with one's own fears, for "security is not a rescue from danger but freedom from the care of danger" (Constantinou, 2000, p. 292).

Contrastingly, the dominant, liberal version of security is captured in the oft-used phrase "freedom from want and freedom from fear." This freedom from attack on one's person or property can be traced back to the eighteenth century (Rothschild, 1995; see also Williams, 2005). At this time, the security of individuals was subsumed in the security of the nation and eventually the state. It came to be linked to liberty and property in the triad of "liberty, security, and property," introduced in the writings of Adam Smith and popularized in various documents of the era including the declaration of the *Rights of Man* (Neocleous, 2000, p. 9). It is the values, or properties, associated with security that are now worth securing (Edkins, 2002), as can be seen in the addition of descriptors such as "national," "individual," or lately "human" security, which themselves carry a history that should be unpacked. Pointing to tales of security which are "less 'evident,' not merely commuted into accounts of safety and certitude, or in perfect tune with the presence of protection and of knowledge . . . shatters, albeit momentarily, the contemporaneous narrative of security" (Constantinou, 2000, p. 288).

Feminists Narrate Security

Feminist scholars in IR aim to reveal how the personal is political and international. In their quest, they seek out marginalized stories of those far from the centers of power and insist on building knowledge based on everyday experience. Although feminists have been criticized in the past for not casting their net wide enough and basing their theorizing exclusively on the lives of white, heterosexual, middle-class, Western women, the feminism this chapter draws on is intersectional by default (see, e.g., Collins, 1990; Crenshaw, 1991; Lorde, 1984; Yuval-Davis, 2012). Only in the multiplicity of the experiences of variously located women does the feminist security scholar find a variety of narratives that help to challenge accepted visions of security. What is more, the intersectional feminist scholar has to be prepared to interrogate them for their relationships to other social justice movements around race, class and more.

Methodologically, this means the feminist security studies scholar of the critical variety has to not only be willing to seek out a multiplicity of stories and accept the unsettling of his or her own identity that might follow, but he or she has to resist the urge to restrict them to a few massively circulated tales. What is more, rather than smoothing over differences, it is by pointing to them as fissures in the frame that feminist security scholars can challenge accepted meanings for security and begin to make room for feminist security narratives. As I discuss in detail in my book *Feminist Security Studies: A Narrative Approach* (Wibben, 2011), it is in the seeking out of marginal stories—those that are not included in the chronicles of official state historians and whose version of normality differs from that of mainstream culture—that feminists develop insights that directly challenge traditional security narratives and the container schema that so crucially defines them.

IR scholars do not normally speak to people, but feminist scholars tend to. Not only do they speak to people, but they also make an effort to accommodate their varied accounts into their research. Feminists have pointed out that subjectivities shift and slide (e.g. Ferguson, 1993; Sandoval, 2000) and that what we can hear/see as well as the stories we tell depend to a large extent on which aspects of our identity are foregrounded in any particular moment. Narratives of security, which are always also narratives of identity—of who we are or want to be (cf. Peterson, 1992)—are contextual. They carry with them a history of effects; understanding them requires an awareness thereof as well as the realization that a text will only speak to us in response to what we ask of it—meaning is to be encountered at the interstices of reader and text.

By definition, marginalized groups are not unproblematically included in the narrative of the imagined nation; indeed, they often suffer oppression as a direct consequence of attempts to present a unified, contained image of what is worth securing (Yuval-Davis, 1997). The complex subject positions that are the result of intersections of class, gender, race, sexuality, religion and more explode the confines of the container and continually challenge its neat boundaries. From this perspective, protection does not call up benign images of shelter from harm but serves to restrict movement and limit options for those who do not belong to the imagined community. Protection, then, becomes contingent on fitting in (the container) and serves to police the behavior of those whose version of normality differs from that of the mainstream. The state is no longer innocent or even benevolent, but does indeed evoke images of a protection racket (Peterson, 1992). Familiarity with the violence inherent in the production of the imagined community of the state (and national security) makes it easier for marginalized populations to imagine the ramifications of violence projected outward (and inward) in the name of protection.

Because fear and vulnerability are already a facet of everyday life, an attack from the outside, such as the events of September 11, 2001, can appear as more of the same. Feminists, attuned to the effects of militarism, have long stressed the need to theorize war as a presence and not an event. Chris Cuomo argues that, aided by spatial metaphors that refer to war as a separate sphere or an event with beginning and end, there is a tendency to think of war mainly in abstract terms, as removed from "normal" life. When "wars become conceptual entities—objects for consideration—rather than diverse, historically loaded exemplifications of the contexts in which they occur" (Cuomo, 1996, p. 36), the pervasiveness of military practices and institutions in everyday life becomes invisible. Consequently, feminist 9/11 narratives do not begin on, nor mark this moment with enough significance to divide the world into a pre- and post-9/11 world as the dominant US 9/11 narrative does. Whereas most official accounts of the events constitute it as a fundamental break with the past, feminists have learned to place emphasis on locating issues on a continuum and making connections between seemingly disparate events.

At the same time that the events usher in a new era for some—"most Americans have probably experienced something like the loss of their First-Worldism as a result of September 11 and its aftermath" (Butler, 2004, p. 39)—others, who do not share the same privilege, and whose everyday lives are marked by intersecting oppressions, whether in the US or elsewhere, experience a different reality. As Mattingly, Lawlor and Jacobs-Huey (2002) note in an article on how race, gender and cultural identity shape reactions to 9/11, their respondents "repeatedly emphasize that they know how to live with fear in a racially charged environment, this was already part of their routine" (p. 747). The loss experienced by some segments of the US population, "the loss of the prerogative, only and always, to be the one who transgresses sovereign boundaries of other states, but never to be in the position of having one's own boundaries transgressed"

(Butler, 2004, p. 39) is not, therefore, a shared experience even within the US or the West. The first world is not unified; the container is a fiction.

The framing of events in a particular narrative always has implications for action because it includes and excludes options and actors while also limiting what can be thought or said, thus eventually imposing silences. The framing "decides, in a forceful way, *what we can hear*, whether a view will be taken as explanation or exoneration, whether we can hear the difference and abide by it" writes Judith Butler (2004, p. 5). The dominant framing of 9/11 by the George W. Bush administration as " 'uncaused' cause" (Zehfuss, 2003, p. 521) consequently "works both to preclude certain kinds of questions, certain kinds of historical inquiries, and to function as a moral justification for retaliation" (Butler, 2004, p. 4). Drawing on traditional, militarized security framings, the Bush administration quickly set the stage for perpetual war, eschewing any alternatives such as a humanitarian or a criminal framing.[13]

In what ways could listening to narratives from the margins contest the US response to the events of September 11, 2001? How might it challenge the way we imagine and study security? When feminists insist on narrating the multiplicity and variety of women's lived experience, they are directly undermining the insistence on a unified, contained space that is knowable and worth securing. As this chapter has tried to outline, however, their narratives of security cannot be heard unless the broader structures of knowledge production in the field of IR, and security studies, are challenged at the same time. Insisting on the inclusion of analyses of narrative and metaphor is a crucial element in this challenge, which has implications not just within these disciplines, but also for our visions of science more broadly.

Notes

1 As is often the case in IR, scholars do not keep up with developments in the fields that initially inspire them such as the field of economics, in which rational actor models have been debated at length (e.g., in the work on cognitive bias by Nobel Prize–winner Daniel Kahneman, 2001).
2 Feminists have paid much attention to the protection metaphor (although not generally specifically calling it a metaphor), see Elshtain (1982, 1987), Stiehm (1982), and Young (2003).
3 This has been a topic of debate among feminists with regard to violence against women—the focus on criminalizing rape (and a focus on its most violent iterations) has led to unproductive distinctions in which rape that does not involve physical force—or takes place within an established relationship—is, more often than not, trivialized (cf. Kelly, 1988; Kelly & Radford, 1990)
4 The other image schemas he points to are path/journey, force and link ((Chilton, 1996, pp. 50–55)
5 This reconceptualization is "embodied in and institutionalized in the National Security Act of 1947, as protected by the McCarran-Walter Act of 1952, and as reconstituted by the first, and subsequent National Security Council meetings of the second, cold war" (Der Derian, 1995, p. 42).

6 Indeed, even within the academy these intersecting developments produced the effect that security largely became equated with military strategy.

7 "No doubt strategists are inclined to think too readily in terms of military solutions to the problems of foreign policy and to lose sight of the other instruments that are available. But this is the occupational disease of any specialist and the remedy for it lies in entering into debate with the specialist and correcting his perspective" (Bull, as cited in Baldwin, 1995, p. 138).

8 It might be of interest to note that classical realists devoted much more attention "to the relationship between national security and domestic affairs, such as the economy, civil liberties, and democratic political processes" (Baldwin, 1995, p. 122), something that has been revived in particular at the end of the Cold War and in critical security narratives.

9 Although there are certainly arguments to be made that concerns other than those currently at the top of the security studies agenda should be considered more seriously; for example, many feminist will suggest that violence against women deserves sustained attention.

10 Another important contribution made by Wæver (1995) is to ask whether it is always a good idea to speak of particular issues in terms of security—he notes, "critics normally address the *what* and the *who* that threatens, or the *whom* to be secured: they never ask whether a phenomenon *should* be treated in terms of security because they don't look into 'securityness' as such, asking what is particular to security, in contrast to non-security, modes of dealing with particular issues" (p. 57).

11 Note that the framework Buzan et al. (1998) propose is not a critical approach in the tradition of Cox (1981) and others, because it does not attempt to challenge the status quo, but simply to find a better way to inquire into and assess the traditional security studies agenda.

12 There are a number of other (earlier) discussions of security and identity, using poststructuralist approaches: Der Derian (1992), Der Derian & Shapiro (1989), Dillon (1990), Luke (1991), and Shapiro (1992).

13 See also Butler's contribution to the documentary *After 9/11* (more information is available at www.watsoninstitute.org/infopeace/after911).

References

Baldwin, D. A. (1995). Security studies and the end of the Cold War. *World Politics*, 48(1), 117–41.

Bobrow, D. B. (2001). Visions of (in)security and American strategic style. *International Studies Perspectives*, 2(1), 1–12.

Butler, J. (2004). *Precarious life: The powers of mourning and violence.* London: Verso.
———. (2009). *Frames of war: When is life grievable?* London: Verso.

Buzan, B. (1987). *An introduction to Strategic Studies: Military technology and International Relations.* New York: St. Martin's Press.

Buzan, B., Wæver, O., & de Wilde, J. (1998). *Security: A new framework for analysis.* Boulder, CO: Lynne Rienner.

Campbell, D. (1998). *Writing security: United States foreign policy and the politics of identity* (Rev. Ed.) Minneapolis: University of Minnesota Press.

Chilton, P. (1996). *Security metaphors: Cold war discourse from containment to common house.* New York: Peter Lang.

Collins, P. H. (1990). *Black feminist thought: Knowledge, consciousness, and the politics of empowerment.* New York: Routledge.

Constantinou, C. M. (2000). Poetics of security. *25 Alternatives: Social Transformation and Humane Governance*, *3*, 287–306.

Cox, R. W. (1981). Social forces, states and world orders: Beyond international relations theory. *Millennium: Journal of International Studies*, *10*(2), 126–155.

Crenshaw, K. W. (1991). Mapping the margins: Intersectionality, identity politics, and violence against women of color. *Stanford Law Review*, *43*(6), 1241–1299.

Cuomo, C. J. (1996). War is not just an event: Reflections on the significance of everyday violence. *Hypatia*, *11*(4), 30–45.

Currie, M. (1998). *Postmodern narrative theory*. New York: St. Martin's Press.

Der Derian, J. (1992). *Antidiplomacy: Spies, terror, speed, and war*. Cambridge, England: Blackwell.

———. (1995). The value of security: Hobbes, Marx, Nietzsche, and Baudrillard. In R. D. Lipschutz (Ed.), *On security: New directions in world politics*. New York: Columbia University Press.

Der Derian, J. & Shapiro, M. (1989). *International/ intertextual relations: Postmodern readings of world politics*. Lanham: Lexington Books.

Dillon, M. (1990). The alliance of security and subjectivity. *Current Research on Peace and Violence*, *13*(3), 101–124.

———. (1996). *Politics of security: Towards a political philosophy of continental thought*. London: Routledge.

Edkins, J. (2002). After the subject of international security. In J. Valentine & A. Finlayson (Eds.), *Politics and Post-structuralism: An introduction* (pp. 66–80). Edinburgh, Scotland: Edinburgh University Press.

Elshtain, J. B. (1982). On beautiful souls, just warriors and feminist consciousness. *Women's Studies International Forum*, *5*(3/4), 39–57.

———. (1987). *Women and war*. New York: Basic Books.

Enloe, C. (2004). *The curious feminist: Searching for women in a new age of empire*. Berkeley: University of California Press.

Ferguson, K. E. (1993). *The man question: Visions of subjectivity in feminist theory*. Berkeley: University of California Press.

Foucault, M. (1980). *Power/ knowledge: Selected interviews and other writings, 1972-1977*. Brighton: Harvester Press.

Grondin, J. (1991). *Einführung in die philosophische Hermeneutik* [Introduction to philosophical hermeneutics]. Darmstadt: Wissenschaftliche Buchgesellschaft.

Harding, S. G. (1986). *The science question in feminism*. Ithaca, NY: Cornell University Press.

Huysmans, J. (1998). Security! What do you mean? From concept to thick signifier, *European Journal of International Relations*, *4*(2), 226–255.

Kahneman, D. (2011). *Thinking, fast and slow*. New York: Farrar, Strauss and Giroux.

Kelly, L. (1988). *Surviving sexual violence*. Minneapolis: University of Minnesota Press.

Kelly, L., & Radford, J. (1990). "Nothing really happened": The invalidation of women's experiences of sexual violence. *Critical Social Policy*, *10*(30), 39–53.

Klein, B. S. (1994). *Strategic studies and world order*. Cambridge: Cambridge University Press.

Krause, K., & Williams, M. C. (1996). Broadening the agenda of security studies: Politics and methods. *Mershon International Studies Review*, *40*, 229–254.

————. (1997). From strategy to security: Foundations of critical security studies. In K. Krause & M. C. Williams (Eds.), *Critical security studies: Concepts and cases* (pp. 33–59). Minneapolis: University of Minnesota Press.

Lorde, A. (1984). *Sister outsider: Essays and speeches.* Trumansburg, NY: Crossing Press.

Lugones, M. C. & Spelman, E. V. (1983). Have we got a theory for you! Feminist theory, cultural imperialism and the demand for the woman's voice. *Women's Studies International Forum, 6*(6), 573–581.

Luke, T. (1991). The discipline of security studies and the codes of containment: Learning from Kuwait. *Alternatives, 16*(3), 315–344.

Mattingly, C., Lawlor, M., & Jacobs-Huey, L. (2002). Narrating September 11: Race, gender and the play of cultural identities. *American Anthropologist, 104*(3), 742–753.

Neocleous, M. (2000). Against security. *Radical Philosophy, 100,* 7–15.

Peterson, V. S. (1992). Security and sovereign states. What is at stake in taking feminist seriously? In V. S. Peterson (Ed.), *Gendered states: feminist (re)visions of international relations theory* (pp. 31–64). Boulder, CO: Lynne Rienner.

Polkinghorne, D. (1988). *Narrative knowing and the human sciences.* Albany: State University of New York Press.

Rothschild, E. (1995). What is security? *Daedalus, 124*(3), 53–98.

Sandoval, C. (2000) *Methodology of the oppressed.* Minneapolis: University of Minnesota Press.

Shapiro, M. J. (1992). That obscure object of violence: Logistics, desire, war. *Alternatives, 17*(4), 453–477.

Snyder, C. A. (1999). Contemporary security and strategy. In C. A. Snyder (Ed.), *Contemporary security and strategy* (pp. 1–12). New York: Routledge.

Stern, M. (2001). *Naming in/security—constructing identity: "Mayan women" in Guatemala on the eve of "peace"* (PhD dissertation). Peace and Development Research Institute, Gothenburg University, Gothenburg, Sweden.

————. (2005). *Naming security—constructing identity: "Mayan women" in Guatemala on the eve of "peace."* Manchester: Manchester University Press.

Stiehm, J. H. (1982). The protected, the protector, the defender. *Women's Studies International Forum, 5*(3/4), 367–376.

Walker, R. B. J. (1993). *Inside/ outside: International relations as political theory.* Cambridge: Cambridge University Press.

Walt, Stephen (1991). The renaissance of security studies. *International Studies Quarterly, 35*(2), 211–239.

Wæver, O. (1995). Securitization and desecuritization. In R. D. Lipschutz (Ed.), *On security: New directions in world politics* (pp. 46–86). New York: Columbia University Press.

————. (1997). *Concepts of security* (PhD dissertation). University of Copenhagen, Copenhagen, Denmark.

————. (1999). Securitizing sectors? A reply to Eriksson, *Cooperation and Conflict, 34*(4), 334–340.

Wibben, A. T. R. (1998). *Narrating experience: Raymond Aron and feminist scholars revis(it)ed—a subversive conversation* (MA thesis). University of Tampere, Tampere, Finland.

————. (2008). Human security: Toward an opening. *Security Dialogue, 39*(4), 455–462.

————. (2011). *Feminist security studies: A narrative approach*. London: Routledge.

Williams, M. C. (2005). *The realist tradition and the limits of international relations*. Cambridge: Cambridge University Press.

Wolfers, A. (1962). *Discord and collaboration: Essays in international politics*. Baltimore: Johns Hopkins Press.

Young, I. M. (2003). Feminist reactions to the contemporary security regime. *Hypatia*, *18*(1), 223–231.

Yuval-Davis, N. (1997). *Gender & nation*. London: Sage.

————. (2012). *The politics of belonging: Intersectional contestations*. London: Sage.

Zehfuss, M. (2003). Forget September 11. *Third World Quarterly*, *24*(3), 513–528.

6 A Conversation with Mark Danner

Michael Hanne and Mark Danner

"Warring with Words" was originally a symposium held at Claremont Gradu-ate University in March 2012. Eminent journalist and media professor Mark Danner was invited to participate, but a research trip to Athens to investigate the Greek financial crisis precluded his attendance. This interview was there-fore conducted later in the year to elicit his thoughts on the themes raised at the symposium.

Michael Hanne: We've called this project "Warring with Words" and it focuses on the use of narrative and the use of metaphor, by political actors, by journalists and commentators on politics, and by scholars writing political his-tory and political theory. Our assertion is that narrative and metaphor are to be found everywhere in the discourse that surrounds politics and that both exercise great influence on our thinking and action. What is novel about what we are attempting is that we are bringing the narrative perspective and the metaphor perspective together, because, while there are a number of people writing on narrative in politics and a number of people writing on metaphor, there are not many people writing on both.

Mr. Danner, you're internationally known for your intensively researched and morally forceful analyses of painful political situations, but, in particular, I wanted to speak to you because I know that you are an extraordinarily impres-sive creator or fabricator of narratives *and* metaphors for representing political events and policies, but equally that you illuminate and analyze with great rigor the deluded or deceptive narratives and metaphors that political leaders employ to legitimize their actions. So, clearly you are acutely aware of the power of narrative and metaphor.

What I want to do in this conversation is tease out with you some of the ways in which you employ narrative and metaphor, but also how you go about analyzing and critiquing the use of narrative and metaphor by key political actors for deceptive purposes. Can we start with the big picture? Amongst the many roles you play, you are a historian of contemporary events. Just as the academic historian poses questions about the origins of the Second World War, so you pose questions about the origins of the Second Iraq War, the origins of the ongoing misery of life in Haiti, the process by which torture came to be the norm in US military practice etc., etc. You have a preoccupation with tracing and recounting what has happened in some of the most troubled and complex communal and international situations of recent years: the war in Yugoslavia, especially in Bosnia, events around the earthquake in Haiti, the Second Iraq War, the Israel-Palestine conflict. So now I come to my first question.

You describe yourself as a storyteller. You said in one interview: "I try to tell the story, to get it right, and to tell it well." Can you amplify on your account of Mark Danner as storyteller?

Mark Danner: Well, that's a very large question. That, it seems to me is a primary kind of task, which is trying to put events into some narrative logic for readers who are looking at a situation that is often painful and grotesque, or very strange and frightening. It might involve mass killing or atrocities of various kinds that too many people are simply incomprehensible. And I think one of your first jobs is to try to make the story itself comprehensible. When I say comprehensible, I mean that we want readers to understand what happens, in a sense, *beyond* good and evil. I want to get beyond the narrative that says, or implies, "There are simply these bad people, and these bad people came and killed other people, and isn't that horrible—and of course there will always be evil in the world."

I suppose I don't really think that is the way the world works. I believe with Solzhenitsyn that people are made up of good and evil: you don't simply have evil people. And when we look at motives—why people do things—we have to look first at ourselves to understand why people act the way they do. That is my goal as a storyteller, to make things comprehensible, particularly horrible things, and vivid, of course; and comprehensible means not only understanding people's motives, but understanding how events unfolded and what made them possible.

MH: The narrative faculty is extraordinary in the sense that we can build into a story—and anyone listening to a story will perfectly well understand—an immense variety of features, which can include character, events, sequence, social and physical context, motivation, causality and so on. Somehow we can absorb all of that, if a story is well told, all in one package.

Mark Danner: That's very true. It is clear we do possess a fundamental kind of understanding that is built around narrative, that in some fundamental way we understand events using a logic of causality that lets us make sense of the world—which is to say, we understand the world in stories. Storytelling: Kant may not have listed it as one of his primary faculties, but I think it is in a sense a primary faculty of human beings. When we look at the world we understand one thing as having caused another. And I agree with you: this mode of understanding can carry with it an immense amount of information. I mean, one thing we can certainly say about stories is that they are extraordinarily efficient conveyors of information. They can carry vast multitudes of facts and impressions and pictures, and that is a remarkable thing.

What a reporter does is *construct* narratives—and yet because of this ideology of "objectivity" in journalism, there is this predisposition to think that people just sort of . . . *find* stories: that stories somehow already exist in the world and people, good reporters, go out and find them. Of course they're not *creating* them—how could they be? they are "objective journalists," after all—they are finding them. They don't create stories. No.

But in fact this is not true. I've always been fascinated that you can sit here in New York or California, wherever, and watch the Iraq War, and the news coming from it. You can have very strong opinions. You know precisely what's going on. You know why. You're certain about what's happening. But when you arrive in Iraq, after the corkscrew landing that the plane makes in order to avoid the missiles and rocket-propelled grenades, and you strap on your body armor and get in your armored car and speed at 100 miles per house down that notorious airport road, where all the car bombs have been attacking, into the devastated city; where the store fronts all are closed and the hulks of blown-out cars are everywhere; and you talk to people who don't want to talk to you, read the fear on the streets, listen for the bombs that are going off, the suicide bombings, look for the plumes of oily smoke that come of out of those attacks about the cityscape. And within a day or two days or three days, after you take in this blizzard of sense impressions, of sights, of sounds, of different narratives coming from people you talk to—after a matter of days, you go from the person who knew everything sitting in New York to the person who knows precisely nothing sitting in Baghdad. I find it a voluptuous process, actually, finding your inner ignorance. Having stripped away all this false "knowledge," you find this inner ignorance and then, with that *tabula rasa* that you've managed to achieve by actually going to this place, you begin, slowly, painfully, to construct a picture of what you think, maybe, possibly, is going on. You build that picture on the skeleton of a narrative: a constructed logic tying together events. You put it together out of your own efforts as a reporter, a seeker after knowledge: out of the stories people tell you, out of the things you have seen, the things you've heard, the details that strike you as bizarre, and strange, and striking. And those are the motley pile of materials out of which you build the skeleton of a story. And that act of construction is, to me, what is exciting about storytelling.

When you arrive at the question of figuration, of figurative language, part of the need for it arises out of the practical necessity to convey vividly what you are seeing and experiencing: what you are looking at. But part of it, antecedent even to the need to convey experience vividly, is rooted in the effort to understand—to understand what is happening *yourself*. To me the primary narrative function of metaphor is, first and foremost, to understand it yourself: to understand what you are seeing; what is in front of you; how, indeed, it looks. You know, I remember one early morning Baghdad, driving to an interview with the top intelligence official in the American army. She had not given an interview before, and she was one of the few female generals in the American army at the time. It was quite a coup to get her to agree to meet with me and I was driving along, thinking about what I would ask her, and before I knew what was happening an enormous shockwave jerked the entire car up in the air. The explosion—it was so loud I never actually heard it—was conveyed to me only by the absence of sound (it had blown out my ears) and then, after a few moments of utter silence, the tinkling of all windows in their sashes along this main street in Baghdad. A kind of little symphony of tinkling glass emerging out of the blank silence. I remember thinking at the time that that abrupt wrenching jerking movement of the car up into the air could only be compared to a horse bucking. The galloping horse had bucked abruptly, his head and back had been wrenched back, and suddenly you, the rider, rushing forward, are being seized as if in an enormous hand and jerked up. At the time, sitting in the car, feeling my hearing return and trying to catch my breath and figure out what had happened, I was asking myself, "What exactly is this like? How do I understand what has just happened?" And the metaphor came out of an effort at self-understanding, before I eventually used it in a description of that morning—and the suicide bomber's attack on the Red Cross a block away, which had wrenched my car into the air.

MH: Often I think metaphors assist the listener or the reader, who has never had an experience like the one you are describing, so you've got to give them some metaphor, something familiar, such as the bucking of a horse, something they feel they know.

Mark Danner: Yes, absolutely. Metaphor is very often a bridge from the unfamiliar to the familiar. It's one of the reasons Orwell, who wrote about the effective use of metaphors in his great essay "Politics and the English Language," argued for using what he called "homey" metaphors, to use homey comparisons, which would be familiar to everyone, and Orwell himself would compare things metaphorically to the falling of snow, or the way coffee grounds choke the drain in sink: literally, a most "homey" image. I'm not sure I would entirely agree with Orwell that these are the most powerful metaphors, but I do agree that metaphors are particularly powerful if they are disjunctive enough: if they are both surprising, like the horse, and familiar at the same time. So I think in context you want them to be surprising, to be fresh and striking, but in order for them to convey what you want to convey they have to be, at least to some extent, familiar.

MH: Staying with narrative for the moment, it seems to me that one of the challenges you must face every day, especially when you are writing shorter pieces, is: how do you insert the historical background, the backstory, in a way which will be comprehensible, manageable to your reader or to your listener? How do you handle the long history? I'm thinking of your writings on Haiti, for instance, in which you really do take the reader right back to the slave revolution and before and say you can only understand Haiti today if you look at the history of the last 200 years and more.

Mark Danner: You are quite right. Many of the places I've written about are incomprehensible without understanding the history. And understanding the history is a way, not least, to start to understand the country as Haitians, or Bosnians, or others, understand it themselves. These peoples are steeped in their history, a history about which outsiders generally are ignorant. It's one strong difference in the points of view between how outsiders see them and how they see themselves. Haitians, for example, are deeply aware of their remarkable past. In Haiti the past is everywhere: Their astonishing history is central to their worldview; it's who they are. I was fortunate enough, in writing about Haiti for *The New Yorker* and also for *The New York Review of Books*, to be writing "long form" and thus to have enough space to "do the history," as it were. I remember that, when the second piece in my *New Yorker* series, as edited, was entirely about the history, I worried: would the reader be able to stay with this? Or would it be like that first couple of chapters of a biography that goes back into the family past—a barrier to the juicy parts of the narrative that the reader is tempted to skip? Robert Gottlieb, the remarkable *New Yorker* editor of the time, bless him, was absolutely confident. He reassured me, "This history is amazing, don't worry about it a bit. It's absolutely compelling. It carries itself on its own interest alone and our readers will appreciate this." And, of course, he proved to be entirely right.

Much more recently, I wrote a piece on Haiti for the *Times* op-ed page, quite a long piece for them, which was given over almost entirely to Haiti's history and its intertwining with the present—with the earthquake, in particular—and went into it rather in depth. In a sense, in this case, the history *was* the drama. I was able to do an 1,800-word piece about Haiti's history because the present tragedy of Haiti, post-earthquake, was so much in the foreground; thus, the history could be put forward, in a sense, as an explanation for a narrative that readers already knew. The history was essentially a critique of the narrative that readers were already familiar with, which was a narrative of Haiti as a fatalistically suffering land, punished by the gods: Haiti as the sacrificial lamb of nations. My intention in treating its history was to show that Haiti's suffering is made not by the gods but by men and women. In order to understand that, you have to see how that came about and in order to see how it came about, you have to understand how we got to the present moment—which is, of course, all narrative. It all comes down, once again, to storytelling. One of the great strengths of writing about Haiti and writing about so many of the other places I have been lucky enough to write about, is that the history is so powerful and colorful, so stocked with remarkable characters, and so infused with an almost inherent drama. When writing about Haiti, I used the phrase "operatic politics"—this kind of high-colored, intensely dramatic, scene of heroes and heroines, walking heavily and portentously upon the stage of the nation. This has always been the way the country has thought of itself: led by these heroes who trace their lines to the heroes who walked the land in the Napoleonic era, the era of the Great Men who carried off the Great Haitian Revolution, the only successful slave revolution in history which produced the only free black republic of its time. The country remains, in a sense, in the grandeur of the Napoleonic era in the way that it thinks of itself.

MH: In addition to being an outstanding storyteller, you are also an analyst and critic of so many kinds of official storytelling, the conventional histories, of the kind you mention in relation to Haiti, and the official stories of, for instance, the American administration, and it seems to me that involves you in chipping away at a story you've come not to trust and eventually substituting your own story for that. Can you give examples of how you go about that chipping away process, the getting behind, getting around stories that, to you, are clearly not right?

Mark Danner: Do you mean in the process of reporting? Or do you mean . . .

MH: I mean the process of thinking through before the reporting.

Mark Danner: Well, I'm not, I suppose, fond of writing that assumes from the beginning that officials are lying. I believe in general that the reader needs to undertake a journey, to follow a path, to realize that there is a difference between what officials are saying and what is actually happening. The sort of piece in which you are showing the difference between what is being said by officials and what the truth is describes a journey from trust to skepticism and then to certainty about what the story really is, and what its relationship is to the official version. I've done a fair amount of that.

Writing on torture, for example, largely begins with an examination of the official story, whether it's Abu Ghraib or the "black sites," and then placing alongside it what happened to people there, for example, in the "Voices From the Black Sites" piece in the *New York Review*, the story of people who had been tortured in the black sites and who had told their stories to representatives of the Red Cross. I contrasted their accounts to the Red Cross with what had been said publicly by administration officials, including President Bush, and I was in the fortunate position of being able to publish the actual Red Cross document, which had been secret up to then, and thus to use their actual stories. The larger arc of the story was really the narrative of Abu Zubaydah, and to some extent that of Khalid Sheikh Mohammed, and what they experienced in captivity at the black sites, and to contrast those stories with what had been claimed publicly about how they'd been treated. Their stories were so powerful that one felt compelled to contrast it with the official versions. George W. Bush, then President, helpfully supplied the official version in his speech of September 6, 2006, when he delivered a speech from the White House defending torture—a remarkable speech, perhaps the only historic speech he ever gave, which I think will be more appreciated as the years go on. So President Bush supplied—and members of the CIA and others supplied—the contrary story.

In the end, I think the most difficult part of writing that piece was to refrain from appearing in any way sarcastic and to try to set out the story clearly, and let the reader draw his or her conclusions. The vivid power of the foreground became simply a potent argument that undermined the background, which was of course the official version. When I consider some of the other pieces I've done in that general mode, for example, writing about the Downing Street memo and its revelations about the run-up to the Iraq War, I think again that it was a question of restraint—of trying to bring out, carefully and dispassionately, what the texts of the memo actually said and then to compare it in a rather methodical way to what the public, official version of those same events had been, drawn principally, again, from President Bush himself.

There is, I believe, an underlying problem here, what I've called the "frozen scandal." When I was growing up, I remember my political awakening came with the Watergate hearings in the early 1970s, which led to the fall of President Richard Nixon, the first and still the only American President ever to resign. Those were extraordinary events where wrongdoing was uncovered, was revealed initially, by journalists; where a full-scale investigation was undertaken the government, by the Senate and House Congressional Committee and by the judiciary, and then, as the third step after revelation and investigation, there was punishment—call it expiation. Nixon resigned; powerful White House officials were fired, lost their jobs; some were prosecuted and went to prison. The point is that in this scandal one saw an almost systematic, stately progression leading from revelation to investigation and from investigation to expiation. Looking back, this was a kind of grand procession from wrongdoing to justice—a kind of American Oresteia, if you will.

As I have written elsewhere, it seems to me one of the characteristics of the present era—call it the post-9/11 era—is that we have the first of those steps, revelation, and sometimes a bit of the second, investigation, but we never do get to the third stage. There is no punishment, no expiation. So we actually go on living with these states of wrongdoing, subsisting in a state of permanent scandal. Torture, I think, is one example of that—perhaps the most vivid. Following the Watergate model, which I took in as a very young man, as a teenager, the writer's role is to reveal, to initiate a process by which the society, through investigation and expiation, goes on to cleanse itself. But what about a situation in which the society, for whatever reason—we can debate that—doesn't *want* to cleanse itself, where it is willing to put up with torture, as long as it's the torture of someone else, where it is willing to put up with lies about weapons of mass destruction. In that case, you are living in what I've described as a case of frozen scandal—a scandal that just sits there in front of us, fully revealed, poisonous, noxious and . . . permanent. To me, unfolding the narrative, official lies are one thing; but what if revealing them leads to no consequence?

MH: It seems to me that in addition to that story, you've told the story of how torture has become acceptable to the American public as long as the reasons for it are perceived to be right, that there has been a kind of moral shift. That is a parallel story, isn't it? That, in a sense, is the public story. Aren't you exposing that moral shift as much as you are the deceit on the part of the administration?

Mark Danner: I think that's true. What you've identified, I think, is extremely important. In a sense, it's a harder story to tell. To begin with "What is this thing we call 'the public,' and how indeed do we determine that it has in fact changed 'its' attitudes?" We have public opinion polls, which at the end of the day are very blunt instruments. Fifty years ago when Daniel Boorstin in his classic study, *The Image* (1961), coined the term "pseudo-events"—events created in order *to be* news events—he listed as one of his categories of pseudo-events public opinion polls. Today, interestingly enough, we regard polls as scientific tools of inquiry, but they are, as I say, rather blunt instruments; so the actual telling of the story of that "moral shift," as you called it, if moral shift it is, from a public that would presumably have rejected those sorts of interrogation techniques to one that is willing to accept them, is very hard. I've written about it, glancingly as it were, but I don't think I've actually told it with any degree of depth or accuracy.

MH: Can we shift our attention a little in relation to narrative now and focus on the way in which you have suggested the political commentator or journalist necessarily uses strategies learned from imaginative writing, imaginative literature. You've talked about your father telling you stories from Homer and so many others. Can you say more about that and particularly how you pick and choose among the strategies the ones which *are* legitimate and the ones which *aren't* legitimate in what you call "fact-based writing," nonfictional writing?

Mark Danner: Well, one can give examples of things that would be wrong: One, obviously, is to write a sentence that in fact is not true, that conflicts directly with the facts as you know them. Such sentences comprise a tiny category of all the sentences you are likely to write about a given subject. There are many ways to be misleading, to give an exaggerated impression, without actually coming in direct conflict with the known facts. To put it another way, there are all sorts of flavors of the subtly "not-true," beyond the clearly not true. So we're talking here much more in the realm of the arts than of the sciences. We find ourselves with these strange divisions, strange categories: fiction and nonfiction, for example—a very oddly drawn distinction, I think. Calling a piece of writing "nonfiction" is akin to calling an object "non-alive." Identifying some writing as "nonfiction" doesn't really tell you what that writing *is*. Because at the end of the day, fact or fiction, we are talking about writing and there is an enormous variety of that. At one time or another the writer of fact-based texts finds himself using many, many, perhaps most, of the techniques of the fiction writer—in order to convey a vivid impression of place, to construct and maintain narrative suspense, to make clear the causal joints of narrative, to sketch and color in pictures that compel and affect the reader.

All of these techniques form part of the toolbox of the fiction *and* the nonfiction writer. The single clarifying difference is that in the work of the nonfiction writer there should not be sentences that distinguish themselves as not according with the facts, that are not true—and such sentences, as I say, form a very small subgroup. Look at "genre-busting" works such as *The Emperor* by my old friend Ryszard Kapuściński, which is a book that has long been criticized for not being "true." To me, *The Emperor* is a brilliant work of writing, and I am sensitive to criticisms of it that claim parts of it do not accord with the facts, but I am not sensitive to criticisms that it is not really an authoritative work on Haile Selassie. It's not meant to be an authoritative work on

Haile Selassie; it's meant to be a meditation on power and many other things. There exist biographies of Haile Selassie, and *The Emperor* isn't one of them. Or look at *Heartburn*, a novel by Norah Ephron, a friend who has just died, alas—they are both gone now—which tells the story of an affair, a real affair, thinly disguised, which "everyone" in Washington knew about, that ended the marriage between Norah and Carl Bernstein, the great journalist and exposer, along with Bob Woodward, of the Watergate Scandal. Norah and Carl were well known as a couple, they had a very public breakup, and she wrote a novel about it—a roman à clef, and it may well be true that many more sentences in that piece of "fiction" were true, that is, true to the facts of what happened in that affair, though the names were changed, than in Kapuściński's nonfiction study of Haile Selasse, even though Kapuściński's was a nonfiction book, and what had happened leading up to the end of his rule in Ethiopia.

So these categories are indistinct, changeable, metamorphic: They rely on implied rules that are made to be broken. I think what we use as writers are very similar tools; the fiction writer can create characters, can use models, but can take as many liberties as he or she wants, and the nonfiction writer obviously can't; but many of the techniques that underlie the creation of the story—the techniques of plotting, the building of suspense, of description and exposition and so on—all draw from the same universe of tools that we use in the creation of effective storytelling.

MH: I was thinking especially of the issue of character. I know you have interviewed the former Bosnian Serb leader Radovan Karadžić, for instance, and I wondered whether there were issues about the depiction of character, the handling of character in your writing, as opposed to what the novelist can do, for instance, ways in which the novelist can get right inside the character and that you can't. You can make a whole lot of suppositions and observations, but you can't get right inside a character, can you? How do you handle character?

Mark Danner: I think again there is a degree of restraint you try to impose on yourself. Dr. Karadžić was such an overflowing, overwhelming character, with this huge cascade of hair sprouting from his head, from his ears, his nose, and with an irrepressible boisterousness and, I regret to say, charm. You know, he asked me, regarding the market massacre, which I had witnessed two days before in Sarajevo—a mortar shell launched by Karadžić's men had killed, dismembered, eviscerated, 68 people—he asked me, "Did you check for ice in their ears?" Karadžić was implying that the massacre had been trumped up, that the corpses were actually bodies that the Bosnian intelligence people had taken out of the morgue to create this kind of a fake massacre. I was stunned by this, didn't know what to say. Karadžić was just in another world—call it, since we were talking about fiction, the world of magical realism. And you are right: I didn't try to look inside his head. But I did draw from his biography certain facts that I thought were rather fascinating: for example, about his aspirations to be a poet, about his attempt to take the world of Sarajevo poetry by storm. When Karadžić made his debut, his first big reading in Sarajevo, he was kind

of laughed off the stage, or so the legend has it, and many people drew from
this a rather simplistic narrative: Karadžić in besieging Sarajevo and raining
shells down on his former colleagues and neighbors was wreaking his revenge
on Sarajevo for the Sarajevans' rejection of him, for their disdain. I think you
can just report that without seeking to assert that you know it to be a fact. So I
don't know whether my portrait of him could constitute a fully described and
realized and believable person. It mostly relies on outward description of him
and also what other people told me about him, including, of course, Dr. Ceric,
Karadžić's training analyst. Because Karadžić; of course was a psychiatrist.
I do recall vividly how at Sarajevo's Kosovo Hospital, with the shells raining
down from the Serb gunners in the hills, Dr. Ceric shook his head ruefully and
told me, "Ah, Radovan. Radovan always had a problem with his sense of personal grandiosity."

MH: I think we can probably all agree with that! Can we move on now to
discussion of your deployment of metaphor. Within and among the extraordinary stories that you tell are a number of metaphors which illuminate your
argument like lightning flashes. You construct or come up with extraordinarily
vivid and persuasive and illuminating metaphors. I'll give you just three or
four examples if I may. Writing of 9/11 you say, "To Americans, those terrible
moments stand as a brightly lit portal through which we were all compelled
to step together into a different world." That seems to me an extraordinarily
illuminating metaphor. You talk elsewhere of the "hydraulics of politics"—the
idea of politics being a plumbing system is wonderful. And then an almost
casual metaphor you throw in: you are talking about the threat matrix, the security presentation that is made to the president each morning. You say it is a document "listing every threat directed at the US that has been sucked up during
the last 24 hours by the vast electronic and human vacuum cleaner of information that was US intelligence." And then the blind-man-in-the-cage metaphor.
You say, "It is possible for most people to live their lives without taking note
of these practices at all except as phrases in the news—until, every once in a
while, like a blind man who lives, all unknowingly, in a very large cage, one
or another of us stumbles into the bars." Those are, as I say, fantastically vivid,
illuminating metaphors. Do you simply find those, do they just come into your
head, or do you perform some quite hard imaginative work before you come up
with each of those metaphors.

Mark Danner: Goodness, I don't really know. I think the "portal" metaphor occurred to me as a metaphor of transfiguration. The imagery surrounding
9/11, and in particular the physical transformation of the towers, was so striking to me. You have these impossibly huge structures that I remember being
built when I was a kid—these astonishingly huge buildings. I remember the
first time I finally saw them when I was sixteen or seventeen: how enormous
they seemed: not only their height but their size. These vast towers were transformed in an instant or two into . . . smoke, into these great plumes of smoke
heading up into the sky. It always seemed to me such an unimaginable, almost

religious moment of transfiguration. And I think the idea of metamorphosis lay behind that image: you know, a portal through which you walk and in so doing become something else. That is what I was trying to convey in that image, that we are now, having walked through that portal, in a state of exception, a state of emergency, and that we have become so accustomed to it that we no longer notice. So I think the "portal" metaphor fit in with a larger metaphorical structure with which I was, consciously or not—and who knows where these ideas actually originate—approaching 9/11.

The "hydraulics of politics" is a phrase I've used, I think, often to bring out the kind of subsystem of needs and desires that really drives our political reality. There is a phrase that professional politicians use: "Policies don't win elections; constituencies win elections." I've always loved that phrase, because intellectuals, in discussing politics, tend to talk about policies: "When it comes to Obama and his health-care policy" they'll begin, and then move quickly to "he sold himself for political gains, when he didn't push for a public option." The discussion almost instantly centers on integrity and authenticity—which, to me, almost always gets it completely wrong, because politics usually isn't about that. It's about interests and constituencies, about appealing to people whose support you need, and whose interests are tied to yours by the "hydraulics of politics"—the underlying substructure which is the means by which the vital life-giving water actually gets from one place to another.

Another example of this phrase comes from post-invasion Iraq, when you heard constant chatter from American occupation officials about "democracy-building" and economic liberalization and empowering the Shia and so on. The key problem of political hydraulics, though, was how to transform the Sunni, the sectarian minority that had long led Iraq, into a loyal opposition—which is to say, an opposition that was secure and thus was willing to accept a non-violent role in the new Shia-led dispensation. By their actions—including abruptly dissolving the Iraqi army, and de-Baathifying all governing institutions—it is clear leaders of the American occupation not only had no idea how to solve this basic problem of political hydraulics but failed even to recognize its centrality. (We can add that the very same problem—how to reassure a ruling political minority of its security so it will leave power—currently faces us in Syria, where the Alawi regime of the Assad family is fighting to cling to power.)

As for the "blind-man-in-the-cage" metaphor, I think I'd had that image somewhere in my mind for a long time: How do you convey the idea of secret limitations? To me the remarkable thing about our current "state of exception" is that most Americans don't even notice it and that's what makes its prolongation possible. If people noticed it and were aware of it all the time and it obstructed them in some way, the state of exception probably could not survive. So the idea of being in a cage, being somehow restricted, but not knowing that you are—blinded to the bars surrounding you—seemed to me to convey that idea. For all of these images, I think the question comes down to "How do you convey something vividly to readers in a way that will stop them, arrest them, make them think?" You seek an image that is somehow arresting and that will succeed in conveying a central truth. You are suffering under a regime that is restrictive, and whether you see it or not, it continues to exist.

I wish I could be more illuminating on the actual genesis of ideas like this. I have to go back to what I said earlier, which is that metaphor, before it becomes a tool of expression, is a tool of conception, of understanding. A lot of people, of course, have written about this. In classical times, metaphor was thought of as a rhetorical strategy that was essentially decorative, but I think in our own day we understand it much more as a tool of apperception as well as expression, and I think all the examples you've asked about are images which came to me as means of understanding before they became ways of expressing.

MH: I found another example, which, I think, probably illustrates just what you are saying here. You say in one of your essays, the Bush administration believed Saddam Hussein had weapons of mass destruction and felt they "needed only to dramatize it a bit to make it clear and convincing to the public, like cops who, certain they have the killer, plant a bit of evidence to frame a guilty man." Now I think that's the kind of metaphor which is just going to make the reader think, "Wow! Yeh, that's it. That's just what it is like." In fact that's a simile, of course, not just a metaphor, but extraordinarily illuminating. Something else you do is quote people whose metaphors you approve of and think are valid: Menachem Begin saying that "terrorism is about dirtying the face of power." And then you say that the American response to 9/11 sought above all to "wipe clean that dirtied face." You also quote an intelligence official who said that the task of defending the country was "like playing goalie in a game in which the goalie must stop every shot, in which all the opposing players and the boundary lines, and the field are invisible." It's a flash of understanding, a conceptual metaphor.

Mark Danner: I think it's true, when you find a metaphor that's powerful, like the Begin one, it's irresistible. One characteristic of metaphor, of course, is that it conveys an enormous amount of information in a very small number of words. It has, as it were, a kind of explosive value, the hidden bombs in language; an effective metaphor has a kind of inherent power and the Begin metaphor of "dirtying the face of power" is a good example of that. The extended "goalie" metaphor is wonderful because it brings home so clearly the feeling of vulnerability that gripped national security officials after 9/11, the notion of being blindfolded and waiting for the shot to hit you—and also, of course, there is an eerie echo in that image, which I bring out in the same passage. The official I was quoting also mentioned a feeling of having loud rock music, Led Zeppelin, I think, playing all the time, and it's fascinating, because we are talking here about both hooding and blindfolding and loud music—the very techniques that were used on prisoners—and comparing that to the constant vulnerability and exposure felt by US officials facing the threat of a second attack. There is a fascinating "mirroring" going on there, which I find rather intriguing. What was the first image you quoted?

MH: The Bush administration framing Saddam Hussein, as a cop framing a guilty man.

Mark Danner: What I love about that image is that it's not only vivid on its own terms, but it's an example of a figurative passage that serves to show the motivations of people, that shows they had reasons for acting beyond just inherent deviousness, or evil. I am always interested in answering the basic question of "Why did these people do what they did? What was their motivation? What were they thinking?" The notion of cops convinced of the justness of their cause planting evidence to make sure the criminal doesn't beat the case in court suggests answers to those questions.

I did a public dialogue recently at Boalt Hall at Berkeley with my old colleague Raymond Bonner, a wonderful reporter, who along with Alma Guillermoprieto did the original reporting on the massacre at El Mozote, which I wrote about in my first book. Ray recently published a powerful book about capital punishment in which he describes a particularly horrible example of cops framing a guy, managing to convict him of a crime he didn't commit and get him on to death row in this awful case in Georgia. That, indeed, was a case of the cops framing what they thought was a guilty man—and why did they do it? Not simply because they were nefarious human beings and wanted to kill this innocent man. They believed sincerely that he had done it and they thought, "Why should we let the fact that there is a lack of evidence admissible in the courtroom lead to a further injustice, which would be releasing a guilty man? If we frame this guilty man, we therefore we get justice." I think in the case of the war in Iraq and weapons of mass destruction, many Bush administration officials believed precisely the same thing. If we have to exaggerate the evidence we have of these weapons, what does it matter? Saddam has them—and even if he doesn't have them, he's going to get them again soon. So in their view the underlying justice of the case was there from the beginning: Therefore, we're not really making up evidence, we're simply doing something that will lead to a just outcome. I've disagreed with some people on the Left—I remember an interview on Air America, a short-lived liberal radio network here, with Janeane Garofalo, who was just so convinced that Bush officials *knew* there were no weapons of mass destruction in Iraq. I've always thought this argument was completely irrational. If they had known there were no weapons of mass destruction in Iraq, they wouldn't have used them as their major argument in the case for war. So I do love that metaphor, of the cops framing a guilty man, because it does bring one to the same point—which is that in both cases the people committing injustice believed that it was the way, eventually, to get to justice.

MH: Just as you are an outstanding teller of stories and an analyst and critic of defective and deceptive stories, so you are also both a wonderful exponent of metaphor and a debunker of misleading metaphors. You've already mentioned the article "To Heal Haiti, Look to History, not Nature" (2010), and you start that article with a series of metaphors which you then show to be deceptive: "Haiti is everybody's cherished tragedy," "the great earthquake struck the country like a vengeful god," "Haiti has taken its place as a kind of sacrificial victim among nations, nailed in its bloody suffering to the cross of unending destitution." And then you say, "No! It's not any of these. It's actually history we have to go to. Don't be satisfied with inadequate or presumptuous metaphors." And I think that's an extraordinarily important and valid process that you go through there: the debunking of metaphors with which people have wrongly become satisfied.

Mark Danner: Well, I think it is true that metaphor is an extremely powerful tool to shape our thinking. These tools are often used with great effectiveness by politicians—think of the "War on Terror," for example, or the "War on Drugs," or the "War on Poverty." We could go on. Such phrases are used by politicians to great effect because they can be immensely powerful and that power is used to convey an impression that is false or overly simplistic. We find the same stories—there are a limited number of plots in the world—in the narratives we tell ourselves to explain various places. The "cursed land," for example, or the "land cursed by nature and by God" is a particularly powerful variant of that story, that of the "suffering land." This image goes back at least to Sophocles, to Thebes under Oedipus, for heaven's sake, in which the curse has been handed down. Or I suppose one could go further back, beyond Thebes and Oedipus to Egypt and Moses, and beyond that to Gilgamesh and his 'cursed city.' So I think, in writing about Haiti, a country trapped and imprisoned in such metaphors, one must sometimes begin by trying to identify these images and then go on to smash them, to show how misleading they are and how they tend to embody an interest that the press may have in telling a story, in trying to find an inherent drama in the story, a drama that's powerful and moving and satisfying, and also of course simplistic and misleading. History very often is complicated while these little parables of good and evil are simple and easy to tell and satisfying. So I do agree that many times in trying to tell a story accurately and vividly you have to clear away the detritus that's before you, the heaps of stories and images that are lying there on the ground, obscuring the view of what's really in front of you. Haiti is a place that everywhere you look is obscured by heaps of stories and heaps of metaphors. So that little essay about Haiti and history did begin with an attempt to clear away that detritus and offer some clarity and logic. In place of the metaphor, the idea was to offer a causal, logical view of history, and how that trail led from then to now.

MH: Talking of metaphors used by politicians to manipulate their audiences, I don't know whether you saw a recent quote from Bashar al-Assad in which he compared the activities of his security forces to the work of a surgeon. He said, "When a surgeon. . . cuts and cleans and amputates, and the wound bleeds, do we say to him your hands are stained with blood? Or do we thank him for saving the patient?"

Mark Danner: It's a stunning analogy. Of course, there is a long history to that particular metaphorical construction. It goes back to the Cold

War and no doubt beyond in its application to insurgencies in general: the comparison of insurgents to a cancer and the logical implication that you must cut out the cancer in order to save the patient and thus heal the body *politique*. I heard generals in El Salvador use the same image. In many areas where you had insurgencies during the Cold War, the figure was used as a kind of explanation—an excuse for killing children, for example; though these children may seem innocent, they are still part of the same cancer, destined to become malignant, and thus they must be excised. So Bashar when he uses this figure is working along one branch of a venerable rhetorical tree. By now the image is very well elaborated.

MH: Particularly so in that he has a medical background himself, as he was training as a consultant ophthalmologist when he was in London. It's a particularly sick irony.

Mark Danner: Yes, he is a doctor, it's true, and thus joins a number of doctors, including Duvalier and Karadžić among others, who became dictators. Bashar never thought that he would actually have this job, of course, and perhaps it perplexes him that he finds himself in this position, trapped fighting in the most ferocious way for the survival of a regime from an office he clearly never wanted for himself.

MH: How do you think narrative and metaphor in the sort of context that we are discussing relate to each other? For instance, does narrative generate metaphor, or does metaphor generate narrative? There's a good deal of discussion about this among theorists in the narrative field and the metaphor field. Or is it sometimes one way and sometimes the other? Can I give you an example? When you are talking about Haiti, you do seem to want to use the metaphor "to *heal* Haiti." Now "healing" entails a whole lot of possible narratives and kinds of narrative. Is it the narratives you discover and put together in relation to Haiti that generate the metaphor of "healing" or is it the metaphor that generates the productive narratives that might follow, or are they somehow just so intimately involved with each other that you can't separate them?

Mark Danner: I think perhaps there is a kind of feedback loop operating there, though in truth I don't know, with the one you cite in particular, where the starting point was, or whether one could be identified. Behind the figure "healing Haiti" we can set out a number of equivalencies: Haiti as "the sick patient," Haiti as "diseased by poverty," Haiti as "passive sufferer" of a malady contracted from outside. As so often that kind of capital metaphor has beneath it all sorts of predicate assumptions. The headline writer in particular prizes a metaphor like that with such a compacted, dramatic potential to draw the reader in, for it contains within it a wealth of predicates while producing in readers' imagination a plethora of potent images: sick patient, lurid sickness, morbidity, you name it. It's a vivid comparison, though, again, I am not sure whether you can say that one produces the other or vice versa. I don't know whether I chose that headline, I don't think I did actually. I'm not sure I would have chosen the verb "to heal," had it been my choice.

MH: I'm sure you know Robert Reich's book, *Tales of a New America*, of 1987, in which he outlined what he called the four morality tales which he saw as underlying American politics at that time, and which he entitled "The Mob at the Gates," "The Triumphant Individual," "The Benevolent Community," and 'The Rot at the Top." His very striking insight was that these narratives embodied bedrock beliefs of Americans and were upheld by both liberals and conservatives, serving equally as resources for both sides, even if they were understood quite differently by the two sides. So, the story of "The Benevolent Community" is interpreted by liberals to justify the maintenance of a social welfare system to care for those who get into difficulty and by conservatives to mean that, since we will always look after our neighbors, there is no need for a general social welfare structure funded by taxation. Do you have any thoughts on such bedrock national narratives?

Mark Danner: I have enormous respect for Bob Reich, and I remember when he was working on that book, I was working at *The New York Review of Books*, where he was first publishing many of those ideas. Reich was then a regular contributor and, as an editorial assistant, I used to take down his galley corrections. Of course, various other writers have worked in this area. George Lakoff, the great linguist and my colleague at Berkeley, writes about the different uses of what he calls framing, but his point is in many ways quite similar to Reich's. Americans certainly have cherished ideas about themselves that each political faction, if we wanted to divide them into two, shares but interprets quite differently. Ideas about how America acts in the world—the greatest power in the history of the world and so on—reveal certain assumptions about the United States that Americans share but express quite differently and those differences can be vivid and consequential. The US as an "exceptional power," for example, the idea of American exceptionalism, which has now become a kind of whip with which to flog President Barack Obama, because he is perceived by Republicans not to be sufficiently enthusiastic about the idea of America as the great exceptional power. I can't help finding this a bit amusing, the notion that if you want to be a legitimate leader in the United States, you must not only accept the idea of America as a great power but proclaim it as "exceptional." Or as Madeleine Albright put it during the Clinton administration, "America is the indispensable power," which I remember well since a friend of mine, James Chace, the wonderful biographer of Dean Acheson, came up with that phrase and supplied it to Albright. The "indispensable power," the "indispensable nation," is, I think, a remarkable notion, but it is an assumption shared by almost all Americans. Beneath it is this unquestioned assumption of overwhelming, unlimited power, which, no matter how many times it is proved wrong—as it has been rather frequently during the last decade—those of almost all political persuasions in America are loath to relinquish.

MH: To round this conversation off, in the Coda to your book *Stripping Bare the Body: Politics, Violence, War*, you quote a Bush administration official, whom you identify as almost certainly Karl Rove, talking about how political commentators are in the "reality-based community" whereas those who work for the empire "create our own reality," concluding that, "We're history's actors . . . and you, all of you, will be left just to study what we do." You clearly hope and believe that you and other political commentators can do more than that. You are a little more optimistic than that . . . I hope?

Mark Danner: I do believe we can do more than that, though, to be candid, the events of the last decade, in particular atrocities like torture that remain "frozen scandals," have chastened a bit that optimism. The Karl Rove quote about the "reality-based community"—pointing to academics and journalists as people who are trapped in the reality-based community, as people who haven't recognized how power changes facts—is to me the signal, the capital quote of the Bush era, and perhaps of the era we are still living. The notion that power is the all-important thing, that power can change reality, can change facts. In the same piece, I believe, I point to the moment where President Bush awarded the Medal of Freedom, the highest award the US can bestow, on George Tenant, Paul Bremer, and General Tommy Franks. It was an astonishing image: the president putting the most distinguished medal on the director of central intelligence who had presided over the failure to detect the September 11 attacks, and also the failure of claiming that Iraq had weapons of mass destruction, the casus belli of the Iraq war; on the director of the Iraq occupation authority, who had presided over an enormous fiasco that included a huge insurgency and civil war; and on the general who had led the invading army into Iraq, into this quagmire, and had failed to plan in any way for the occupation that was to follow. All of them were being recognized—by the president, in a public, televised ceremony—for having achieved these brilliant victories. And I remember watching this ceremony televised and thinking, "This is the illustration of Karl Rove's quotation about the imperial power creating reality, rather than recording it." In the same essay, or the same speech—it was originally delivered as a commencement address at Berkeley—I quoted Orwell, who remarked that "From the totalitarian point of view history is something to be created rather than learned." I remember thinking that Orwell's point was rather similar to Rove's. This is not to say that the US is a totalitarian power, but it is to say that the attitudes about power here expressed are the same. Power can create "facts," and those in the reality-based community Karl Rove was disdaining are not unable to identify what the real facts are but simply impotent when it comes to convincing the public that there's a distinction between what they are writing and what the administration is saying.

As I have said, when it comes to torture and other lingering scandals, that situation persists. What if you point to obvious wrongdoing and no one pays attention? What if people read what you write and then say, "You're right, very heroic. Thanks—great article!" But in fact at the same time the president who actually presided over the torture of prisoners writes in his memoirs that when he was asked, by his director of central intelligence, whether he would permit waterboarding of Khalid Sheikh Mohammed, his answer was "Damn right!" (his exclamation point). What if the president, the vice-president, and other officials of the former administration go on proudly proclaiming the waterboarding and other techniques they ordered used on prisoners in those interrogation rooms on the other side of the world, techniques which are now identified as illegal by the current president and attorney general and other officials of the current administration? How exactly does that situation persist? And how can people who write about such things, once they have done the work of exposing them, go on and do anything else, if the exposure leads to no consequences—which is precisely the situation we are in right now?

So the Karl Rove quotation about the reality-based community takes on a slightly different cast, which is that we can write it, we can say it, we can gesture toward it, but the reality that they created persists and the reality that we perceive and try to point to coexists with it but is unable to supplant it. I think is a remarkable fact. It's as if we are living in a science-fiction movie where you have two worlds existing side by side, one of them mocking the other. And the question is, "What is the consequence for someone who's trying to write about those two worlds and finds himself trapped behind the glass, pounding on it, finds himself trapped in the reality-based community?" So I do believe that Rove's is the signal quote of our time and we are still living under its shadow.

MH: I'd really like to give you rather than Karl Rove the last word. Narrative is a competitive device, isn't it? One story can trump another story, can't it? Getting people to understand your story rather than the contrary story that has been told—it's not only in the law court that that is seen as crucial, but presumably in your field as well. So does it come down in part to who tells the best story?

Mark Danner: Well, that's an interesting way to put it. It is one of those questions that leads quite inexorably to a further question which is, "How do we define 'the best story'? What is the best story? Is the best story defined pragmatically as the story that . . . wins out?" What then is the intellectual content of calling it "best"? Are we simply saying, "Well, the best story is the one that triumphs"? To find out what are the characteristics that the best story has and whether those are something inherent in the story itself, or whether it's a fact that the person with the biggest trumpet who can put the most power behind his story is the one who triumphs. If that is the way we define it, we are perilously close simply to acknowledging that "history is written by the winners." One of the fascinating things about officials of the Bush administration in particular was that they understood very well who their audience was and they acted accordingly. They didn't, in a sense, care what *The New York Times* said—I'm exaggerating a bit for effect here, but not much. What they cared about was getting their message out to those they perceived to be their audience. It's the first administration in my lifetime that was able to act with that kind of discipline. The Bush people believed that the best story was the story they could tell to convince a certain number of people who supported them. So we are brought back to your deceptively simple-sounding question: Is that the best story?

MH: Well, I was hoping and, on the basis of all you've said before, that it would be the story which had the greatest degree of truth and the greatest degree of humanity to it. I'm sure that's the kind of storytelling that you are always attempting, isn't it?

Mark Danner: As my mother would say, "Your lips to God's ear." I fervently wish it were true that the best story, the story that triumphs, would always be the story that has the most truth and the most humanity. How beautiful to have faith and conviction that the story with the most truth and the most humanity wins out in the end. Perhaps we saw that play out in Iraq, for example. In a piece from Baghdad early on during the war I wrote eventually Americans would realize this war was a disaster because that is what was happening on the ground and that truth could not be kept from people for ever. This was in essence a statement of faith in just that principle that you have set out. The true story would triumph. People would perceive the truth and, indeed, in Iraq they eventually did—though it took a long time and many deaths. But other stories, some of which you and I have talked about, like the story of post-9/11 torture, would seem to convey the opposite message. And if you look at a place like Argentina, a story I was very interested in as a very young man, while I was still at university and the "dirty war" there was still raging, you find that 30 years later more people, Argentine military officers, are being convicted of torture. This is an extraordinary thing and perhaps suggests—certainly one could take it to suggest—that your definition of the best story, the story destined to triumph, as the story with the most truth and the most humanity is the correct one. In the long run that is the story that will triumph: I would love to believe that. Of course, one is immediately confronted with Keynes's tart observation that "In the long run, we are all dead." How long is the long run? How many lifetimes must we wait for truth to win out—and after how many of those lifetimes can we still be justified in calling it a triumph?

References

Boorstin, D. J. (1961). *The Image: A guide to pseudo-events in America.* New York: Harper and Row.

Danner, M. (2009). *Stripping bare the body: Politics, violence, war.* New York: Nation Books.

———. (2010, February 22). To heal Haiti, look to history, not nature. *New York Times.* Retrieved January 3, 2014, from www.nytimes.com/2010/01/22/opinion/22danner.html?pagewanted=all&_r=0

Kapuściński, R. (1984). *The Emperor* (W. R. Brand and K. Mroczkowska-Brand, Trans.). London: Pan.

7　Metaphors of International Cooperation

Michael P. Marks

Metaphors serve as common framing devices in international relations (IR) theory.[1] Scholars of linguistics have now firmly established that human cognition relies on metaphors to make sense of the world.[2] As in other academic disciplines, metaphors in IR indicate areas of interest, pose theoretical problems, define concepts, suggest hypotheses, and frame analytical inquiry. Although metaphors are part of the conceptualization of international cooperation, their use in the area of international security is often more obvious, perhaps in part because of the prioritization of international security through the metaphorical division that often is drawn between "high" and "low" politics in the field of IR.[3] The narrative of international security in international relations theory is built on the centrality of the metaphor of "anarchy," which is seen by IR scholars as an integral (if metaphorical) structure of the international system.[4] The dilemma countries face in maintaining their security is a theoretical precept made possible in large part because of the foundational metaphor of "anarchy" from which theoretical propositions are deduced. It is possible for scholars to relate this narrative of insecurity once the metaphor of "anarchy" is set in place. Similarly, politicians who practice the arts of Realpolitik and "balance of power" politics in diplomacy and international affairs customarily accept the premise of metaphorical "anarchy" enshrined in international relations theory.

Delving into the realm of "low" politics, one finds that the narrative of international cooperation, as is true for the narrative of insecurity, is also built on an accumulation of metaphors. These metaphors are as central to analyses of international cooperation as they are to the study of international security. Although often framed as the problem of "cooperation under anarchy" (Oye, 1986, p. 1), the primary metaphor used to conceptualize international cooperation is the image of "governance." This contrast between metaphors of "anarchy" and "governance" represents a fundamental ontological distinction between the study of international security and international cooperation, respectively. Security metaphors such as those pertaining to "balances of power," alliances, and war pose more pressing problems than the "governance" metaphor that dominates metaphors of international cooperation. For scholars of international relations, governance is preferable to anarchy. The relegation of cooperation to the realm of "low" politics is part of the narrative that while anarchy is a "problem," "governance" is less problematic in terms of the prospects for finding satisfactory outcomes to political disputes. Likewise, for political leaders who seek cooperation on matters of "low politics," the metaphor of "governance" as framed by international relations theory makes such cooperation seemingly easier to obtain than issues that are subject to the pressures of "anarchy."

My premise in this chapter is that scholars and political practitioners alike weave together a narrative of international cooperation through the conceptual metaphors that frame political issues. Narrative and metaphor are interrelated mental activities. On one hand, metaphors themselves "carry explicit narrative structure within them, insofar as they are spelled out narratively" (Johnson, 1993, p. 158). In a larger sense, narratives tell stories, and thus political narratives (both in theory and in practice) can draw on and elaborate discrete conceptual metaphors. Thus, as Donald Polkinghorne (1988) notes, "The narrative explanation . . . answers [a categorical question] by configuring a set of events into a storylike causal nexus" (p. 21). The contrasting narratives of international security and international cooperation are built on equally contrasting metaphors of "anarchy" and "governance" and thus help explain why often distinct theoretical paradigms are employed to account for the behaviors of actors and international outcomes in the areas of international security, on one hand, and international cooperation, on the other.[5] This chapter focuses on metaphors that scholars use to give meaning to the origins and nature of international cooperation. Given space limitations, the analysis focuses on two prominent areas of study, international regimes, and metaphors of European integration. In many ways, the framing of international cooperation by the language of "governance" supplies conceptual metaphors to the narrative by which analyses of international cooperation are undertaken.

Metaphors in the Study of International Regimes

A specific type of international cooperation is conceptualized in international relations theory using the narrative of governance by way of what is known metaphorically as "international regimes." In the now standard formulation, international regimes are defined as "sets of implicit or explicit principles, norms, rules, and decision-making procedures around which actors' expectations converge in a given area of international relations" (Krasner, 1983, p. 2).[6] On one hand, in this definition the concept of a "regime" is presented in very specific, literal, and technical terms.[7] On the other hand, in her contribution to the Krasner volume, Susan Strange (1983) highlights the "woolly" nature of the regime concept and its analytical imprecision (pp. 337, 342–343). More important, Krasner's seemingly straightforward definition of international regimes (which generally has been adopted by scholars of international relations) betrays underlying metaphorical frames. Specifically, although in the field of IR regimes are conceptualized as arrangements of international cooperation, in the larger political sense a regime typically is understood as a system of government.[8] In this sense, as applied to international cooperation, the term *regime* is used metaphorically. International cooperation, which is not synonymous with international law, is with the term international "regime" conceptualized only metaphorically as governance.

Moreover, the very term *regime* is telling as people tend to think of regimes as particularly strong forms of government. This terminology indicates a potential desire by international relations scholars to tell the narrative of international cooperation with metaphors of governance-like organizations because of a preference for cooperation over anarchy. Can "anarchy" ever be overcome? Only if it is by means of "strong" forms of governance, that is, metaphorical international "regimes."[9] Krasner (1983) further reifies the metaphor when he refers to "regime-*governed* behavior" (p. 3, emphasis added). Here the metaphor of "regime" is linguistically fused with the concept of governance in such a manner that they cannot be analytically disentangled. The definition of regimes that most readily acknowledges this metaphorical aspect is the one offered by Robert Keohane and Joseph Nye (1977), who define regimes as "sets of governing arrangements" (p. 19).[10] The metaphor itself has dictated how this particular sort of international cooperation is conceptualized and what results are theorized to emanate from it.[11]

The metaphorical qualities of international regimes have not gone entirely unnoticed. The early literature on regimes included debates on the veracity of the concept itself. Presumably the type of international cooperation eventually branded with the label "regimes" had existed for a long time. The effort to give a name to this type of cooperation is relatively recent and reflects debates over how to frame the concept. Early works on regimes thus reflect debates over the multiple narratives of international cooperation that could be elaborated around the metaphor of "governance" the regime trope implies. In his aptly titled contribution to Krasner's edited *International Regimes*, "Words Can Hurt You; Or, Who Said What to Whom About Regimes," Ernst Haas points out that the aforementioned standard definition of regimes pointedly excludes two other important terms, specifically, *order* and *system*. This is because *order* and *system* represent the outcome and context, respectively, of regimes.[12] To treat *regime*, *order*, and *system* as synonymous would, of course, create a tautology. For Haas it is important to keep terms distinct.

Haas points out that if the type of cooperation described by the term "regime" were instead known as international "order" or an international "system" the deductions and conclusions that would follow would be influenced by these terms, not the term *regime*. This is because *order* and *system* here would be every bit as much metaphors (not literal descriptions of the cooperation in question) as the word *regime* is. As for how those deductions and conclusions would be different if "order" or "system" provided metaphors for this particular type of international cooperation as opposed to "regime," Haas (1983) observes that "order" and "system" imply naturally occurring conditions, whereas "regimes are man-made arrangements (social institutions) for managing conflict in a setting of international interdependence . . ." (p. 26). Thus, for Haas regime theory is colored by the implications that follow from distinguishing certain types of international cooperation as man-made contrivances as opposed to spontaneously arising phenomena.

Further highlighting the multiple narratives that could be created from the base "regime" metaphor, Haas (1983) goes on to discuss how regime theorists generally fall into two categories, those who subscribe to an organic metaphor of international regimes and those who follow a mechanical metaphor of regimes (pp. 30–52). "The *mechanical* metaphor is pessimistic. It sees the world in steady state, closed, its future determined by its constituent elements and the laws that govern them. . . . The hope held out by adepts of the *organic* metaphor is based on their conviction that the processes embedded in their system are essentially harmonious. The system is open, moving, and dynamic" (ibid., p. 33, emphasis in the original). Haas asserts that adherents of these two metaphorical approaches to international regimes are as much practitioners of politics as they are scholars. As practitioners, "devotees of the organic metaphor show great concern for the future of mankind, but they make short shrift of the political arrangements necessary for assuring this future. Followers of the mechanical metaphor reverse the emphasis; they are sophisticated about politics and economics, but they fail to show much interest in the substantive *problématique* to which politics and economics might be applied" (ibid., p. 52).

Haas (ibid.) suggests an alternative metaphor revolving around the concept of "process." "The actors' perceptions of reality result in policies that shape events; these effects create a new reality whose impact will then be perceived all over again, ad infinitum" (p. 57). Unlike the organic and mechanical metaphors of international regimes, which Haas says fix certain perceptions about life in place (tending towards harmonious equilibrium in the case of organic metaphors and tending towards stale and sterile automation in the case of mechanical metaphors), Haas's "process" metaphor envisions regimes as the product of ongoing and continuous human reevaluation of social interaction. This is much as metaphors themselves work, namely, as linguistic referents that lead to ongoing re-creation of humans' relationship to the world and to themselves. Ultimately, Haas's contribution to regime theory is an explicit attention to the metaphorical aspects of regimes and the way his particular process metaphor is "agnostic about the finality of social laws and about the links between scientific discovery and social design" (ibid., p. 59).

Once arrangements of international cooperation have been imagined metaphorically as "regimes," what does this do for theoretical and empirical analysis of the arrangements in question? The short answer is that these arrangements are treated a priori as systems of government, and thus theories and rules of empirical analyses of government borrowed from other areas of politics then apply. This is demonstrated in Donald Puchala and Raymond Hopkins's contribution to the Krasner-edited *International Regimes*. Puchala and Hopkins (1983) situate regimes in an explicitly political context and define them in terms of things typically associated with governments: "For every political system, be it the United Nations, the United States, New York City, or the American Political Science Association, there is a corresponding regime. Regimes constrain and regularize the behavior of participants, affect which issues among protagonists move on and off agendas, determine which activities are legitimized or condemned, and influence whether, when, and how conflicts are resolved" (p. 62).

Interestingly, not every entity listed by Puchala and Hopkins is strictly speaking a political system. The American Political Science Association, for example, hardly qualifies in most people's book as a political system inasmuch as it barely governs people's lives, if it governs them at all. Puchala and Hopkins have moved from the regime metaphor to that which it is designed to illuminate and, in doing so, have—as is so often the case with metaphors—transferred from the metaphor to the target domain qualities associated with the metaphor that make qualities in the target domain appear to be literally true.

To put it another way, as noted earlier, the salient aspect of the metaphor of "regime" is that, owing to the association the word *regime* has with formal government, the regime metaphor imputes to certain types of international cooperation government-like qualities. In the passage from Puchala and Hopkins earlier, the authors associate with regimes governing qualities of things such as agenda setting and legitimation. Although it is true that the type of international cooperation now known by the expression "international regimes" may incorporate these phenomena, it also includes other activities and practices that are seen as secondary features by regime theorists. Had what are now known as international regimes been called something else (i.e., as Haas suggests, "orders," "systems," or "processes"), the qualities associated with these terms would have been given primacy over secondary qualities; for example, those associated with government as implied by the word *regime*. In this case, researchers would focus their energies on identifying and analyzing these newly primary aspects of the phenomenon in question. The point is that the very association of a certain type of international cooperation with the metaphor of "regime" dictates much, if not most, of the empirical research that ensues. Thus, for example, regimes are said to provide a "governance" solution to dilemmas posed in a variety of game theoretic scenarios.

Although the governance aspect of the regime metaphor is primary, any number of secondary metaphors emanate from it. Among these is the notion that regimes respond to and provide a government-like solution for metaphorical economic "market failure." A good example of this is found in Robert Keohane's (1983) contribution to the aforementioned *International Regimes*. Keohane makes this analogy between the conditions in international relations that create a consumer-like "demand" for international regimes and economic markets: "Like imperfect markets, world politics is characterized by institutional deficiencies that inhibit mutually advantageous coordination" (Keohane 1983, p. 151). Keohane continues later, saying, "Insofar as regimes are established through voluntary agreements among a number of states, we can interpret them, at least in part, as devices to overcome the barriers to more efficient coordination identified by theories of market failure" (ibid.).

Like the central regime metaphor that privileges the government-like aspects of international regimes, the market failure metaphor has significant implications for what conclusions are drawn about regimes. In economics theory, consumer demand is treated as an essential element of economic behavior, preceding even the very market in which demand operates. By using the economic market as a metaphor for the context in which international regimes are created, Keohane (1983) assumes as part of his theory that states (the relevant actors for the authors who contributed to the book *International Regimes*) have innate demands that can be assumed a priori simply on the basis of their existence. What these demands are assumed to be depends on the assumptions about states which theorists bring to the table. For Keohane, the template appears to be neoliberal international relations theory, which assumes that states are self-interested actors seeking to maximize their individual benefits. This certainly seems to be the case from the overtly economic metaphorical language Keohane employs. The following passage suffices to illustrate this: "Neither international agreements nor international regimes are created spontaneously. Political *entrepreneurs* must exist who see a potential *profit* in organizing collaboration" (ibid., p. 155, emphasis added).

The irony is that Keohane and other regime theorists are not dealing with economic rewards, strictly speaking, when utilizing economic metaphors to help conceptualize international regimes. Indeed, Keohane (1983) goes on to discuss how regimes respond to states' demand for principles, norms, and information (pp. 157–161). This is not in itself unsurprising, inasmuch as the economic market metaphor is just that, a metaphor, not a one-to-one analogy for the elements of international relations it is designed to illuminate. What is interesting is the way that the economic language of the market metaphor constrains scholars' thinking so that they conceptualize states' shared perceptions and information as just so many commodities designed to further their narrow self-interests. Thus, whereas the analytical category at play—international cooperation—might imply the creation of communal practices, the economic language of the market metaphor limits theorists' thinking to the narrow implications of economic behavior, and marginalizes other behaviors that might be suggested (but are not) from alternate (but not utilized) metaphorical images.

Within regime theory exist secondary metaphors that also frame theoretical analysis. Among them is the metaphor of "linkage" either in the form of "linked regimes" or within regimes the concept of "issue linkage."[13] When scholars say that regimes or issues are "linked" what they mean is that policy makers see inherent connections between one policy and others. The main hypothesis suggested by assumptions about issue linkage is that if issues are linked within a regime, regime members will see an interest in furthering cooperation in one issue linked to another. Most of the theories dealing with this hypothesis focus on the aforementioned interests. One could ask if the "linkage" metaphor is an attempt to see international cooperation in similar terms to "alliances," one of the few theorized areas of "cooperation under anarchy."

Similar to issue "linkage" is the metaphor of "nested" issues or regimes. To some extent these metaphors deal with the same concept, that is, issues that are connected to each other in such a way that it is hypothesized that policy in one issue area has an effect on policy in another. Indeed, this might be one area in which the metaphors are somewhat redundant, yet there exist distinct strands of research and scholarship that utilize these metaphorical images. "Nested" issues are ones around which policy shifts in one area logically entail policy shifts in another since the two policies fall within the same political purview. The metaphor here is distinctly spatial in nature since the "nest" image implies that one issue is located within the scope of another. Anyone who can visualize two nests, one resting inside the other like a series of stacked bowls, can easily see how the metaphor immediately calls to mind a "within" quality to what is being imagined. Obviously real political issues have no physical space; the notion of an "issue" is an abstraction encompassing certain realms of government administration. So in a literal sense it makes no sense to think of one policy "resting within" another like so many nests stacked together. The power of the metaphor is to impute to issue areas a connection that then logically suggests the hypothesis that when policies are "nested" governments have no choice but to deal with them as a group. This is a good example of an instance in which a metaphor ("nesting") tends to entail a specific narrative about international cooperation, in this case, international cooperation within international regimes represents a type of governance because of the expansion of governing functions from one agency to another.

Another way of metaphorically representing the connections between issue areas in international regimes is the concept of a policy "network."[14] Unlike issue "linkage" that imagines issues strung together in a chain with just two directions, and issue "nesting" that also implies a two-dimensional space with issues moving towards one or another end, a "network" implies a spatial connection with multiple points of contact. A "network," after all, is a metaphor drawing on the shape and form of a net or a web involving interconnected strands crisscrossing each other at multiple junctures or points of connection. This suggests a more multifaceted (to use another metaphor) image of policy making within international regimes. As two scholars have imagined them in the context of European integration, "policy networks are conceptual tools of public policy analysis. They help describe and explain decision-making which 'shapes' policy away from the limelight. The term 'policy network' is a metaphor for a cluster of actors, each of which has an interest, or 'stake,' in a given policy sector and the capacity to help determine policy success or failure" (Peterson & Bomberg, 1999, p. 8). As this quotation suggests, in addition to issues radiating out in a variety of directions, the policy network metaphor also implies a variety of actors and, therefore, as in the "nesting" metaphor, a narrative of governance involving multiple functional agencies.

In sum, the connotations of the "regime" metaphor for conceptualizing international cooperation are not insignificant. Four main metaphorical concepts are highlighted by thinking in terms of "regimes." First, the "regime" metaphor implies a system of governance involved with processes of international cooperation. Regimes are conceptualized as sets of governing principles, norms, rules, and decision-making procedures that mimic the ideational and institutional arrangements found in formal government. The hypotheses that derive from this lead towards theories of international cooperation which propose that cooperation in the realm of international relations mimics formal procedures for cooperation in institutionalized government settings. Second, as Ernst Haas (1983) has suggested, the metaphorical language of regimes, whether it is mechanical or organic in nature, fixes interests in ways that a language of "processes" does not. The hypotheses deriving from this lead to theories of international cooperation overlook the social quality of international interactions.

Third, in addition to the metaphorical frame of regimes grounded in images of governance, the metaphorical language of regimes draws on images of a government-regulated economic market and imputes to states interests consistent with market-based behavior. The hypotheses that derive from this lead to theories of international cooperation in which interests are treated as objective, fixed, and prior to interactions with others. Finally, the market metaphor within regime theory suggests secondary metaphors of linkage, nesting, and networks that frame the way connections among issues of international cooperation are conceptualized. What was previously an unnamed arrangement of international cooperation is baptized through metaphor as a government-like "regime," equipped with mechanisms for regulating states' interests conceived of metaphorically in terms of a regulated economic market.

Although the term *regime,* as applied to a certain type of international cooperation, originated in academia, its narrative of governance resonates with policy makers keen on fostering formal institutions to resolve issues of cooperation in international affairs. There are hundreds of international organizations classified as regimes ranging from the International Whaling Commission to the World Trade Organization to the International Air Transport Association. Although these types of institutions vary in terms of the rules and enforcement mechanisms associated with them, and although they therefore differ regarding the degree of informal versus formal governance they provide to member states, the purpose of regimes of this nature is to impose on members binding commitments of the sort citizens bound by governments experience. The narrative of governance inherent in the regime trope frames international cooperation in ways that advance the aims of policy makers to enhance what otherwise might be seen as merely informal cooperative arrangements. The scholarly concern with elevating realms of "low" politics and the political interest in enhancing cooperation among states thus coincide with the regime metaphor providing a common narrative theme.

Metaphors of European Integration

Because of the relatively unprecedented nature of European integration, metaphors are common in the conceptualization of processes associated with it. Early theories of European integration are notable in that they assumed a metaphorical blank slate with which nascent processes of political and economic convergence in Europe were imagined. The very names of the institutions of European integration bear metaphorical roots, often by design. The first institution created—the European Coal and Steel Community (ECSC)—contains within it a metaphorical framing in the form of the term *community* as does the name of successor organizations the European Economic Community (EEC) and the European Community (EC).[15] By the same token, the present name of the umbrella organization for these institutions is known metaphorically as the European "Union" (EU).[16] By "community," what is meant metaphorically is that the member states of the EC form a group of actors with commonalities sufficient enough to comprise a singularity with shared interests and concerns. The metaphor "union" goes even further, as was the intent of the framers of the Treaty of European Union, because it connotes unification or a process of uniting. Thus, many of the terms associated with European integration are a function of the goals of European leaders, that is, to create a sense of unity among European governments and citizens alike.

This is not necessarily to say that metaphorical discourse within the European Union is unified or without disagreement. As the debates about European integration following the financial crisis of 2008 well illustrate, politicians and other commentators within the EU often find themselves at odds about to frame European integration both for their own purposes as well as for public consumption. As Cris Shore (1997) points out, "studying discourses on European integration—particularly metaphors—can reveal a great deal about the cultural differences and ideological rifts underlying current debates and disagreements between member states over the future shape and direction of the European Union" (p. 127). Thus, for example, Shore (ibid.) discusses how European leaders attempted to frame aspects of European integration using metaphors such as "Europe à la carte," "variable geometry," "concentric circles," "two-tier" integration, and policy implementation that is either "multi-track" or "multi-speed" (pp. 140–145). Other scholars have identified similar efforts by European officials to use metaphors to define the contours of European integration. For instance, Mika Luoma-aho (2004) chronicles how European leaders advanced competing metaphors of "arm" versus "pillar" to situate matters of European security relative to other areas of European integration. Likewise, a variety of European leaders have sought to couch European integration in terms of a common European "home" or "house," yet these metaphors can meet resistance from those skeptical of the scope or pace of European integration.[17] Drawing on the "home" and "house" metaphors, leaders can speak metaphorically of "building a new Europe" (Shore, 1997, p. 129), but if the "home" and "house" metaphors are contested, the "building" metaphor will only exacerbate opposition to European integration where it is to be found. According to Shore (ibid.), "the key question . . . of Europe is *whose* meanings prevail?" (p. 145, emphasis in the original). Part of the answer to that question resides in how metaphors in the practice of European politics are taken up by scholars who study this topic. Scholars are sensitive to the political language of those they study whereas political leaders are not immune to the metaphorical language of scholarly discourse focused on what they practice.

Just as the choice of framing language, including metaphors, reflects either an explicit or an implicit set of *political* calculations for policy makers (as the change from "community" to "union" illustrates), for scholars, too, the choice of analytical language, including metaphors, reflects either an explicit or an implicit set of *theoretical* formulations. Even more so than in the case of international regimes, the language of cooperation regarding European integration is explicitly a narrative of "governance," yet how to conceptualize this nonetheless raises theoretical questions. The implications that policy language has for scholarly analysis can be illustrated by the way that theorists have taken a metaphorical term such as *community* and conjugated it in an effort to explain evolution in the policy realm.[18] Notably, the early theorist of European integration Karl Deutsch et al. (1957) conceptualized the nascent European federation as constituting an emerging "security-community" (p. 5).[19] As discussed earlier, the framing of European supranational institutions as a "community" indicates a metaphorical imagination of Europe as a group of actors with common interests. Likewise, the choice of the word *security* reflects a metaphorical conception of actors' goals, namely, the desire to be "secure."[20] For Deutsch (ibid.), security-communities could take two forms, "pluralistic" security-communities and "amalgamated" ones (pp. 29ff., 56ff.). *Pluralistic*, of course, comes from the root word *plural*, which is a straightforward English manifestation of the Latin *plūrālis*, which itself comes from the Greek *polus* meaning "much" or "many." In studies of politics, the term *pluralism* is a fairly literal term implying the involvement of many voices in the policy-making process.[21]

The concept of "amalgamation," on the other hand, is more intriguing. In conceptualizing economic and political integration in Europe that goes beyond simply coordinating functions of governance Deutsch (1957) emphasizes the emergence of a common identity among Europeans—what Deutsch famously termed a "we-feeling" (p. 36).[22] To amalgamate something is to "combine into a unified or integrated whole" or alternately to create an amalgam which is a "combination of diverse elements; a mixture" (*American Heritage Dictionary*, 1992, p. 56). In metallurgy, an amalgam, like any other metal alloy, renders the constituent elements of the combined alloy unrecognizable, at least on the surface, because its qualities have been altered at the molecular level bringing about a new formulation with its own properties. Unlike, say, a machine composed of various individual parts, once an amalgam has been created one cannot easily separate out the constituent parts if it is possible at all. Deutsch et.al. (1957) define the concept thus: "By AMALGAMATION we mean the formal merger of two or more previously independent units into a single larger unit, with some type of common government after amalgamation" (p. 6, small capitals in the original). To view a fully integrated Europe as a metaphorical "amalgamated" community is to create a category in which certain assumptions about the potential for new identities are theorized. Deutsch has given a metaphorical name—amalgamated security-communities—in which the name of this entity, composed as it is of three metaphorical elements ("amalgamated," "security," "community"), is given qualities that are not yet observed but imply features that follow inexorably from the metaphors that give rise to the concept. An amalgamated security-community comprises a group of actors with a common identity and common interests that make them secure.

Other early theories of European integration have framed analysis in a similar fashion, most notably functionalist theory and the concept of "spillover." As an image used to conceptualize a political phenomenon, the spillover metaphor captures the notion that once agencies are created that have been designed to coordinate among two or more European countries regarding one issue of governance typically reserved for states, coordination concerning additional issues of governance will "spill over" from the first issue to others. Once the metaphorical "tide" of coordinating functions of governance is set in motion, it is only natural and inevitable that functions of government, like metaphorical bodies of water, will spill over from one area of governance to another, creating one large government at the European level. Ernst Haas (1958) sums up the image of spillover as follows: "Economic integration—with its evident political implications and causes—then becomes almost a universal battlecry [*sic*], making complete the 'spill-over' from ECSC to Euratom and its promise of independence from oil imports, from sector common markets to the General Common Market" (p. 298).[23]

The "spillover" metaphor is one of the most well known in the annals of international relations theory, but it is also one of the most contentious perhaps in part because it was consciously contrived by theorists attempting to give form to both an incipient political process and a new area of theorizing in the realm of world affairs. *Neo*functionalism rests on the contention that European integration, in fact, does not reflect a kind of *automatic* or *uncontrolled* "spilling over" from one function of governance to another, but rather, a process that requires the conscious efforts of policy makers and policy advocates acting deliberately to bring about coordination in European policy areas. The spillover metaphor is retained, signaling that as a theoretical concept it continues to inform hypotheses asserted by the theory, but those hypotheses are refined so as to reflect the perception that spillover is the result of deliberate political actions.

Interestingly, proponents of neofunctionalist theory were dissatisfied with the automaticity assumption of the original functionalist theory yet for the most part stuck with the spillover metaphor that made automaticity a working assumption. This illustrates the hold that metaphors can have on the theoretical process. Despite the ill fit between the theoretical implications of the imagery of spillover and neofunctionalist theory, which was designed precisely to avoid the assumptions of automatic integration inherent in the spillover metaphor, no new metaphorical concepts were proposed by neofunctionalist theorists to replace the spillover image. Thus, in many ways, neofunctionalism does not represent a major departure from functionalist theory, and this perhaps was the intent of neofunctionalists who, after all, retained the *functionalist* root after adding the *neo–* prefix.

Other theories also rely on governance metaphors to imagine European integration, most notably the theory of "intergovernmentalism." Relations among the individual members of the European Union do not necessarily result in governance at the EU level that is recognizable as such unless it is narrated with the *metaphor* of "governance," something desired among international relations scholars who see international cooperation conceived of metaphorically as "governance" as a way to overcome the anarchy *problématique*. Such governance includes additional key metaphorical concepts such as the notion of "side payments" within the European Union. Andrew Moravcsik (1991) writes that in negotiations within the EU "small states can be bought off with side-payments" (p. 25).[24] Although the usage of the term *side payment* in economics is fairly straightforward, it relies on a spatial image to conceptualize a somewhat abstract concept. Specifically, the term imagines economic transactions being made metaphorically to the "side" of some other more "central" economic exchange. Economic transactions can be made with any number of means of exchange from bartered goods to services rendered to paper or metal currency to purely electronic movements of stores of value as is common in the digital age.

The notion of a payment being made to the metaphorical "side" of another larger transaction is even more important for understanding the theoretical implications of intergovernmental institutionalist theory. As articulated by Moravcsik, the importance of side payments in European integration is that they reflect the distribution of power among member states of the European Union. Succinctly, more powerful states in the EU are able to determine the shape of European integration and, to secure the consent of weaker states, offer them payments "on the side" to get them to go along. It is critical to this theoretical formulation that the metaphorical "centrality" of certain negotiations be established so as to verify the predictions of intergovernmental institutionalism that stronger states get their way. The predictions of intergovernmental institutionalism are further shown by the fact that when supposedly weaker states benefit, they do so only because they are being paid to the metaphorical "side" of more important "central" transactions. In fact, the validity of intergovernmental theory depends precisely on "proving" that the distribution of power within the EU determines outcome by indicating which states benefit from metaphorical "central" negotiations and which states are being paid off on the "side."

Like many metaphors in the study of international relations, the metaphor of side payments is more suggestive than it is analytically useful. If used as a measure of power within the EU, the concept of side payments is non-falsifiable. Regardless of what negotiations are transacted in the EU, those in which predetermined "strong" states prevail could be said to be central transactions while those in which predetermined "weak" states get their way could be said to be "side payments." What is "central" to one state may be a "side payment" to another state; there is no way to prove which is which. It also relies on ex post facto observations to decide that a transaction was central to EU negotiations because "strong" states won or that a transaction was a "side payment" because supposedly "weaker" states benefitted. Which actors are deemed "strong" states and which are "weak" in the EU is determined based on whether the transaction that produced benefits for the state in question was either a central issue or whether it was a "side payment."

Also embodying the metaphor of governance in the study of European integration is the notion of "multi-level governance," which additionally contains the metaphors of spatially separated "levels." The concept of multi-level governance in the study of European integration was introduced by Gary Marks in 1992. Offering a critique of state-centric approaches to European integration, Marks (1992) offered a spatial conceptualization of political authority that echoes the metaphorical language of levels of analysis: "Instead of a neat, two-sided process involving member states and Community institutions, one finds a complex, *multilayered*, decisionmaking process stretching *beneath* the state as well as *above* it" (p. 221, emphasis added). Marks (1993) later refined and defined this concept, coining the term "multilevel governance," supplementing the spatial metaphor of layers or levels with that of nested placement of political authority: "I suggest that we are seeing the emergence of *multilevel governance*, a system of continuous negotiation among *nested* governments at several territorial *tiers*—supranational, national, regional, and local—as the result of a broad process of institutional creation and decisional reallocation that has pulled some previously *centralized* functions of the state *up* to the supranational level and some *down* to the local/regional *level*" (p. 392, emphasis added except for "multilevel governance," which is italicized in the original).[25]

The theory of multi-level governance borrows heavily from the concept of "levels of analysis" in international relations theory. The basic similarity is that both metaphors rely on a spatial visualization of political organization. In the case of multi-level governance, local and regional politics are located at the metaphorical "bottom," domestic politics within the 27 EU member states in the "middle," and politics among EU institutions at the "top."

Several interesting observations can be made about Marks's original metaphorical formulation of multi-level governance (aside from the changed convention of inserting a hyphen into the term). First, Marks initially suggested the concept as a heuristic device, which has later been refined both in terms of its exact meanings as well as the metaphorical images which it conjures up. For example, in his 1993 definition Marks invokes the metaphor of "nesting" in association with multi-level governance, but by 1996 he and his collaborators assert that in the multi-level model "political arenas are interconnected *rather than* nested" (G. Marks, Hooghe, & Blank, 1996, p. 346, emphasis added). This is not an insignificant metaphorical shift. In the "nested" view, political actors occupy spaces of political authority that are metaphorically self-contained as well as situated within other realms of political authority. Seen from the metaphorical perspective of "interconnectedness" "subnational actors operate in both national and supranational arenas, creating transnational associations in the process" (ibid.). In other words, the metaphor of "multi-level governance" specifies that "levels" of political authority allow for interests to be articulated, coalitions formed, and policy made *across* offices, agencies, and elected bodies rather than solely *within* any one of them as the "nested" metaphor would suggest.

Second, by "levels," G. Marks and his coauthors mean political authority defined both by geographic location as well as by kind. In his original 1993 formulation, Marks indicates that political levels mean governments operating in national, regional, and local contexts. This is repeated by G. Marks and Hooghe (2004) when they define multi-level governance as "the dispersion of authoritative decision making across multiple *territorial* levels" (p. xi, emphasis added). Yet, Marks and his fellow authors also include as a "level" of governance "supranational" entities by which are meant the institutions of the European Union (and its earlier incarnations, e.g., the European Community). This is accentuated when Marks, Hooghe, and Blank (1996) specify institutions at the supranational "level" EU institutions, "above all, the European Commission, the European Court, and the European Parliament" which are not territorial in nature, but rather, represent different forms of political decision making (p. 346). Thus, "level" as a metaphor indicates two analytically distinct ways of categorizing political authority.

Third, and in a related sense, the metaphor of "multi-level" governance is set forth as a way to specify that European integration is no longer (if it ever was) the exclusive purview of the state. Refining their 2001 definition, G. Marks and Hooghe (2004) identify multi-level governance as involving the dispersion of "formal authority . . . from central states both up to supranational institutions and down to regional and local governments" (p. 15). In this formulation, in addition to supranational institutions of European integration and regional and local governments, nonstate forums such as transnational regimes and public/private networks are included as aspects of multi-level governance that supplement traditional state authority. Metaphorically, the image of multiple "levels" perhaps has too wide a scope, and as Marks and Hooghe (ibid.) concede, the metaphor of multi-level governance exists alongside a variety of other terms including "multi-tiered governance, polycentric governance, multi-perspectival governance, functional, overlapping, competing jurisdictions (FOCJ), fragmentation (or spheres of authority), and consortio and condominio, to name but a few" (ibid.).[26] Ironically, although Marks and Hooghe argue that the study of multi-level governance includes entities aside from the state, what political units are included continue to be understood metaphorically in terms of formal governance.

In sum, the arguably unique nature of European integration in the realm of international relations makes it especially susceptible to metaphorical formulations, in particular, metaphors that frame the processes of European integration in terms of formal governance. This is not necessarily surprising. On one hand, European integration is an area of international relations that perhaps is qualitatively distinct from other areas of international affairs. As I have discussed elsewhere, metaphors are particularly useful for theorizing in that they can provide a heuristic function (M. Marks, 2004, 2011). That metaphors of governance are pervasive in theorizing about European integration demonstrates the way that thinking about novel areas of international relations that is empirically distinct and in many ways unprecedented in contemporary world affairs relies on metaphors of the familiar, that is, formal governance.

On the other hand, European integration is an area of international cooperation where theory and practice meet. Since the creation of the ECSC in 1951, proponents of European integration within policy and political circles have endeavored to construct agencies of cooperation that would eventually serve as forms of governance either supplementing or perhaps eventually replacing the governmental functions of individual European states. The metaphors of "community" and "union" that frame European integration resonate with scholars who see in organizations such as the EU the promise for cooperation that eludes states trapped in a metaphorical condition of "anarchy." As scholars have sought to theorize European integration, they have added to these metaphors a narrative of governance through metaphorical concepts such as "security communities," "spillover," "intergovernmentalism," and "multi-level governance." The assumption by policymakers and scholars alike that cooperation can be achieved when framed in ways different from the problem of metaphorical "anarchy" provides the basis for a narrative portraying European integration as an example of cooperation understood in terms of the metaphor of "governance."

Concluding Thoughts

The purpose of this chapter has been to extend the findings of my previous work analyzing the role metaphors provide in the narratives that shape international relations theory (M. Marks, 2011). In that book I opined that the very "problems" that IR scholars seek to solve are framed by metaphorical conceptualizations of the core topics in the field. In my research in that volume, it was not surprising to find that issues of power and security are imagined in IR scholarship to a much greater extent than in international cooperation through a vast series of metaphorical frames. I took this as a reflection of the primacy that "high politics" enjoys in the study of international relations. Because power and conflict are considered more pressing matters than other issues of world affairs (hence the "high" politics label, to suggest a high priority), scholars devote greater attention to how to imagine these matters using metaphors that conceptualize multiple facets of the "problems" associated with international security. Furthermore, the realm of metaphorical high politics is imagined metaphorically in dire terms, that is, within the context of a metaphorical problem of "anarchy" among states.

Questions of international cooperation also are conceptualized metaphorically, specifically, via the metaphor of "governance." Just as "anarchy" is not meant literally, but rather metaphorically in terms either of a "void" or a "state of nature,"[27] so, too, is "governance" used in a metaphorical sense. In a literal sense, what is typically understood by governance involves formal rules, laws, and enforcement mechanisms. As applied to international cooperation, and as illustrated in this chapter, governance is used metaphorically to describe relations among international actors characterized less by formal governance and more by informal conventions, regularized expectations, and habituated compliance. Whether it is the study of international regimes or in analyses of European integration, metaphors of governance establish an ontological basis for scholarship just as the metaphor of anarchy provides a starting point for theorizing about international security.

The inescapable conclusion is that the facts of international relations do not present themselves unambiguously. Once a concept has been labeled, in virtually every case with a metaphor, the implications of that labeling reflect the metaphors that are chosen. How scholars think about the world before they have arrived at theoretical conclusions is part of how they approach the subject from the start. International cooperation has to this point been relegated to the realm of metaphorical "low politics," in part because, when compared to the dire threats posed to international cooperation by a metaphorical "anarchy," the metaphors used to conceptualize international cooperation draw on the comparatively tamer concept of "governance." When compared to the danger of metaphorical anarchy, the *problématique* of international cooperation, framed as it is through the conceptual metaphor of "governance," seems far less pressing and is hence relegated to the metaphorical level of "low politics" in the study of international relations.

Notes

1 For a fuller account of the role of metaphors in international relations, see my previous work (M. Marks, 2011).
2 Research on the role of metaphors in human cognition is now legion in the field of linguistics. For a primer on the cognitive theory of metaphors, see especially

the works of George Lakoff, Mark Johnson, and Mark Turner, in particular Lakoff (1987, 1993), Lakoff and Johnson (1980a, 1980b, 1999), Lakoff and Turner (1989), Johnson (1981, 1987, 1993), and Turner (1987).

3   The division of international relations into "high" and "low" politics indicates the prioritization of international security over other significant aspects of international relations such as international cooperation, which frequently are afforded a lesser status. The order of chapters in introductory textbooks on international relations illustrates this phenomenon; in almost every case, chapters on security precede chapters on international cooperation.

4   On the centrality of the anarchy *problématique* to the study of international relations, see Ashley (1988).

5   On the use of different paradigms to explain different ontological problems, see Lake (2011).

6   Examples of international regimes include the International Whaling Commission, the World Health Organization, and the International Atomic Energy Agency.

7   The standard definition of international regimes is explicated in some detail. After defining international regimes, Krasner (1983) goes on to define their constituent components: "Principles are beliefs of fact, causation, and rectitude. Norms are standards of behavior defined in terms of rights and obligations. Rules are specific prescriptions or proscriptions for action. Decision-making procedures are prevailing practices for making and implementing collective choice" (p. 2).

8   The first two definitions of regime in the *American Heritage Dictionary* (1992) define regime as a "form of government. A government in power; administration" (p. 1520).

9   It is worth observing that it is thought that security regimes are harder to create than regimes in other areas precisely because of the difficulty of "anarchy."

10 Oran Young (1983) affirms this, stating, "regimes are social institutions *governing* the actions of those interested in specifiable activities (or accepted sets of activities)" (p. 93, emphasis added).

11 Once imagined metaphorically as systems of government, what are now known as international "regimes" are hard to conceptualize in any other way. Such is the power of metaphors; once they have gained a literal sense, they influence how people think of the concept and make other formulations almost unimaginable.

12 "Order, then, refers to the benefits a regime is to provide; system refers to the whole in which collaboration toward an order takes place" (Haas, 1983, p. 27).

13 On issue linkage generally see, for example, Tollison and Willett (1979), McGinnis (1986), and Conconi and Perroni (2002). On issue linkage in European integration see, for example, Weber and Wiesmeth (1991) and Da Conceição-Heldt (2008).

14 On policy networks in Europe see, for example, Kriesi, Adam, and Jochum (2006) and Moschitz and Stolze (2009).

15 The name of the European Coal and Steel Community in the languages of the founding member states incorporates the equivalent for the English word "community:" *Communauté* Européenne du Charbon et de l'Acier (French); Europäischen *Gemeinschaft* für Kohle und Stahl (German); *Comunità* Europea Del Carbone E Dell'Acciaio (Italian); and Europese *Gemeenschap* voor Kolen en Staal (Dutch).

16 In French the organization is known as the "Union Européenne," whereas in German it is the "Europäische Union" and in Italian it is the "Unione Europea." In virtually all of the languages of the current 27 EU member states, the English word *union* translates into their linguistic equivalent.

17 For works on metaphors in the language used by policymakers to frame European integration (including the aforementioned "pillar" versus "arm" and "house" metaphors) see, for example, Chilton and Ilyin (1993), Thornborrow (1993), Cattaneo and

Velo (1995), Chilton (1996), Schäffner (1996), Fierke (1997), Shore (1997), Hyman (2001), Musolff (2001, 2004), Luoma-aho (2004), and Mason and Penksa (2004).

18 For example, the noun *community* has morphed into the contrived verb *communitize* to account for transference of policy-making authority to the institutions of European integration.

19 Deutsch et.al. (1957) define a security-community as "a group of people which has become 'integrated.'" "Integration" is subsequently defined as "the attainment, within a territory, of a 'sense of community' and of institutions and practices strong enough and widespread enough to assure, for a 'long' time, dependable expectations of 'peaceful change' among its population." Further, by "sense of community," Deutsch et.al. "mean a belief on the part of individuals in a group that they have come to agreement on at least this point: that common social problems must and can be resolved by processes of 'peaceful change.'" Finally, by "peaceful change" is meant "the resolution of social problems, normally by institutionalized procedures, without resort to large-scale physical force." All quotes are from Deutsch et.al. (1957, p. 5).

20 On the metaphorical qualities of the term *security*, see Chilton (1996).

21 "The PLURALISTIC security-community . . . retains the legal independence of separate governments. The combined territory of the United States and Canada is an example of the pluralistic type. Its two separate governmental units form a security-community without being merged" (Deutsch et al., 1957, p. 6, small capitals in the original).

22 "The kind of sense of community that is relevant for integration, and therefore for our study, turned out to be rather a matter of mutual sympathy and loyalties; of 'we-feeling,' trust, and mutual consideration; of partial identification in terms of self-images and interests; of mutually successful predictions of behavior, and of cooperative action in accordance with it . . ." (Deutsch, et.al., 1957, p. 36).

23. An ironic aspect of the spillover metaphor is that some of the images it brings to mind hardly suggest the positive qualities of European integration commonly associated with it. Students in a class I teach on European politics and foreign policy once discussed the spillover metaphor in the context of the ill-fated steamship RMS. *Titanic* and its less-than-water-tight compartments, the flooding of one spilled over to the next dragging the ship to the bottom of the ocean. Although the concept of spillover suggests an accretion of European government institutions to foster greater peace and prosperity in Europe, the spillover image can just as easily be brought to bear on a metaphor that imagines European integration as a process that takes the European "ship of state" to its watery grave. Some observers have noted that the worldwide financial crisis that began in 2008 perhaps has resulted in a worse situation for some EU states than would otherwise be the case as a consequence of European monetary integration. The crisis in individual countries "spilled over" into others because of the creation of a single currency for EU countries within the eurozone, hence limiting the ability of individual EU member states to solve their problems using a full range of monetary measures.

24 Moravcsik (1991) also writes that states in the European Union engage in "widespread use of linkages and logrolling," among other metaphorical practices of European integration (p. 25). For more on side payments see, for example, Mayer (1992) and Friman (1993).

25 Since Marks coined the term "multilevel governance" it has been employed widely throughout the literature on European integration. See, for example, the chapters in Bache and Flinders (2004).

26 Within each of these metaphorical formulations, there are also nuances. For example, G. Marks and Hooghe (2004) identify "general purpose" political jurisdictions that operate at "international, national, regional, meso, [and] local" levels and "task-specific" jurisdictions "that, for example, provide a particular local service, solve a

common pool resource problem, select a product standard, monitor water quality in a particular river, or adjudicate international trade disputes" (pp. 16–17).
27 On the construction of anarchy in metaphorical terms in the study of international security, see M. Marks (2011, especially pp. 30–34).

References

American heritage dictionary of the English language. (1992). 3rd ed. Boston: Houghton Mifflin.
Ashley, R. K. (1988). Untying the sovereign state: a double reading of the anarchy problematique. *Millennium, 17*(2), 227–262.
Bache, I., & Flinders, M. (Eds.). (2004). *Multi-level governance.* New York: Oxford University Press.
Cattaneo, C., & Velo, D. (1995, May). *Variable geometry Europe: An interpretation of the European integration development.* Paper presented at the biennial conference of the European Union Studies Association, Charleston, South Carolina, USA.
Chilton, P. A. (1996). *Security metaphors: Cold war discourse from containment to common house.* New York: Peter Lang.
Chilton, P. A., & Ilyin, M. (1993). Metaphor in political discourse: The case of the "common European house." *Discourse and Society, 4*(1), 7–31.
Conconi, P., & Perroni, C. (2002). Issue linkage and issue tie-in in multilateral negotiations. *Journal of International Economics, 57*(2), 423–447.
Da Conceição-Heldt, E. (2008). Assessing the impact of issue linkage in the Common Fisheries Policy. *International Negotiation, 13*(2), 285–300.
Deutsch, K. W. et.al. (1957). *Political community and the North Atlantic area: International organization in the light of historical experience.* Princeton, NJ: Princeton University Press.
Fierke, K. M. (1997). Changing worlds of security. In K. Krause & M. C. Williams (Eds.), *Critical security studies: Concepts and cases* (pp. 223–252). Minneapolis: University of Minnesota Press.
Friman, H. R. (1993). Side-payments versus security cards: Domestic bargaining tactics in international economic negotiations. *International Organization, 47*(3), 387–410.
Haas, E. B. (1958). *The uniting of Europe: Political, social, and economic forces 1950–1957.* Stanford, CA: Stanford University Press.
———. (1983). Words can hurt you; or, who said what to whom about regimes. In S. D. Krasner (Ed.), *International regimes* (pp. 23–59). Ithaca, NY: Cornell University Press.
Hooghe, L., & Marks, G. (2001). *Multi-level governance and European integration.* Lanham, MD: Rowman and Littlefield.
Hyman, R. (2001). European integration and industrial relations: A case of variable geometry? *Antipode, 33*(3), 468–483.
Johnson, M. (1981). Introduction: Metaphor in the philosophical tradition. In M. Johnson (Ed.), *Philosophical perspectives on metaphor* (pp. 1–47). Minneapolis: University of Minnesota Press.
———. (1987). *The body in the mind: The bodily basis of meaning, imagination, and reason.* Chicago: University of Chicago Press.
———. (1993). *Moral imagination: Implications of cognitive science for ethics.* Chicago: University of Chicago Press.

Keohane, R. O. (1983). The demand for international regimes. In S. D. Krasner (Ed.), *International regimes* (pp.141–171). Ithaca, NY: Cornell University Press.

Keohane, R. O., & Nye, J. S. (1977). *Power and interdependence*. Boston: Little, Brown.

Krasner, S. D. (1983). Structural causes and regime consequences: Regimes as intervening variables. In S. D. Krasner (Ed.), *International regimes* (pp.1–21). Ithaca, NY: Cornell University Press.

Kriesi, H., Adam, S., & Jochum, M. (2006). Comparative analysis of policy networks in Western Europe. *Journal of European Public Policy, 13*(3), 341–361.

Lake, D. A. (2011). Why "isms" are evil: Theory, epistemology, and academic sects as impediments to understanding Progress. *International Studies Quarterly, 55*(2), 465–480.

Lakoff, G. (1987). *Women, fire, and dangerous things: What categories reveal about the mind*. Chicago: University of Chicago Press.

———. (1993). The contemporary theory of metaphor. In A. Ortony (Ed.), *Metaphor and thought* (2nd ed., pp. 202–251). New York: Cambridge University Press.

Lakoff, G., & Johnson, M. (1980a). *Metaphors of everyday life*. Chicago: University of Chicago Press.

———. (1980b). *Metaphors we live by*. Chicago: University of Chicago Press.

———. (1999). *Philosophy in the flesh: The embodied mind and its challenge to Western thought*. New York: Basic Books.

Lakoff, G., & Turner, M. (1989). *More than cool reason: A field guide to poetic metaphor*. Chicago: University of Chicago Press.

Luoma-aho, M. (2004). "Arm" versus "pillar": The politics of metaphors of the Western European Union at the 1990–91 Intergovernmental Conference on Political Union. *Journal of European Public Policy, 11*(1), 106–127.

Marks, G. (1992). Structural Policy in the European Community. In A. M. Sbragia (Ed.), *Euro-politics: Institutions and policymaking in the "new" European Community* (pp. 191–224). Washington, DC: Brookings Institution.

———. (1993). Structural policy and multilevel governance in the EC. In A. W. Cafruny & G. G. Rosenthal (Eds.), *The State of the European Community, Volume 2. The Maastricht debates and beyond* (pp. 391–410). Boulder, CO: Lynne Rienner.

Marks, G., & Hooghe, L. (2004). Contrasting visions of multi-level governance. In I. Bache & M. Flinders (Eds.), *Multi-level governance* (pp. 15–30). New York: Oxford University Press.

Marks, G., Hooghe, L., & Blank, K. (1996). European integration from the 1980s: State-centric v. multi-level governance. *Journal of Common Market Studies, 34*(3), 341–378.

Marks, M. P. (2004). *The prison as metaphor: Re-imagining international relations*. New York: Peter Lang.

———. (2011). *Metaphors in international relations theory*. New York: Palgrave Macmillan.

Mason, W., & Susan, P. (2004, March). *The variable geometry of security cooperation: A policy framework for European integration*. Paper presented at the annual meeting of the International Studies Association, Montreal.

Mayer, F. (1992). Managing domestic differences in international negotiations: The strategic use of internal side-payments. *International Organization, 46*(4), 793–818.

McGinnis, M. D. (1986). Issue linkage and the evolution of international cooperation. *Journal of Conflict Resolution, 30*(1), 141–170.

Moravcsik, A. (1991). Negotiating the Single European Act: National interests and conventional statecraft in the European Community. *International Organization, 45*(1), 19–56.

Moschitz, H., & Stolze, M. (2009). Organic farming policy networks in Europe: Context, actors and variation. *Food Policy, 34*(3), 258–264.

Musolff, A. (2001). The metaphorisation of European politics: *Movement* on the *road* to Europe. In A. Musolff et al. (Eds.), *Attitudes towards Europe: Language in the unification process.* (pp. 179–200). Aldershot, England: Ashgate.

———. (2004). *Metaphor and political discourse: Analogical reasoning in debates about Europe.* London: Palgrave Macmillan.

Oye, K. A. (Ed.). (1986). *Cooperation under anarchy.* Princeton, NJ: Princeton University Press.

Peterson, J., & Bomberg, E. (1999). *Decision-making in the European Union.* New York: St. Martin's Press.

Polkinghorne, D. E. (1988). *Narrative knowing and the human sciences.* Albany: State University of New York Press.

Puchala, D. J., & Hopkins, R. F. (1983). International regimes: Lessons from inductive analysis. In S. D. Krasner (Ed.), *International regimes* (pp. 61–91). Ithaca, NY: Cornell University Press.

Schäffner, C. (1996). Building a European house? Or at two speeds into a dead end? Metaphors in the debate on the united Europe. In A. Musolff, C. Schäffner, & M. Townson (Eds.), *Conceiving of Europe: Diversity in unity* (pp. 31–59). Aldershot, England: Dartmouth.

Shore, C. (1997). Metaphors of Europe: Integration and the politics of language. In S. Nugent & C. Shore (Eds.), *Anthropology and cultural studies* (pp. 126–159). London: Pluto Press.

Strange, S. (1983). *Cave! Hic dragones*: A critique of regime analysis. In S. D. Krasner (Ed.), *International regimes* (pp. 337–354). Ithaca, NY: Cornell University Press.

Thornborrow, J. (1993). Metaphors of security: A comparison of representation in defense discourse in post-cold war France and Britain. *Discourse and Society, 4*(1), 99–119.

Tollison, R. D., & Willett, T. D. (1979). An economic theory of mutually advantageous issue linkages in international negotiations. *International Organization, 33*(4) 425–449.

Turner, M. (1987). *Death is the mother of beauty: Mind, metaphor, criticism.* Chicago: University of Chicago Press.

Weber, S., & Wiesmeth, H. (1991). Issues linkage in the European Community. *Journal of Common Market Studies, 29*(3), 255–267.

Young, O. R. (1983). Regime dynamics: The rise and fall of international regimes. In S. D. Krasner (Ed.), *International regimes* (pp. 93–113). Ithaca, NY: Cornell University Press.

8 From *Saving Private Ryan* to Building *Team America*

US Presidential Oratory and the Art of Interpellation

Susan Wright and Cris Shore

Introduction: Presidential Oratory and the Art of Interpellation[1]

Narratives and metaphors are ways by which people make sense of experience (or construct meaning), but they are also instruments by which political leaders seek to legitimize their policies and mobilize public support (or wield power). In this chapter we analyze key political speeches by Presidents Bush and Obama on particular ceremonial occasions in order to explore the connections between language, oratory and power. More specifically, we examine how both presidents deal with the issues of war and US national security and identify some of the continuities and contrasts in their uses of narrative and metaphor. As anthropologists, we are not just interested in analyzing these as texts; we also consider the wider social and cultural context in which these speeches were delivered, and the symbolism and semiotics of these ritual occasions. Taking up Bloch and Parry's (1975) concepts of "linguistic ritual" and "formalized codes," we ask, "How are these presidential speeches made authoritative? How do they narrate 'America'? How do they explain the failures of the past and envision the future? More specifically, how do they convey their political messages about homeland security and threats to the nation? And how do they hail or interpellate their audiences in their attempts to manufacture consent?"

We suggest that whereas President Bush's rhetoric tended to emphasize fear and hatred, shock and awe, American military might and unilateralism, President Obama, at least initially, downplayed belligerence and the flouting of international law and emphasized the importance of teamwork and international cooperation. Bush sought to rally Americans behind their president as a commander-in-chief engaged in an all-out "war" on terror. Obama, by contrast, drew on a different repertoire of military values—covering each other's backs, leaving no one behind and disinterested service to one's country—and transposed these "Team America" ideals into a model of the civilian sociality needed to forge a multicultural America that is "built to last." Obama's change in tone differed radically from that of Bush, initially capturing the enthusiasm of the American—and global—public tired of permanent war. He was rewarded in 2009 with the Nobel Peace Prize for promoting a "new climate" in international relations and "reaching out to the Muslim world." Contrary to expectations, Obama has continued to use the war-on-terror apparatus that Bush created; however, by shifting the focus away from conventional "troops on the ground," he and Secretary of Defense John Kerry are able to claim that this is "not war" because it involves "no attempt to take over the country" (Lakoff, 2013). Instead, he has relied on secret "kill lists," unmanned drone attacks, extrajudicial killings and undercover operations all based on undisclosed or "classified" legal opinions (Scahill, 2013). This "limited war" approach recalls the sanitized "surgical strike" metaphors of the first Gulf War (Lakoff, 1991, 2013).

Our aim is to analyze how Bush and Obama's narratives and metaphors combine within political oratory to become elements of linguistic rituals and how they work as interpellative devices to forge hegemony and legitimize presidential authority. Central to establishing hegemony, as Asad (1979) argues, is the ability of leaders to create a generalized vision of the social order that is normative, and then to draw on state institutions to make that vision authoritative. Even so, as Gramsci (1971) observed, a hegemonic position has to be continually reinforced and sustained. Power is most effective when it goes unquestioned and unnoticed and when its ideological agenda succeeds in becoming naturalized as "common sense." As Bourdieu (1977) put it, "[e]very established order tends to produce . . . the naturalization of its own arbitrariness" (p. 164). A hegemonic position exhibits fragility if its proponents have to repeatedly restate its premises and arguments: then it is clearly man-made, and can more easily be contested. An important question, therefore, is, How exactly do leaders try to normalize their agenda so that their position or vision becomes "naturalized" as taken-for-granted common sense? More specifically, what role does metaphor and narrative play in the symbolic constructing of that common sense?

Putting Text in Context: Speech Acts and Performative Oratory

Linguists usually start by establishing a "corpus" of texts. In our case, we have chosen to focus on selected key speeches of George Bush and critical events during the period immediately after the 9/11 (2001) terrorist attacks on the World Trade Center and extending up to the fifth anniversary speech in September 2006. This period covers the start of the war in Afghanistan and the passing of the PATRIOT Act in October 2001, the claim that there was an "Axis of Evil" in January 2002, attempts to get a UN mandate for war in Iraq during 2002–2003, the attack on Iraq, starting in March 2002, and in November, the establishment of the Department of Homeland Security. Bush was reelected as president in November 2004, while the wars continued, with the scandal of mistreatment of Iraqi prisoners and the senate report that allies went to war on "flawed" information, followed by reports of rendition of terror suspects (and Hurricane Katrina) in 2005. Our timeline ends with President Bush making a series of speeches to justify his war on terror in the run-up to the elections for the Senate and the House of Representatives in 2006. In particular we analyze in detail his speech "Planning for victory" given at the US Naval Academy at Annapolis on 30 November 2005 and his televised Oval Office address to the nation, "A war unlike any we have fought before" on 9 September 2006.

We compare these speeches with three speeches by Barack Obama that speak to similar themes of nationhood, security and war: his first State of the Union address in February 2009, his speech later that year to cadets at the West Point military academy explaining his policy of a temporary "troop surge" and escalation of the war in Afghanistan, and his election-year State of the Union address in 2012 setting out his administration's record of achievements and vision for a second term.

These speeches are contextualized socially and historically by referring to the written texts of other speeches and legislation, television coverage of the speeches and media reports. We supplement this material with empirical observations made by one author while living in the US in 2002 and by visits to the US by both authors in 2005.[2] Following Victor Turner's (1967) prescriptions on how to analyze rituals anthropologically,[3] we examine the speech acts themselves, the interpretations of these given by "ritual specialists," and the wider context in which these events occurred (see the Appendix to this chapter). We also focus on the political tactics and personal and institutional resources that politicians use to try to interpellate their imagined audience and to make their vision hegemonic and authoritative.[4]

Our approach draws on social linguistics and critical discourse analysis, particularly in its focus on the rhetorical structure of speeches (Barker and Breezer, 1983; Lloyd-Jones, 1981; Seidel, 1997). But it is also important to recognize that public speeches are "speech acts" that have strong elements of rhetoric, ritual and symbolism. As anthropologists Bloch and Parry (1975) noted, in every society there exists a limited and highly ritualized set of metaphors, references and images that political rulers will seek to "tap into" in order to endow their oratory with authority and cultural legitimacy. These "speech acts," their narratives and metaphors, gain meaning not only in the event itself but also from their location within sequences of events. Within anthropology, "event analysis" has recently become a focus of major theoretical interest as a way of exploring "moments of social life in the very process of formation" (Kapferer, 2005, p. 102). As Kapferer (2005) sums it up,

> An event is a site of creativity whose analysis leads to understanding of the potentialities of social forces or structural processes that are not yet apparent in the lived environment or the larger contexts of the event's occurrence. (p. 104)

In a similar vein, Sally Falk Moore (1987, p. 727) argues that anthropological fieldwork is "current history" in which the focus is change-in-the-making and the core question is not just "How was the present produced?" but more importantly "What is the present producing?" This line of reasoning can equally apply to the analysis of policy and the consequences and effects that a policy produces. As we have argued elsewhere (Shore & Wright, 1997), governments typically frame policy problems in a way that makes only one "solution" seem feasible or rational (see also Bacchi, 2009). This discursive framing that permits only one policy response is nowhere more clearly illustrated than in the presidential speeches of George W. Bush.

The USA PATRIOT Act

Within a month of the terrorist attacks on the World Trade Center and the Pentagon in September 2001, a hastily drafted antiterrorism bill was presented to Congress. This heralded a new era of "security" with draconian new state powers. Known as the "PATRIOT Act" (its full title being the "Uniting and Protecting America by Providing Appropriate Tools Required to Intercept and Obstruct Terrorism Act"), the new bill rapidly passed into law on 26 October 2001. According to both supporters and critics of the legislation, it laid the foundations for a domestic intelligence-gathering system of unprecedented scale and technological prowess. Among its provisions, the PATRIOT Act empowered the government to shift the primary mission of the Federal Bureau of Investigation (FBI) from solving crimes to gathering domestic intelligence; it charged the Treasury Department with building a financial intelligence-gathering system whose data can be accessed by the Central Intelligence Agency (CIA); and, for the first time ever, it gave the CIA authority to influence FBI operations inside the US and obtain evidence gathered by wiretaps and federal grand juries. The act permitted a vast array of covert information gathering, effectively giving the Central Intelligence Agency and National Security Agency license to spy on Americans. In doing so, it overturned measures taken to curb abuses of state power, including the legal firewall erected after the Watergate scandal exposed presidential abuses of domestic intelligence gathering against political activists. The CIA's ability to spy on American citizens had been specifically restricted as a result of Operation CHAOS in the 1970s in which the CIA was caught illegally spying on anti-Vietnam war protesters, so-called black nationalists and student activists (McGee, 2001). A few weeks after the PATRIOT act was passed, President Bush signed an order empowering him to authorize military trials in the US and abroad for international terrorists and their collaborators. These military tribunals can impose sentences as severe as death on a two-thirds vote, hold trials in secret and rely on evidence that would be rejected in a civil court. Furthermore, Bush's order does not allow for judicial review. Some legal experts argued that the order was an attempt by the President to suspend the right of habeas corpus for those accused of plotting against the US.

The speed with which the PATRIOT Act was ratified reflected the ability of the Bush administration to capitalize on the bipartisan mood in Congress created by the climate of wartime politics. By then, the US was leading a massive military campaign to achieve regime change in Afghanistan as part of its "war on terror," which was fuelled by fear of further terrorist attacks and talk of "Weapons of Mass Destruction." At its signing, President Bush (2004) described the PATRIOT Act as "an essential step in defeating terrorism, while protecting the constitutional rights of all Americans" which would "give intelligence and law enforcement officials important new tools to fight a present danger." However, many critics opposed the bill, particularly the way it redrew the line between civil liberties and national security. Reflecting on the history of intelligence abuses, Senator Frank Church warned that domestic intelligence gathering was a "new form of power", unconstrained by law, often abused by presidents and always inclined to grow (McGee, 2001). Even conservative Republicans, such Robert L. Barr Junior, characterized the government's plans as ethnic profiling, power grabbing and overzealous law enforcement. Others denounced the military tribunals and secret evidence as "Third World" practices (Lardner, 2001).

The Bush administration countered these criticisms with accusations that opponents were using delaying tactics in a moment of crisis and were unpatriotic. Attorney General John Ashcroft rebuffed questions about the legislation with the slogan "Talk won't prevent terrorism," adding that he was deeply concerned about the rather slow pace of the legislation (*New York Daily News*, 2001). Republican senator Orin Hatch voiced similar frustration with an attempt to debate the proposal in the Senate: "[Delays] are very dangerous things. It's time to get off our duffs and do what's right" (ibid). Such statements equated patriotism with blind obedience to government and state. They permitted no space for those who might appeal to an earlier American meaning of patriotism as the duty to defend one's nation against a corrupt or overly powerful government (Ball, Farr, & Hanson, 1989).

In the event, the PATRIOT Act passed with little vocal opposition. Most critics either stonewalled or simply caved in to pressure to vote for the bill for fear of being deemed "soft on terrorism" and, by implication, weak on defense of the American nation. *Insight* magazine reported that only a few copies of the bill were made available in the hours just before its passage, and most representatives admitted to voting for the bill without even seeing it, let alone reading it. As one Republican critic of the bill (Texas representative Ron Paul) complained,

> The insult is to call this a "patriot bill" and suggest I'm not patriotic because I insisted upon finding out what is in it and voting no. I thought it was undermining the Constitution, so I didn't vote for it—and therefore I'm somehow not a patriot. That's insulting. (O'Meara, 2001)

What is anthropologically interesting about the PATRIOT Act is precisely the language in which it was presented to senators and the American public.

The dominant discourse was "national security" and the new threat posed by global networks of terrorists who, in George W. Bush's (2001) words, "recognize no barrier of morality," "have no conscience," and "cannot be reasoned with." This language echoes a much older narrative about piracy, which as Thorup (2009) points out, stems from Cicero's *De Officiis* and was prevalent in Europe from the early colonial conflicts for global dominance of the seas, until the Paris Declaration of 1856. Whereas conventional war was between states that recognized each other's legitimacy, followed rules of war, and concluded hostilities with negotiations and a treaty, pirates embodied the antithesis of these characteristics. They entered hostilities for private profit and their violence, lacking the legitimacy of a state, was deemed criminal. Pirates were also often referred to as "the enemies of humanity" who were outside the rules of war and ordinary morality, and with whom it was "impossible to negotiate." They could be hunted down anywhere, and their extermination was the only way to bring peace. Like modern-day terrorists, they too were an asymmetrical enemy, an enemy without rights, with whom the state did not need to keep its word and who could be fought with "unconventional" methods. Thorup (2006, p. 75) argues that the war against pirates took on the very characteristics it set out to defeat. Similar constructions are seen in the Bush administration's rejection of diplomacy and its reliance instead on war as the basis of foreign policy. The policy narrative was filled with metaphors of "danger," "the urgency of a nation at war," and the need to "bring down walls" between intelligence gathering and law enforcement. A recurring motif in the discourse of the US government was that these measures were "necessary tools" to enable "our nation's law enforcement, national defense and intelligence personnel" to "bring terrorists and other dangerous criminals to justice" (US Department of Justice 2004, p. 1). The very identification of these kinds of threats and crises in public policy serves as a foil against which national identity is consolidated and dissent pushed aside (Feldman, 2005). The Bush administration managed to mobilize fears among legislators that if they questioned the legislation, and especially if they suggested it was undermining the very principles of freedom and the rule of law that they were trying to preserve, they would be labeled as unpatriotic and incapable of taking decisive action to defend the nation against the enemies of humanity. By these means the Bush administration got the PATRIOT Act through Congress and Senate and thereby drew on the security services and law enforcement agencies of the state to make their view of the world authoritative. But were they able to make their vision of a nation under permanent threat from terrorists *hegemonic*?

Making the Case for War on Iraq: Constructing "Coalitions of the Willing" Among the American Public

What is striking in this case study of the evolution of US policy regarding the war on terror is the curious reversal of the normal procedures used by political leaders to construct a hegemonic policy narrative. In most circumstances, key agenda-setting policy speeches are made before the enactment of a particular piece of legislation because the aim is usually to garner consent and lend legitimacy so that the proposed legislation can pass into law. However, most of Bush's key speeches making the case for the war on terror were made *after* the PATRIOT Act had been signed into law in October 2002. Bush had succeeded in getting his controversial legislation approved by US senators and congresspersons so that he could draw on the institutional power of the state and the new duties placed on private companies to make the law authoritative; the challenge now was to win over US public opinion.

Although critics derided President Bush for his linguistic gaffes and inappropriate remarks, his speeches on the "war on terror" are masterpieces in the manipulation of political symbols and the strategic deployment of political shibboleths and well-placed slogans, "masterpieces," that is, in the sense of trying to create a compelling narrative for justifying continuing US military involvement in Iraq, and for mobilizing large sections of the American public, for whom his words were designed to hold particular emotional resonance and appeal. While some might view these speeches as hackneyed and banal, they merit closer scholarly attention if we are to understand how neoconservative policy elites sought to maintain hegemony over the American public. Analysis of Bush's major public speeches also provides insight into the structure of contemporary American political culture and neoconservative ideology. Although we would hesitate to claim, pace Clifford Geertz (1973, 1983), that "thick description" and interpretive analysis can provide a window into the "psyche" of a particular people, they do nonetheless reveal important cultural patterns—and in this case, they show us how Presidents have sought to govern the US and the linguistic and ideological registers deployed towards these ends.

Following the US-led invasion of Afghanistan in October 2001 (Operation Enduring Freedom) and the defeat of the Taliban regime, the Bush administration turned its attention to Saddam Hussein and Iraq. The sequence of events and speeches leading up to the declaration of war against Iraq on 20 March 2003 were part of a well-orchestrated campaign to prepare the US public for the inevitability of conflict and to discredit the idea of a diplomatic solution. The invasion of Iraq was completed some six weeks later. On 1 May 2003, speaking on the deck of the aircraft carrier *Abraham Lincoln*, a triumphant Bush declared that the main part of the war in Iraq was now over. This was the point at which public support for the Bush administration's war against terror was at its highest. In November 2004 Bush won a second term in office. However, the tide of public opinion was beginning to turn. This was largely the result of two critical events: first, the furor that erupted in May 2004 over pictures showing the abuse of Iraqi prisoners in US custody at Abu Ghraib that forced President Bush and defense secretary Rumsfeld to apologize publicly for the mistreatment, and second, the publication in July 2004 of a Senate report saying that the US and its allies had gone to war in Iraq on "flawed" information. This was followed by an independent report into the September 11 attacks that high-lighted deep institutional failings in the intelligence services and government. In August 2005, the credibility of the Bush administration was further shaken by the floods that destroyed New Orleans following the devastation wrought by Hurricane Katrina. The levees, especially those protecting the poorest parts of town, were known to be too weak, and a program of repairs should have been completed, but the Department of Homeland Security had deflected the repair budget to pay for the war on terror. Although the government sought to portray those left homeless by the floods as "refugees," critics challenged that narrative, arguing instead that they were victims of political violence (Mesque-lier, 2006).

In November 2005, in the run up to elections in Iraq, President Bush made a series of four speeches to try to convince domestic audiences he had a plan and it was working well. The following year, President Bush made a similar series of speeches in the run-up to the US elections. It is against the backdrop of these events, and President Bush's attempts to mend the "legitimacy breaches" in his own regime, that we now turn to examine one of his speeches from each of these series in 2005 and 2006.

"Planning for Victory in Iraq": President Bush Addresses the Nation

On 30 November 2005, some 8,000 anthropologists were gathering at the Hilton Hotel in Washington for the 104th annual meeting of the American Anthropological Association. A short distance away, at the United States Naval Academy in Annapolis, Maryland, President George W. Bush was outlining his strategy for Victory in Iraq before an audience of US midshipmen, naval com-manders and academy personnel. Accompanying the president were the secre-tary of defense (and a "Navy aviator"), Donald Rumsfeld, and the chairman of the Senate Armed Services Committee, Senator John Warner. From our hotel, we sat watching the speech as it was broadcast live on TV, an experience tinged with both fascination and alarm. Like Saddam Hussein when he was president of Iraq, the American president had chosen to speak to the nation in his capac-ity as commander-in-chief of the armed forces, flanked by a disciplined audi-ence that could be guaranteed to give him a rapturous welcome. There was no risk of dissent from this captive audience.

After his opening joke about how pleased he was to have provided the assembled students with an excuse to miss class, Bush reminded them that this was the "first war of the 21st century" and part of "the global war on terror" being fought on many fronts, "from the streets of Western cities, to the moun-tains of Afghanistan, the islands of Southeast Asia and the Horn of Africa." The terrorists, he declared, had "made it clear that Iraq is the central front in their war against humanity" and "every man and woman who volunteers to defend our nation," he continued, "deserves an unwavering commitment."

Who exactly was this enemy? The president portrayed them as a combination of Sunni rejectionists, former regime loyalists ("Saddamists") and terrorists affiliated to al Qaeda and led by Abu Mussab al-Zarqawi.

Critics of the US invasion of Iraq had long rejected government and CIA attempts to link Saddam Hussein with al Qaeda. Against this, Bush warned that al-Zarqawi and his terrorists had "pledged allegiance to Osama bin Laden":

> Their objective is to drive the United States and coalition forces out of Iraq, and use the vacuum that would be created by an American retreat to gain control of that country. They would then use Iraq as a base from which to launch attacks against America, and overthrow moderate governments in the Middle East, and try to establish a totalitarian Islamic empire that reaches from Indonesia to Spain. (Bush, 2005)

Drawing on a centuries-old Orientalist narrative (Said, 1978) evoking fears of a resurgent Islamic empire overwhelming Christendom[5] and aiming for world domination, the president went on confidently to predict its inevitable failure on the grounds that "the will to power is no match for the universal desire to live in liberty (Applause)." Reiterating the link among Iraqi insurgency, the 9/11 attacks and other terrorist atrocities, and evoking the piracy discourse referred to above, he continued:

> The terrorists in Iraq share the same ideology as the terrorists who struck the United States on September the 11th. Those terrorists share the same ideology with those who blew up commuters in London and Madrid, murdered tourists in Bali, workers in Rhyadh, and guests at a wedding in Amman, Jordan. Just last week, they massacred Iraqi children and their parents at a toy give-away outside an Iraqi hospital. This is an enemy without conscience—and they cannot be appeased. If we were not fighting and destroying this enemy in Iraq, they would not be idle. They would be plotting and killing Americans across the world and within our own borders. (Bush, 2005)

In the remainder of his 43-minute speech the president went on to highlight two further planks of his Planning for Victory policy: the training of the Iraqi security forces to replace US troops on the streets and, related to this, the need to "stay the course" and not set any timetable for withdrawal, a decision that would be driven by "conditions on the ground . . . and the good judgment of our commanders—not by artificial timetables set by politicians in Washington (Applause)". This latter comment was in response to those Democrats and critics who were demanding the troops be brought home.

His closing remarks spoke of bringing "justice to our enemies" and the "unstoppable power of freedom" that would defeat the "hateful ideologies that use terror" He reminded his audience that "we" had "seen freedom conquer evil and secure the peace before," notably in Japan and Germany but also in the case of the Soviet Union during the Cold War. He also reminded them that war demands sacrifice:

> Many of you know comrades and classmates who left our shores to defend freedom and who did not live to make the journey home. We pray for the military families who mourn the loss of a loved one. We hold them in our hearts—and we honor the memory of every fallen soldier, sailor, airman, Coast Guardsman, and Marine. (Bush, 2005)

This was then exemplified by the case of Marine Corporal Jeff Staff, a "fallen hero" who had left a note on his laptop stating that it was an honor to die for such a noble cause as the fight for freedom against dictators and tyrants. Bush finished his oration, as though concluding a sermon, by thanking his audience for "wearing the uniform" and calling on God to bless you all and to bless the United States of America.

Beyond these ritual invocations of the military values of honor, patriotism, and service to one's country, the main theme of Bush's narrative is a story of a peaceful and reluctant "America" compelled to defend itself against an evil and fanatical enemy intent on "killing Americans" and imposing a "totalitarian Islamic empire." Bush evokes a figure called "America" by drawing on these lexical triggers for what Esch (2010, p. 358) identifies as the two main political myths at the heart of American political culture: "American Exceptionalism" (the idea that America has a unique role to play in the world) and "Civilization v. Barbarism" (the dualism that constructs American national identity against an "evil other"). However, what distinguishes Bush's approach to these tropes is his insistence that in order to combat global terror, "America" must suspend the rules of war (as well as civil rights) and embark unilaterally on an aggressive crusade to take the war to the enemies beyond its national borders.

"A War Unlike Any We Have Fought Before": President Bush's Oval Office Speech, September 2006

In our second example, Bush's speech from the Oval Office nearly a year later, on 9 September 2006, the fifth anniversary of the 9/11 attacks, the ritualistic, religious, and formalized structure of Bush's political oratory is even more pronounced. Here Bush appears not as commander-in-chief but as president, seated at an enormous polished wooden table and surrounded by the regalia of the presidential office. Dressed in a somber black suit with white shirt and red tie, he stares earnestly into the camera. Flanking him on either side of the table are two framed portraits of members of the Bush family: his two daughters, his wife, his mother and his father, George Bush senior. To his left hangs the draped flag of the United States and, to his right, the presidential seal and flag:

a spread-winged bald eagle surrounded by a circle of 50 stars. The semiotics of the scene ring loud and clear with the visual message that this president, who is clothed in the mantle of nationhood and addressing you from the Oval Office live on prime-time television, is also a loved and loving father, husband and son. The camera angle is also slightly offset so that these stars form an arc around the president's head, like a halo. The visual imagery is perfectly aligned to reinforce the key message of Bush's speech, an emotive call for Americans to rally in defense of family, nation and God.

Whereas the "Preparing for Victory in Iraq" speech moved from the jocular to the somber culminating in the sacred, this speech was pitched from the outset in the register of the reverential and the religious. Indeed, it had striking structural similarities to a Christian sermon. The key aim of this 17-minute speech was to evoke the memory of the September 11 victims in order to garner support for the war in Iraq. September 11 had been "seared into America's memory"; the attack had been "a barbarity unequalled in our history," directed against "the entire free world," and on "this solemn night" he had come "to discuss the nature of the threat still before us." Like his "Victory in Iraq" speech with its themes of "freedom," "threat" and "sacrifice", this also had three main messages ("threat," "civilization" and "sacrifice") and deployed simple binary oppositions that contrasted "Us" (American citizens, freedom-loving people, ordinary individuals who, when pushed, are capable of extraordinary feats, etc.) against "Them" (the terrorists, murderers, tyrants, zealots who would impose their fanatical Islamic creed on the whole world).

What We Saw on September 11, 2001: Our Nation Is Being Tested

> On 9/11, our nation saw the face of evil. Yet, on that awful day, we also witnessed something distinctly American: ordinary citizens rising to the occasion and responding with extraordinary courage. . . . We saw courage in passengers aboard Flight 93, who recited the 23rd Psalm—and then charged the cockpit. And we saw courage in the Pentagon staff who made it out of the flames and smoke—and ran back in to answer cries for help. (Bush, 2006)

Since 9/11, we had also learned more about the enemy. As the president summed up,

> We have learned that they are evil and kill without mercy, but not without purpose. We have learned that they form a global network of extremists driven by a perverted vision of Islam: a totalitarian ideology that hates freedom, rejects tolerance and despises all dissent. And we have learned that their goal is to build a radical Islamic empire where women are prisoners in their homes, men are beaten for missing prayer meetings, and terrorists have a safe haven. (Bush, 2006)

188   *Susan Wright and Cris Shore*

This idea of "being tested," which is repeated twice in the speech, recalls another Biblical theme (e.g., in the story of Job or in the story of Saint Peter). Although Bush sought to compare the present situation with the Cold War, he also emphasized how this threat was unlike anything encountered before: "The war against this enemy is more than a military conflict. It is the decisive ideological struggle of the 21st Century and the calling of our generation." This enemy is "determined to bring death and suffering into our homes" and if America did not defeat the extremists, the Middle East would be "overrun by terrorist states and radical dictators armed with nuclear weapons." These arguments are followed immediately with Bush's explanation of why "we" (i.e., the president and his government) have "resolved that we would go on the offense against our enemies and we would not distinguish between the terrorists and those who harbor or support them." This logic, it should be noted, recalls the principle of "collective punishment," which the Geneva Convention classifies as a war crime. Bush also reiterated his new defense doctrine of preemption, first expounded in his speech at West Point in June 2002, that is, that the "America must confront threats before they reach our shores" and has a right to launch preemptive strikes against countries that pose a potential threat.

A Struggle for Civilization

The elevation of the US occupation of Iraq to a war of historical and Biblical proportions is the second key theme of the speech. Bush makes a clear reference to Samuel P. Huntington's (1993) simplistic thesis that future conflicts in the world will be based on a clash of civilizations between Christianity and Islam. However, for Bush there is only one civilization:

> This struggle has been called a clash of civilizations. In truth, it is a struggle for civilization. We are fighting to maintain the way of life enjoyed by free nations. And we're fighting for the possibility that good and decent people across the Middle East can raise up societies based on freedom and tolerance and personal dignity. (Bush, 2006)

The Pax Americana is portrayed not only as the struggle for "dignity" and "freedom," but for "civilization" itself. Once again, Bush's oratory draws on a rich but highly selective set of cultural referents and collective historical memories: D-Day, Nazi Germany, Iwo Jima, Imperial Japan, Soviet aggression, Harry Truman, and the Berlin Wall. Iraq is depicted as simply the latest episode in a heroic quest by the leader of the free world, for liberty and justice against the forces of tyranny and oppression. Further Biblical imagery is used to emphasize this point when Bush tells his audience (in almost "eschatological" language) that

> America looks to the day when the people of the Middle East leave the desert of despotism for the fertile gardens of liberty . . . And when that

good day comes, the clouds of war will part, the appeal of radicalism will decline, and we will leave our children with a better and safer world. On this solemn anniversary, we rededicate ourselves to this cause. (Bush, 2006)

After quoting the words of a "proud mom" (RoseEllen Dowdell) whose husband was a victim of the 9/11 attacks and whose sons recently graduated from the US Army and the New York City Fire Academy, respectively, the speech ends on a crescendo of religious zeal as Bush proclaims, "Our nation is blessed to have young Americans like these" and that the terrorist attacks were "meant to bring us to our knees" but instead "Americans united in prayer." Calling on God to bless you all, he ends with the words "we go forward with trust in that spirit, confidence in our purpose, and faith in a loving God who made us to be free" (Bush, 2006).

Five Years After 9/11, Americans Are Safer—But We Are Not Yet Safe

The third "campaign" message is a warning to the American public that the clear and present danger to the nation (and, thus, the ongoing "state of emergency") will continue. In this part of the speech Bush outlined all the policy actions taken to protect the homeland from terrorists, including the creation of the Department of Homeland Security; the removal of privacy laws that kept law enforcement and secret intelligence services separated; the tightening of security screening at seaports, airports and borders and programs to allow increased use of covert phone tapping and the monitoring of "enemy bank records." These highly controversial measures—which were condemned by civil rights activists and undermined many of the previously accepted norms of liberal democracy—were glossed over as actions necessary to "give the men and women who protect us every resource and legal authority they need to do their jobs."

From a semiotic perspective of the Barthes (1957) kind, the structure of the speech has a compellingly simple logic: our nation—America—is fighting evil; this is a war for civilization itself; we are blessed by God with young Americans who are prepared to lay down their lives for their loved ones; I am your leader, a father, and I speak for you and for the memory of the 9/11 victims; my policies are making our land safe, but we are not safe yet.

Not surprisingly, the speech was widely condemned by the opposition Democrats. Their main complaint, however, was less against Bush's rhetoric than the apparent misuse of his incumbency to make party-political points on prime-time television during what should have been a bipartisan day of remembrance. As Senator Edward Kennedy expressed it,

The President should be ashamed of using a national day of mourning to commandeer the airwaves to give a speech that was designed not to unite the country and commemorate the fallen but to seek support for a war in Iraq that he has admitted had nothing to do with 9/11. (Kennedy, cited in Pickler, 2006)

Significantly, earlier that day US senators and members of Congress from both parties had put aside campaigning and joined on the steps of the Capitol to remember the attacks. They also sang "God Bless America" as they had five years earlier. By contrast, press reaction was more muted and skeptical. The *Washington Post* noted how the president's capacity to move the public had become severely diminished thanks to falsely optimistic predictions of progress. Despite the rhetoric of remembrance and overt attempts to recall the language Bush had invoked five years earlier when he united a stricken nation looking to him for both comfort and leadership, the *Post* concluded that "a majority of Americans question fundamental elements of the President's argument, including his contention that Iraq is the central front in the campaign against terrorism" (Balz and Abramowitz, 2006).

The *New York Times* went further, mocking Bush's assertions about the strength of democracy in Iraq as "delusional," adding that even if a strategy existed to stabilize a fractured, disintegrating country and end the violence, it was unlikely that Mr. Bush could see it "through the filter of his fantasies." "Iraq," it concluded, "had nothing to do with the war on terror until the Bush administration decided to invade it" (*New York Times*, 2006).

Interpreting Bush's Political Oratory

How should we analyze Bush's oratory and its meanings? How was he trying to interpellate his American audience? What tactics was he using to try to make his position hegemonic? In their work on "political oratory in traditional society," Bloch and Parry (1975) noted the highly formalized and ritualistic nature of certain forms of public speaking, and how traditional political leaders (particularly those whose authority depends on their oratorical abilities) typically attempt to imbue their oratory with symbolic forms and linguistic protocols that have a particular cultural, historical, emotional and religious saliency for the society in question. The effect of these "formalized codes," as Bloch and Parry call them, is to create a form of "linguistic ritual" in which both speaker and audience enter into a culturally sanctioned and well-choreographed set of speech acts and responses, somewhat akin, perhaps, to the relationship formed between a charismatic preacher and an audience of believers. By tapping into this repository of key symbols and culturally charged references the speaker is able to shift the discourse from the mundane and everyday to the plane of the sacred and the universal in which speakers and listeners are obliged to draw upon a very limited—and highly ritualized—set of images, metaphors and references. One of the consequences of this is to bind the listeners to the speaker and to strengthen the latter's authority by rendering opposition virtually impossible (because one cannot legitimately argue against the "proper"—or sacred— order of things).

Analysis of the rhetorical strategies used in such ritual occasions enables us to see more clearly how Bush uses genres, narratives and metaphors to interpellate his audience. He deploys many of the features of what in Aristo-telian rhetoric is termed an "epideictic genre," that is, a form of address asso-ciated with ritual occasions, in which contemporary events are set within a longer view of the past and the future and are explained in terms of the values and behaviors that should be praised or blamed. Thus, Bush enjoins his fellow Americans to reflect on what they are witnessing, and commemorate the virtues they hold dear. This genre harnesses emotional attachments to personal and shared cultural values, rather than logic or reason. Success depends on making a persuasive appeal that draws on the ethos of the speaker, whose words incar-nate the virtues that inspire the community. To engender his audience's trust (and his ethos appeal), Bush relies heavily on pathos (the audience's feelings for the topic). As we illustrate in the following, he does this by drawing on two key narratives; those of "piracy" and "security."

We Must Fight for Justice and Freedom Against an Enemy Without Conscience

The first major narrative constructs a stark "us" versus "them" dualism. The evil and immorality of the enemy (who would go to any lengths, including the massacre of women and children and the bombing of hospitals to advance their nefarious ambitions), is contrasted with the humanity and nobility of "our" soldiers and those heroic Iraqi volunteers fighting for Iraq's freedom. Bush seems to address the terrorists directly when he promises "America will find you, and we will bring you to justice"—but a form of justice appropriate to his new category of "unlawful enemy combatant" (aka pirate), who is not given the protection of codes of conduct of war or entitled to civil justice. His reassuring message to the American public is that the terrorists in captivity have been transferred to Guantanamo Bay, "so they can be held to account for their actions." This discourse of "justice and freedom" is steeped in "Ameri-can Exceptionalism" (Esch, 2010)—the US image of itself as global sheriff whose long reach will bring liberty and the rule of law to those parts of the world where lawlessness prevails (and buttresses the often unspoken beliefs that, in a lawless society, one may go beyond the limits of "due process" and that "might is right"). This narrative is also linked to the popular notion (highly prevalent during the Cold War) that the United States is engaged in a global struggle for freedom against the forces of totalitarianism. First, it was British colonialism, then German and Japanese fascism, then the threat of Soviet communism, and now Islamic extremism and terrorism. All of these historical battles represent episodes in the ongoing struggle between good and evil. Using strong visual images and metaphors, Bush proclaims there is only one "good," one civilization; al Qaeda and the Islamic people and states where they are found are not only evil but beyond civilization—they become pirates. Bush looks to the day when the "people of the Middle East" will leave the desert and join the fenced gardens of civilization. Combining the narrative of piracy with the myth of American Exceptionalism, the Bush administration gave its own distinctive twist to the idea that the United States has a responsibility (perhaps even a "manifest destiny") to intervene on the world stage in order to "defend freedom" and "export democracy" wherever these are believed to be at risk.

Homeland Security: We Must Defend Our Nation Against the Forces of Terror

In the wake of 9/11, "homeland security" became the chosen motif under which US internal security efforts were to be organized. The choice of the word "homeland," with its inclusionary and exclusionary connotations, was significant. The idea of the motherland under attack is one that has been promulgated repeatedly by the Bush administration to justify its more pro-active policy of "preemptive strikes" against suspected terrorists, or what is termed "bringing the war to the terrorists." The discourse is highly gendered, with mothers associated with motherland and domestic security. Hence, the choice of the phrase "homeland security" rather than "homeland defense" was also significant. Whereas "defense" implies a known threat that, armed or standing on the ramparts (or levees?), one can repel or defend oneself against, "security" denotes an unknown danger against which one must mobilize to pre-empt or deter (Fosher, 2009, p. xx). This narrative is presented through metaphors not only of motherland, homeland and security but also of repeated references to homes, shores, and harbors. These metaphors are made relevant and substantial when Bush's 2006 speech ends with reference to a real mother and her sacrifice via the service of her sons for homeland security.

Bush's Ethos Appeal

Through his accounts of the issues facing the country (his pathos appeal) he depicts himself as displaying the virtues and values that accord with those of his imagined audience. He is ready for a fight, while also being a Christian—a combination that took on negative connotations when he explicitly used the term *crusader*. On his shoulders rest the virtues of freedom and justice that will stand up against the illegitimacy and ruthlessness of a (partly) boundariless global terror and (partly) the "Middle Eastern" site of timeless threats to western civilization. But he does not just don a combat jacket or a leather flying suit; he also represents himself as the father surrounded by pictures of his family. Using the topoi that associate father with leader, he projects himself as the father/president and commander-in-chief who has taken on the obligation to defend all mothers in making safe their motherland. He successfully monopolizes the domain of homeland security in a way that is difficult to contest or oppose. His speeches focus on the ethos he draws of himself and of the space where he thinks he meets his audience. Having set up that ethos in his early speeches, he has to act in accordance with it in his later speeches. However, by that time its virtuous foundations are undermined by controversies over government deception ("dodgy dossiers"), illegal practices (extraordinary rendition) and human rights violations (including waterboarding and the torture of prisoners at Abu Ghraib prison)—which increasingly resemble the piracy and evil that he/America had pledged to defeat.

President Obama's Narrative of America: War and Homeland Security

Contrary to Bush, the narrative of "America" in Obama's presidential speeches had a far less belligerent, apocalyptic or Orientalist tone. Of central importance, "America" is not defined in opposition to a lawless, ruthless "other" that reflexively implies America's virtues. Instead, American values are set out without an external referent. Obama's first State of the Union address on 24 February 2009 struck a note of optimism and outlined an ambitious agenda for economic recovery through investment. Standing before a large US flag, he proclaimed the "day of reckoning has arrived"—which he meant in accountancy rather than eschatological terms—and now was the time "to build a new foundation for lasting prosperity" (Obama, 2009a). The main theme of his speech was the US economy and the need for America to "pull together" and "take responsibility for our future once more." Like many of Bush's speeches, he evoked the idea of a "covenant" with the American people, only this time in the form of a "promise to the children of America" that every child will have "access to a complete and competitive education": "This is a promise we have to make to the children of America." The emphasis on education is underpinned by its economic utility and the recognition that "countries that out-teach us today will out-compete us tomorrow." Describing his recovery plan as "a vision for America" and "a blueprint for our future," he set out an ambitious new goal: "By 2020, America will once again have the highest proportion of college graduates in the world."

As with many of Bush's key speeches, Obama singled out the military for praise. Americans, he declared to rapturous applause and a standing ovation, "are united in sending out one message: we honor your service; we are inspired by your sacrifice; and you have our unyielding support" (Obama, 2009a). This prefaced his announcement of increases in the number of soldiers and Marines and a pay rise for the military and health care for veterans "to keep our sacred trust with those who serve." However, unlike Bush, Obama's message on foreign policy was a call for more international diplomacy and consensus ("we cannot shun the negotiating table"). He concluded with a call for national unity by citing an inspirational example of local heroism of a South Carolina school-child and her determination to raise funds to rebuild her decrepit school: her message, "we are not quitters" provides a segue for Obama's message that the "American people expect us to build common ground" (Obama, 2009a).

Obama's "Troop Surge" Speech, December 2009

A direct comparison can be made between President Bush's speech at Annapolis and President Obama's televised speech delivered in December 2009 to the US cadets at the West Point Military Academy. In this speech, Obama announced his plan to send 30,000 additional US troops to Afghanistan and then start withdrawing them in July 2011. Even in this speech to announce the escalation of war, rather than defining America in opposition to the supposed characteristics of the enemy, he focused on amplifying the themes of national unity and military sacrifice seen in his previous speech. Speaking of the responsibility he felt as commander-in-chief, he set out the case that Islamist extremism in the region remains an enduring threat to American security. This speech was among the most important of his presidency, as he sought to prepare the country for heavier fighting and higher casualties in the months ahead. The speech was largely a technical explication of his strategy and a reminder of the reasons why the US had taken up arms against the Taliban ("a ruthless, repressive and radical movement that had seized control of the country"). The troop surge would build capacity to enable "a responsible transition of our forces out of Afghanistan" and "to prevent a cancer from once again spreading through that country." Only toward the end of his speech did he shift register by eulogizing the character and resilience of the American people:

> America will speak out on behalf of their human rights, and tend to the light of freedom and justice and opportunity and respect for the dignity of all peoples. That is who we are. That is the source, the moral source of America's authority. (Obama, 2009b)

Addressing the US public beyond the hall, he declared, "we are still heirs to a noble struggle for freedom" (ibid.). The United States, he added, had "underwritten global security for over six decades" and

> unlike the great powers of old, we have not sought world domination. Our union was founded in resistance to oppression. We do not seek to occupy other nations. We will not claim another nation's resources or target other peoples because their faith or ethnicity is different from ours. (ibid.)

The setting for Obama's speech had striking parallels to Bush's "Strategy for victory in Iraq" address. Like Bush, he stands between the US eagle symbol and the US flag, facing an audience of smartly uniformed military cadets. But whereas Bush sought to rally the nation for a crusade-like war against terrorists and foreign enemies, Obama adopts a more placatory tone, reminding the audience of the need for diplomacy, partnership and building alliances—even with the Muslim world—rather than unilateralism. He also emphasizes the link between economic and military security:

Our prosperity provides a foundation for our power. It pays for our military. It underwrites our diplomacy. It taps the potential of our people, and allows investment in new industry. And it will allow us to compete in this century as successfully as we did in the last. That's why our troop commitment in Afghanistan cannot be open-ended—because the nation that I am most interested in building is our own. (ibid.)

Like Bush, Obama also ends by invoking the national virtues of resilience and determination, and locates the present as a period in which America is being "tested":

America—we are passing through a time of great trial. And the message that we send in the midst of these storms must be clear: that our cause is just, our resolve unwavering. We will go forward with the confidence that right makes might, and with the commitment to forge an America that is safer, a world that is more secure, and a future that represents not the deepest of fears but the highest of hopes. (Applause)

Thank you. God bless you. God bless our troops. May God bless the United States of America. (Applause) (ibid)

There are important differences from Bush, not just by twisting "might is right" into "right is might," but in seeking security not only for America but also the world, and a future not based on sustained fear, but on the keyword from his election campaign, hope.

Obama's 2012 State of the Union Address

From the point of view of the work of metaphor and narrative in presidential oratory, President Obama's State of the Union address three years later is one of his most interesting public speeches (2012a). It is also one in which the metaphors of "homeland," "security" and "America" all feature prominently, words also used frequently by Bush, but to different effect.

Obama begins by reminding his audience of his foreign policy successes: welcoming home US troops from Iraq, eradicating Osama Bin Laden and other top Al Qaeda leaders and military victories against the Taliban in Afghanistan. This provides the platform for developing the two main themes of his speech: a tribute to the heroism of the armed forces on the one hand, and a eulogy about the importance of working together as a "team" to overcome the threats and obstacles facing the American nation. Those foreign policy achievements were

a testament to the courage, selflessness, and teamwork of America's Armed Forces. At a time when too many of our institutions have let us down, they exceed all expectations. They're not consumed with personal ambition. They don't obsess over their differences. They focus on the mission at hand. They work together. (Obama, 2012a)

What we see here is an explicit emphasis on the army and its values as a model for US society. With echoes of John F. Kennedy's famous 1961 inauguration speech ("Ask not what your country can do for you"), Obama uses the history of US combat to tell a story about the importance of teamwork, cooperation and a shared vision that transcends party politics. Like his 2009 State of the Union address discussed earlier, the main themes of this speech were the US economy and delivering America from recession through a plan of strategic government investment to reinvigorate the country's industrial base to create "an America built to last." This metaphor evokes a golden age when the US led the world as a manufacturer of industrial goods—a position that (by implication) the Bush administration had squandered through its costly wars, short-termism and narrow self-interest. Against this selfishness, Obama projects a message of national unity: "from the coalitions we've built to secure nuclear materials, to the missions we've led against hunger and disease . . . to the enduring power of our moral example, America is back." But unlike the Bush era, this is "an America built to last [that] insists on responsibility from everybody" (Obama, 2012a).

Towards the end of the speech, he shifts register to celebrate American values, particularly those that are embodied in the US military. Once again, the military are singled out for special praise:

Above all, our freedom endures because of the men and women in uniform who defend it. As they come home, we must serve them as well as they served us. That includes giving them the care and benefits they have earned—which is why we've increased annual VA spending every year I've been President. And it means enlisting our veterans in the work of rebuilding our Nation. (ibid.)

Whereas Bush's references to the US military typically serve to justify violence and promote "militarism"—that "tense social process in which civil society organizes itself for the production of violence" (Lutz, 2002, p. 723)—Obama's speeches convey a different narrative; one in which the army becomes a symbol for unity and the nation pulling together.

Obama's Rhetorical Appeal

Obama's speeches engage his audience in a very different way to those of Bush. They create what we have called a policy narrative (Shore & Wright, 1997, p. 15), one that gives an account of the past to define a problem of the present in such a way that it posits one and only one solution for the future. To convey this policy narrative, Obama uses a less epideictic and more deliberative genre and adopts a more pedagogic tone. In his 2009 State of the Union speech (2009a), for example, he spends the first half carefully explaining the causes of the weak economy and how to increase oversight, combat waste and fraud, get credit flowing and increase employment. He continues with the same "logos" appeal in the second half by going on to explain the problems with energy, health care and education and the solutions to those problems. He repeatedly refers to causes, facts and truth, which he presents in a straightforward, reasoned way. In presenting his well-reasoned positions, Palaima (2009) suggests that Obama is moving the meaning of "argument" away from "controversy" and towards its root of "making things clear." Palaima refers to Obama's "feeling tone" through which he appeals to his audience: "He is an 'I' who is part of the 'we' who see large problems in life and choose the hard work and personal sacrifice it takes to try and solve them" (2009, p. 38). This feeling tone is conveyed not just through his words but the "total, spontaneous, involuntary expressiveness that can't be faked" (Palaima, 2009, p. 35). He seems relaxed and dignified and appears willing to be honest, to be "real" with a sense of common decency. In contrast, Bush never achieved a convincing "feeling tone": Palaima, quoting Lewis Black, says, "When he speaks, his words don't match his face. Something is askew"—he talks about the war with a "fraternity-brother smirk" whereas he should at least mimic somber concern (2009, p. 39). Palaima attributes Obama's feeling tone to his acquisition of the political art of making an instantaneous calculation of immediate and long term interests, and then choosing measured words to suit the moment—or in Cato's aphorism, "Grasp the matter; the words will follow." This gives Obama a presence of candid and relaxed self-containment" (Palaima, 2009, p. 35).

Obama's "ethos" appeal arises not just from the delivery but also from the construction of his speeches. In his 2009 State of the Union speech, in each phase of setting out his argument about the cause of problems and the route to solutions, he wove in an ethos appeal to "America" as the space he shares with his audience. For example, he says it will be possible to get out of current difficulties because "This is America. We don't do what's easy. We do what's necessary to move this country forward." At times he refers to "a responsibility we have to our children"; at other times he hits an abstract note: "We are a nation that has . . . claimed opportunity from ordeal. We must be that nation again" or "America does not torture" (Obama, 2009a). Obama presents the values he stands for and shares with his audience not as everlasting moral values, but as ones reinforced by practical wisdom (phronesis) on which to build a renewed "America."

This "America" is not set in opposition to any external "Axis of Evil." Indeed, Obama's speech in Cairo in June 2009 (Obama, 2009c) marked a break with the western construction of itself through portraying the evils of the Orientalist "other": "I have come here to seek a new beginning between the United States and Muslims around the world; one based upon mutual interest and mutual respect . . . This cycle of suspicion and discord must end." To make the point even clearer, "I consider it part of my responsibility as President of the United States to fight against negative stereotypes of Islam wherever they appear . . . That is what it means to share this world in the 21st century. That is the responsibility we have to one another as human beings" (ibid).

Nor does Obama's "America" arise from Bush's everlasting national character traits. Rather, Obama is highlighting political values from America's past that need resurrecting and rebuilding to form a social and political economy that will fulfill this vision of the future. This he develops in the 2012 State of the Union speech (Obama, 2012a). This "America," which leads the world in educating its people, attracting high-tech jobs, controls its own energy, security and prosperity, is "within our reach" and will "win the race for the future." It depends on keeping alive the "basic American promise" of rewarding hard work and responsibility. Instead of a society in which the incomes of a shrinking number at the top rise as never before while hardworking Americans barely get by, the "America built to last" depends on "restoring an economy where everyone gets a fair shot, everyone does their fair share, and everyone plays by the same set of rules." These he claims are not party political but "American" values. "Americans," he later says, "know it's not right" for some to get tax breaks that seniors, students and struggling families have to pay for. And "they know" that "past generations felt a responsibility to each other, and to their country's future, and they know our way of life will only endure if we feel that same sense of responsibility." He refers to the project of building "an America to last" as a battle (having ended the real wars in Iraq and planned the end of the Afghanistan war) and extends the metaphor by "learning from the service of our troops." They do not think about politics, or themselves, but just their mission, united by a clear vision, teamwork and comradeship. Once again, the military are singled out for special praise and the "service of our troops" becomes a model that the rest of society "can learn from":

> When you put on that uniform, it doesn't matter if you're black or white; Asian or Latino; conservative or liberal; rich or poor; gay or straight. When you're marching into battle, you look out for the person next to you, or the mission fails. When you're in the thick of the fight, you rise or fall as one unit, serving one Nation, leaving no one behind. (Obama, 2012a)

Obama tells his audience that one of his proudest possessions is the flag that the US Navy SEAL team took with them on the mission to get Osama bin Laden. On it each Marine had put his signature. And on that day, no one thought about politics or about themselves: all that mattered was the mission. He ends, "So it is with America":

> Each time I look at that flag, I'm reminded that our destiny is stitched together like those fifty stars and those thirteen stripes. No one built this

country on their own. This Nation is great because we built it together. This Nation is great because we worked as a team. This Nation is great because we get each other's backs. And if we hold fast to that truth, in this moment of trial, there is no challenge too great; no mission too hard. (Obama, 2012a)

This projection of an America based on opportunity, cooperation, a strong middle class and a "relentless focus on the future" as "both morally right and good economics," as against the Republican "alternative universe" where "every politician wants every voter to believe he was born in a log cabin he built himself" was the focus of Bill Clinton's (2012) speech nominating Obama as the Democratic presidential candidate for a second term. Accepting that nomination, Obama (2012b) repeated much of the argument, even the same phrases, from his State of the Union address. America honors individual initiative, "the strivers, the dreamers, the risk-takers . . . the engine of growth and prosperity" but "we also accept . . . certain obligations to each other and to future generations." This he calls "citizenship." "As citizens, we understand that America is not about what can be done for us. It's about what can be done by us, together, through the hard and frustrating but necessary work of self-government. So you see, the election four years ago wasn't about me. It was about you. My fellow citizens—you were the change." In his inaugural address the reelected president makes a further shift and now addresses not "America," or "fellow citizens," but "we, the people." In setting out his political vision of liberal democracy, he simultaneously shifts his own position in relation to his audience. Whereas he starts by ventriloquizing about what "America" thinks or believes, he starts his second term by locating himself with his audience in a shared space, a renewed "we" based on empathy, where "the preserving of our individual freedoms ultimately requires collective action."

Conclusion

The questions posed at the beginning were how have presidents Bush and Obama used narratives and metaphors about war and national security in speeches made on ceremonial occasions? And in particular, how have they sought to interpellate their audiences and mobilize public support? To a large extent, the answer appears to lie in the persuasive rhetoric of their oratory. According to Althusser's (1971) theory of identity-formation, "interpellation" is a process by which individuals are "hailed" within an ideologically structured field, and thereby acquire their self-awareness as subjects and as actors positioned in appropriate social roles. One need not necessarily agree with Althusser's deterministic views about "ideological and repressive state apparatuses" to appreciate that certain discourses can exert a powerful influence in shaping subjectivities. Both Bush's and Obama's speeches also exemplify the way "formalized codes" work to shift the register onto the plane of the sacred.

Bush's doctrine of "preemptive attack" was skillfully portrayed in terms of a "clash of civilizations" between "free nations" and an organized network of Al Qaeda extremists "who will kill all those that stand in the way of their totalitarian ideology." But there is a striking difference in how, rhetorically, the two presidents created an ethos appeal and invoked a sense of trust in the speaker. Bush built up imagery of a leader/father figure enabling the motherland to be made secure against an everlasting threat from ruthless, irrational and puritanical Middle Easterners bent on devastation and mayhem. This rhetorical strategy worked for a surprisingly long time, but ultimately he could not sustain the virtuous figure he drew of himself against the reports of dodgy dossiers, torture and actions that undermined the very American values he purported to stand for. In contrast, Obama announced a clear break with divisive discourses (and wars) whether abroad or at home and presented himself as reasoning his way towards a new American political economy and a society based on empathy and resurrected values of liberal democracy. He invokes trust by a relaxed gravitas and appearance of speaking honestly, as if there is nothing "dodgy" about his administration.

The heroic figure of the "citizen-soldier" features prominently in the speeches of both Bush and Obama, and for both presidents the armed forces are used to symbolize the virtues and values of American society. However, they take different lessons from these virtues and their images of "America" are quite different. For Bush, the armed forces are a signifier of an abstract idea of national unity and cohesion, where valor is found in the exceptional virtues exhibited in dire circumstances by ordinary people, as if it is an innate quality of Americans. Although Obama always praises the virtues of members of the services who are "in harm's way," for him the armed forces are an exemplar of the characteristics of focusing on the mission for America rather than on private profit and for constructing relations of empathy and solidarity—watching each other's backs—that are at the core of his liberal democratic vision of an America built to last. This metaphor is maybe not surprising, because the army is one of the few institutions of US society in which social citizenship is realized in practice and in which individuals can enjoy the rights and benefits of secure employment, medical care and a pension (at least while they remain in uniform).

Both presidents also draw on Biblical imagery, but they do so in different ways. Obama often fixes his audience's attention by using the techniques of preachers in African-American churches. He quotes and appropriates lines from the Bible, just as he does from the rhythms and refrains of famous blues songs and the speeches of Martin Luther King (Palaima, 2009). Bush, in contrast, drew on the lexicon of evangelical Christianity and eschatology to describe the "war on terror." Curiously, fundamentalist Protestants share with some strands of Shia Islam (e.g., found in the speeches of President Ahmadinejad of Iran) an excitement over mayhem that might herald the end of the world and the return of the messiah or the hidden imam. In Bush's case, repeated Biblical references to the Apocalypse, Rapture and Armageddon helped to lift a materialist and secular policy agenda onto the realm of the sacred. They also normalized and naturalized the discourse of terror. For example, it has become commonplace even among critical observers to treat the phrase "war on terror" as an unproblematic given. As Diane Nelson (2003, p. 21) points out, "terror is not a thing but a relationship." The more appropriate question to ask is "terrifying for whom?" Like "homeland security," the "war on terror" is a semantic sleight of hand that gives unity, fixity and concreteness to a set of processes and relationships that are dis-united, fluid and abstract.

If Bush's use of religious discourse helped to normalize the war on terror, it also had inherent weaknesses. His rhetoric about living with continual fear drew on the central dilemma of perpetual uncertainty about one's salvation with which Fundamental Christians live (Gould, 2006). But this worldview, when presented from the position of the president, undermines a central tenet about the role of the secular state. To argue for a perpetual state of emergency in a war that can never be won is to admit that the state can never regain control of the means of organized violence or secure the safety of its citizens. All the state can do is advocate vigilance and keep everyone on "orange alert." The Marxist critic Walter Benjamin (1968) once wrote that the " 'state of emergency' in which we live is not the exception but the rule" (p. 257). We suggest (perhaps more optimistically than Benjamin) that although the "state of emergency" principle is indeed a much-used tool of contemporary governance, the hegemony required to maintain such a state cannot be easily sustained in the longer term.

One of the most notable effects of the "war on terror" has been to increase the capacity of the state to intervene in the lives of ordinary citizens. In this respect, "combating terror" also serves as a useful instrument for "governing *through* terror." As Elaine Scarry (2002) writes, speed has repeatedly been invoked by governments over the past 50 years to centralize power, counter ethical, legal or constitutional objections, and sidestep the democratic process in the United States. Historians would no doubt point to other examples of this, such as the anticommunist witch hunts and "red-scares" that were engineered by Richard Nixon and other Republicans during the McCarthy era.

Whereas Obama distanced himself from Bush's "national security" rhetoric that became the dominant political discourse post 9/11, one continuity, despite appearances, is that Obama has not dismantled the security apparatus of the PATRIOT Act. Obama stated clearly from the start that he would not allow torture and it seems that rendition of prisoners to other countries that allow torture has now ended. Obama announced the closure of Guantanamo Bay and has been able to blame Congress for not carrying that out. Apart from these publicized policies, the practices permitted by the PATRIOT Act have quietly continued. The secret services still have their expanded roles that undermine many of America's civil liberties. Overseas, the Obama administration has vastly increased the use of drones for extralegal killings and to terrorize populations in Afghanistan, Pakistan and Yemen (Stanford Law School/NYU, 2012;

Reprieve, 2013). In a recent US Department of Justice White Paper, government lawyers asserted that the government need not have specific intelligence that an American citizen is actively engaged in a terror plot in order to "be cleared for targeted killing" (Scahill, 2013) and several US citizens have now been assassinated in US overseas "targeted killing operations" (Wolf, 2013). "Hypothetically" according to Attorney General Eric Holder, the president can also order drone attacks on US territory (Calamur, 2013). Rhetorically, Obama has shifted the focus to rebuilding America's political society and economy, taking attention away from governing through terror. But in the face of the mounting public criticism of the terror brought to civilians by drone attacks, it is unlikely that Obama's administration can sustain the reputation for honesty it once enjoyed.

What our case studies illustrate is that despite differences in ethos and register, there are striking similarities in the narratives used by Bush and Obama to construct their vision of America. Both draw on an exalted ideal of the "citizen-soldier" who, like Captain Tom Miller in *Saving Private Ryan*, epitomizes the "American" soldierly virtues of loyalty, heroism, self-sacrifice and duty to one's country. In the case of Bush, that narrative combined with the discourses of national security, and "state of emergency" and a new political doctrine of pre-emption, easily triumphed over rival discourses of civil liberties and diplomacy. That triumph also owed much to the mobilization of rhetorics about risk and danger, as well as to patriotism, xenophobia and republican populism. Although antiforeigner sentiments and Islamophobia also helped to mobilize many Americans behind the Bush administration, it was the narrative of "homeland security" and "our nation at war" that sanctified the PATRIOT Act and against which oppositional voices struggled to be heard. Like policy in general, the PATRIOT Act bound together a wide variety of actors, institutions and agendas in new and ambiguous relationships as subjects of terror. However, although gaining institutional authority is an important aspect of hegemony, it is not the whole story. As both the Bush and Obama speeches show, hegemony is a continually contested process of trying to assert one's way of seeing and defining problems in ways that then prescribe certain actions in order to produce particular outcomes. Even when a dominant position has been made authoritative its hegemony is not assured. If the formalized codes that Bush drew on after 9/11 succeeded in interpellating the American public and making war in Iraq seem like the only viable course of action, by 2005 the rising death toll of American troops in Iraq and Afghanistan and the botched relief operation after Hurricane Katrina had dramatically reduced the appeal of that narrative. Thereafter, Bush struggled to make his view of the world hegemonic as Obama successfully contested the meanings that Bush had sought to attribute to the symbolic keywords of US presidential oratory, from *liberty*, *freedom* and *democracy* to *civilization* and *the rule of law*. The art of interpellation and hegemony, it would seem, lies in successfully claiming the "title deeds" to these master symbols, while also sustaining an ethos appeal, a sense of trust and shared values with the audience. But, as Bush's presidency clearly demonstrated, and as we are perhaps seeing the first signs in Obama's, the power of political oratory and the spell it may cast over the American public has a limited life span.

Notes

1 We wish to thank Signe Pildal Hansen for reading an early draft of this chapter and giving us the benefit of her expertise in rhetorical analysis, as well as several useful references.
2 Between August 2002 and January 2003, Cris Shore and his family lived in Cambridge, Massachusetts. This was the period prior to the start of Operation Iraqi Freedom and the full-scale bombing of Iraq on 20 March 2003, during which American public opinion was being primed for war.
3 Turner (1967, p. 20) suggests we can work out the structure and properties of rituals using three classes of data: First, the external form and observable characteristics; second, the interpretations offered by specialists and laypeople; and, third, the "significant contexts," which are largely worked out by the anthropologist.
4 Other aspects of an anthropology of policy include the ways policies, often via "political technologies," try to refashion institutions, their professions and the subjectivities of clients and citizens; how such processes are contested, with multiple perspectives entering into the ways the institutions and figures on the political landscape are continually reimagined and enacted; and how, out of such a process of contestation, new forms of governance emerge.
5 This is a recurrent and ancient discourse about "infidels" overrunning Christendom, stemming from alarm that, within 100 years of the founding of Islam, the caliphate had conquered an empire from Spain to Persia. Christendom responded with the Crusades and ultimately by expelling the Moors from Spain, but the discourse makes Islam into the expansionist and cruel aggressor and paints Europe as the civilized victim. Perhaps the strongest trope in this discourse is "The Gates of Vienna," when the new Ottoman-Turk empire tried to capture Vienna, the capital of the Holy Roman Empire in the heart of Europe. Two attempts in 1529 and 1566 failed. Then in 1683, the Ottomans with 250,000 troops laid siege to Vienna and settled in a luxurious tent camp outside the city walls. Before going into battle, the Polish military leader John Sobieski, addressed his 60,000 Christian fighters: "It is not a city alone that we have to save, but the whole of Christianity, of which the city of Vienna is the bulwark. This war is a holy one." The Muslim army was routed, but ever since, "the Gates of Vienna" has been used to denote the fear that Islam could overrun Christendom. Retrieved from www.crf-usa.org/bria/bria20_1b.htm.

References

Althusser, L. (1971). *Lenin and philosophy*. London: New Left Books.
Asad, T. (1979). Anthropology and the analysis of ideology. *Man* (NS), *14*(4), 607–627.
Bacchi, C. (2009). *Analyzing policy: What is the policy represented to be?* Frenchs Forest, New South Wales, Australia: Pearson.
Ball, T., Farr, J. & Hanson, R. (Eds.). (1989). *Political innovation and conceptual change*. Cambridge: Cambridge University Press.
Balz, D. & Abramowitz, M. (2006, September 12). President tries to win over a war-weary nation. *Washington Post*, p. A17. Retrieved from www.washingtonpost.com/wpdyn/content/article/2006/09/11/AR2006091101416.html

Barker, M. & Breezer, A. (1983). The language of racism—an examination of Lord Scarman's report on the Brixton riots. *International Socialism, 2*(18), 108–125.

Barthes, R. (1957). *Mythologies.* London: Paladin.

Benjamin, W. (1968 [1940]). *Theses on the Philosophy of History reprinted in his Illuminations.* New York: Schocken Books.

Bloch, M., & Parry, J. (Eds.). (1975). *Language and oratory in traditional society.* London: Academic Press.

Bourdieu, P. (1977). *Outline of a theory of practice.* Cambridge: Cambridge University Press.

Bush, G. W. (2001, October 26). Remarks by the president at signing of the Patriot Act [Press Release]. Retrieved from www.whitehouse.gov/news.releases/2001/10/print/20011026–5.html

———. (2005). President outlines strategy for victory in Iraq, United States Naval Academy, Annapolis, Maryland [Press release]. Washington, DC: The White House. Retrieved from www.whitehouse.gov/news/releases/2005/11/print/20051130–2.html

———. (2006). The Fifth Anniversary of September 11, 2001, US President's Address to the Nation [Press release]. Washington, DC: The White House. Retrieved from www.whitehouse.gov/news/releases/2006/09/print/200609011–2.html

Calamur, K. (2013, March 6). Holder: President could order drone strike inside US. *Reader Supported News.* Retrieved from http://readersupportednews.org/news-section2/345-justice/16347-focus-holder-president-could-order-drone-strike-inside-us

Clinton, B. (2012, September 5). Transcript of Bill Clinton's speech to the Democratic National Convention. Retrieved from www.nytimes.com/2012/09/05/us/politics/transcript-of-bill-clintons-speech-to-the-democratic-national-convention.html?pagewanted=all&_r=0

Esch, J. (2010). Legitimizing the "war on terror": Political myth in official-level rhetoric. *Political Psychology, 31*(3), 357–391.

Feldman, G. (2005). Culture, State, and Security in Europe: The Case of Citizenship and Integration Policy in Estonia. *American Ethnologist, 32*(4), 676–695.

Fosher, K. (2009). *Under construction: Making homeland security at the local level.* Chicago: University of Chicago Press.

Geertz, C. (1973). Thick description: Toward an interpretive theory of culture. In *The interpretation of cultures* (pp. 3–30). New York: Basic Books.

Geertz, C. (1983). *Local knowledge: Further essays in interpretive anthropology.* New York: Basic Books.

Gould, C. (2006). *Fear in America* (Unpublished Ph.D. thesis). University of Birmingham, England.

Gramsci, Antonio (1971). *Selections from the Prison Notebooks.* New York: International Publishers.

Huntington, S.P. (1993 Summer). The clash of civilizations? *Foreign Affairs, 72*(3), 22–49.

Kapferer, B. (2005). Situations, crisis, and the anthropology of the concrete. The contribution of Max Gluckman, *Social Analysis, 49*(3): 85–122.

Kruglanski, A. W., Crenshaw, M., Post, J. M., & Victoroff, J. (2008). What should this fight be called? Metaphors of counterterrorism and their implications, *Psychological Science in the Public Interest, 8*(3), 97–133.

Lakoff, G. (1991). (Part 1 of 2) Metaphor and war: The metaphor system used to justify war in the gulf. *Viet Nam Generation Journal and Newsletter, 3*(3). Retrieved from www2. iath.virginia.edu/sixties/HTML_docs/Texts/Scholarly/Lakoff_Gulf_Metaphor_1. html; (Part 2 of 2) Metaphor and war: The metaphor system used to justify war in the gulf.?*Viet Nam Generation Journal and Newsletter, 3*(3). Retrieved from www2. iath.virginia.edu/sixties/HTML_docs/Texts/Scholarly/Lakoff_Gulf_Metaphor_2.html

Lakoff, G. (2013). Obama Reframes Syria: Metaphor and War Revisited. Huffington Post, 9 June. Retrieved February 2, 2013, from www.huffingtonpost.com/george-lakoff/obama-reframes-syria-meta_b_3879335.html

Lardner, George (2001, November 16). On left and right, concern over anti-terrorism moves. *Washington Post*.

Lloyd-Jones, D. (1981). The art of Enoch Powell: the rhetorical structure of a speech on immigration. In R. Paine (Ed.), *Politically speaking.* (pp. 87–111). Philadelphia: Institute for the Study of Human Issues.

Lutz, C. (2002). Making war at home in the United States: Militarization and the current crisis. *American Anthropologist, 104*(3), 723–735.

McGee, J. (2001, November 4). An intelligence giant in the making. *Washington Post*, p. A4.

Mesquelier, A. (2006). Why Katrina's victims aren't *refugees*: Musings on a "dirty" word. *American Anthropologist, 108,* 735–743.

Moore, S. F. (1987). Explaining the present: Theoretical dilemmas in processual ethnography. *American Ethnologist, 14*(4), 727–736.

Nelson, D. (2003). Relating to terror: Gender, anthropology, law, and some September Elevenths. *Duke Journal of Gender Law and Policy, 10,* 195–210.

New York Daily News (2001, October 3). Ashcroft hits Congress says committee's pokey on anti-terror bill. Retrieved January 7, 2014, from www.nydailynews.com/archives/news/ashcroft-hits-congress-committee-pokey-anti-terror-bill-article-1.934126

New York Times. (2006, September 12). Editorial: President Bush's reality. Retrieved from www.nytimes.com/2006/09/12/opinion/12tue1.html?_r=0

Obama, B. (2009a, February 24). President's State of the Nation address to joint session of Congress. Retrieved from www.whitehouse.gov/the_press_office/Remarks-of-President-Barack-Obama-Address-to-Joint-Session-of-Congress

———. (2009b, December 1). Remarks by the President in address to the nation on the way forward in Afghanistan and Pakistan. The White House, Office of the Press Secretary, Washington. Retrieved from www.whitehouse.gov/the-press-office/remarks-president-address-nation-way-forward-afghanistan-and-pakistan

———. (2009c, June 4). Full text of President Obama's speech in Cairo, Egypt, titled "A new beginning." Retrieved from www.huffingtonpost.com/2009/06/04/obama-egypt-speech-video_n_211216.html

———. (2012a, January 24). State of the Union 2012: Full transcript of President Obama's speech. Retrieved from www.guardian.co.uk/world/2012/jan/25/state-of-the-union-address-full-text

———. (2012b, September 6). Transcript: President Obama's convention speech. Retrieved from www.npr.org/2012/09/06/160713941/transcript-president-obamas-convention-speech

———. (2013, January 21). President Barack Obama's inaugural address—full text. Retrieved from www.guardian.co.uk/world/2013/jan/21/barack-obama-2013-inaugural-address

O'Meara, K. (2001, November 9). Police state. *Insight Magazine.* Retrieved February 2, 2013 from http://911review.org/Wget/www.insightmag.com/main.cfm.bk

Palaima, T. (2009, April 2). The tools of power, *Times Higher Education,* pp. 32–39.

Pickler, N. (2006, September). Bush invokes 9/11 to argue for Iraq war. ABC News. Retrieved January 7, 2014, from www.freerepublic.com/focus/news/1699929/posts

Reprieve. (2013, March 6). Drones in Yemen causing a "psychological emergency", psychologist tells MPs. Retrieved from www.reprieve.org.uk/press/2013_03_05_drones_in_yemen_psychological_emergency/

Said, E. (1978). *Orientalism.* New York: Pantheon Books.

Scahill, J. (2013, October 29). Perpetual war: How does the global war on terror ever end? *Reader Supported News.* Retrieved February 12, 2013 from http://reader-supportednews.org/opinion2/266-32/20137-focus-perpetual-war-how-does-the-global-war-on-terror-ever-end

Scarry, E. (2002, Oct./Nov.). Citizenship in emergency. *Boston Review.* Retrieved January 7, 2014, from http://new.bostonreview.net/BR27.5/scarry.html

Seidel, G., & Vidal, L. (1997). The implications of "medical", "gender in development" and "culturalist" discourses for HIV/AIDS policy in Africa. In C. Shore & S. Wright (Eds.), *Anthropology of policy: Critical perspectives on governance and power* (pp. 59–87). London and New York: Routledge.

Shore, C., & Wright, S. (Eds.). (1997). *Anthropology of policy: Critical perspectives on governance and power.* London and New York: Routledge.

Stanford Law School/NYU (2012). Living under drones. The aftermath of drone attacks. Retrieved from http://livingunderdrones.org/

Thorup, M. (2006). Menneskehedens fjende. Om pirater og terrorister. *Kritik, 180,* 71–82.

———. (2009). Enemy of humanity: the anti-piracy discourse in present day anti-terrorism. *Terrorism and Political Violence, 21*(3), 401–11.

Turner, V. (1967). *The forest of symbols: Aspects of Ndembu ritual.* London: Cornell University Press.

US Department of Justice (2004, July). Report from the field: the U.S. PATRIOT Act at work, Washington: US Department of Justice Retrieved January 7, 2014, from www.justice.gov/olp/pdf/patriot_report_from_the_field0704.pdf

Wolf, N. (2013, February 3). JSoc: Obama's secret assassins. *Guardian.* Retrieved from www.theguardian.com/commentisfree/2013/feb/03/jsoc-obama-secret-assassins

Appendix

Time Line of Key Events Regarding the War in Iraq: 2001–2006

2001 September 11—Four passenger aircraft are hijacked, two are crashed into the World Trade Center in New York, one into the US Defense Department—the Pentagon—in Washington, D.C., and the fourth into a field in Pennsylvania; 3,025 people are killed in the attacks.

2001 October 8—US leads a massive campaign of air strikes against Afghanistan and later sends in special forces to help opposition forces defeat the Taliban regime and find Saudi-born dissident Osama Bin Laden, who is suspected of masterminding the 11 September attacks.

2001 October—USA PATRIOT Act is approved by the Senate, giving the government greater powers to detain suspected terrorists, eavesdrop on communications and counter money laundering. In November, President Bush signs a directive to try suspected terrorists in military tribunals rather than the courts.

2001 December—US Army assault on Osama bin Laden's hideout, the Tora Bora caves in Afghanistan, ends in ignominious failure.

2002 January 29—In the first State of the Union address after the September 11 attacks on America, US president George Bush says Iraq is part of an "Axis of Evil." He vows that the US "will not permit the world's most dangerous regimes to threaten us with the world's most destructive weapons."

2002 June 2—President Bush publicly introduces the new defense doctrine of preemption in a speech at West Point. In some instances, the president asserts, the U.S. must strike first against another state to prevent a potential threat from growing into an actual one: "Our security will require all Americans . . . [to] be ready for pre-emptive action when necessary to defend our liberty and to defend our lives."

2002 September 12—President Bush addresses the UN to put the case for war against Iraq. Bush sets the war clock ticking.

2002 September 24—Britain publishes a dossier saying Iraq could produce a nuclear weapon within one or two years, if it obtains fissile material and other components from abroad. Blair claims the British

Secret Intelligence Service has hard evidence of Iraq's secret nuclear processing facilities.

2002 November—President Bush signs into law a bill creating a Department of Homeland Security, the biggest reorganization of federal government in more than 50 years. The large and powerful department is tasked with protecting the US against terrorist attacks and natural disasters.

2002 December 2—The British government publishes a dossier documenting human rights abuses in Iraq. It is attacked by Amnesty International for being "opportunistic and selective." Critics say it uses longstanding human rights abuses to achieve current military goals, and ignores US and UK support for Saddam at the time of some of the worst atrocities.

2002 December 21—President Bush approves the deployment of US troops to the Gulf region. By March an estimated 200,000 troops will be stationed there. US creates an alliance of the willing. British and Australian troops join them over the coming months.

2003 January 6—Saddam Hussein says he is ready for war, accuses UN weapons inspectors of being spies and calls his enemies the "friends and helpers of Satan."

2003 January 28—In his State of the Union address, President Bush announces that he is ready to attack Iraq even without a UN mandate.

2003 February 5—Colin Powell uses satellite photographs, tapes of intercepted conversations and newly opened CIA files to make the United States' case against Iraq in a determined attempt to win over international opinion.

Iraq War

2003 March 17—All diplomatic efforts cease when President Bush delivers an ultimatum to Saddam Hussein to leave the country within 48 hours or else face an attack.

2003 March 20—Missile attacks on targets in Baghdad mark the start of a US-led campaign to topple the Iraqi leader Saddam Hussein. US forces advance into central Baghdad in early April.

2003 May 1—Speaking on the deck of the aircraft carrier Abraham Lincoln, President Bush's speech "Mission Accomplished" declares that the main part of the war in Iraq is over. Meanwhile US troops oversee the dismantling and looting of Iraqi state institutions and the U.S. appointed Governor Paul Bremer gives out contracts for their rebuilding.

2004 May—Furor over pictures showing the abuse of Iraqi prisoners in US custody. President Bush and defense secretary Rumsfeld—who is questioned by Congress about the scandal—apologize for the mistreatment.

2004 July—Senate report says US and allies went to war in Iraq on "flawed" information. Independent report into 11 September 2001 attacks highlights deep institutional failings in intelligence services and government.

Bush Second Term

2004 November 2—Presidential elections: George W Bush wins a second term. He is inaugurated on 20 January 2005.

2005 August—Hurricane Katrina, the most destructive storm to hit the US in decades, sweeps through Gulf Coast states. Much of the city of New Orleans is submerged by floodwaters, and hundreds of people are killed. The levees, especially those protecting the poorest parts of town, were known to be too weak, but the Department of Homeland Security had deflected the repair budget to pay for the war on terror.

2005 November—Reports of the rendition of terror suspects captured or kidnapped abroad, via secret CIA flights, to prisons in countries where torture is practiced.

2005 November—President Bush makes a series of four speeches in the run-up to the Iraqi elections on December 15, including the November 30 "Plan for victory in Iraq" speech at US Naval Academy, Annapolis, and the December 7 "A hopeful future" speech on the war on terrorism to the Council on Foreign Relations, Washington, D.C.

2006 March—Congress renews the USA PATRIOT Act, a centerpiece of the government's fight against terrorism, after months of debate about its impact on civil liberties. The government agrees to some curbs on information gathering.

2006 May—The only man to be charged over the September 11 attacks, self-confessed Al-Qaeda conspirator Zacarias Moussaoui, is sentenced to life in jail.

2006 September—President Bush makes a series of speeches in run up to the US elections including 7 September on terrorism in Atlanta and 11 September "A war unlike any we have fought before" in the Oval Office.

2006 November—Democratic Party wins control of the Senate and House of Representatives in mid-term elections. Defense secretary Donald Rumsfeld steps down.

2007 January—President Bush announces a new Iraq strategy; thousands more US troops will be dispatched to shore up security in Baghdad.

2008 November—Iraq and the United States sign an accord requiring the withdrawal of American forces by the end of 2011. The Iraqi government is given authority over the US mission for the first time, replacing a UN Security Council mandate.

Election of Obama

2009 March—Newly inaugurated president Barack Obama announces a plan to end US combat operations in Iraq by September 2010. Up to 50,000 will stay on until the end of 2011 to advise Iraqi forces and protect US interests.

2009 December—President Obama announces that he has approved a surge of 30,000 troops to be sent to Afghanistan, adding to the 17,000 additional troops sent nine months earlier

2011 January—After Congress blocks plans to bring Guantanamo Bay detainees to the US to be tried, the Obama administration abandons its plans to close the detention center and approves plans to resume military tribunals.

2011 May—President Obama announces that Osama bin Laden was killed by Navy SEALs during a raid on his compound in Abbottabad, Pakistan

2011 October—Iraq's prime minister Nouri al-Maliki wins support from political blocs on keeping US troops as trainers, but they reject Washington's request to grant US troops immunity. The Pentagon reports there have been more than 4,400 US military deaths in Iraq since the 2003 invasion.

2011 December—President Obama welcomes home some of the last US troops from Iraq at Fort Bragg, North Carolina.

9 Nation Building Through Historical Narratives in Pre-Independence India

Gandhi, Nehru, Savarkar, and Golwalkar as Entrepreneurs of Identity

James H. Liu and Sammyh S. Khan

Recently, Hammack and Pilecki (2012) have made the claim that narrative represents an ideal "root metaphor" for political psychology that transcends disciplinary boundaries to link mind and society in a way that offers solutions to political dilemmas (see Sarbin, 1986, more generally). Consistent with Bruner's (1986) classic formulation, they define narrative as a story that involves sense-making for minds in society with one another. Hammack and Pilecki (2012) argue that narrative is useful for political psychology because it provides an analytical frame that speaks to people's need for personal coherence and identity as they work for collective solidarity and shared meaning. Liu and Hilton (2005) similarly drew on Bruner (1990), fusing his ideas with those of Moscovici (1961/2008, 1988) to describe social representations of history as a source of "narratives that tell us who we are, where we came from and where we should be going. It defines a trajectory which helps construct the essence of a group's identity, how it relates to other groups, and ascertains what its options are for facing present challenges" (Liu & Hilton, 2005, p. 537). Narratives can link the individual to collectives in a fluid manner through structures that enable analysis of how communication of shared beliefs mediates and motivates political action (see László, 2008).

The purpose of the present chapter is to elaborate on a narrative theory of history and identity (Liu & László, 2007) through analysis of the structure and language of competing narratives of Indian national identity prior to independence. Liu and Sibley (in press) have recently argued that history provides claims to societal legitimacy that are not duplicated by any other basis of argument. Therefore, political leaders, especially in times of crisis and transition are motivated as identity entrepreneurs (Reicher, Haslam, & Hopkins, 2005; Reicher & Hopkins, 2001) to articulate an account of the history of their group (in this case, the nation) as a means of legitimizing their political agendas for the future.

In the first part of the 20th century, the problem facing all indigenous political leaders in the Indian subcontinent was how to deal with the overwhelming fact of British colonization from above, and the treacherous terrain of sectarian divisions on the ground below. Our focus here is on historical narratives of India written by Indian National Congress (INC) leaders Mohandas Gandhi

(1910) and Jawaharlal Nehru (1946), and their Hindu nationalist competitors Veer Savarkar (1923) and M.S. Golwalkar (1939).[1] These have served to provide "myths of origin" (Malinowski, 1926) or "master narratives" (Thorne & McLean, 2003; Fivush, 2010) of Indian national identity as a *story trajectory* from the past through transition to independence. They condition conceptions of Indian nationhood to this day (Sen & Wagner, 2005). The central theme of their narratives is different: Gandhi argues for Indian Home Rule (Hind Swaraj), whereas Savarkar and Golwalkar make an argument for Hindutva (loosely translated as Hindu nationalism). Among the four, only Nehru is explicitly writing a history of India. However, each of the authors makes a significant use of history as a central component of their argument of how to define India as a nation for the present and future. Each of them was highly political, and definitely could be considered as identity entrepreneurs (Reicher & Hopkins, 2001).

According to Reicher, Hopkins, Levine, and Rath (2005), social identity is *the* critical source of soft power (or social influence): "the definition of who is included in the category (category boundaries) will determine the extent of the mobilization, the definition of what it means to be a category member (category content) will determine the direction of the mobilization, and the definition of who best exemplifies the category (category prototypes) will determine the leadership of the mobilization" (p. 626). Marrying social identity theory/self-categorization theory (Tajfel & Turner, 1979; Turner, Hogg, Oakes, Reicher, & Wetherell, 1987) to social representations of history (Liu & Hilton, 2005), we argue that history provides crucial information during times of crises that determine category *content*—what it means to be and to act as an Indian through *story trajectory* (following Propp, 1968).

Despite the polemical politics between the Indian National Congress (or INC) and the Hindu nationalists today (represented politically by the Bharatiya Janata Party, or BJP), in the early 20th century they shared common cause in wanting to get the British out of India. To achieve this purpose, the four leaders located the point of origin for India as a nation in strikingly similar ways: the distant Vedantic past and the ancient language of Sanskrit. None of them emphasized the times or the people before this "golden age," so in this sense, the Vedantic past could be regarded as a "myth of origin" according to Malinowski (1926). However, unlike the historical charter of Malinowski, which is relatively immutable, these histories extend from the distant past to a more clearly remembered historical time that is narrated in a dynamic and contestable manner (see Bottici, this volume; Liu & Hilton, 2005). The two rival factions of identity entrepreneurs differed in how they defined the historically mandated out-group, and this difference in defining category boundaries has shaped the formation of states in the modern subcontinent of India. We will show that social representations of history (Liu & Sibley, in press) in concert with the social identity theory of identity entrepreneurship (Reicher, Haslam, & Hopkins, 2005; Reicher & Hopkins, 2001) provides fresh insight into a central problem for narrative theory: conceptualizing to what extent narratives (or representations) are shared, and the importance of the different forms and functions of the sharing. In other words, what are the critical elements of shared narrative required for a better understanding of what binds and what differentiates the political psychology of a people?

From narrative theory we draw two strands of analysis, one synchronous and one asynchronous. The theory of history and identity (Liu & Sibley, 2009) is endowed with overall structural frames designated as narrative templates by Wertsch (2002) as well as micro-level devices for analyzing the specific forms of language (Liu & László, 2007) used to communicate details of the story (László, 2008). Following Propp (1968), among the most important overall frames for the analysis of historical narratives is its temporal structure (e.g., Bottici, this volume; White, 1987), rendered by Propp (1968) as a linear sequence. While Propp (1968) focused on small invariant story elements of the Russian folktale as functions of dramatic personae, we do not require rigid adherence to such a scheme here. The theory of history and identity (Liu & Hilton, 2005; Liu & László, 2007) analyzes narrative as dynamic, contested, and variable. However, we concur with Propp (1968) that the choice of a beginning, middle (or technical climax), and end to an historical narrative, that is, its *story trajectory*, is absolutely essential to its functions in communicating history as a storied sequence with causal implications linking past to present and connecting the individual to the collective as a social identity.

The central premise of the present chapter is that the construction of an historical trajectory constitutes a critical feat of identity entrepreneurship by political leaders. This defines the group prototype (Turner et al., 1987) as an historical ideal rather than as a product of present-day social comparisons. It is extremely important because it enables subordinate groups to avoid disadvantageous social comparisons versus a dominant group in the present (Tajfel & Turner, 1979). Rather, a more favorable comparison can be made between an out-group in the corrupted present against the in-group in a distant and idealized past. This *temporal alternative* appears to be an important tactic for subordinate groups (Kus, Liu, & Ward, 2013).

We examine the narrative choices made by Nehru, Savarkar, and Golwalkar, all of which structure their political arguments historically. Gandhi's text by contrast is diachronic. His *Hind Swaraj (Indian Home Rule)* takes the form of a Socratic dialogue. But within the diachronic form of a wide-ranging dialogue, there are historical sections with structural similarities to the other three. Out of the temporal structure of a historical narrative a plot, or historical trajectory (see also Laszlo, 2008), can be ascertained. This mobilizes the direction of social identification and provides a *story sequence* to drive the work of a national identity project (Bauer & Gaskell, 1999; Reicher & Hopkins, 2001). The plot of a nation's history is a historically derived argument for the legitimacy of the author's political agenda (Liu & Hilton, 2005; Liu & Sibley, in press). The driving plot lines of popular representations of history, as Liu and colleagues have reported in multiple studies (Liu et al., 2005, 2009; and central to the plot structure of the Russian folktale as rendered by Propp, 1968) involve conflict. Conflict serves to define the in-group and the out-group (Tajfel & Turner, 1979). The critical feat of identity entrepreneurship, as articulated by Reicher and colleagues (Reicher & Hopkins, 2001; Reicher, Hopkins, Levine, & Rath, 2005) is to identify the in-group and out-group in a manner that is congruent with the political agenda of the identity entrepreneur, and includes as many as possible while also targeting an out-group for exclusion.

The second strand of analysis is asynchronous (or diachronic) and concerns the use of metaphor in narrative. We theorize that metaphor might serve as a psychological mechanism to create moments of sharing that activates political identity in a different way. The asynchrony of metaphor, by intuitively grasping together disparate and not necessarily logically or temporally connected parts, may serve as a particular means for activating an identity project (Bauer & Gaskell, 1999; Turner et al., 1987) within a body of text. Although narrative itself must be received synchronously (i.e., it takes time for a story to unfold), and some narratives unfold as temporal structures, their organization in human memory after reception, as Fivush (2010) has noted, can be multimodal. That is, they can leave memory traces that may be implicit and/or explicit, and episodic (e.g., retaining the temporal form of the story) and/or semantic (i.e., extracting a more general meaning). Gandhi, in particular employs metaphor throughout *Hind Swaraj*, to such an extent that this device largely replaces chronological narrative as the primary argument for his feats of identity entrepreneurship. He likens Western civilization to a disease and the British Parliament to a prostitute. The other three, who seek to create more apparently logical arguments, make far less use of metaphor. Nehru in fact apologizes for using metaphor to describe India as a woman, or its civilization as having a soul; this attempt to adhere to scientific discourses is shared to some degree in the texts of the two Hindu nationalists. We explore the extent to which the use of metaphor by our four identity entrepreneurs may create meaning that activates identity in a more implicit and semantically holistic way than in the more explicit and episodic reception of the temporal structure and plot elements of narrative.

The second premise of this chapter is hence that metaphor, with its diachronic and less than analytical form of argumentation, can mobilize emotions and clinch an argument in a way that a more temporally structured argument cannot (Ortony, 1975). Metaphor can thus be a discursive strategy that shifts the grounds of argument from logic and power to intuition and feeling, especially when employed by a master of symbolic meaning such as Gandhi.

The full historical context of the writings to be examined cannot be addressed in the brief space of our chapter (see Bandyopadhyay, 2004, 2010 for excellent histories). However, we can provide a little background to help interpret these materials. Gandhi had just about finished honing his protest politics against the racist policies of the British Empire in South Africa when he wrote *Hind Swaraj* in 1909 in Gujarati while on a boat between London and South Africa. He would soon be going home to his epoch-making activities in India as a fresh new political leader against the British Raj. Savarkar wrote *Hindutva—Who*

Is a Hindu? in 1921–1922 while in prison for revolutionary activities against the British Raj; later, as leader of Hindu Mahasabha, a third political party opposed to both Muslim separatism and Gandhi's secular INC, he would be accused of conspiring to assassinate Gandhi. Golwalkar was a major force in turning the Rashtriya Swayamsevak Sangh (RSS) into a formidable grassroots organization promoting the values of Hindu Nationalism.[2] He wrote *We, or our Nationhood Defined* in 1938 to cement his credentials as the right-hand man of the founder of the organization. Finally, Nehru was anointed by Gandhi as his protégé in the INC and became the founder of the greatest political dynasty in the history of modern India. He wrote *Discovery of India* while in prison from 1942 to 1946 (Churchill had no patience for the protest politics of the INC while the British Empire was engaged in a life and death struggle with the Axis powers). Nehru had the last laugh, however, as he ruled India for decades as its first prime minister after independence came to India in 1947. Although the other three are relatively short treatises, his is a full-length book whose merit is comparable to that of Churchill, who once wrote, "History will be kind to me, for I intend to write it."

We do not attempt a complete textual or discursive analysis of the four seminal texts; for detailed thematic analyses of the Hindu nationalist canon, see Khan (2011). Rather, we examine (1) the narrative agenda and structure of the texts—that is, how they put together their argument for the form of national identity or nationalism they advocate. Together with narrative structure and agenda, we essay an analysis of (2) the temporal structure (i.e., chronology) of the four texts. We loosely follow Propp's (1968) linear sequential analysis, identifying gross structural features of the texts as moves while eschewing the details of his syntagmatic approach (which is appropriate only for a more homogeneous selection of short stories within the genre of folk tales). We derive the concept of an *historical trajectory*, defined as a temporal plot that uses history to define an in-group (and its structure) and its out-groups in a manner that legitimizes an identity project.

Setting the Context for the Texts and Their Authors

Gandhi and especially Nehru, who were both famous at the time when they were writing, open their texts with prefaces that orient the reader to themselves and their political projects. Gandhi (1910) writes memorably in his preface that "The British Government in India constitutes a struggle between the Modern Civilisation, which is the Kingdom of Satan, and the Ancient Civilisation, which is the Kingdom of God." (p. 2). He adopts the stance of Editor, who instructs an impatient young activist Indian Reader through a Socratic dialogue.

Nehru's (1946) opening paragraph is more poignantly personal: "It is more than twenty months since we were brought here, more than twenty months of my ninth term of imprisonment." (p. 15). He writes of his opposition to fascism and his sympathy for China from imprisonment in Ahmadnagar Fort. As his argument unfolds, Nehru acknowledges that "it is a curious turn of fate's wheel that I, and people like me, should spend our days in prison while war against fascism and Nazism is raging . . ." (p. 19). "I wanted India to take an eager and active part in the mighty conflict, for I felt that high principles would be at stake . . . But I was convinced that only as a free country and an equal could she function in this way" (p. 19). So he burnishes his credentials as an anti-fascist by way of introduction as he and the other Congress leaders (including Gandhi) were in prison. They had time to contemplate history as a call to action:

> Yet the past is ever with us and all that we are and that we have comes from the past. We are its products and we live immersed in it. Not to understand it and feel it as something living within us is to not to understand the present. To combine it with the present and to extend it into the future, to break from it where it cannot be so united, to make of all this the pulsating and vibrating material for thought and action—that is life. (Nehru, 1946, p. 21)

Savarkar, who was less famous and who was in jail for sedition as he was writing, could afford no such grand gestures. He published his work under a pseudonym (A. Maratha),[3] and without irony opens his text with an appeal to Shakespeare's fair maid of Verona about the importance of a name: the central premise of his text is to define Hindutva. Golwalkar's (1939) opening move in his preface is to apologize to the INC for what he is about to do (claiming common cause with them in desiring to throw the British out). He then inserts a lengthy (25-page) foreword (of a total 148-page text in .pdf form) from a respected Indian professor who writes academically about nationalism in a much more measured tone than himself. Clearly, they are less confident than were their INC counterparts, needing some form of academic warrant of legitimacy to augment their arguments.

Setting the Narrative Agenda and Articulating Identity Projects: Opening Moves

Gandhi had not yet assumed a leading role within the INC. But he nevertheless positions it as a vehicle or product of India's desire for Home Rule in his first chapter: "To treat the Congress as an institution inimical to our growth as a nation would disable us from using that body" (Ghandi, 1910, p. 8). Not only does he thus co-opt the organization to his purpose (by no means in 1910 were all INC members supporters of Home Rule—in fact Gandhi himself recruited volunteers to fight for the British Army in World War I), he also claims the historical legacy of the previous generation of Indian political leaders, even those who were pro-British: "Had not the Grand Old Man of India prepared the soil, our young men could not have even spoken about Home Rule." In this way, Gandhi is as inclusive as he can be in terms of defining his political project. Being Gandhi, he even includes a few British: "Many Englishmen desire Home

Rule for India. That the English people are somewhat more selfish than others is true, but that does not prove that every Englishman is bad" (p. 7). Gandhi makes no attempt to define the identity boundaries of his political agenda in his opening move, but positions his political party the INC (Congress) as the instigator of action. His is the least academic of the four texts, written originally in Gujarati with the intention of reaching a popular audience with the idea of *Hind Swaraj* (Indian Home Rule).

Savarkar is an identity entrepreneur with the difficult task of following in the wake of Gandhi's massive popularity in 1921–1922 with a competing project. His project is to create a conception of the nation as "Hindutva" that is similar to but different from Hinduism: "To this category of names which have been to mankind a subtle source of life and inspiration belongs the word Hindutva, the essential nature and significance of which we have to investigate into. The ideas and ideals, the systems and societies, the thoughts and sentiments which have centered round this name are so varied and rich, so powerful and so subtle, so elusive and yet so varied that the term Hindutva defies all attempts at analysis. Forty centuries, if not more, had been at work to mould it as it is." (Savarkar, 1923, pp. 3–4). Unlike Gandhi who only claims to build on the work of a previous generation of Indian political leaders, Savarkar (1923) claims 40 centuries as the warrant of antiquity for his nation building: "Hindutva is not a word but a history," he writes. "Not only the spiritual or religious history of our people as at times it is mistaken to be by being confounded with the other cognate term Hinduism, but a history in full. Hinduism is only a derivative, a fraction, a part of Hindutva" (p. 4). He argues that "Hindutva embraces all the departments of thought and activity of the whole Being of our Hindu race" (p. 5). This is rooted in Vedic religion: "long before the ancient Egyptians, and Babylonians had built their magnificent civilization, the holy waters of the Indus were daily witnessing the lucid and curling columns of the scented sacrificial smokes and the valleys resounding with the chants of Vedic hymns" (p. 4). Savarkar, like Gandhi, does not define the boundaries of inclusion and exclusion in his opening, but he is much more explicit that he is defining an identity project rather than a political agenda. He is meticulous about shaping his narrative in a manner that will allow maximum inclusion of his targeted audience within his key definition of *Hindutva*.

Having both Savarkar and Gandhi before him, Golwalkar builds a more polemical case in 1938. Hindu nationalism was by this time firmly ensconced as a political power, the hammer to the All-India Muslim League's anvil on which the souls of two nations were to be partitioned in blood and fire. On his behalf the academic in the preface asks, "What is Swaraj and whose independence is our goal? Do we strive to make our "nation" independent and glorious, or merely to create a "state" with certain political and economic powers centralized in other hands than those of our present rulers? Do we clearly perceive that the two concepts—the nation and the state—are distinctly different?" (Golwalkar, 1939, p. 38). Golwalkar's idea of nationhood begins with the Vedas, and the two great epics of the Vedic period, the *Ramayana* and the *Mahabharata*. He is happy to aggrandize his in-group past with a massive (and unsubstantiated) warrant of antiquity:

> Undoubtedly, therefore, we—Hindus—have been in undisputed and undisturbed possession of this land for over 8 or even 10 thousand years[4] before the land was invaded by any foreign race. Thus apart from any consideration of the Hindu i.e. Aryan race being indigenous or otherwise, of one thing we are certain, that the very first page of history records our existence as a progressive and highly civilized nation—the only nation in the then world, in this land, which, therefore, came to be known as Hindusthan, the land of the Hindus." (Golwalkar, 1939, p. 42)

He is dismissive of criticism: "And after all what authority is there to prove our immigrant nature? The shady testimony of Western scholars? Well, it must not be ignored that the superiority complex of the 'White Man' blurs their vision . . . Till yesterday they wandered wild in the wildernesses, their nude bodies weirdly tattooed and painted. They must need show, therefore, that all peoples of the world were at that time in the same or worse state" (p. 43). Golwalkar's narrative agenda of defining Hindu nationalism appears to fuse Savarkar's intellectual content with Gandhi's political purpose of throwing the British out.

Nehru (1946) rounds out our quartet with a more philosophical orientation to the past that never mentions his competitors, and yet foregrounds their injudicious use of the past: "The burden of the past, the burden of both good and ill, is over-powering, and sometimes suffocating, more especially for those of us who belong to very ancient civilizations like those of India and China. As Nietzsche says: 'Not only the wisdom of centuries—also their madness breaketh out in us. Dangerous is it to be an heir.' What is my inheritance? To what am I an heir?" (p. 36). Nehru's orientation is depicted as a quest (Campbell, 1968) whereas for Savarkar and Golwakar, the answer is presented a priori as part of their ideology of Hindu nationalism. Nehru writes that

> India was in my blood and there was much in her that instinctively thrilled me. And yet I approached her almost as an alien critic, full of dislike for the present as well as for many of the relics of the past that I saw. To some extent I came to her via the West, and looked to her as a friendly westerner might have done. I was eager and anxious to change her outlook and appearance and give her the garb of modernity. (p. 50)

The metaphor of India as a woman is sustained throughout his book, and here finds full expression in the signal question of modernity versus tradition that has perplexed indigenous academics and politicians alike (e.g., Hwang, 2003; Sinha, 1989; Yang, 2003). As feminist scholars have noted, the positioning of nation as a women empowers the male politician to act on her behalf (e.g.,

Einhorn, 2006; Jayawardena, 1986; McClintock, 1997). Although not religious, Nehru (1946) is no less a nationalist than the others: "at almost any time in recorded history, an Indian would have felt more or less at home in any part of India, and would have felt as a stranger and alien in any other country" (p. 62). He is syncretic and assimilationist: "Those who professed a religion of non-Indian origin or, coming to India, settled down there, became distinctively Indian in the course of a few generations . . ." (p. 62), and "It would seem that every outside element that has come to India and been absorbed by India, has given something to India and taken much from her; it has contributed to its own and to India's strength" (p. 146).

And yet, there is a high level of reflexivity here, in self-positioning as an alien critic and friendly westerner (Harré & van Langenhove, 1991). He further probes his psyche: "And yet doubts arose within me. Did I know India?—I who presumed to scrap much of her past heritage? There was a great deal that had to be scrapped, and must be scrapped; but surely India could not have been what she undoubtedly was, and could not have continued a cultured existence for thousands of years, if she had not possessed something vital and enduring, something that was worthwhile. What was this something?" (Nehru, 1946, p. 50). Nehru's (1946) narrative agenda with respect to the past is that of the seeker, the asker, the searcher in Joseph Campbell's (1968) *Hero of a Thousand Faces* looking for renewal of society. Nehru signals that he is going to take the reader on a long journey rather than write a short political treatise as the other three.

All four identity entrepreneurs essentialize Indian identity (Yzerbyt, Judd, & Corneille, 2004) albeit under different aliases and with competing boundaries (to be defined). They are Indian nationalists who cannot accept the Western scholarly contention articulated by Mill (1918) that India was never fully a nation before British colonization (see Anderson, 1983, for a general theory of nation as "imagined community"). All four use the past as a warrant of legitimacy; three of the texts are in the genre of narrative history, with a temporal structure after the introduction moving from distant past to the present. Gandhi is the only one of the four whose genre is a dialogue rather than history, and so he reverses the temporal sequence by establishing the out-group in the present before defining the in-group as an historical ideal.

Gandhi: Establishing the Present Out-Group as the Source of Corruption

Home rule (*Hind Swaraj*) is the narrative agenda of "what" is to be accomplished according to Gandhi. In his first sustained metaphor (opening chapter 3), it requires the sleeper to awaken: "When a man rises from sleep, he twists his limbs and is restless. It takes some time before he is entirely awakened." (Ghandi, 1910, p. 11). The metaphor of the recent period of Indian history as torpor or decay is also taken up by the other three writers; a period of decay is the natural historical trajectory following a Golden Age, which is a central narrative device for all the authors except Nehru. It helps to explain how a great people came to be colonized.

Arising from a condition of sleep, Gandhi (1910) challenges the Reader to define Swaraj in chapter 4: "You and I and all Indians are impatient to attain Swaraj, but we are certainly not decided as to what it is . . . Why do you want to drive away the English?" (p. 12). After a series of questions where the Reader is unable to describe an autonomous agenda for Home Rule, Gandhi concludes: "You have drawn the picture well. In effect it means this: that we want English rule without the Englishman. You want the tiger's nature, but not the tiger; that is to say, you would make India English. And when it becomes English, it will be called not Hindustan but Englishtan. This is not the Swaraj I want" (p. 13).

The Reader admits he wants to copy the British Parliament for India. Gandhi spends the rest of his book demolishing this argument and making his case for Swaraj as a spiritual condition. He uses metaphorical language to make his case that modern civilization is a disease. Gandhi (1910) likens the British Parliament to "a sterile woman and a prostitute" (p. 14) because "without outside pressure, it can do nothing." He dismisses parliamentary democracy as "simply a costly toy of the nation" (p. 14) whose members are "hypocritical and selfish" with fear as their guiding motive, and whose views "swing like the pendulum of a clock and are never steadfast" (pp. 15–16).

People who have never read Gandhi and believe his public image as a saintly old man have no idea of the unyielding nature of his political positions. Gandhi (1910) rejects all technological accomplishments of the Europeans, saying, "This civilization is irreligion, and it has taken such a hold on the people in Europe that those who are in it appear to be half mad. They lack real physical strength or courage. They keep up their energy by intoxication. They can hardly be happy in solitude. Women, who should be the queens of households, wander in the streets or they slave away in factories" (pp. 18–19). At the root of his discontent is the material basis of Western civilization: "Formerly, men were made slaves under physical compulsion. Now they are enslaved by temptation of money and of the luxuries that money can buy" (p. 19). His language is intemperate: "According to the teaching of Mohammed this would be considered a Satanic Civilization. Hinduism calls it a Black Age . . . Parliaments are really emblems of slavery . . . Civilization is not an incurable disease, but it should never be forgotten that the English are at present afflicted by it" (p. 19). Quoting Napoleon, Gandhi calls the British "a nation of shopkeepers" for whom "money is their God" (p. 21).

Gandhi (1910) claims that "Railways, lawyers and doctors have impoverished the country so much so that, if we do not wake up in time, we shall be ruined" (p. 24). He devotes a chapter to blasting each of the three.[5] He claims that railroads are responsible for famines (by moving food according to market pricing) and a general decline in morality ("Good travels at a snail's pace—it can, therefore, have little to do with railways"; p. 25). His firm opinion is that "lawyers have enslaved India, have accentuated Hindu-Mohammedan dissensions and have confirmed English authority" (p. 32). His accusation is that "doctors induce us to indulge, and the result is that we have become deprived of self-control and have become effeminate" (p. 36). Using metaphor again, Gandhi describes the two as "parasitical" branches of a tree whose root is "immorality" (p. 32).

By way of temporal contrast, shifting to ancient times, Ghandi (1910) argues that

> our leading men traveled throughout India either on foot or in bullock-carts . . . They learned one another's languages and there was no aloofness between them . . . they saw that India was one undivided land so made by nature. They, therefore, argued that it must be one nation. Arguing thus, they established holy places in various parts of India, and fired the people with an idea of nationality in a manner unknown in other parts of the world. (p. 25)

Gandhi's Swaraj is a spiritual nation: "we Indians are one as no two Englishmen are. Only you and I and others who consider ourselves civilized and superior persons imagine that we are many nations. It was after the advent of railways that we began to believe in distinctions, and you are at liberty now to say that it is through the railways that we are beginning to abolish those distinctions" (pp. 25–26).

Gandhi (1910) bet the lives of 1 million Hindus and Muslims on his story that all divisions of people in India were the product of Western civilization. His critical social comparison between groups is temporal, between a corrupt present and an idealized past. "You have described to me the India of the pre-Mohammedan period, but now we have Mohammedans, Parsis and Christians. How can they be one nation?" (p. 26), the Reader asks. Gandhi blames the divisions on railways (breakers of natural partitions between people), lawyers (bloodsucking instruments of colonial misrule), and doctors (facilitators of self-indulgence). He first claims pragmatically that "The Hindus, the Mohammedans, the Parsis and the Christians who have made India their country are fellow countrymen, and they will have to live in unity, if only for their own interest. In no part of the world are one nationality and one religion synonymous terms; nor has it ever been so in India" (p. 27). Adopting the doctrine of assimilation, he argues that "India cannot cease to be one nation because people belonging to different religions live in it. The introduction of foreigners does not necessarily destroy the nation, they merge in it." He refuses to acknowledge historical enmity between Muslims and Hindus: "The Hindus flourished under Moslem sovereigns and Moslems under the Hindu. Each party recognized that mutual fighting was suicidal, and that neither party would abandon its religion by force of arms. Both parties, therefore, decided to live in peace. With the English advent quarrels recommenced" (p. 28). Gandhi's willingness to subvert facts about history to his political agenda is slightly exceeded by the Hindu nationalists.

The Golden Age of the Vedas: The Basis for Hind
Swaraj and Hindutva but Not Nehru's India

Savarkar (1923) treats the events of the *Ramayana* (and *Mahabharata*) not as mythology, but as historical fact: "The day when the Horse of Victory returned to Ayodhya unchallenged and unchallengeable, the great white Umbrella of Sovereignty was unfurled over that Imperial throne of Ramchandra, the brave, Ramchandra the good, and a loving allegiance to him was sworn, not only by the Princes of Aryan blood but Hanuman,[6] Sugriva, Bibhishana from the south—that day was the real birth-day of our Hindu people" (p. 7). The timeless, living nature of ritual enactments from the *Ramayana* has been used in political campaigning by the Hindu nationalist movement in India recently, and has been remarked on by many scholars (see Jaffrelot, 1996, 2007; Katju, 2003; Ludden, 2003).

Savarkar (1923) glorifies Buddhism and Jainism within his big tent of *Hindutva* in principle as a beacon of international enlightenment: "the great and divine mission that set in motion 'the wheel of the law of Righteousness' made India the very heart—the very soul—of almost all the then known world" (p. 9). But he also rejects their doctrine of non-violence or *ahimsa* as disastrous in practice:

> The Indians saw that the cherished ideals of their race—their thrones and their families and the very Gods they worshipped—were trampled under foot, the holy land of their love devastated and sacked by hordes of barbarians, so inferior to them in language, religion, philosophy, mercy and all the soft and human attributes of man and God—but superior to them in strength alone—strength that summed up its creed, in two words—Fire and Sword! The inference was clear. Clear also was the fact that Buddhistic logic had no argument that could efficiently meet this new and terrible dualism—this strange Bible of Fire and Steel. (pp. 10–11)

He holds up nonviolence as an impossibly naïve ideal, never once mentioning Gandhi who by then had become famous for *ahimsa*: "Nobly did she try to kill killing by getting killed—and at last found out that palm leaves at times are too fragile for steel!" (p. 11).

He claims that Vedic warriors expelled the foreign invaders, leading to a golden age where "peace and plenty reigned. The blessings of freedom and independence were shared by the princes and peasants alike. The patriotic authors go in rapture over the greatness and the happiness that marked this long chapter of our history extending over nearly a thousand years or so" (Savarkar, 1923, p. 19). Savarkar's (1923) contemporary nationalism is thus warranted by an ancient ideal: "The Vedic State based on and backed up by the Vedic Church must be designed by the Vedic name, and—so far as it was then possible-identified with the Vedic lines" (p. 14). He marks the Indus River as the boundary of Vedic civilization: "The best country of the Aryans is known as Sindhusthan[7] whereas the Mlecch country lies beyond the Indus" (p. 14).

Golwalkar (1939) attempts to develop (before giving up) a story about the Aryans originating from the North Pole (pp. 44–45) before finally stating:

> Out of the heap of hypotheses we reject all and positively maintain that we Hindus came into this land from nowhere, but are indigenous children of the soil always, from times immemorial and are natural masters of the country. Here we compiled our inimitable Vedas, reasoned out our Philosophy of the Absolute—the last word on the subject, built our sciences and arts and crafts. Here we progressed in cultivation, industries and trade, flourished and prospered—a great nation of a great race—propounded the one religion, which is no make belief but religion in essence, and built up a culture of such sublime nobility that foreign travellers to the land were dumbfounded to see it, a culture which made every individual a noble specimen of humanity, truth and generosity, under the divine influence of which, not one of the hundreds of millions of the people, ever told a lie or stole or indulged in any moral aberration; and all this long before the west had learnt to eat roast meat—instead of raw! And we were one Nation— "Over all the land from sea to sea one kingdom!" is the trumpet cry of the ancient Vedas! (p. 47–48)

An international conference between Savarkar and Golwalkar and historians specializing in the invention of tradition (Hobsbawm & Ranger, 1983) would have been quite some battle!

Nor was Gandhi immune from telling tales of the golden age. When asked by the Reader to define true civilization, Gandhi's (1910) Editor replies, "[T]he civilization India has evolved is not to be beaten in the world. Nothing can equal the seeds sown by our ancestors. Rome went, Greece shared the same fate; the might of the Pharaohs was broken; Japan has become Westernized; of China nothing can be said; but India is still, somehow or other, sound at the foundation" (p. 37). Gandhi takes a step further than the Hindu nationalists and provides a moral definition of civilization that refuses to entertain the notion of progress:

> What we have tested and found true on the anvil of experience, we dare not change. Many thrust their advice upon India, and she remains steady. This is her beauty: it is the sheet-anchor of our hope. Civilization is that mode of conduct which points out to man the path of duty. Performance of duty and observance of morality are convertible terms. To observe morality is to attain mastery over our mind and our passions. So doing, we know ourselves. The Gujarati equivalent for civilization means "good conduct". If this definition be correct, then India, as so many writers have shown, has nothing to learn from anybody else, and this is as it should be. (p. 37)

The Bhagavad Gita was the final word for Gandhi, although he read with it the Bible and the Koran at his prayer meetings.

The Home Rule of Gandhi is a self-imposed moral limit to material indulgences. "Our ancestors, therefore, set a limit to our indulgences. They saw that happiness was largely a mental condition. A man is not necessarily happy because he is rich, or unhappy because he is poor" (Ghandi, 1910, p. 38). Like the Hindu nationalists, he romanticizes the past: "We have had no system of life corroding competition . . . The common people lived independently and followed their agricultural occupation. They enjoyed true Home Rule" (p. 38). When the Reader mentions child widows, polyandry, child prostitution, and animal sacrifice, Gandhi (1910) admits that no one mistakes them for ancient civilization. But his clinching argument is that "[t]he tendency of the Indian civilization is to elevate the moral being, that of the Western civilization is to propagate immorality. The latter is godless, the former is based on a belief in God. So understanding and so believing, it behooves every lover of India to cling to the Indian civilization even as a child clings to the mother's breast" (p. 39). These religious binaries are not ordinarily associated with Gandhi, but they might have interfered with his attempts to negotiate a peaceful transfer of power from the British Raj. Western negotiators found him to be intransigent and unpredictable.

Alone among the four, Nehru abstains from a narrative of a Golden Age of the Vedas. To the contrary, he claims a secular view of them instead: "I have always hesitated to read books of religion. The totalitarian claims made on their behalf did not appeal to me. The outward evidences of the practice of religion did not encourage me to go to the original sources" (Nehru, 1946, p. 77). His world is resolutely human, and situated in real time: "I could not approach these books, or any book, as Holy Writ . . . Looking at scripture then as a product of the human mind, we have to remember the age in which it was written, the environment and mental climate in which it grew, the vast distance in time and thought and experience that separates it from us" (p. 78). Yet he admits their staying power: "From these dim beginnings of long ago flow out the rivers of Indian thought and philosophy, of Indian life and culture . . . During this enormous span of years they changed their courses sometimes, and even appeared to shrivel up, yet they preserved their essential identity . . . That staying power need not necessarily be a virtue; it may well mean, as I think it has meant for India for a long time past, stagnation and decay" (p. 81). In this metaphor of the river he emphasizes a changing continuity layered with syncretism: "There is in the *Mahabharata* the polytheism of the Vedas, the monism of the Upanishads, and deisms, and dualisms, and monotheism . . . In the Mahabharata there are references to beef or veal being offered to honoured guests" (p. 108). He celebrates the philosophy of the Vedas while decrying the caste system they inspired.

Nehru (1946) refutes the Golden Age narrative as follows:

A country under foreign domination seeks escape from the present in dreams of a vanished age, and finds consolation in visions of past greatness. That is a foolish and dangerous pastime in which many of us indulge. An equally questionable practice for us in India is to imagine that we are still spiritually great even though we have come down in the world in other respects. Spiritual or any other greatness cannot be founded on lack of freedom and opportunity, or on starvation and misery. (p. 81)

Among all the old stories, the one he identifies with most is the Buddha Story (p. 130): "the nation and the race which can produce such a magnificent type must have deep reserves of wisdom and inner strength" (p. 132), one who was "against all forms of metaphysics" (p. 128) as the secular Nehru himself. What a remarkable partnership there must have been between Gandhi and Nehru, to be so different in temperament and philosophy, yet united in action.

Identifying the Out-Group

It is in the subject positions that Nehru offers to the Muslims and the British in his narrative that his alliance with Gandhi becomes evident. Like Gandhi, he downplays historical conflict between the religious groups: "It is thus wrong and misleading to talk of a Moslem invasion of India or of the Moslem period in India, just as it would be wrong to refer to the coming of the British to India as a Christian invasion. Islam did not invade India; it had come to India some centuries earlier" (Nehru, 1946, p. 241). He writes of a new synthesis of Afghan and Hindu styles with the arrival of Islam, as Persian crept into popular use. Of the greatest of the Mughal emperors he writes,

> Babar is an attractive person, a typical Renaissance prince, bold and adventurous, fond of art and literature and good living. His grandson Akbar is even more attractive and has greater qualities. Daring and reckless, an able general, and yet gentle and full of compassion, an idealist and dreamer, but also a man of action . . . As a warrior he conquered large parts of India, but his eyes were set on another more enduring conquest, the conquest of the hearts and minds of the people . . . In him, the old dream of a united India again took shape, united not only politically in one state but organically fused into one people. (p. 259).

This likening of Mughal emperors to Renaissance princes is remarkable, and probably only possible with the secular orientation that Nehru adopts. But he goes further about Akbar: "He married a Rajput princess, and his son and successor, Jehangir, was thus half Mughal and half Rajput Hindu. Jehangir's son, Shah Jehan, was also the son of a Rajput mother, Thus racially, this Turko-Mongol dynasty became far more Indian than Turk or Mongol" (p. 259). Nehru casts the best of the Muslim princes as in-group members!

Contrast this with Savarkar (1923), who ends his golden age narrative with the advent of the Muslims:

> But as it often happens in history this very undisturbed enjoyment of peace and plenty lulled our Sindhusthan, in a sense of false security and bred a habit of living in the land of dreams. At last she was rudely awakened on

the day when Mohammad of Gazni crossed the Indus, the frontier line of Sindhusthan and invaded her. That day the conflict of life and death began. Nothing makes Self conscious of itself so much as a conflict with non-self. Nothing can weld peoples into a nation and nations into a state as the pressure of a common foe. Hatred separates as well as unites. Never had Sindhusthan a better chance and a more powerful stimulus to be herself forged into an indivisible whole as on that dire day, when the great inconoclast crossed the Indus. (p. 19).

In a textbook instance of self-categorization identity entrepreneurship (Reicher & Hopkins, 2001; Reicher et al., 2005), he defines the in-group by enmity with the out-group:

> Sanatanists, Satnamis, Sikhs, Aryas, Anaryas, Marathas and Madrasis, Brahmins and Panchamas—all suffered as Hindus and triumphed as Hindus . . . The enemies hated us as Hindus and the whole family of peoples and races, of sects and creeds that flourished from Attock to Cuttack was suddenly individualised into a single Being . . . This one word, Hindutva, ran like a vital spinal cord through our whole body politic and made the Nayars of Malabar weep over the sufferings of the Brahmins of Kashmir. (p. 20)

Savarkar, who is seeking intellectual credibility, employs metaphor very little, but here he uses the language of the Hindu nation as one being with a spinal cord through the body politic to great effect. The entire premise of Savarkar's idea of nationhood excludes Muslims. It is constructed on differentiation from Muslims. He does not talk about the British at all—they appear to be irrelevant to his nation-building project, in marked contrast to Gandhi and Nehru.

Nehru (1946), with his Oxford education and his elegant English prose, is, by contrast, scathing of British rule: "The feudal landlords and their kind who came from England to rule over India had the landlord's view of the world" (p. 292). Memorably, he calls the Raj's Indian Civil Service "the world's most tenacious trade union" and a "rigid and exclusive" caste who thought "They ran India, they were India, and anything that was harmful to their interests must of necessity be injurious to India" (p. 292). He identifies British rule with plunder, famine, debt, and the destruction of Indian industry. It was thus "the real, the fundamental, cause of the appalling poverty of the Indian people" (p. 300). Like Gandhi (but without his technophobia), Nehru claims that "Nearly all of our major problems to-day have grown up during British rule and as a direct result of British policy" (p. 306).

Golwalkar's (1939) focus of attention is more on the in-group than on the out-group, although he identifies both the Muslims and the British as foes:

> Overindividualization [associated with Buddhism] in the field of religion followed the consequence was that the individual became more

prominent than the society, the Nation . . . And yet the race-spirit did not wholly die out. The Race Spirit is too tenacious to be dead so easily. And when the first real invasions of murdering hordes of Mussalman free-booters occurred, they indeed found the nation divided against itself and incapable of stemming the tide of devastation they brought in their wake. (p. 49)

But the fault is within the in-group, not the out-group: "All through the centuries, since the Moslems first tread upon this land, it is this want of National Consciousness, which has been the cause of our ills" (p. 126).

The reason for this is that he sees the battle as not just a three-way conflict: "As a matter of fact we have in Hindusthan a triangular fight, we, Hindus, at war at once with the Moslems on the one hand and Britain on the other" (Golwalkar, 1939, p. 56). There are deeper issues at stake. Golwalkar (1939) refutes syncretism and assimilation: "The Moslems are not misled. They take themselves to be the conquering invaders and grasp for power. In our self-deception, we go on seceding more and more, in hopes of 'Nationalising" the foreigners and succeed merely in increasing their all-devouring appetite" (p. 56). He then identifies Gandhi and Nehru's Congress Party as race traitors: "The Congress, they [the British] founded as a safety valve to seething nationalism, as a toy which would lull the awakening giant into slumber, an instrument to destroy National consciousness, has been, as far as they are concerned, a success. Our own "denationalization" under the name of Nationality is nearing its consummation. We have almost forgotten our Nationhood" (p. 59).

From these writings, we can see clearly the narrative dimensions to one of the great tragedies of the 20th century, the partition of India, where almost 1 million perished. Today, Pakistan and India are hostile, nuclear-armed neighbors who define one another by mutual enmity (Svensson, 2013; Wolpert, 2010). This was not just a two-way or three-way conflict. There was a four-way conflict, between the British, the All-India Muslim League, the Congress Party, and the Hindu Nationalists, and this was to be a trigger for insoluble violence.

Mobilizing the Past for the Present

We have examined the narrative framing of history by four of the most influential writers about nation-building in pre-Independence India. What is most striking about the four writers is that they define their agendas in the outset of their writings, each invoking history as providing lessons from the past to resolve a crisis of the present. Although Gandhi invokes history diachronically, the four authors all make use of a comparable reservoir of events, transitions and periods in Indian history for the purposes of their respective agendas. This is in accord with previous research on popular representations of history where the content of critical events is not disputed so much as their relevance and interpretation (Liu, Sibley, & Huang, 2013; Liu & Sibley, 2009). This type of hegemony of content but not meaning appears to be typical. The construction of boundaries for inclusion and exclusion in the national category thus adhered to a common "narrative template" (Wertsch, 2002) for Indian history. The main differences between the writers lay in the sequencing and interpretation of key historical moments and junctures.

The key common elements of narrative invoked as a "historical warrant of legitimacy" (Liu & Sibley, in press) could be classified as consisting of (1) a historical moment referring to the existence of a golden age (or, in Nehru's case, an immemorial national consciousness) embodying the desired (or imagined) national culture and (2) historical junctures referring to the meeting and interaction among three groups (or civilizations: the British, Muslims/Moghuls, and Indians) that represent critical junctures in the historical trajectory of nationhood defined.

The invocation of an historical moment as a "Golden Age" functions to define the characteristics of the in-group, especially for the three religiously oriented identity entrepreneurs. Gandhi is the most explicit here: his metaphor for the British-dominated present is as a disease, with the British Parliament as a whorehouse, and doctors and lawyers as branch parasites of a tree whose root is immorality. For all three of the religious identity entrepreneurs, the golden age of ancient Indian history forms a historical prototype, the temporal ideal which the in-group should draw important characteristics from for self-categorization (Turner et al., 1987). Savarkar and Golwalkar are actually more diffident about this than is Gandhi, because they make no wholesale claims for rejecting Western modernity. They do, however, clearly demarcate the golden age of the Vedas as the be all and end all of their definition of nationhood. They mark the shift to the nonviolence of Buddhism both as a glorious accomplishment of Vedic civilization but also as an important indicator of decline. Gandhi's account locates the golden age as pre-British, but does not limit it to any particular epoch. Even the secular Nehru, who does not make claims about a golden age, still claims the existence of an underlying national consciousness by recounting an inherently syncretic civilization at the core of Indian nationality. Thus, all four identity entrepreneurs claim history's warrant of antiquity for their identity projects by locating the origins of Indian nationality in the distant past with sacred values.

Although the historical moment of a golden age might implicitly demarcate an out-group by defining the in-group, a second critical element of the historical trajectory articulated by the identity entrepreneurs is a *historical juncture*, or a conflict/crisis that lends itself directly to explicit definition of an out-group. For all four writers, the out-group was a foreign invader. Tragically for the 1 million people who lost their lives during the partition of India and Pakistan, they disagreed about who the self-defining out-group was.

Although the meeting between Hinduism and Islam is acknowledged by both Gandhi and Nehru, it is not demarcated as the critical historical juncture in their writings. Nehru, who characterizes the national culture as inherently syncretic and secular, goes so far as to claim that the historical interaction between

Hinduism and Islam produced some of the finest examples of Indian culture and nationhood. In a similar vein, Gandhi refused to acknowledge any historical tensions between the Hindu and Muslim communities of India, attributing any existing tension to British and Western influences. The period that the two INC leaders mark as representing the historical ideal thus stretched beyond the Vedic era to include interaction between Hinduism and Islam in India. For both these identity entrepreneurs, this extended period illustrates the syncretism of Indian national culture. For Gandhi and Nehru, the arrival of the British, and not Muslims, represents the critical juncture/turning point in the historical trajectory of India.

Conversely, Savarkar and Golwalkar clearly demarcate Vedic civilization as the golden age and the meeting between Hinduism and Islam as the critical historical juncture for their identity projects. However, in defining the in-group, they still use the same strategy as Nehru and Gandhi in that they define it is as widely as possible (see Reicher et al., 2005), including Buddhism, Sikhism and Jainism as branches within the Sanskrit-derived tree. They valorize the Hindu warrior spirit more than the pacifism of Buddhism. Notably, they also ascribe some of the same syncretic characteristics to the national culture as Nehru does, but do not extend these to encompass the historical meeting between the Hindus and Muslims. The colonization of India is thus a fact for all writers, but for the Hindu nationalists the oppression begins not with the British, but with the arrival of Islam.

Metaphor is used as a major argument and structuring device only by Gandhi among the four authors. The Hindu nationalists generally attempt to use more historical and analytical arguments to burnish their credentials. They do employ the familiar device of likening the nation to a body in places (see Hanne, this volume), but it is the chronological historical narrative and not the diachronic use of metaphor that is the heart of their argument. The secular and avuncular Nehru similarly apologizes for his use of metaphor to characterize India as a woman and to claim that its civilization has a soul. A rational construction of author legitimacy is thus attempted by three of the four authors, with Gandhi alone using the more intuitive and nonchronological appeal of metaphor to make his major points. This may be because only Gandhi was aiming at a popular audience (originally writing in Gujarati) with his book, whereas the other three may have been aiming at a more highbrow audience. Future research may well examine the use of metaphor to reach different audiences in different forms of political communication.

Conclusion

Besides the secession of Pakistan, independence meant that the INC's vision for the nation could be realized within the borders of the Republic of India as it adopted secular democracy and constitutionalized religious rights as a guiding principle for nation building. However, rather than separating religion from state, which secularism entails in the West, the INC adopted an indigenous variation of secularism requiring state involvement in religious affairs, entailing special rights and protection of religious minority communities. More concretely, the principle led to the provision of ten articles in the constitution for the benefit and protection of religious minorities (Articles 15–17 and 24–30). India also maintained its separate family and family laws for different religious groups, most markedly *Shariat* for its Muslim citizens.

On the other hand, the secession of Pakistan arguably vindicated the views of Savarkar and Golwalkar as well. According to the Hindu nationalist movement, India being a Hindu nation was the only logical consequence after Pakistan had been established as a Muslim state. However, as a result of its alleged involvement in the assassination of Gandhi (see Noorani, 2002), the Hindu nationalist movement was marginalized and stigmatized for the first three decades after Indian independence and dedicated itself to nation-building from the grass-roots. It was not until 30 years after independence that the RSS established a political wing (the Bharatiya Jana Sangh [BJS], predecessor of the BJP) to directly challenge the INC's hegemony to state power through electoral politics. Until then, the RSS believed strictly in sociocultural reform of Hindu people and culture. Golwalkar, who served as supreme leader for the movement between 1940 and 1977, implemented the principle of *Saravangeena Unnati* (All-Round-Development). What the principle came to entail for the RSS was the establishment of a network of 44 affiliate organisations across societal domains and spheres central to the building of Hindu nationhood. Together the network of affiliate organisations is referred to as the *Sangh Parivar* (Family of Organisations). Amongst these the BJP and Vishwa Hindu Parishad (VHP; organisation dedicated to consolidating and strengthening Hindu values and society) have arguably been most central to the propagation of Hindu nationalism in India (see Bhatt, 2001, and Jaffrelot, 1996, for elaborate accounts of the Hindu nationalist movement).

The Hindu nationalist movement most markedly resurfaced at the forefront of Indian politics during the Shah Bano affair in 1978. The case involved a 62-year-old Muslim woman who had been granted alimony under the common criminal code by a High Court, and then the Supreme Court of India, after her husband appealed against the High Court decision. Having been granted alimony under the common criminal code as opposed to Muslim personal law effectively meant that her ex-husband had to pay her a higher amount of alimony (see Engineer, 1987, for an elaborate account of the case). Leaders of the orthodox Muslim community were outraged by the decision and argued that it was an encroachment upon the jurisdiction and autonomy of the All-Indian Muslim Personal Law Board (AIMPLB). Rajiv Gandhi, then-president of the INC, ended up yielding to the pressure of the orthodox Muslim clergy and passed The Muslim Women (Protection of Rights on Divorce) Act 1986. This essentially meant that divorced Muslim women were no longer under the jurisdiction of the common criminal code.

The Hindu nationalist movement, spearheaded by the BJP, was fast to exploit the alleged double standard of the INC. Whereas the orthodox Muslim community perceived the original verdict as an attack on Muslims, Hindu nationalists perceived the overruling of the verdict as discriminatory against non-Muslims, who still had to pay a higher amount of alimony in a divorce, and stressed the necessity of a uniform civil code. Many had already questioned the separate Muslim personal law, but the overturning of a Supreme Court decision placed the separate legal system and its functions under even more scrutiny. Fearing he had lost Hindu voters to the BJP as a consequence of his appeasement of the orthodox Muslim clergy, Rajiv Gandhi lifted previous access restrictions to the site of the Babri Mosque, allowing Hindu pilgrims to worship at the site that had been claimed to be the birthplace of Lord Ram in Ayodhya (Engineer, 1987). His decision arguably sparked the contemporary Ayodhya movement, which was the most significant event for the revitalisation of the Hindu nationalist movement, and the success of the BJP being elected into national government in 1998. Compared to previous campaigns that had invoked Hindu mythology to propagate the Hindu nationalist vision of a homogenous and unified Hindu nation with limited success, the Ayodhya dispute came to represent the ideal opportunity for the movement to mobilise its vision of Hindu nationhood by combining the historical moment of a Vedic golden age with the historical juncture of the meeting between Hindus and Muslims in the same manufactured event.

Historically, the birthplace of Lord Ram[8] was believed to be signified by a small platform adjacent to the Babri mosque, built in 1528 by the first Mughal emperor of India, Babur (1483–1581). The site remained undisputed until 1853, when local worshippers of Lord Ram claimed that the mosque had been built on the birthplace itself. Requests were made by local Hindu priests to have a temple built on the platform, but these were rejected by the British colonial administration because of its proximity to the mosque. The dispute did not lead to any conflict at the time; instead, a compromise was reached between Hindu and Muslim worshippers, whereby devotees were allowed to worship Lord Ram on the platform next to the mosque. Only 60 years after this did the issue resurface in the context of the partition. In 1949, someone broke into the mosque and installed idols of Lord Ram, his wife Sita and his most trusted companion, the monkey god Hanuman. While thousands of Hindu devotees gathered outside the mosque the day after the idols had been installed, Hindu nationalist organizations claimed the event to be a miracle, and that the idols had manifested themselves to reclaim the site. Recognizing the sensitivity of the issue, the state government immediately ordered the removal of the idols to prevent interreligious violence. Following the event in 1949, the issue did not resurface for almost 30 years. The issue was then revived in the 1980s by the VHP with the organization of numerous state and national rallies that called for access to the "shrine" in the Babri mosque where the idols had been installed in 1949. The VHP also made several appeals to different courts demanding access to the mosque and "shrine" (Jaffrelot, 1996; 2007; Katju, 2003; Puniyani, 2003).

Polarization between the Hindu and Muslim communities was already high as a consequence of the Shah Bano case. In addition, the state-owned Indian television station *Doordarshan* began the screening of a 78-episode weekly *Ramayana* television series in 1987, which inadvertently furthered the Hindu nationalist campaign to liberate the birthplace of Lord Ram by reinforcing the view that the town of Ayodhya was his birthplace (Bacchetta, 2000; Rajagopal, 2001). By this stage, even Muslim organizations had begun to organize rallies against Hindu nationalist claims to the Babri mosque. However, the movement was further reinvigorated in 1989, when the BJP (who had previously remained distanced from the Ayodhya movement) joined the movement in the lead-up to the 1989 general elections. In the same year, the BJP passed a resolution making the *Ramjanmabhoomi* (birthplace of Lord Ram) its main campaign issue (Jaffrelot, 1996; 2007; Katju, 2003; Puniyani, 2003).

The BJP resolution was followed by L. K. Advani's (then president of the BJP) infamous Rath Yatra (Chariot March) in 1990. The Rath Yatra was led by a Toyota GMC truck that had been decorated to resemble an ancient Indian chariot (portrayed in the screening of the *Ramayana*), but instead of Lord Ram, Advani addressed the public through loudspeakers from a platform behind the driver's cab. The procession covered 10,000 miles and 10 states, and along its course, almost 300 interreligious riots erupted across India, the most since the partition of India (Jaffrelot, 1996, 2007; Katju, 2003; Puniyani, 2003). Such theater using the metaphor of Advani as Ram and the BJP as the spearhead of the sacred Indian nation was a most powerful form of propaganda. Although less celebrated internationally for obvious reasons, for Hindu nationalists this could be likened to the metaphorical impact of Gandhi's march to the sea to make salt in defiance of the British Raj. Anecdotally, it appears that metaphor, especially in the guise of political theater, is capable of inspiring powerful social movements in India.

However, the Rath Yatra comprised only one component of a larger Sangh Parivar campaign to gather support for the construction of a Ram temple. During the same period, members of the RSS and VHP were recruiting *Kar Sevaks* (Spiritual Volunteers) to assist in the construction of the planned Ram temple. In this endeavour, the RSS, VHP and BJP launched the Ramshilapujan campaign whereby bricks for the Ram temple were blessed in religious ceremonies across the country, and were to be sent with Kar Sevaks to Ayodhya. An estimated 297,705 such ceremonies were held in India and abroad (Katju, 2003).

The agitations of the Hindu nationalist movement culminated on the December 6, 1992, when an estimated 150,000 Hindu nationalist activists and Kar Sevaks gathered for a rally outside the mosque. While the crowds were being addressed by several prominent Hindu nationalist leaders, a small group of activists managed to break through the barricades protecting the Babri mosque. This encouraged thousands of other activists in the crowd to follow suit, and within minutes, the mosque was surrounded by activists, who hurled stones at the police and shouted Hindu-nationalist slogans. The police protecting the mosque eventually retreated and refrained from opening fire. Thousands of activists then began climbing the mosque using sledgehammers and iron rods to destroy the structure. Triangular saffron flags, representing the Hindu nationalist movement, were also hoisted onto the domes of the mosque. Within hours, large parts of the mosque were razed to the ground. Interreligious riots erupted in most major northern Indian cities in the aftermath of the demolition, resulting in nearly 1,500 deaths across the country.

The Ayodhya movement and the circumstances leading up to the demolition of Babri Mosque have been extensively analyzed amongst both political commentators and academic scholars. Although there seems to be an agreement about the role that wider political and economic factors played in the episode (see Kinnvall, 2004; Lochtefeld, 1996; Varshney, 1993), there is a consensus that the combination of Hindu mythology and Hindu–Muslim history in the same campaign proved to be a compelling recipe for success for the Hindu nationalist movement. Not only did widely shared understandings of the *Ramayana* enable the Vedic period to be portrayed and mobilized as a golden age for the Hindu people; the historical meeting between Hindu and Muslim, embodied through the invasion by Babur, also enabled the Hindu nationalist movement to define the out-group exactly as narrated by Savarkar and Golwalkar. The Babri mosque thus came to represent a metaphor embodying Muslims as foreign invaders compromising the sacred integrity of the "pure" and ancient Indian nation.

Thus, besides containing the critical ingredients of a Vedic golden age and the critical historical juncture of Muslims conquering India (represented by Babur), the success of the Ayodhya campaign for the Hindu nationalist movement appeared to be contingent on the fact that its mythological content is widely shared among Hindus and other religious sects in India. Not only is Lord Ram one of the most significant deities in Hindu mythology as the principal character and hero of the widely read *Ramayana*; the Ayodhya campaign also coincided with a 78-episode weekly television screening of the epic.

Nevertheless, it is important to keep in mind that the success of the *Sangh Parivar* was temporary. Although the BJP is the second largest political party in India today, it lost in a landslide to the INC in the general elections of 2004. In 2004, the theme of the BJP's election campaign was "India Shining." The campaign was intended to promote feelings of economic optimism amongst the Indian population, but also to promote its 8% growth rate and booming information technology and service industries attracting foreign investment internationally. The campaign cost 20 million US dollars and was outsourced to the US advertising company Grey Worldwide. The campaign was largely a failure as the BJP lost the general elections to the INC. It was felt that the economic policies of the BJP—together with its "India Shining" campaign—were the main causes for its setback. The economic policies of the BJP and its campaigns appealed to the wealthy sections of Indian society and big business, but had in the process lost touch with the middle classes and poor of India. Even the leaders of the BJP, including Vaypajee and Advani, have admitted that their economic policies and campaign had failed by neglecting the realities of large sections of Indian society that had bought into their mythological reading of history a few years before (e.g., McGuire & Copland, 2007).

The massive irony in these outcomes cannot have escaped notice by the astute reader. The Hindu nationalists finally came to political power by using the re-enactment of a metaphor (the Chariot March) to carry an historical narrative pioneered by their intellectual ancestors Savarkar and Golwalkar and replayed on TV. They lost it again in subordinating this narrative to one of liberal progress. The INC view of India as a syncretic and multicultural whole continues to be the dominant form of national identity, even though Gandhi's Luddite views against technology and Western forms of progress have become a mere historical footnote to his legend as a humanitarian and freedom fighter. As the dominant political party, the INC very rarely revisits the historical narratives of its forefathers Gandhi and Nehru, for these men achieved their aims of getting the British out of India, and founding a secular and pluralistic state.

Notes

1 Unfortunately, due to space limitations, we will not be able to elaborate on the critical role played in independence (and partition) by All-Muslim League leader Muhammad Ali Jinnah
2 The RSS was allied to the Hindu Mahasabha and was banned for a time after Gandhi's assassination; it has been accused of fomenting sectarian violence on other occasions.
3 The Marathas were tribal peoples of the Deccan plateau who warred against the Moghuls and effectively stopped their advance into southern parts of the Indian subcontinent
4 Note the slight matter of four millennia of difference between the warrants of antiquity claimed by Savarkar and Golwalkar. But what's 4,000 years between friends?
5 He was trained in India as a lawyer, although his performance was inept.
6 Hanuman and Sugriva are monkey kings who assisted Rama in his battles.
7 This is a difference in spelling and pronunciation only: Sindusthan in Sanskrit equals Hindustan in Hindi. *Mlecch* or *Mleccha* is non-Vedic for "barbarian," a term historically used to refer to foreigners.
8 Lord Ram is one of the most significant deities in Hindu mythology and is the principal character and hero of the ancient Sanskrit epic, the *Ramayana*, widely known by the greater Hindu community.

References

Anderson, B. (1983). *Imagined communities*: *Reflections on the origins and spread of nationalism*. London: Verso.

Bacchetta, P. (2000). Sacred space in religious-political conflict in India: The Babri Masjid affair. *Growth and Change*, *31* (2), 255–284.

Bandyopadhyay, S. (2004). *From Plassey to partition: A history of modern India*. New Delhi: Orient Longman.

Bandyopadhyay, S. (2010). *Nationalist movement in India. A reader*. New Delhi: Oxford University Press.

Bauer, M. & Gaskell, G. (1999). Towards a paradigm for the study of social representations, *Journal for the Theory of Social Behaviour*, *29*, 162–186.

Bhatt, C. (2001). *Hindu nationalism: Origins, ideologies and modern myths*. Oxford, England: Berg.

Bruner, J. (1990). *Acts of meaning*. Cambridge, MA: Harvard University Press.

Campbell, J. (1968). *The hero of a thousand faces*. Princeton, NJ: Princeton University Press.

Einhorn, B. (2006). Insiders and outsiders: Within and beyond the gendered nation. In K. Davis, M. Evans, & J. Lorber (Eds.), *Handbook of gender and women's studies* (pp. 89–112). London: Sage.

Engineer, A. A. (1987). *The Shah Bano controversy*. New Delhi: Orient Longman.

Fivush, R. (2010). Speaking silence: The social construction of silence in autobiographical and cultural narratives, *Memory*, *12*, 88–98.

Gandhi, M. K. (1910). *Hind Swaraj*. Phoenix, South Africa: International Printing Press.

Golwalkar, M. S. (1939). *We, or our nationhood defined*. Nagpur, India: Bharat Publications.

Hammack, P., & Pilecki, A. (2012). Narrative as a root metaphor for political psychology. *Political Psychology*, *33*, 75–103.

Harré, R., & van Langenhove, L. (1991). Varieties of positioning. *Journal for the Theory of Social Behaviour*, *21*, 393–407.

Hobsbawm, E., & Ranger, T. (Eds.). (1983). *The invention of tradition*. Cambridge: Cambridge University Press.

Hwang, K. K. (2003). Critique of the methodology of empirical research on individual modernity in Taiwan. *Asian Journal of Social Psychology*, *6*, 241–262.

Jaffrelot, C. (1996). *The Hindu nationalist movement and Indian politics: 1925 to the 1990s*. London: Hurst & Co.

Jaffrelot, C. (Ed.). (2007). *Hindu nationalism: A reader*. Princeton, NJ: Princeton University Press.

Jayawardena, K. (1986). *Feminism and nationalism in the third world*. New Delhi: Kali for Women.

Katju, M. (2003). *The Vishwa Hindu Parishad and Indian politics*. Hyderabad, India: Orient Longman.

Khan, S. S. (2011). *Hindutva: A social psychological examination of the structure, content and intergroup consequences of Hindu nationalism in India*. (Unpublished doctoral dissertation). Victoria University of Wellington, New Zealand.

Kinnvall, C. (2004). Globalization and religious nationalism: Self, identity, and the search for ontological security. *Political Psychology*, *25*, 741–767

Kus, L., Liu, J. H., & Ward, C. (2013). Relative deprivation versus system justification: The past as a cognitive alternative to the *status quo* in a post-Soviet society. *European Journal of Social Psychology, 43*(5), 423–437.

László, J. (2008). *The science of stories: An introduction to narrative psychology*. London: Routledge.

Liu, J. H., Goldstein-Hawes, R., Hilton, D. J., Huang, L. L., Gastardo-Conaco, C., Dresler-Hawke, E., Pittolo, F., Hong, Y. Y., Ward, C., Abraham, S., Kashima, Y., Kashima, E., Ohashi, M., Yuki, M., & Hidaka, Y. (2005). Social representations of events and people in world history across twelve cultures. *Journal of Cross-Cultural Psychology, 36*(2), 171–191.

Liu, J. H., & Hilton, D. (2005). How the past weighs on the present: Social representations of history and their role in identity politics. *British Journal of Social Psychology*, *44*, 537–556.

Liu, J. H., & László, J. (2007). A narrative theory of history and identity: Social identity, social representations, society and the individual. In G. Moloney & I. Walker (Eds.), *Social representations and identity: Content, process and power* (pp. 85–107). London: Palgrave Macmillan.

Liu, J. H., Paez, D., Slawuta, P., Cabecinhas, R., Techio, E., Kokdemir, D., Sen, R., Vincze, O., Muluk, H., Wang, F. X., & Zlobina, A. (2009). Representing world history in the 21st century: The impact of 9–11, the Iraq War, and the nation-state on the dynamics of collective remembering. *Journal of Cross-Cultural Psychology*, *40*, 667–692.

Liu, J. H., & Sibley, C. G. (2009). Culture, social representations, and peacemaking: A symbolic theory of history and identity. In C. Montiel & N. Noor (Eds.), *Peace psychology in Asia* (pp. 21–42). New York: Springer.

Liu, J. H., & Sibley, C. G. (in press). Social representations of history: Theory and applications, methods, measurement and results. In G. Sammut, E. Andreouli, G. Gaskell (Eds.), *Resistance, stability, and social change: A handbook of social representations*. Cambridge: Cambridge University Press.

Liu, J. H., Sibley, C. G., & Huang, L. L. (2013). History matters: The impact of culture-specific symbols on political attitudes and intergroup relations. *Political Psychology*. Advanced online publication. Doi:10.1111/pops.12027

Lochtefeld, J. G. (1996). New wine, old skins: The Sangh Parivar and the transformation of Hinduism. *Religion*, *26*, 101–118.

Ludden, D. (Ed.). (2005). *Reinventing India*: *Liberalization, Hindu nationalism and popular democracy* (2nd ed.). Delhi: Oxford University Press.

Malinowski, B. (1926). *Myth in primitive psychology*. London: Kegan Paul, Trench, Trubner.

McClintock, A. (1997). No longer in a future heaven: Gender, race, and nationalism. In A. McClintock, A. Mufti, & E. Shohat (Eds.), *Dangerous liaisons: gender, nation, and postcolonial perspectives* (pp. 196–213). Minneapolis: University of Minnesota Press.

McGuire, J., & Copland, I (Eds.) (2007). *Hindu nationalism and governance*. New Delhi: Oxford University Press.

Mill, J. (1818). *The history of British India*. London: Baldwin, Cradock and Joy.

Moscovici, S. (1961/2008). *Psychoanalysis: Its image and its public*. Malden, MA: Polity Press.

Moscovici, S. (1988). Notes towards a description of social representations. *European Journal of Social Psychology*, *18*, 211–250.

Nehru, J. (1946). *The discovery of India*. Oxford, England: Oxford University Press.

Noorani, A. G. (2002). *Savarkar and Hindutva: The Godse connection*. New Delhi: Left Word Books.

Ortony, A. (1975) Why metaphors are necessary and not just nice. *Educational Theory*, *25*(1), 45–53.

Propp, V. (1968). *The morphology of the folktale*. Austin: Texas University Press.

Puniyani, R. (2003). *Communal politics*: *Facts versus myths*. New Delhi: Sage.

Rajagopal, A. (2001). *Politics after television: Hindu nationalism and the reshaping of the public in India*. Cambridge: Cambridge University Press.

Reicher, S. D., Haslam, S. A., & Hopkins, N. (2005). Social identity and the dynamics of leadership: Leaders and followers as collaborative agents in the transformation of social reality. *Leadership Quarterly, 16*, 547–568.

Reicher, S., & Hopkins, N. (2001). *Self and nation*. London: Sage.

Reicher, S., Hopkins, N., Levine, M., & Rath, R. (2005). Entrepreneurs of hate and entrepreneurs of solidarity: Social identity as a basis for mass communication. *International Review of the Red Cross, 87*, 621–637.

Sarbin, T. R. (1986). The narrative as a root metaphor for psychology. In T. R. Sarbin (Ed.), *Narrative psychology: The storied nature of human conduct* (pp. 3–21). New York: Praeger.

Savarkar, V. D. (1923). *Hindutva—Who is a Hindu?* Bombay, India: Veer Savarkar Prakashan.

Sen, R., & Wagner, W. (2005). History, emotions and hetero-referential representations in inter-group conflict: The example of Hindu-Muslim relations in India. *Papers on Social Representations, 14*, 2.1–2.23.

Sinha, D. (1998). Changing perspectives in social psychology in India: A journey towards indigenisation. *Asian Journal of Social Psychology, 1*, 17–32.

Svensson, T. (2013). *Production of postcolonial India and Pakistan: Meanings of partition*. Abingdon: Routledge.

Tajfel, H., & Turner, J. C. (1979). The social identity theory of intergroup behaviour. In S. Worchel & W. Austin (Eds.), *Psychology of intergroup relations* (pp. 33–48). Chicago: Nelson-Hall.

Thorne, A., & McLean, K. C. (2003). Telling traumatic events in adolescence: A study of master narrative positioning. In R. Fivush & C. A. Haden (Eds.), *Autobiographical memory and the construction of a narrative self: Developmental and cultural perspectives* (pp. 169–186). Mahwah, NJ: Erlbaum.

Turner, J. C., Hogg, M. A., Oakes, P. J., Reicher, S. D., & Wetherell, M. S. (1987). *Rediscovering the social group: A self-categorization theory*. New York: Basil Blackwell.

Varshney, A. (1993). Contested meanings: Hindu nationalism, India's national Identity, and the politics of anxiety. *Daedalus, 122*, 227–261.

Wertsch, J. V. (2002). *Voices of collective remembering*. Cambridge: Cambridge University Press.

White, H. (1987). *The content of the form: Narrative discourse and historical representation*. Baltimore: The Johns Hopkins University Press.

Wolpert, S. (2010). *India and Pakistan: Continued conflict or cooperation*. Los Angeles: University of California Press.

Yang, K. S. (2003). Methodological and theoretical issues on psychological traditionality and modernity research in an Asian society: In response to Kwang-Kuo Hwang and beyond. *Asian Journal of Social Psychology, 6*(3), 263–285.

Yzerbyt, V., Judd, C., & Corneille, O. (2004). *The psychology of group perception: Perceived variability, entitativity, and essentialism*. New York: Psychology Press.

10 Responses to Metaphors in Politics

Continued Explorations of the Metaphor Extension Hypothesis

Jeffery Scott Mio

On September 18, 1986, President Corazon Aquino addressed a joint session of Congress, becoming only the second foreign dignitary ever to do so in the history of the United States. The purpose of the speech was to report on the "people power revolution" that the Philippines had successfully completed just half a year before her address to the Congress. A second—and more important—purpose of the speech was to ask for foreign aid to help her country pay off the foreign debts accumulated by her predecessor, President Ferdinand Marcos. Despite the fact that the Philippines had been the third leading recipient of US foreign aid at the time, it turned out that President Marcos had diverted these funds into his private offshore bank accounts, leaving the Filipino treasury empty.

By all accounts, President Aquino's speech was highly effective. In fact, Speaker of the House Tip O'Neill stated that it was the best political speech he had ever heard. As President Aquino was leaving the chambers of the Congress, *Time* magazine reported, "Senate Majority Leader Robert Dole said to Mrs. Aquino, 'Cory, you hit a home run.' Without missing a beat, Aquino smiled and shot back: 'I hope the bases were loaded.'" (Sherrill, 1986). Later that day, the House of Representatives voted to allocate $200 million in emergency foreign aid to the Philippines.

The Filipino people's revolution and Mrs. Aquino's subsequent address to a joint session of the U.S. Congress were clearly major occurrences in world history, as the revolution demonstrated how democratic rule can be wrested from dictators, and Mrs. Aquino's address was only the second time in U.S. history that a foreign dignitary addressed a joint session of Congress. However, these incidents also marked a turning point in my personal professional career. I had been interested in conducting research on metaphors, but I was uncertain how to pursue this interest. As a clinical psychologist, I had some interest in examining metaphors that arose in therapy sessions, but this would require the consent of the therapist and client and also timely transcriptions of the sessions. As a sports fan, I had been aware of how many metaphors are used in sports broadcasting and reporting, but this pursuit seemed to be of little consequence. However, winning political arguments had some real-world implications, so

I decided to pursue this endeavor. Moreover, at the time of this occurrence, many political news programs, such as *The McNeil/Lehrer News Hour* on PBS or ABC's *Nightline*, offered transcripts for a fee. Also, if one could wait a few months after a major speech, *Vital Speeches of the Day* printed speeches such as presidential nomination acceptance speeches and states of the union. Therefore, studying rhetoric in the political arena was much easier to do than studying language in therapy and it had some real-world consequence.

While I pursued various endeavors on metaphors in politics, I kept thinking of how deftly President Aquino responded to Senator Dole. I was aware that much of the research on metaphor and political persuasion yielded conflicting results, with some studies finding support for the use of metaphors as persuasive devices (e.g., Bowers, 1964; Bowers & Osborn, 1966; Read, Cesa, Jones, & Collins, 1990; Reinsch, 1971), and others not finding such support or finding equivocal support for the efficacy of metaphors in political persuasion (e.g., Bosman, 1987; Bosman & Hagendoorn, 1991; Johnson & Taylor, 1981).

As time went on, I began developing what I called the "Metaphor Extension Hypothesis" (MEH). Rather than studying the general effectiveness of metaphors in political persuasion, I concentrated on the context of political interactions or debates (Mio, 1996, 1997). The MEH suggests that metaphors are particularly effective when they extend a conversational partner's or debate opponent's metaphor. President Aquino's metaphorical response is a perfect example of such an extension. She could have responded in a literal manner, such as, "Thank you, Senator, I hope I was effective," or in a manner using a different metaphor, such as, "Thank you, Senator, I hope you Americans pour your hearts out to us." However, the fact that she extended Senator Dole's home run metaphor by hoping that the bases were loaded when she hit the home run was so effective that it was used as the basis of the title of the article in *Time* magazine: "The Philippines Cory Hits a Grand Slam" (Sherill, 1986).

Why Metaphors?

As most social psychologists know, Hovland and his associates (Hovland, Janis, & Kelley, 1953) studied factors involved in persuasion. Their studies identified four major components of a persuasive message: the speaker, the message, the medium of the communication, and the audience receiving the message. Besides the speaker needing to be seen as a credible source of information, the message is one aspect of a persuasive communication under the control of the designers of the communication.

With respect to the message, Petty and Cacioppo (1986) asserted that there were two routes to persuasion: the central route and the peripheral route. The central route of persuasion is a logical, rational presentation of arguments in favor of one position. It is more persuasive if the audience is motivated to make a good decision and will expend some effort on paying attention to the message and even generate counterarguments to the message to stretch the limits of the points being made. The peripheral route of persuasion is an emotional, irrational presentation of a position. It is more persuasive if the audience is not involved with the central issue and will not want to expend much effort into paying attention to the speaker. The audience quite often uses rules of thumb heuristics to make decisions or is swayed by catchy phrases or colorful, superficial cues. Petty and Cacioppo found that the central route tends to lead to enduring agreement with the persuasive message, whereas the peripheral route tends to lead to only temporary agreement.

In their review of the attitude change literature, Chaiken and Stangor (1987) concluded that metaphors are particularly interesting linguistic devices in that they had the ability to combine both the central and peripheral routes of persuasion. On the surface, metaphorical arguments would seem to utilize the peripheral route of persuasion in that the metaphor can be seen superficially or as merely a clever way of presenting one's argument. However, metaphors can also suggest a logical path towards a solution characterization of an issue. For example, in the famous political advertisement given credit for turning around people's impression that Ronald Reagan was too old to continue being president in 1984, the ad using the metaphor "It is morning in America" suggested that although the darkness of night had left the country uncertain about its future, morning had broken, and the early light of the sun gave assurance that things were going to get better in the country after a long period of recession.

My First Studies on the Metaphor Extension Hypothesis

In the spring of 1990, Lithuania was in a struggle to break away from the Soviet Union. President Mikhail Gorbachev sent in the Soviet Army to suppress the uprising, killing and injuring numerous Lithuanians and blowing up buildings with tanks that roamed the streets of Lithuania's capital, Vilnius (Sherrill, 1990). In a subsequent ABC *Nightline* program (see Mio, 1996), a Soviet representative explained that the Soviet Union and Lithuania were in something akin to a divorce, in that they first needed to have a trial separation to determine if the two countries could survive without one another. He further explained that Lithuania's highly productive factories were dependent upon cheap Soviet Union oil, so the two regions' respective economies were intertwined. The Lithuanian representative on the program said that the two countries were not in a divorce because they were never married, Lithuania was simply raped. He further went on to explain that because Lithuania bordered Russia during World War II, when Nazi Germany invaded Lithuania, Russia became concerned that it was going to be the next target of German invasion. In order to keep Russia out of the war for the time being, Germany gave Lithuania to Russia to serve as a buffer zone.

This Lithuanian "rape" metaphor was a good example of a metaphor extension, so I decided to study it systematically to determine if metaphor extensions were truly more effective in convincing an observing audience in the context of a debate. As I reported previously (Mio, 1996), this was indeed the case, lending support for the MEH. However, in studying language, one must guard against overinterpreting one specific exchange because there may be something special about the particular dialogue being studied. There may have been something particularly convincing about the rape metaphor in this context. Therefore, I began collecting more debates illustrating metaphor extensions in the latter part of the George H. W. Bush administration and the beginning part of the Bill Clinton administration.

I identified 12 debates in the early 1990s where a second speaker extended the metaphor of the first speaker, turning it against the first speaker in an attempt to win the debate. Such segments included the preceding *divorce–rape* metaphor, a metaphor exchange about not intervening in the Bosnia-Herzegovina civil war as merely *tattering* our reputation a little bit versus *ripping it to shreds*, a senator criticizing President Clinton's first budget by saying that he felt *like a mosquito in a nudist colony not knowing where to strike first*, and a colleague criticizing this senator for contributing to the budget problem and saying that the first senator was more *like a nudist in a mosquito colony not knowing what to cover up first*. There were also some rhyming metaphors that I called "homomets" to be akin to homophones (e.g., *their* and *there*). An example of these homomets was trying to deal with all of the nuclear weapons in the aftermath of the downfall of the Soviet Union and one person saying that we did not have the resources to conduct another *Marshall Plan* to help Russia deal with these nuclear weapons, and the debate opponent saying that he would rather have a *Marshall Plan* than *martial law*. Another example of a homomet was the intervention in Somalia's civil war that resulted in a Black Hawk helicopter being shot down and our soldiers being killed and dragged through the streets of Mogadishu, Somalia. One speaker defended our intervention, saying that it was appropriate to try to act like the *Red Cross* to help starving citizens of Somalia, but the opponent saying that while we tried to act like the *Red Cross*, we become caught in the *crossfire* of local disputes.

We assembled these debate segments into booklets in which we asked participants to pretend they were Speaker 2 in a political debate with Speaker 1, and they were to circle the option they felt would be the more effective in response to a position taken by Speaker 1. Some of the options had Speaker 2 saying either a metaphor extension or a metaphor nonextension, some had Speaker 2 saying either a metaphor extension or a literal response, some had Speaker 2 saying either a homomet or a literal response, and some debate segments did not have Speaker 1 presenting a position containing a metaphor. Table 10.1 is an example of some of the stimuli we used.

Of course, all the relevant counterbalancing was conducted in this study, with the extending metaphors being the first alternative sometimes and second at other times, and the homomet being first sometimes and second at other times. Moreover, participants were asked to take a "liberal" position on half the items and a "conservative" position on the other half. Finally, we also

Table 10.1 Examples of Stimuli Comparing Presented to Speaker 2

Extending metaphors versus nonextending metaphors

Speaker 1: We see our relationship with Lithuania as a divorce, and like a divorce, there needs to be a slow process of separation, then a fair and equitable division of common property.

Speaker 2:

    a. Our relationship with the Soviet Union is not like a divorce, because we were never married, we were simply raped. We demand our freedom immediately.

    b. Our relationship with the Soviet Union is not like a divorce, it is more like we are prisoners in an illegal regime. We demand our freedom immediately.

Speaker 1: Our failure in dealing with the Bosnian situation merely means that our prestige got tattered a little bit.

Speaker 2:

    a. It was more than tattered a little bit, it was ripped to shreds.

    b. It was more than tattered a little bit, it was tarnished considerably.

Speaker 1: Looking at President Clinton's economic program, I feel like a mosquito in a nudist colony. The real question is where to strike first.

Speaker 2:

    a. Speaker 1 is more like a nudist in a mosquito colony, not knowing what to cover up first.

    b. Speaker 1 is more like a man in a glass house throwing stones at the president's plan.

Extending metaphors versus literal responses

Speaker 1: We see our relationship with Lithuania as a divorce, and like a divorce, there needs to be a slow process of separation, then a fair and equitable division of common property.

Speaker 2:

    a. Our relationship with the Soviet Union is not like a divorce, because we were never married, we were simply raped. We demand our freedom immediately.

    b. Our relationship with the Soviet Union is not like a divorce because we were forced to join the union against our will. We demand our freedom immediately.

Speaker 1: Our failure in dealing with the Bosnian situation merely means that our prestige got tattered a little bit.

Speaker 2:

    a. It was more than tattered a little bit, it was ripped to shreds.

    b. It was more than tattered a little bit, it was harmed considerably.

Speaker 1: Looking at President Clinton's economic program, I feel like a mosquito in a nudist colony. The real question is where to strike first.

Speaker 2:

    a. Speaker 1 is more like a nudist in a mosquito colony, not knowing what to cover up first.

    b. Speaker 1 should not criticize the president's plan before he examines his own contribution to the budget problem.

Homomets versus literal responses

Speaker 1:   We do not have the money nor the resources to do a Marshall Plan for Russia.

Speaker 2:

      a. Given Russia's nuclear weapons, I would rather have a Marshall Plan than martial law.

      b. Given Russia's nuclear weapons, a Marshall Plan is preferable to the army taking control of the country.

Speaker 1:   I feel it is appropriate that we serve as a Red Cross to help those starving people.

Speaker 2:

      a. The problem is that we started out as the Red Cross, but we got caught in the crossfire.

      b. The problem is that we started out as the Red Cross, but we got caught in internal disputes.

had a brief paragraph explaining the context of the debates, given that most undergraduates may not be well versed in history or politics. For example, we informed our participants about the complex history between the Soviet Union and Lithuania, and we informed our participants what the Marshall Plan was. Our results were somewhat equivocal, as the metaphor extensions were clearly preferred over metaphor nonextensions (see Table 10.2), but literal responses were preferred over metaphor extensions by our female participants, whereas the male participant preference of metaphor extensions was much more attenuated (see Table 10.3). Neither male nor female participants preferred homomets over their literal counterparts (see Table 10.4). However, we also happened to ask participants which three debates they felt were the *most* convincing of the 16 debate segments in the booklet (there were four filler items that did not contain any metaphors in them). This question was crucial in that there was unequivocal support for the MEH by both male and female participants (see Table 10.5).

Taken as a whole, these results offer support for the MEH. In the context of a political debate, metaphor extensions are more effective responses to an opponent's otherwise convincing metaphor. I say "otherwise convincing metaphor" because as we are all aware, some people seem to use poor metaphors or ones that are not apt for a particular situation. As I reported in my 1996 study (Mio, 1996), I created a nonextending metaphor as one of the responses to the Soviet–Lithuania divorce metaphor that was not very well received by the participants. Moreover, we can all recall metaphors that are poorly selected that result in ridicule by political analysts. For example, I recall Ronald Reagan criticizing a Democratic plan by saying, "That's like a boat drifting aimlessly at sea down the wrong way of a one-way street." This metaphorical expression both employed mixed metaphors (*boat drifting* and *one-way street*) and was contradictory in that going down a one-way street implies a particular direction

Table 10.2 Metaphor Extensions Versus Nonextensions

	Males	Females
Metaphor Extensions	71	101
Metaphor Nonextensions	49	65

Table 10.3 Metaphor Extensions Versus Literal Responses

	Males	Females
Metaphor Extensions	63	74
Literal Reponses	58	93

Table 10.4 Homomets Versus Literal Responses

	Males	Females
Homomets	101	110
Literal Responses	141	223

Table 10.5 Three Most Convincing Arguments

	Males	Females
Metaphor Extensions	25	33
Metaphor Nonextensions	4	9
Literal Responses	8	5
Homomets	14	7
Literal Responses	13	16

but drifting at sea has no intentional direction. If one's opponent in a debate were to use poorly selected metaphors, it would be best just to allow the audience to come to a negative assessment without your assistance using an extending metaphor. Again, however, if your opponent uses a metaphor that was particularly effective, your best response would be to use a metaphor extension.

To further examine the MEH, I decided to allow research participants to generate their own responses to an opponent's position, some of which included metaphors. I embedded the 12 metaphors in the preceding study within other political issues, asking participants to pretend that they were in the position of being Speaker 2, and they had to respond to Speaker 1's position to convince an observing audience of their position. Again, about half of the positions that Speaker 2 had to take were the liberal position and half were the conservative position. Participants overwhelmingly responded literally to Speaker 1's positions, but when they *did* use metaphors, they used about eight times more extending metaphors than nonextending metaphors (see Table 10.6). Table 10.7

Table 10.6 Response Generation to Metaphors in the 1990s

	Literal	Extending Metaphors	Nonextending Metaphors
Males	8.67	2.56	.33
Females	8.69	2.69	.54

Table 10.7 Examples of Participant-Generated Extending Metaphors

Speaker 1: We see our relationship with Lithuania as a divorce, and like a divorce, there needs to be a slow process of separation, then a fair and equitable division of common property.
Speaker 2 (Participant): A slow divorce like what you propose would set us back for decades while we try to remarry another country.

Speaker 1: The engine driving our health care system is broken and needs to be fixed.
Speaker 2 (Participant): No, the engine needs a tune-up, but runs fine otherwise.

Speaker 1: The administration and environmentalists are having a love affair.
Speaker 2 (Participant): Some love affair; the administration has cheated occasionally.

Speaker 1: Looking at President Clinton's economic program, I feel like a mosquito in a nudist colony. The real question is where to strike first.
Speaker 2 (Participant): Speaker one is like a mosquito, except he sucks your money instead of your blood.

displays a few examples of the kinds of metaphor extensions that our participants generated.

Politicians are used to engaging in verbal sparring, so metaphor extensions may be somewhat natural—or at least a learned skill—to them. Therefore, it might not be surprising that our participants mostly responded literally to the metaphors presented by Speaker 1 in the debate encounters in the study. However, as stated earlier it was particularly pleasing to me that when the participants did use metaphors, they overwhelmingly used metaphor extensions as opposed to metaphor nonextensions. This was true both for our male *and* female participants and at approximately the same percentages. This was pleasing because our first study using multiple debate encounters yielded somewhat equivocal data, with women seeming to prefer literal responses over extending metaphorical ones overall, although they did feel that extending metaphors were the *most* persuasive responses. These participant-generated responses to metaphors gave me much more confidence in the MEH.

Participant-Generated Responses to Metaphors in the Post-9/11 Era

In the early 2000s, I conducted a study in collaboration with a colleague who was interested in a different topic. We decided to embed her topic among a list

Table 10.8 Participant-Generated Responses in the Post-9/11 Era

	Literal	Extending Metaphors	Nonextending Metaphors
Males	3.27	1.00	.27
Females	3.23	1.00	.15

Table 10.9 Examples of Participant-Generated Metaphors in the Post-9/11 Era

Speaker 1: We need to construct fences around the U.S.–Mexican border in order to close the door on illegal immigration.

Speaker 2 (Extending Metaphor): Closing the door on illegal immigration means closing one's mind to what America is all about.

Speaker 2 (Nonextending Metaphor): We need to allow the transition of immigrants to this country in a way that welcomes them to the land of the free.

Speaker 1: The Bush Administration keeps saying that we have turned the corner in Iraq, but I don't see where we turned the corner.

Speaker 2 (Extending Metaphor): One corner does not necessarily mean it is the right corner, so perhaps the Bush Administration hasn't found the right corner.

Speaker 2 (Nonextending Metaphor): It's hard to see the light at the end of the tunnel, but you know it's there so we have hope and continue on.

of nine topics characterized by metaphors in the post-9/11 era. Half the topics were presented in their metaphorical forms, and the other half were presented in their literal forms. Therefore, some booklets had four metaphors to which participants could respond, and some booklets had five metaphors to which participants could respond. Otherwise, the 55 participants (15 males and 40 females) followed the procedures we used in our previous study where they were to generate their own responses in the context of a debate, with half of their stances taking a liberal position and the other half taking a conservative position. As can be seen in Table 10.8, most responses were literal, but consistent with our previous study, when a metaphor *was* used, it was more likely to be an extending metaphor as opposed to a nonextending metaphor.

Again, just to give the reader a sense of the kinds of metaphors the participants generated, Table 10.9 is a sample of these responses. Because the disparity between extending and nonextending metaphors was not as large as in our previous study, we are presenting both kinds of metaphors in response to Speaker 1's metaphors.

Participant-Generated Metaphors During the First Year of the Obama Administration

Feeling confident in the consistency in our results, we decided to continue collecting data on participant-generated responses in order to demonstrate the prominence of metaphor extensions. We identified 18 metaphors that arose in articles in *Time* and *Newsweek* magazines in the first year of the Obama administration. These 18 metaphors represented seven different topics: health care, Afghanistan, international relations other than Afghanistan, the economy, political relations between Democrats and Republicans, the prosecution of Bush officials for war crimes, and Sarah Palin (with health care and the economy being the most represented topics because of their prominence during that year). Table 10.10 displays a sampling of the metaphors pulled from these two publications.

We created booklets that contained these 18 topics, half of which preserved the original metaphors and the other half of which had literal versions of the statements. For example, the metaphor of "playing political football" was changed to its literal likeness of "callously arguing back and forth," and the metaphor of "our financial house needed to be built on a rock, not sand" was changed to "the policies needed to be secure and enduring, not temporary." Metaphorical and literal statements were alternated in each booklet for counterbalancing. Of the 78 participants in the study, 34 were male and 44 were female.

Unfortunately, our results were quite different from our past studies. Similar to our past studies, the majority of responses that participants generated were literal. However, unlike our past studies, there was only a slight preference for extending metaphors over nonextending metaphors. Table 10.11 depicts our results, and Table 10.12 displays some responses.

As stated earlier, consistent with our past studies, most responses were literal. However, unlike our past results, there was an attenuated disparity between metaphor extensions and nonextensions. When metaphors *were* generated, most were metaphor extensions as opposed to metaphor nonextensions

Table 10.10 Examples of Metaphorical Statements Arising During the Obama Administration

The Republicans and Democrats are playing political football with our health care system.

So few people are identifying with the Republican Party that Republicans are becoming an endangered species.

The Obama health care bill will create a death panel that will pull the plug on grandma.

The stimulus package needed to be so large because our financial house needed to be built on a rock, not sand.

Increasing troops in Afghanistan is putting our fist in a hornet's nest.

President Obama has been trying to find the middle ground between Republicans and Democrats. They see the middle ground as the high ground.

Sarah Palin is a rock star.

Table 10.11 Participant-Generated Responses from Topics Arising in the Obama Administration

	Literal	*Extending Metaphors*	*Nonextending Metaphors*
Males	6.28	1.28	1.11
Females	6.76	1.11	.67

Table 10.12 Metaphorical Generated Responses from Participants

Metaphor Extensions

Speaker 1: The unrealistic increase of the stock market is an indication that investors are on a sugar high.
Speaker 2: We need to ride that high before it goes back down. That's how the market works; up and down.

Speaker 1: The stimulus package needed to be so large because our financial house needed to be built on a rock, not sand.
Speaker 2: Wrong, the stimulus package needed to be so large because the house itself was shuttered and buried far beneath the depths of the sand to begin with, and it takes such a large necessary fund to recover it.

Speaker 1: The Obama health care reform bill will create a death panel that will pull the plug on grandma.
Speaker 2: If there is a plug on grandma, she isn't really alive on her own in the first place and no one would pull the plug on her; it's a family's choice.

Metaphor Nonextensions

Speaker 1: Sarah Palin is a political rock star.
Speaker 2: She is a political buffoon. . . . I mean really, she "can see Russia from her house"?!

Speaker 1: The Republicans and Democrats are playing political football with our health care system.
Speaker 2: We need to work out all the kinks first.

Speaker 1: President Obama has been expanding his powers so much he is a Hitler taking away our freedoms.
Speaker 2: President Obama came into power when our government had already been shred to pieces. In order for him, or any person, to regain order in America, [he] has to expand his power in every aspect possible.

for both men and women, but rather than large disparities such as the 8-to-1 difference found in our first study on this topic during the early 1990s or even the 4-to-1 difference found during the George W. Bush years, our differences were only a 3-to-2 ratio for our current study for the early stages of the Obama era. These conclusions are still consistent with the predictions of the MEH.

We must acknowledge, however, that we took much more care in selecting our metaphorical segments in our original study. We collected numerous debates using metaphors that actually arose during the 1990s. Perhaps these metaphors had much more apparent metaphorical responses than the metaphors we used in the present study. In this last study, we found our metaphors by combing through *Time* and *Newsweek* magazines as opposed to political debates. Thus, the metaphors were identified by political writers who were trying to encapsulate complex issues as opposed to politicians who were engaged in political debates with fellow politicians. Such a difference may be important and worthy of study in future years.

References

Bosman, J. (1987). Persuasive effects of political metaphors. *Metaphor and Symbolic Activity, 2,* 97–113.

Bosman, J., & Hagendoorn, L. (1991). Effects of literal and metaphorical persuasive messages. *Metaphor and Symbolic Activity, 6,* 271–292.

Bowers, J. W. (1964). Some correlates of language intensity. *Quarterly Journal of Speech, 50,* 415–420.

Bowers, J. W., & Osborn, M. M. (1966). Attitudinal effects of selected types of concluding metaphors in persuasive speeches. *Speech Monographs, 33,* 147–155.

Chaiken, S., & Stangor, C. (1987). Attitudes and attitude change. *Annual Review of Psychology, 38,* 575–630.

Hovland, C. I., Janis, I. L., & Kelley, H. H. (1953). *Communication and persuasion: Psychological studies of one on one.* New Haven, CT: Yale University Press.

Johnson, J. T., & Taylor, S. E. (1981). The effect of metaphor on political attitudes. *Basic and Applied Social Psychology, 2,* 305–316.

Mio, J. S. (1996). Metaphor, politics, and persuasion. In J. S. Mio & A. N. Katz (Eds.), *Metaphor: Implications and applications* (pp. 127–146). Mahwah, NJ: Erlbaum.

Mio, J. S. (1997). Metaphor and politics. *Metaphor and Symbol, 12,* 111–133.

Petty, R. E., & Cacioppo, J. T. (1986). *Communication and persuasion: Central and peripheral routes to attitude change.* New York: Springer-Verlag.

Read, S. J., Cesa, I. L., Jones, D. K., & Collins, N. L. (1990). When is the federal budget like a baby? Metaphor in political rhetoric. *Metaphor and Symbolic Activity, 5,* 125–149.

Reinsch, N. L., Jr. (1971). An investigation of the effects of the metaphor and simile in persuasive discourse. *Speech Monographs, 38,* 142–145.

Sherrill, M. S. (1986, September 29). The Philippines Cory hits a grand slam. *Time.* Retrieved from www.time.com/time/magazine/article/0,962428,00.html

Sherrill, M. S. (1990, April 2). Soviet Union war of nerves. *Time.* Retrieved from www.time.com/tim/magazine/article/0,9171,969736,00.html

11 Cognitive Coherence in Politics

Unifying Metaphor and Narrative in Civic Cognition

Lori D. Bougher

How do citizens make sense of the political world? Previous research has reiterated that citizens often lack detailed information when it comes to politics, revealing "a high variance in political awareness around a generally low mean" (Zaller, 1992, p. 18).[1] Instead, citizens use cognitive shortcuts (heuristics) to "simplify cognitively taxing demands and to respond quickly to new information" (Jacobs & Shapiro, 2011, p. 14; see also Lau & Redlawsk, 2006; Taber, 2011). Although a full review of this literature is outside the scope of this chapter, "[t]here is no question that citizens use heuristics to simplify their information processing; there is considerable uncertainty, however, about whether such shortcuts allow them to behave competently" (Taber, 2011, p. 380). Although heuristics enable citizens to overcome cognitive limitations by making use of existing knowledge structures, they also leave citizens susceptible to bias and manipulation. Placing normative evaluations of heuristic usage temporarily to the side, there is still substantial merit in understanding the cognitive processes that can generate this susceptibility (see also Chong & Druckman, 2011). In the United States, for example, focus has shifted from "attributing failures of American democracy to the ignorance and stupidity of the masses" (Schattschneider, 1960, p. 135) to securing richer, descriptive accounts of civic behavior and rationales (e.g., Lupia, Levine, Menning, & Sin, 2007; Lupia, McCubbins, & Popkin, 2000), and to more critical assessments of the media and political leaders (Shapiro & Jacobs, 2011).

In general, citizens use a number of cognitive tools to efficiently navigate the uncertainty, ambiguity, and complexity of the political world. Metaphor and narrative are not simply linguistic flourishes or persuasive devices in political rhetoric; they are effective reasoning tools in civic cognition. Both devices provide constructs for categorizing and making sense of incoming information and experiences in the political world, satisfying our need for cognitive coherence. Despite similarity in the cognitive functions of metaphor and narrative, few attempts have been made to integrate the two concepts into a unified cognitive model. This chapter reviews why metaphor and narrative are important for civic reasoning and cognition, how they are similar, and how they are likely to be related. The discussion highlights the cognitive nature of language, the need for an integrated model of civic cognition that includes both metaphor and narrative, prospects for the more explicit incorporation of metaphor and narrative in civic education, and the inextricability of political cognition from its social context. Because they shape political identities, frame political issues, and offer the potential to enhance civic tolerance and reflection, metaphor and narrative feature prominently in civic cognition and merit further investigation.

Metaphor and Narrative in Civic Cognition

One as the Other: The Cognitive Similarities Between Metaphor and Narrative

Metaphor and narrative are both useful devices for navigating the political world (for overviews, see, e.g., Bougher, 2012; Patterson & Monroe, 1998, respectively). They share a similar history in that they are linguistic constructs that have each been increasingly recognized for their centrality in human cognition (e.g., Bruner, 1986, 1991; Gentner, 2003; Lakoff & Johnson, 1980). Metaphor and narrative provide psychological structures that allow us to piece fragments of information together into a cohesive whole. With metaphor, we piece together bits of information by relying on our existing knowledge structures in other domains; with narrative, we try to fit fragments into a running storyline. In both instances, we use embedded knowledge structures, grounded in everyday life, to make sense of our social world. Metaphor and narrative allow us to draw causal inferences and make predictions based on limited information (Colhoun & Gentner, 2009; Costabile & Klein, 2008). Consequently, they provide efficient heuristics for filling gaps in knowledge, including those we witness in the political realm.

Metaphor and narrative can help citizens make sense of political events, including campaigns and wars, candidates, policy issues, and so on. The metaphor of a "dogfight," for example, enables citizens to capture not only the severity of electoral competitions but also the candidates' desperation. When it comes to policy issues, the narrative of a "death panel" dissuaded some American citizens from supporting President Obama's health care plan. Metaphors can be equally influential in guiding policy preferences. Research has demonstrated that citizens can view healthcare in the metaphoric templates of community obligation, a societal right, employer responsibility, marketable commodity, and professional service (Lau & Schlesinger, 2005; Schlesinger & Lau, 2000), or view obesity metaphorically as a sin, disability, eating disorder, food addiction, reflection of time pressure, manipulation of commercial interests, or consequence of a toxic food environment (Barry, Brescoll, Brownell, & Schlesinger, 2009). These "policy metaphors" not only structure how citizens view the relevant issues and its causes but also guide the types of interventions citizens support.

Metaphor and narrative also provide an integrative structure that allows citizens to identify themselves and others in political terms. Narratives weave together chronological events, ensuring coherence over time and space, "becom[ing] recipes for structuring experience itself, for laying down routes into memory, for not only guiding the life narrative up to the present but directing it into the future" (Bruner, 2004, p. 708). As such, narratives facilitate coherence in personal as well as group identities, including national identity (e.g., Hammack & Pilecki, 2012). Narratives "allow individuals and communities to make sense of actions and events by telling stories" (Farquhar, 2010, p. 10; see also Ricoeur, 1992). Similarly, metaphors provide cognitive frameworks that can integrate values, beliefs, attitudes, and behavior into cohesive political identities. Lakoff (2004), for example, has notably argued that the NATION-AS-FAMILY conceptual metaphor underlies ideological identity in American politics—with conservatives adopting a morality system that is metaphorically like a Strict Father model of the family (e.g., emphasis on self-discipline and punishment for bad behavior) and liberals adopting a morality system that is more like a Nurturant Parent model of the family (e.g., emphasis on compassion and respect). Metaphors can also dynamically shape our conversations about political matters (see, e.g., Cameron, 2010; Gibbs & Cameron, 2008). Through metaphor and narrative, "humans have agency to create new meanings and new understandings of ourselves" (Farquhar, 2010, p. 22).

Both devices enable citizens to not only integrate political fragments into cohesive wholes, but metaphor and narrative also help citizens *categorize* new information more efficiently. Metaphor and narrative act as cognitive frames and "[f]rames function like political categories" (Nelson, 2011, p. 198.). "Categories are mental containers in a world that has only continua" (Stone, 2011, p. 381), and framing "refers to the process by which people develop a particular conceptualization of an issue or reorient their thinking about an issue" (Chong & Druckman, 2007, p. 104). As frames, metaphor and narrative simplify the complex by focusing attention to particular attributes of an object, issue, or event, while masking others.

Although the framing process facilitates cognitive efficiency, it leaves individuals susceptible to bias, misperception, and manipulation. More specifically, an adopted frame guides the subsequent search for and interpretation of new information, and "if the facts do not fit a frame, the frame stays and the facts bounce off" (Lakoff, 2004, p. 17). To illustrate, Thibodeau and Boroditsky (2011) found that the alternative metaphoric frames of crime-as-a-beast or crime-as-a-virus not only influenced the crime policy interventions respondents supported (e.g., enforcement vs. structural reforms, respectively), but the frames exerted an early effect by biasing the information search. Berinsky and Kinder (2006) similarly found that American perceptions of the Kosovo crisis were skewed according to whether study participants received the humanitarian or risk-to-America narrative, and the storied frames once again affected how information was sought and remembered.

The heuristic nature of metaphoric and narrative frames means that facts can be omitted, distorted, or misremembered, and citizens can draw incorrect inferences. For example, viewing former British prime minister Tony Blair as "America's lapdog" during the Iraq War underestimates the role his own convictions and motivations played in his decision making (see, e.g., Azubuike, 2005). Similarly, the narrative of US Senator and former presidential hopeful John McCain as a "maverick" may disproportionately attribute his political successes to his assertive, rebellious attitude when his capacity to forge political relationships was likely to be just as important. Revising frames or beliefs in light of conflicting information can be cognitively taxing. Because competing narratives and metaphors place different "spins" on the same information, these devices can contain the balance of power—with the "warring with words" resulting in the "winning with words," as balance shifts to the side holding the dominant metaphor or narrative (see, e.g., Nelson, 2011). Ryan and Gamson (2006) similarly asserted that "[f]acts take on meaning by being embedded in frames, which render them relevant and significant or irrelevant and trivial. The contest is lost at the outset if we allow our adversaries to define what facts are relevant" (p. 14). Consequently, metaphor and narrative help explain collective divisions, including those based on ideology, partisanship, ethnicity, and nationality. In the case of national or ethnic conflicts, for example, opposing groups often adopt narratives that cast their own group as the victim or protagonist and the other group as perpetrator or antagonist, omitting the negative attributes of their own group, thereby limiting its accountability. In this sense, narrative can act to perpetuate a group-serving bias.

With their role in structuring how citizens see the political world, metaphor and narrative can also be used to promote social change or justify the status quo and governmental decisions. Narratives become vehicles for action because they organize "plans, schemes, projects, and goals . . . providing a means for future actions" (Farquhar, 2010, p. 69). Narratives give coherence to the personal lives of social activists, but also help other citizens make sense of why things are the way they are, as in the case of Palestinian and Israeli youths (Hammack & Pilecki, 2012). Metaphoric frames have been used to make some government initiatives more palatable to the public, such as George W. Bush's "War on Terror" (e.g., Steuter & Will, 2008). One factor that makes metaphor and narrative powerful devices for promoting social change or securing public support is their emotional content (see, e.g., Blanchette & Dunbar, 2001). For example, in the recent US presidential election, Mitt Romney's campaign ran an emotionally arousing commercial titled "Dear Daughter," in which a mother narrated a dismal picture of the country and its prospects by piecing together fragments of statistics when welcoming her newborn child "to America." Both metaphor and narrative demonstrate the difficulty of separating affect from cognition, further challenging the ideal notion of a "disembodied Cartesian citizen" (see Fischman & Haas, 2012).

Because of the perceptual biases they can instill and the values, beliefs, and motivations they embody, metaphor and narrative provide crucial predispositions in civic cognition. As motivated reasoners (Taber & Lodge, 2006), citizens process new information and events with adopted storylines or meta-phoric source analogs; citizens do not "treat new information evenhandedly" (Taber, 2011, p. 380). Metaphor and narrative structure previous knowledge and experience into influential resources for political understanding, enabling citizens to see how various pieces fit together, formulate worldviews, derive explanations, attribute causation, and make predictions—whether accurate or not. Despite their powerful influence in structuring political understanding, empirical research on the roles of metaphor and narrative in civic cognition is not exhaustive. For example, empirical work on metaphor in politics has predominately examined the influence of "given" metaphors as found in elite discourse or priming experiments, emphasizing metaphor's capacity in persua-sion rather than reasoning (Bougher, 2012). Similarly, more empirical work is needed on narrative's role in shaping individual subjectivity, including the effects of elite narratives and moving away from the predominant focus on the formation of national identity (Hammack & Pilecki, 2012). Part of the chal-lenge in elaborating the roles of cognitive constructs such as metaphor and narrative in civic cognition is that their influence can operate automatically and largely outside of conscious awareness (i.e., they are implicit; see, e.g., Bougher, 2012). Whereas unconscious processing can tackle more complex decisions with greater efficiency and fewer cognitive limitations (Taber, 2011), devising empirical methods that capture the extent of implicit procedures in civic understanding and cognition is far more difficult.

Bridging the Cognitive Divide

The field needs more extensive explorations of the individual roles metaphor and narrative play in civic cognition, but there should also be a greater effort to integrate the two constructs. Although metaphor and narrative are both pow-erful devices for integrating various fragments of the political world into a coherent picture, the irony is that metaphor and narrative have been examined predominantly in isolation from one another (Bezeczky, 2000; Hanne, 1999, 2011). Metaphor's main components are source analog, target analog, and mapping, whereas narrative includes, for example, a plot, characters, and set-ting. The essence of metaphor is the *cross-domain* transfer of knowledge; the essence of narrative is storytelling. These concepts are neither mutually exclu-sive, nor are they the same.

Research suggests a symbiotic relationship between metaphor and narra-tive. First, metaphor can provide a structure that guides narrative, infusing texts with symbolic meaning. As Stone (2012) summarized, "on the surface, [meta-phors] draw a comparison between one thing and another, but in a more subtle way they usually imply a larger narrative story and a prescription for action" (p. 171). Narrative is often implicit in studies that have focused exclusively on metaphor. Simply hinting at a metaphor (e.g., crime as a virus) can help citizens build a fuller story from the information given (see Thibodeau & Boroditsky,

2012). However, metaphors seem to only function as narrative frames when they are included early on in a text (ibid.). The capacity of metaphor to give text a cohesive narrative structure is so strong that a weak metaphoric comparison can make a storyline less compelling (Thagard, 2011). Because metaphors can help citizens fill in information not provided in texts, they also provide compact versions of narrative. The metaphoric frames of "genocide" and "captive liberation," for example, will "activate divergent stories of the US War in Iraq" (Ottati, Renstrom, & Price, 2012, p. 14). At the same time, metaphor can supplement narratives by presenting elaborated flourishes within a given text. To illustrate, the "marketplace" metaphor for economics has often been "further flanked by a number of other metaphorical clusters," including those based on the military, sports, or religion (Hanne, 1999, p. 46).

Narrative likewise can structure metaphor. Just as metaphors can elaborate certain points in a narrative, narrative can give meaning to a mix of seemingly unrelated metaphors. In addition, narrative itself can serve as an influential source analog for metaphoric transfer. Dehghani, Gentner, Forbus, Ekhtiari, and Sachdeva (2009) found that Iranian participants applied popular cultural narratives to make sense of moral dilemmas that shared structural similarity to collective myths. Just mentioning characters from popular narratives can also prompt individuals to apply that narrative as a metaphoric source. For example, mentioning the character of Robin Hood in reference to a political candidate will likely lead citizens to infer that the candidate is an advocate for the poor and disadvantaged.

Overall, metaphor and narrative can act as structuring guides for one another. Citing the work of Daniel Cohen, Hanne (1999) summarized that "it may be useful to think of metaphor as compressed narrative, or, indeed, of narrative as extended metaphor" (p. 39). One caveat is that using metaphor as "narrative shorthand" can mask or demote some features of the narrative itself (ibid., pp. 40–41). The two devices, however, can also act as substitutions when the other fails. Some events, such as 9/11, can be so traumatic that individuals are unable to develop continuous narratives, relying instead on metaphor to help make sense of and express their thoughts and feelings about the event (Brockmeier, 2008; see also, e.g., Angus & Mio, 2011). Although metaphor and narrative clearly interact, future research must more robustly test and clarify the nature of their relationship. Does metaphor help enrich the processing and understanding of narrative, affording citizens a "deeper rationality" or "emotionally focused" grasp (see, e.g., Fischman & Haas, 2012, and Angus & Mio, 2011, respectively) on political issues, events, and situations? Likewise, can narrative help extend the cognitive web of metaphors that link any one political narrative to a number of different life domains (e.g., health, family, work, etc.)? And to what extent do narrative and metaphor facilitate or inhibit the other's role in political learning and comprehension? Questions such as these and their empirical answers will help refine a more unified model of civic cognition.

Metaphor, Narrative, and Political Learning: Suggestions for Civic Education

The pervasive roles of metaphor and narrative in shaping our understanding of the social world make them crucial components for civic education. Although the extent of public malleability and its underlying processes are still under debate, public ignorance does leave citizens susceptible to political manipulation and exploitation (Jacobs & Shapiro, 2000; Shapiro & Jacobs, 2011). Consequently, to safeguard democratic functioning, it is ideal to have a populace that is discriminating, yet not obdurately biased when processing new information (Chong & Druckman, 2011). Metaphor and narrative can help foster the development of critical citizenship through education in three main ways. Not only are they instrumental educational resources in their own right, but metaphor and narrative also offer the opportunity to facilitate critical reflection and civic tolerance.

Metaphor and Narrative as Educational Tools

Metaphor and narrative have long been appreciated as educational instruments. Although a full review of this work is outside the confines of this chapter, it is important to highlight that metaphors and narratives can ease the teaching of abstract or difficult concepts and materials. Because metaphor is a form of analogical reasoning, it is fundamental for abstract learning and causal understanding (Gentner & Colhoun, 2010; Colhoun & Gentner, 2009, respectively), making it particularly instructive when teaching science and mathematics (see, e.g., Duit, 1991; Richland, Zur, & Holyoak, 2007). In general, academic texts contain more metaphors than are found in the news, works of fiction, or conversations (Steen, Dorst, Herrmann, Kaal, & Krennmayr, 2010). Narrative can equally help students integrate chronological events and causal relations in science texts (van den Broek, 2010). Even more, narratives in history textbooks help shape national identities, imbuing historical facts (or fiction) with cultural values, beliefs, practices, and ideals in compacted form (e.g., Hammack & Pilecki, 2012). Metaphors enable teachers to explain complex topics and issues in terms that are more familiar to students; teachers can use narratives to organize a myriad of facts or events into more memorable storylines. In this sense, metaphor and narrative are both instructional tools available to educators, including those teaching history and civic education courses.

Making the Implicit Visible in Individual Cognition and Intergroup Reconciliation

Metaphor and narrative are no doubt useful instructional devices for teachers, but rather than acting simply as supplementary vehicles to convey some other kind of subject material, can metaphor and narrative themselves also be the explicit subject of learning? Because metaphor and narrative are so integral to human cognition, students already frame difficult materials through these lenses without much prompting. For example, students generate their own spontaneous metaphors to make sense of challenging concepts in mathematics and science (e.g., Jakobson & Wickman, 2007; Oehrtman, 2009; Schinck, Neale, Pugalee, & Cifarelli, 2008). The question is whether teaching students more explicitly about how they understand politics and process political decisions can make them think more critically as citizens. Rather than focusing on the repetition of political facts, can drawing their attention to their own biases, misconceptions, erroneous inferences, and susceptibilities to outside influences, such as media persuasion, foster more adaptive and critical civic awareness? This would involve bringing largely implicit processes and dispositions into conscious awareness, "making thinking visible" (see Ritchhart, Church, & Morrison, 2011).

Bringing spontaneous metaphors and narratives into conscious awareness may encourage citizens to think more critically about political issues. This is what happened in an innovative study examining discourse in political blogs (Baumer, Sinclair, & Tomlinson, 2010). A web application called metaViz (Baumer, Sinclair, Hubin, & Tomlinson, 2009) identified conceptual metaphors contained in political blogs and then visually displayed those metaphors to blog readers for comment. The researchers then analyzed the content of the comments left by blog readers and found that bringing metaphors into conscious awareness not only prompted readers to critically reflect on the aptness of the metaphor, but it also facilitated creative thinking about the issue at hand.

Explicit discussions of metaphors and narratives that underlie political cognition may not only help students understand how they themselves make political decisions, but can potentially facilitate the understanding of others' viewpoints and promote more effective communication. Although their work does not deal with civic education or students, Cameron and Maslen (2010) have poignantly argued that political communication can be improved by identifying the metaphors that underlie how different groups understand political issues. In particular, Cameron and Maslen focused on the issue of terrorism and compared the metaphors used by the political elite versus the public. They found that members of the general public were more likely than experts to understand governmental responses to terrorism in terms of body, animal, or physical action metaphors; in addition, although both groups used a balance metaphor, they used it differently, with the public using it to emphasize disruption after a terrorist act and experts using it to convey agency to restore equilibrium. The authors have suggested that experts can mitigate the public's negative feelings, such as helplessness, and promote positive feelings in the event of a terrorist act if they tailor their communication in light of these different applications of metaphor.

The exchange of personal narratives too can help facilitate wider understanding. Not only did volunteering in a soup kitchen expose youths to personal narratives of homelessness that helped correct inaccurate stereotypes and flawed attributional reasoning, but discussing these experiences of volunteering in the classroom also helped students construct their own political identities (Yates & Youniss, 1996). As mentioned, contrasting metaphors and narratives can often underlie deep divisions in political understanding and perception. When individuals exchange personal narratives about political events and issues, this can help mitigate rigid "us" versus "them" dichotomies (Hammack & Pilecki, 2012, p. 91). Oftentimes, "[s]uccessful reframing involves the ability to enter into the worldview of our adversaries" (Ryan & Gamson, 2006, p. 14). Mio (1996) found that political actors were more persuasive when they adopted and extended the metaphoric frames used by their opponent to structure their own counter-arguments rather than when they introduced a different metaphor into the debate. Political arguments are therefore strengthened when the metaphoric frameworks introduced by political opponents are taken into account (see also, e.g., Lakoff & Wehling, 2012). Narrative and metaphor thus offer the potential to both help identify and challenge preexisting ideologies (see, e.g., Alsup, 2003, for an application of this method to teachers themselves).

While many studies document how citizens rely on cognitive heuristics in politics, more empirical work is needed on what happens when individuals are made aware of the biases and processes that underlie their political beliefs, attitudes, and decisions. Fischman and Haas (2012) have contended that "we cannot make much progress by ignoring the unconscious and automatic levels of thinking, which are not easily dissuaded with rational and factual arguments alone" (p. 187). The most educated and engaged citizens are often the most susceptible to bias (e.g., Taber, 2011), and research has shown that political misperceptions can be difficult to correct (Nyhan & Reilfer, 2010; Redlawsk, Civettini, & Emmerson, 2010). These latter studies, however, focus on whether individuals update their political preferences in light of further information. Because we know that citizens seek and incorporate political facts in a biased manner, would it not be more efficient to bring the cognitive biases to their attention rather than simply presenting them with further information?

Although this question still requires empirical study, some findings merit optimism for formal instruction that emphasizes the *how* over the *what* in social, and thereby political, reasoning. For example, formal education—particularly that which includes inferential rules students have already partially induced from their everyday lives—has been found to improve reasoning skills under certain conditions (Lehman, Lempert, & Nisbett, 1988). But even the authors of this research added that "we know very little about reasoning and how to teach it" (ibid., p. 441). Speculating on how to reduce the effects of implicit stereotypes, Banaji and Greenwald (1994) asserted that "drawing social category information into conscious awareness allows mental (cognitive and motivational) resources to overrule the consciously unwanted but unconsciously operative response" (p. 70). Schnall, Haidt, Clore, and Jordan (2008) have similarly questioned whether making individuals aware of extraneous feelings of disgust (i.e., those that are unrelated to the judgment at hand) can limit its heuristic effects on moral reasoning, such as in the case of jurors who may judge a defendant with a facial deformity more harshly because of those displaced feelings of disgust. This idea of testing the effects of bringing biases and heuristics into conscious awareness is likely to attract only further attention in the future because it affects decision making in so many social domains, whether it involve law, economics, politics, and so on. But the question for civic reasoning and cognition remains: Can bringing metaphor and narrative in particular into conscious awareness enhance civic competence, deliberation, communication, and tolerance?

Designing New Benchmarks and Assessments for Civic Education

If research confirmed that citizens can, in fact, improve their political decisions or become more tolerant when they become aware of the processes and biases that underlie their political beliefs and cognition, this would suggest the desirability of reforms in terms of how students are educated for their roles as citizens. Not least, this would further challenge any paradigms that prize the rote memorization of political facts alone. It may be more effective to teach students how to approach political information, rather than presenting information on its own—focusing on the *how* rather than the *what* of political thinking. This focus may be especially important for encouraging critical reflection and social tolerance in an information age during which opinions increasingly infiltrate the media in lieu of "hard facts" (Jacobs & Shapiro, 2011; see also Graber & Holyk, 2011; Jamieson & Hardy, 2011) and during a time when "the burden of democracy has shifted from skepticism about the competence of citizens to doubts and concerns about the wisdom and responsibility of their political leaders" (Shapiro & Jacobs, 2011, p. 726).

Educational approaches that more fully incorporate metaphor and narrative as civic tools complement definitions of civic competence that extend beyond full information alone. For example, Haste (2009) has identified managing uncertainty and ambiguity; managing technological change, agency and responsibility; finding and sustaining community; and managing emotion as five key civic competences. She has defined competence as the "capacity for adaptive responses and for appropriate interpretation of information" (Haste, 2009, p. 207), contending that it "is about effective and adaptive tool use" (Haste, 2009, p. 214). A more explicit recognition and discussion of cognitive frames such as metaphor and narrative may also facilitate open classroom climates, interactive discussions, and exposure to and "grappling with" diverse views—all of which have been identified as important school-based antecedents that foster Western democratic values such as critical reflection, tolerance of dissenting views, and social trust (Ferreira, Azevedo, & Menezes, 2012; Flanagan, Stoppa, Syvertsen, & Stout, 2010; Hess, 2009; McDevitt & Kiousis, 2006; Torney-Purta, Lehmann, Oswald, & Schulz, 2001). Rather than setting the less realistic goal of eradicating the use of heuristics in political understanding, it may be more effective to teach students how to better use those cognitive devices.

Compelling individuals to want to revise their perceptions can be challenging. "The decision to appraise or reconsider the evidence takes time, is effortful, assumes one is somehow aware of having a biased set of considerations in mind, and believes the need to be accurate is worth the effort that will be required to rethink the issue" (Taber, 2011, p. 376). Schools can therefore be the ideal setting for intervention to help train students early on to think more critically about politics. In addition to challenging top-down, knowledge-based pedagogical paradigms (Haste, 2009), there is a need for "a revitalized sense of democracy within early childhood" (Farquhar, 2010, p. 6). By helping students understand their own perceptions of the political world, as well as those of others, and allowing students to generate creative responses, metaphor and narrative foster both interpretation and imagination—two elements that would contribute towards an ethical paradigm for civic education (see Farquhar, 2010; Ricoeur, 1992).

Politics, as noted, represents a dynamic, uncertain, complex, and abstract world. As such, equipping students with a transferable, "adaptive toolbox" (see Gigerenzer & Selten, 2002) may best facilitate the type of critical civic awareness, reflection and deliberation that will foster popular sovereignty and reason-based public talk, reinforcing democratic governance (Jacobs, Cook, & Delli Carpini, 2009; Jacobs & Shapiro, 2011). As it stands, at least in the United States, citizens tend to perform better on questions pertaining to stable elements or anchors in the political domain, such as institutions and political processes, and fare worse on questions regarding dynamic elements, such as candidates and issues (Delli Carpini & Keeter, 1996)—which is, paradoxically, where their vote has the most immediate impact. A shift of focus to adaptive training and tool sets would entail civic education programs adopting new forms of assessment that extend beyond the reproduction of political information. For example, stories themselves can be used as a form of assessment to evaluate how successful students are at integrating various perspectives. The challenge of this mode of curriculum is that it involves "a project of contestable meanings and different understandings giving it meaning in specific contexts," leaving "no objective truth to doing curriculum" (Farquhar, 2010, p. 14). Compounding and paralleling this assessment problem in education is that there is still "no consensus . . . [regarding] the standards that should be applied to evaluating the quality of public opinion" (Chong & Druckman, 2011, p. 182).

More empirical work is required before the aforementioned recommendations for civic education can be taken further. Future work should specify the extent to which tools such as metaphor and narrative can be used to enhance civic reasoning, deliberation, and tolerance. Is it more efficient to try to bring habits into conscious awareness rather than trying to change them by simply providing additional information? Can early intervention train students to become more critical citizens, and do the effects last? It also remains to be seen how novel pedagogical approaches will interact with traditional knowledge-based methods and which sorts of assessments will be required. Overall, a richer descriptive understanding of civic cognition, including the roles afforded to metaphor and narrative, would guide more-effective interventions to achieve civic aims—whether the means of intervention involve education, public policy, or institutional procedures such as deliberation or conflict resolution.

An Agenda for the Future: Towards a Unified Model of Civic Cognition

One consequence of the informational interdependence of the modern information age "is that the content of public attitudes and mechanisms of opinion formation matter and that analyzing the heterogeneity of individuals is critical" (Jacobs & Shapiro, 2011, p. 11). The narratives and metaphors citizens use to guide their political reasoning act as perceptual filters and thus constrain the frames, beliefs, and worldviews they find acceptable. Clarifying the roles of metaphor and narrative as key psychological processes that underpin political reasoning would "[facilitate] the specification of conditions under which effects take place, an empirical question with significant normative implications" (Chong & Druckman, 2011, p. 174). As mentioned, identifying key metaphors and narratives in political cognition, in general, offers the potential to enhance political communication, to foster more-critical civic awareness, and to promote mutual understanding that can bridge societal divisions, whether based on ideology, partisanship, ethnicity, or nationality. However, further research is required before these prospects can fully materialize.

Analyzing Individual Heterogeneity in Metaphor and Narrative

The narratives and metaphors that underlie civic cognition require more systematic study. Although some scholars have turned their attention to exploring how various fragments interact (e.g., Druckman, Hennessy, St. Charles, & Webber, 2010; Huckfeldt, Mondak, Craw, & Mendez, 2005; Lau & Redlawsk, 2001, 2006), the study of public opinion generally lacks a unifying model of decision making that integrates its various components and insights (Druckman, Kuklinski, & Sigelman, 2009). Future studies should more thoroughly investigate individual differences in the application and operation of metaphor and narrative in political cognition, including the roles of moderators and mediators. For example, does the reliance on and use of metaphor and narrative depend on demographic characteristics and cognitive processing preferences (i.e., memory based versus online processing; see, e.g., Druckman et al., 2010), or on motivations such as the need for cognition and affect (Arceneaux & Vander Wielen, forthcoming)? Does issue complexity or level of uncertainty moderate the individual-level effects and functions of metaphor and narrative, and are these effects then mediated by processing preferences? Taber (2011) has pointed out that "the evidence suggests hybrid models that include both online and memory components" (p. 370), which further complicates the task of specifying the individual psychology underlying civic cognition.

Cognitive coherence involves not only the integration of various fragments into a sense-making whole, but it also entails the congruence between behavior and cognition. Cognition not only drives behavior, but behavior can also drive cognition as individuals apply post hoc rationality to justify their thoughts, feelings, or actions (Haidt, 2001). Studies on metaphor and narrative can help further elucidate this bidirectional relationship, particularly in regards to civic agency. Hammack and Pilecki (2012) have reviewed the role of narrative "as a mediator between structure and agency, particularly at the level of the individual," highlighting the bidirectional influence of narrative in mediating "material reality and forms of actions" (p. 91).

A more unified model of civic cognition would allow metaphor and narrative to intervene both before and after behavior, helping citizens make sense of what has already been done, but also guiding them towards action in the future. Can these functions be distinguished empirically, however? And are there individual differences in their execution? Additional questions pertaining to individual differences in the use and application of metaphor and narrative in political cognition remain. For instance, are there also individual differences in the effects of bringing biases into conscious awareness? Do some factors (e.g., political interest, political sophistication, and ideological or partisan strength) moderate this learning process and, if so, which ones?

Because metaphor and narrative provide conceptual frames that integrate but also filter out information, they provide crucial predispositions for navigating the political world (see also, e.g., Bougher, 2012). Although some perceptual frames may dominate, research suggests that this dominance is malleable and "other ways of thinking may often be just beneath the surface" (Bryan, Dweck, Ross, Kay, & Mislavsky, 2009, p. 894). Consequently, future research should also elaborate on how individuals negotiate and reconcile competing metaphors and narratives. As Ryan and Gamson (2006) have explained,

> People carry around multiple frames in their heads. We have more than one way of framing an issue or an event. A specific frame may be much more easily triggered and habitually used, but others are also part of our cultural heritage and can be triggered and used as well, given the appropriate cues. (p. 14)

Individuals adopt stronger frames over weaker ones, but the criteria that determine frame strength remain unclear (Chong & Druckman, 2011). Previous research on political attitudes allocates a role for availability, accessibility, and applicability (ibid.). Elsewhere, I have argued that structural similarity and domain familiarity are likely to be key criteria guiding the selection of competing metaphoric source analogs (Bougher, 2012). However, congruence to core values and political goals are likely to be a further overarching determinant in the selection and formulation of both metaphors and narratives.

Further empirical work is needed to refine the criteria that guide the selection of competing metaphors and narrative and to specify the processes that underlie the resolution of these conflicts. In addition to competing metaphors and narratives, how do metaphors and narratives interact with one another and with other political heuristics in individual psychology? For example, do metaphors and narratives fulfill similar functions in politics, such as persuasion, and do they aid or inhibit one another in the execution of these functions? Do inappropriate metaphors weaken the persuasive effects of a strong narrative, or vice versa? Also, can narrative or metaphor help citizens integrate contrasting information from various political cues, such as a Republican (party identity) who supports a liberal social policy (issue position)? Do citizens gravitate towards certain narratives or metaphoric frames when relayed from candidates who share the same political party as the citizen? Although metaphor research has focused predominantly on metaphors found in elite discourse (Bougher, 2012), individual metaphors have typically been analyzed in isolation from other metaphors and certainly from other heuristic cues. And, "an analysis of the way in which narratives of political leaders impact individual subjectivity remains unstudied" (Hammack & Pilecki, 2012, p. 81).

Context and the Social Construction of Metaphor and Narrative

Examining the effects of elite communication on public opinion, however, requires us to "[look] beyond individual psychology to take account of the context of elite-public interactions" (Chong & Druckman, 2011, p. 179). Chong and Druckman (2011) were referencing multiple frames within a competitive environment, but their point regarding context is poignant for the study of metaphor and narrative as well. Although focus here has been on individual cognition, it is necessary to reiterate that metaphor and narrative involve individuals' dialogic interaction with their environment. As such, a unified model of civic cognition would include considerations of the wider ecological framework. The transactional or dialogic nature of political understanding may be even more pronounced today, at a time when technological advances have made citizens as much a part of news creation as are political elites and the media (Jacobs & Shapiro, 2011). Politics itself is a social construction, resting its organization on *power-in-common* (Ricoeur, 1992); therefore, it is perhaps unsurprising that political understanding, too, is a largely social construction. With political matters, the relevant person is the first person plural, not first person singular, prompting individuals to think to themselves "[w]hat I as a respondent am being asked to decide is what is best, not for me distinctively, but for us collectively" (Sniderman, 2000, p. 80). Likewise, political identity is not "an isolated, static, unchanging endpoint; rather, it is seen as involving continual change and *adaptation in response to others* [emphasis added]" (Farquhar, 2010, p. 5). As individuals interact in the social domain of politics, private thoughts turn public, undergoing a dynamic, dialogic process that shapes political understanding and reasoning (McIntosh & Youniss, 2010).

Adding ecological considerations to models of civic cognition encourages a more nuanced understanding of the development and uses of metaphor and narrative in politics. Causal explanations for political phenomena, including the behavior of citizens, are incomplete when underlying processes or mechanisms are studied in isolation from the context in which they occur (Falleti & Lynch, 2009). Metaphor and narrative may perform different functions at the individual level depending on the context. It may be, for example, that some narratives and metaphors pervade political thinking, traversing a number of political topics, whereas others are issue specific. Priming subjects with a contamination threat using the NATION-AS-BODY metaphor affected attitudes towards immigration, for example, but not minimum wage (Landau, Sullivan, & Greenberg, 2009). Indeed, the same metaphor can have very different meanings depending on the context (e.g., Zinken, 2007), reiterating the need to conduct phenomenon-based research (Landau, Meier, & Keefer, 2010). Similarly, narratives help citizens understand their particular position in society at a specific place and moment in time, or events within a particular context, prompting scholars to increasingly adopt "a multilevel approach to narrative" (Hammack & Pilecki, 2012, p. 77). Further work should continue to empirically expand and better specify the contextual variants (e.g., issue specificity, cultural factors, political uncertainty, out-group threat, etc.) that influence the roles metaphor and narrative play in individual cognition.

Contextual factors are not only likely to moderate how metaphor and narrative function in civic cognition, but social context provides direct and sometimes competing sources for those metaphors and narratives. The local context may send messages that contrast the state-endorsed meta-narratives found in history textbooks or culture, potentially motivating political change (see, e.g., Cole, 2003; Flanagan, Martínez, Cumsille, & Ngomane, 2011; Wertsch, 2008). In addition, the explicit lessons taught in school or other mediating institutions may deviate from the implicit ones individuals learn from their own experiences. Explicit lessons using narratives or metaphors of fairness, for instance, may be challenged if they occur in contexts where individuals personally experience injustice. As Biesta (2007) has argued, "[a] society in which individuals are not able nor allowed to act, cannot expect from its schools to produce its democratic citizens for it" (p. 740). In the case of metaphor, experiences in other life domains can determine political outlooks. More immediate experiences with authority in the family and school act as metaphoric source analogs, for example, by generalizing to evaluations of political authority (Gniewosz, Noack, & Buhl, 2009; see also Fischman & Haas, 2012). Do citizens imbue meta-narratives and universal metaphors with their own personal experiences? How do personal experiences constrain the effects of cultural metaphors and narratives in civic cognition? Future research should further untangle our understanding of how personal sources interact with social ones in the active co-construction of politically relevant metaphors and narratives.

Conclusion

Metaphor and narrative are integral components of human cognition. Metaphor prompts individuals to see one thing as something else. Narrative enables people to tie fragmented elements together into a cohesive story. Both devices enable individuals to make predictions or draw inferences based on what they already know, either in terms of a source analog or ongoing plot development, for example. Although metaphor and narrative provide efficient heuristic devices that facilitate cognitive coherence and categorization, they also leave citizens susceptible to bias. As such, they provide vital predispositions for how citizens make sense of the political world and merit greater scholarly attention.

Citizens are not passive recipients; instead, they actively co-construct metaphors and narratives, but the processes and caveats underlying this relationship require further refinement. Although scholars have made notable efforts to integrate fragmented studies within metaphor (see, e.g., Ottati, Renstrom, & Price, 2012) and narrative research (see, e.g., Hammack & Pilecki, 2012), more work will be required to integrate the two strands not only with one another but with other heuristic-based and cognitive research to establish a more unified model of individual civic cognition. It remains to be seen whether bringing implicit biases and processes into conscious awareness through civic education can help promote more critical civic awareness, deliberation, and tolerance. The scope for future research on metaphor and narrative in civic cognition remains wide, encompassing both individual differences and ecological considerations. Clarifying the complex cognition that underlies civic decision making carries important implications for psychologists, political scientists, policy makers, social institutions, such as schools, and even democracy at large. Metaphor and narrative are two productive research pathways that will help us secure a more unified model of civic cognition.

Note

1 To be sure, some scholars have argued that lapses in civic knowledge have been exaggerated because of methodological flaws (e.g., Mondak, 2001; Mondak & Davies, 2001; Prior & Lupia, 2008), for example, and others have challenged the premise that representative democracies require fully informed citizenries (Althaus, 2006; Esterling, Neblo, & Lazer, 2011).

References

Alsup, J. (2003). English education students and professional identity development: Using narrative and metaphor to challenge preexisting ideologies. *Pedagogy: Critical Approaches to Teaching Literature, Language, Composition, and Culture, 3,* 277–280.

Althaus, S. L. (2006). False starts, dead ends, and new opportunities in public opinion research. *Critical Review*, *18*, 75–104.

Angus, L., & Mio, J. S. (2011). At the "heart of the matter": Understanding the importance of emotion-focused metaphors in patient illness narratives. *Genre*, *44*, 349–361.

Arceneaux, K., & Vander Wielen, R. J. (forthcoming). The effects of need for cognition and need for affect on partisan evaluations. *Political Psychology*.

Azubuike, S. (2005). The "poodle theory" and the Anglo-American "special relationship." *International Studies*, *42*, 123–139.

Banaji, M. R., & Greenwald, A. G. (1994). Implicit stereotyping and prejudice. In M. P. Zanna & J. M. Olson (Eds.), *The psychology of prejudice: The Ontario symposium* (Vol. 7, pp. 55–76). Hillsdale, NJ: Erlbaum.

Barry, C. L., Brescoll, V. L., Brownell, K. D., & Schlesinger, M. (2009). Obesity metaphors: How beliefs about the causes of obesity affect support for public policy. *The Milbank Quarterly*, *87*, 7–47.

Baumer, E. P. S., Sinclair, J., Hubin, D., & Tomlinson, B. (2009). "metaViz: Visualizing Computationally Identified Metaphors in Political Blogs." In *Proceedings IEEE CSE'09, 12th IEEE International Conference on Computational Science and Engineering,* August 29–31, 2009, Vancouver, BC, Canada (pp. 389-394). IEEE Computer Society.

Baumer, E. P. S., Sinclair, J., & Tomlinson, B. (2010). "America is like Metamucil": Fostering critical and creative thinking about metaphor in political blogs. In *Proceedings of the 28th International Conference on Human Factors in Computing Systems (CHI 2010)* (pp. 1437–1446). Atlanta: ACM Press.

Berinsky, A. J., & Kinder, D. R. (2006). Making sense of issues through media frames: understanding the Kosovo Crisis. *Journal of Politics*, *68*, 640–656.

Bezecsky, G. (2000). Metaphor and narrative. *Neohelicon*, *27*, 13–48.

Biesta, G. (2007). Education and the democratic person: Towards a political conception of democratic education. *Teachers College Record*, *109*, 740–769.

Blanchette, I., & Dunbar, K. (2001). Analogy use in naturalistic settings: The influence of audience, emotion, and goals. *Memory & Cognition*, *29*, 730–735.

Bougher, L. (2012). The case for metaphor in political reasoning and cognition. *Political Psychology*, *33*, 121–139.

Brockmeier, J. (2008). Language, experience, and the "traumatic gap": How to talk about 9/11? In L. Hydén & J. Brockmeier (Eds.), *Health, illness and culture: Broken narratives* (pp. 16–35). New York: Routledge.

Bruner, J. (1986). *Actual minds, possible worlds.* Cambridge, MA: Harvard University Press.

Bruner, J. (1991). The narrative construction of reality. *Critical Inquiry*, *18*, 1–21.

Bruner, J. (2004). Life as narrative. *Social Research*, *71*, 691–710.

Bryan, C. J., Dweck, C. S., Ross, L., Kay, A. C., & Mislavsky, N. O. (2009). Political mindset: Effects of schema priming on liberal-conservative political positions. *Journal of Experimental Social Psychology*, *45*, 890–895.

Cameron, L. (2010). The discourse dynamics framework for metaphor. In L. Cameron & R. Maslen (Eds.), *Metaphor analysis: Research practice in applied linguistics, social sciences, and the humanities* (pp. 77–94). London: Equinox.

Cameron, L., & Maslen, R. (2010). Using metaphor analysis to compare expert and public perceptions of the risk of terrorism. In L. Cameron & R. Maslen (Eds.), *Metaphor analysis: Research practice in applied linguistics, social sciences, and the humanities* (pp. 248–256). London: Equinox.

Chong, D., & Druckman, J. N. (2007). Framing theory. *Annual Review of Political Science*, *10*, 103–126.

Chong, D., & Druckman, J. N. (2011). Public-elite interactions: Puzzles in search of researchers. In R. Y. Shapiro & L. R. Jacobs (Eds.), *The Oxford handbook of American public opinion and the media* (pp. 170–203). Oxford: Oxford University Press.

Cole, J. (2003). Narratives and moral projects: Generational memories of the Malagasy 1947 rebellion. *Ethos*, *31*, 95–126.

Colhoun, J., & Gentner, D. (2009). Inference processes in causal analogies. In B. Kokinov, K. Holyoak, & D. Gentner (Eds.), *New frontiers in analogy research: Proceedings of the Second International Conference on Analogy* (pp. 82–96). Sofia: NBU Press.

Costabile, K. A., & Klein, S. B. (2008). Understanding and predicting social events: The effects of narrative construction on inference generation. *Social Cognition*, *26*, 420–437.

Dehghani, M., Gentner, D., Forbus, K., Ekhtiari, H., & Sachdeva, S. (2009). Analogy and moral decision making. In B. Kokinov, K. Holyoak, & D. Gentner (Eds.), *New frontiers in analogy research: Proceedings of the Second International Conference on Analogy* (pp. 168–177). Sofia: NBU Press.

Delli Carpini, M. X., & Keeter, S. (1996). *What Americans know about politics and why it matters*. New Haven, CT: Yale University Press.

Druckman, J. N., Hennessy, C. L., St. Charles, K., & Webber, J. (2010). Competing rhetoric over time: Frames versus cues. *Journal of Politics*, *72*, 136–148.

Druckman, J. N., Kuklinski, J. H., & Sigelman, L. (2009). The unmet potential of interdisciplinary research: Political psychological approaches to voting and public opinion. *Political Behavior*, *31*, 485–510.

Duit, R. (1991). On the roles of analogies and metaphors in learning science. *Science Education*, *75*, 649–672.

Esterling, K. M., Neblo, M. A., & Lazer, D. M. J. (2011). Means, motive, and opportunity in becoming informed about politics: A deliberative field experiment with members of Congress and their constituents. *Public Opinion Quarterly*, *75*, 483–503.

Falleti, T. G., & Lynch, J. F. (2009). Context and causal mechanisms in political analysis. *Comparative Political Studies*, *42*, 1143–1166.

Farquhar, S. (2010). *Ricoeur, identity, and early childhood*. Lanham, MD: Rowman & Littlefield.

Ferreira, P. D., Azevedo, C. N., & Menezes, I. (2012). The developmental quality of participation experiences: Beyond the rhetoric that "participation is always good!" *Journal of Adolescence*, *35*, 599–610.

Fischman, G. E., & Haas, E. (2012). Beyond idealized citizenship: Embodied cognition, metaphors, and democracy. *Review of Research in Education*, *36*, 169–196.

Flanagan, C., Stoppa, T., Syvertsen, A. K., & Stout, M. (2010). Schools and social trust. In L. R. Sherrod, J. Torney-Purta, & C. A. Flanagan (Eds.), *Handbook of research on civic engagement in youth* (pp. 307–329). Hoboken, NJ: John Wiley & Sons.

Flanagan, C. A., Martínez, M. L., Cumsille, P., & Ngomane, T. (2011). Youth civic development: Theorizing a domain with evidence from different cultural contexts. *New Directions for Child and Adolescent Development*, *134*, 95–109.

Gentner, D. (2003). Why we're so smart. In D. Gentner & S. Goldin-Meadow (Eds.), *Language in mind: Advances in the study of language and thought* (pp. 195–235). Cambridge, MA: MIT Press.

Gentner, D., & Colhoun, J. (2010). Analogical processes in human thinking and learning. In A. von Müller & E. Pöppel (Series Eds.) & B. Glatzeder, V. Goel, &

A. von Müller (Vol. Eds.), *On Thinking: Vol. 2. Towards a theory of thinking: Building blocks for a conceptual framework* (pp. 35–48). Heidelberg: Springer.

Gibbs, R.W., & Cameron, L. (2008). The social-cognitive dynamics of metaphor performance. *Cognitive Systems Research*, *9*, 64–75.

Gigerenzer, G., & Selten, R. (2002). *Bounded rationality: the adaptive toolbox*. Cambridge, MA: MIT Press.

Gniewosz, B., Noack, P., & Buhl, M. (2009). Political alienation in adolescence: Associations with parental role models, parenting styles, and classroom climate. *International Journal of Behavioral Development*, *33*, 337–346.

Graber, D. A., & Holyk, G. C. (2011). The news industry. In R. Y. Shapiro & L. R. Jacobs (Eds.), *The Oxford handbook of American public opinion and the media* (pp. 89–104). Oxford: Oxford University Press.

Haidt, J. (2001). The emotional dog and its rational tail: A social intuitionist approach to moral judgment. *Psychological Review*, *108*, 814–834.

Hammack, P. L., & Pilecki, A. (2012). Narrative as root metaphor for political psychology. *Political Psychology*, *33*, 75–103.

Hanne, M. (1999). Getting to know the neighbors: When plot meets knot. *Canadian Review of Comparative Literature*, *26*, 35–50.

Hanne, M. (2011). The binocular vision project: An introduction. *Genre*, *44*, 223–237.

Haste, H. (2009). What is "competence" and how should education incorporate new technology's tools to generate "competent civic agents." *Curriculum Journal*, *20*, 207–223.

Hess, D. E. (2009). *Controversy in the classroom: The democratic power of discussion*. New York: Routledge.

Huckfeldt, R., Mondak, J. J., Craw, M., & Mendez, J. M. (2005). Making sense of candidates: Partisanship, ideology, and issues as guides to judgments. *Cognitive Brain Research, 23*, 11–23.

Jacobs, L. R., Cook, F. L., & Delli Carpini, M. X. (2009). *Talking together: Public deliberation in America and the search for community*. Chicago: Chicago University Press.

Jacobs, L. R., & Shapiro, R. Y. (2000). *Politicians don't pander: Political manipulation and the loss of democratic responsiveness*. Chicago: University of Chicago Press.

Jacobs, L. R., & Shapiro, R. Y. (2011). Informational interdependence: Public opinion and the media in the new communications era. In R. Y. Shapiro & L. R. Jacobs (Eds.), *The Oxford handbook of American public opinion and the media* (pp. 3–21). Oxford: Oxford University Press.

Jakobson, B., & Wickman, P. (2007). Transformation through language use: Children's spontaneous metaphors in elementary school science. *Science & Education*, *16*, 267–289.

Jamieson, K. H., & Hardy, B. W. (2011). The effect of media on public knowledge. In R. Y. Shapiro & L. R. Jacobs (Eds.), *The Oxford handbook of American public opinion and the media* (pp. 236–250). Oxford: Oxford University Press.

Lakoff, G. (2004). *Don't think of an elephant: Know your values and frame the debate*. White River Junction, VT: Chelsea Green.

Lakoff, G., & Johnson, M. (1980). *Metaphors we live by*. Chicago: University of Chicago Press.

Lakoff, G., & Wehling, E. (2012). *The little blue book: The essential guide to thinking and talking democratic*. New York: Free Press.

Landau, M. J., Meier, B. P., & Keefer, L. A. (2010). A metaphor-enriched social cognition. *Psychological Bulletin, 136*, 1045–1067.

Landau, M. J., Sullivan, D., & Greenberg, J. (2009). Evidence that self-relevant motives and metaphoric framing interact to influence political and social attitudes. *Psychological Science, 20*, 1421–1427.

Lau, R. R., & Redlawsk, D. P. (2001). Advantages and disadvantages of cognitive heuristics in political decision making. *American Journal of Political Science, 45*, 951–971.

Lau, R. R., & Redlawsk, D. P. (2006). *How voters decide: Information processing during election campaigns*. Cambridge: Cambridge University Press.

Lau, R. R., & Schlesinger, M. (2005). Policy frames, metaphorical reasoning, and support for public policies. *Political Psychology, 26*, 77–114.

Lehman, D. R., Lempert, R. O., & Nisbett, R. E. (1988). The effects of graduate training on reasoning: Formal discipline and thinking about everyday-life events. *American Psychologist, 43*, 431–442.

Lupia, A., Levine, A. S., Menning, J. O., & Sin, G. (2007). Were Bush tax cut supporters "simply ignorant?" A second look at conservatives and liberals in "Homer gets a tax cut." *Perspectives on Politics, 5*, 773–784.

Lupia, A., McCubbins, M. D., & Popkin, S. L. (Eds.). (2000). *Elements of reason: Cognition, choice, and the bounds of rationality*. Cambridge: Cambridge University Press.

McDevitt, M., & Kiousis, S. (2006). Deliberative learning: An evaluative interactive civic education. *Communication Education, 55*, 247–264.

McIntosh, H., & Youniss, J. (2010). Toward a political theory of political socialization of youth. In L. R. Sherrod, J. Torney-Purta, & C. A. Flanagan (Eds.), *Handbook of research on civic engagement in youth* (pp. 23–41). Hoboken, NJ: John Wiley & Sons.

Mio, J. S. (1996). Metaphor, politics and persuasion. In J. S. Mio & A. N. Katz (Eds.), *Metaphor: Implications and applications* (pp. 127–146). Mahwah, NJ: Lawrence Erlbaum.

Mondak, J. J. (2001). Developing valid knowledge scales. *American Journal of Political Science, 45*, 224–238.

Mondak, J. J., & Davis, B.C. (2001). Asked and answered: Knowledge levels when we will not take "don't know" for an answer. *Political Behavior, 23*, 199–224.

Nelson, T. E. (2011). Issue framing. In R. Y. Shapiro & L. R. Jacobs (Eds.), *The Oxford handbook of American public opinion and the media* (pp. 189–203). Oxford: Oxford University Press.

Nyhan, B., & Reifler, J. (2010). When corrections fail: The persistence of political misperceptions. *Political Behavior, 32*, 303–330.

Oehrtman, M. (2009). Collapsing dimensions, physical limitation, and other student metaphors for limit concepts. *Journal for Research in Mathematics Education, 40*, 396–426.

Ottati, V., Renstrom, R., & Price, E. (2012). *The metaphorical framing model: Political communication and public opinion*. Unpublished manuscript.

Patterson, M., & Monroe, K. R. (1998). Narrative in political science. *Annual Review of Political Science, 1*, 315–331.

Prior, M., & Lupia, A. (2008). Money, time, and political knowledge: Distinguishing quick recall and political learning skills. *American Journal of Political Science, 52*, 169–183.

Redlawsk, D. P., Civettini, A. J. W., & Emmerson, K. M. (2010). The affective tipping point: Do motivated reasoners ever "get it"? *Political Psychology, 31*, 563–593.

Richland, L. E., Zur, O., & Holyoak, K. J. (2007). Cognitive supports for analogies in the mathematics classroom. *Science, 316*, 1128–1129.

Ricoeur, P. (1992). *Oneself as another* (K. Blamey, Trans.). Chicago: University of Chicago Press.

Ritchhart, R., Church, M., & Morrison, K. (2011). *Making thinking visible: How to promote engagement, understanding, and independence for all learners*. San Francisco: Jossey-Bass.

Ryan, C., & Gamson, W. A. (2006). The art of reframing political debates. *Contexts, 5*, 13–18.

Schattschneider, E. E. (1960). *The semisovereign people: a realist's view of democracy in America*. New York: Holt, Rinehart and Winston.

Schinck, A. G., Neale, H. W., Pugalee, D. K., & Cifarelli, V. V. (2008). Using metaphors to unpack student beliefs about mathematics. *School Science and Mathematics, 108*, 326–333.

Schlesinger, M., & Lau, R. R. (2000). The meaning and measure of policy metaphors. *American Political Science Review, 94*, 611–626.

Schnall, S., Haidt, J., Clore, G. L., & Jordan, A. H. (2008). Disgust as embodied moral judgment. *Personality and Social Psychology Bulletin, 34*, 1096–1109.

Shapiro, R. Y., & Jacobs, L. R. (2011). The democratic paradox: The waning of popular sovereignty and the pathologies of American politics. In R. Y. Shapiro & L. R. Jacobs (Eds.), *The Oxford handbook of American public opinion and the media* (pp. 713–731). Oxford: Oxford University Press.

Sniderman, P. M. (2000). Taking sides: A fixed choice theory of political reasoning. In A. Lupia, M. D. McCubbins, & S. L. Popkin (Eds.), *Elements of reason: Cognition, choice, and the bounds of rationality* (pp. 67–84). Cambridge: Cambridge University Press.

Steen, G. J., Dorst, A. G., Herrmann, J. B., Kaal, A. A., & Krennmayr, T. (2010). Metaphor in usage. *Cognitive Linguistics, 21*, 765–796.

Steuter, E., & Will, D. (2008). *At war with metaphor: media, propaganda, and racism in the war on terror*. Plymouth: Lexington Books.

Stone, D. (2012). *Policy paradox: The art of political decision* making (3rd ed.). New York: W. W. Norton.

Taber, C. S. (2011). Political cognition and public opinion. In R. Y. Shapiro & L. R. Jacobs (Eds.), *The Oxford handbook of American public opinion and the media* (pp. 368–383). Oxford: Oxford University Press.

Taber, C. S., & Lodge, M. (2006). Motivated skepticism in the evaluation of political beliefs. *American Journal of Political Science, 50*, 755–769.

Thagard, P. (2011). The brain is wider than the sky: Analogy, emotion, and allegory. *Metaphor and Symbol, 26*, 131–142.

Thibodeau, P. H., & Boroditsky, L. (2011). Metaphors we think with: The role of metaphor in reasoning. *PLoS ONE, 6*, e16782.

Torney-Purta, J., Lehmann, R., Oswald, H., & Schulz, W. (2001). *Citizenship and education in twenty-eight countries: Civic knowledge and engagement at age fourteen*. Amsterdam: International Association for the Evaluation of Educational Achievement.

van den Broek, P. (2010). Using texts in science education: Cognitive processes and knowledge representation. *Science, 328,* 453–456.

Wertsch, J. V. (2008). The narrative organization of collective memory. *Ethos, 36,* 120–135.

Yates, M., & Youniss, J. (1996). Community service and political-moral identity in adolescents. *Journal of Research on Adolescence, 54,* 248–261.

Zaller, J. R. (1992). *The nature and origins of mass opinions.* Cambridge: Cambridge University Press.

Zinken, J. (2007). Discourse metaphors: The link between figurative language and habitual analogies. *Cognitive Linguistics, 18,* 445–466.

12 Useful Strategies in the War of Words

William D. Crano

In the pages that preceded this final chapter, the authors' expressed views were clear, strongly argued, and persuasive, so I feel no need to attempt to summarize each of their important and enlightening insights; rather, I try to show how the work of the symposium has affected my own thinking on an issue that has occupied part of my research agenda for more than a decade, the question of how members of minority groups can move the majority, although they may have little capacity even to make the majority listen, much less comply with their requests and demands. In this sense, this chapter probably anticipates the approaches of many readers, who undoubtedly will appreciate the wisdom of the observations presented and who are concerned with transposing these insights to their own particular arena of concern. In my case, the work presented here is reframed in terms of its relevance to the ways minority groups represent issues that are of central relevance to their vested interests, and with the words its members use to foster the portrayal of their positions. Lacking brute force, the minority must rely on the power of persuasion to make its way to the docket. Moving the multitude to its position is the next, but far from the most important step. How the minority makes its voice heard requires some preliminary exposition, but as will become clear, the preceding chapters have provided important insights, a veritable instruction booklet for how the minority group may mobilize the power of persuasive argument to maximize its chances of succeeding in moving more powerful groups, even though it lacks the coercive power to enforce its will.

How Minorities Prevail

Some years ago, the great French polymath Serge Moscovici took American social psychology to task for focusing its research agenda almost exclusively, he claimed, on the features and actions the majority used to impose its will on the minority (Moscovici, 1985; Moscovici, Mucchi-Faina, & Maass, 1994; Moscovici, Mugny, & Van Avermaet, 1985). Although many (American) social psychologists thought Moscovici had overstated his case, it is true that we knew considerably more about the ways the group holding power, the majority, influenced the minority, than vice versa. The minority, we were to learn, often was characterized by the majority as different, and somehow inferior, numerically, morally and in the power to shape events (Seyranian, Atuel, & Crano, 2008). In contradistinction to the "American" bias, Moscovici cited many examples of minorities, groups and individuals, who were able to change the world although they had little power to demand the majority's acquiescence. Gandhi, Darwin, Martin Luther King, Jr., Betty Friedan, and Hitler (you do not need to be virtuous to be influential), even Moscovici himself, had enormous influence; however, initially they could not back their demands with anything other than moral force, wit, and the power of their words.

Almost all of the various predictive models of minority influence that have evolved from Moscovici's original work make reference in one way or another to the importance of the minority being accepted as a part of the group it seeks to win over (Martin & Hewstone, 2008). One of these, the leniency contract model, has special relevance to the topic of this symposium and, as such, will receive special consideration. The leniency contract is a component of a general theory designed to explicate majority *and* minority influence, which we have called the *Context/Comparison Model* (CCM; Crano & Alvaro, 1998, in press; Crano & Hemovich, 2011). The model is concerned with the questions, "How and why do people bend to the will of the majority?" and "How does the minority make its point heard and, later, accepted?" The leniency contract is a subcomponent of the more general CCM. It is focused specifically on *minority* influence. How and why does the minority prevail in the war of words with the majority, and how does it fail? It was designed to explain and predict the very peculiar patterns of people's responses to a minority group's persuasive attacks. The pattern or response to minority influence that has been detailed in the research literature is quite different from that seen in response to majority influence. It takes one of three possible forms (Crano, 2010; Crano & Hemovich, 2011; Wood, Lundgren, Ouellette, Busceme, & Blackstone, 1994). The most obvious outcome, although one that rarely travels beyond a journal editor's desk, involves no change; the minority, that is, fails utterly in its attempt at influence. A less obvious, more exciting, and not uncommon outcome of much of the published research on minority influence is found in studies that report no immediate acceptance of the minority's position, but rather a change in beliefs on the topic under discussion (often called the *focal issue*). The change, however, is almost never immediate—it occurs and is noticed only after some time has transpired. The indirect change process follows a predictable path: A minority group or a spokesperson makes an argument for a position at odds with that held by the majority. In most studies of this phenomenon, an immediate measure of effect is administered and shows no acceptance of the minority's counter-attitudinal message. Later, sometimes days or weeks later, a remeasure of the majority's position shows a shift in the direction of the minority's earlier argument. This delayed change effect is almost never found in research in which the majority is the source of influence and a minority group is the target (Crano, 2000, 2010; Martin & Hewstone, 2008; Martin, Hewstone, & Martin, 2008). Usually, if the minority is moved, not uncommonly, its compliant response with the majority's position is noted immediately. Reasons for the power of the majority are manifold: The majority can punish or ostracize; it can define right and wrong, and so deviance is sometimes equated with immorality, and it enjoys the power of many heuristics that appeal to the majority as generally being right ("Two heads are better than one," "Fifty million Frenchmen can't be wrong," and so on—but then, as Mark Twain is supposed to have said, "Whenever you find yourself on the side of the majority, it is time to pause and reflect.").

Indirect Attitude Change

Perhaps the most unusual and counterintuitive outcome in minority influence research, and one that dovetails nicely with the themes of this symposium, involves studies that report findings in which there are no focal changes but substantial change on an issue related, but not identical, to the thrust of the minority's persuasive appeal. The changes can occur on issues not even mentioned in the minority's statement, and not obviously related to it (Crano, 2012). For example, in an early study of the indirect minority influence effect, Juan Antonio Pérez and Gabriel Mugny (1987) gathered a group of Spanish high school women as participants in their research, randomly sorted them into three groups, and exposed each group to a message that argued for a liberalization of abortion laws. This statement was contrary to the law of the land at the time, and to the attitudes of most of the participants. For one of the randomly assorted groups, the message was attributed to a majority of their fellow students; for the second group, it was attributed to a small minority of high school *men* (whom the authors believed the female respondents would consider to be an out-group); to the third group, the identical message was attributed to a small minority of participants' fellow (female) students (an in-group minority).

At first glance, the study seemed to fail. It did not appear to matter to which source the communication was attributed. In all cases, the message did not persuade the student respondents, who, as noted, held staunch, pro-life positions. However, the third group, the students who heard the message attributed to the in-group minority (fellow female students) became on average significantly more amenable to contraception. The message source clearly constituted an opinion minority because of its pro-choice position, but in all other ways, this group's members (also) were members in good standing in the majority—they constituted an *in-group* minority. This minority was successful, but only indirectly. Its message appeared to evoke change, but only on an issue obviously related, but obviously not identical, to the focus of the persuasive message. When the identical message was attributed to a different group (e.g., to men, the "out-group"), or to the majority of the student body, no movement was evident on either the focal or the indirect issue (Pérez & Mugny, 1987).

This result was replicated and extended in later studies (Alvaro & Crano, 1997; Crano & Chen, 1998). Alvaro and Crano (1997) showed that the obvious relatedness of the issues, a salient feature of Pérez and Mugny's (1987) study, was not a necessary precondition for the indirect minority influence effect. They demonstrated that an in-group minority with a *strong* message could produce indirect influence effects similar to those found in Pérez and Mugny's earlier research.[1] Even more intriguing, the changes occurred even though the respondents did not believe the two issues were related. Sophisticated statistical assessment had established that the association between the two concepts was strong, even if the respondents themselves did not realize it.

The details of the research deserve attention, as they will help to illustrate the remarkable results uncovered in this study. In Alvaro and Crano's (1997) experiment, research participants read a strong message that argued against allowing gay people to serve in the US military (the study was conducted while the "Don't Ask, Don't Tell" order was under congressional debate during the Clinton administration—*Plus ça change, plus c'est la même chose*). The vast majority of the message audience (undergraduate students at a large state university in the US desert southwest) opposed this position. They were perfectly happy to see gay people serve in the military. The message was attributed to a small minority that was either an in-group (a radical minority group of their fellow students attending the university) or an out-group minority (students from a rival university). It did not appear to matter to which group the message was attributed. Neither had any effect on the respondents' attitudes toward gay people serving in the military. The study apparently failed. However, Alvaro and Crano had established beforehand that students' attitudes toward this critical issue were strongly related to an apparently unrelated topic, namely, gun control. Using the students' own survey responses, however, made it clear that the students themselves were unaware of this mental connection.

As predicted, the strongly argued minority group communication on the issue of gays in the military was resisted by students who held the majority attitude (i.e., that gay people ought to be allowed to serve, if they chose to do so). The researchers also had hypothesized, however, that as a result of a strong message from an in-group minority source, participants would feel pressure to change on a related issue. Thus, they predicted that although the group of students constituting the majority would reject the minority's anti–gays-in-the-military arguments, their attitudes on an issue conceptually related to this focal issue would move in a conservative political direction (i.e., in favor of *less* gun control) that was consistent with the minority's message—and this is exactly what happened. The research participants, in other words, adopted the more conservative gun control attitude after reading a message arguing against allowing gay people to serve in the military, if the message was attributed to an in-group minority. The out-group minority source had no influence whatsoever.

To bolster confidence in these startling results, to ensure that they were not a complete fluke, Alvaro and Crano (1997) replicated the study, but this time switched the focal and indirect issues. The leniency contract does not specify which should be the focal issue, and which the indirect one. They prepared a strong antigun control message (consistent with the views of more conservative individuals) and attributed it either to an in-group minority or to the majority of an important in-group for the students—their fellow university student-peers. The results of this study perfectly replicated the earlier findings. Students who read a strong antigun control message attributed to an in-group minority were not moved to become more resistant to gun control; they were, however, moved in a conservative direction on the issue of gays in the military—that is, they became significantly less favorable to allowing gay people to serve.

As an aside, the results found among respondents exposed to the majority-ascribed message were quite different. Participants exposed to the message attributed to the majority were significantly less in favor of gun control (i.e., more in agreement with the persuasive message) than those who read the identical communication that was attributed to the minority. They showed no evidence of indirect influence, however. Their attitudes toward gays in the military were not affected. In this case, the majority succeeded in moving people on the focal issue, consistent with many earlier studies on majority-based influence (Crano, 2000).

Delayed Focal Change

Crano and Chen (1998) attempted to extend these findings by taking on the issue of delayed focal change, a common result that confounded many, even those involved in minority influence research (Wood et al., 1994). Using different attitude objects from Alvaro and Crano's (1997) earlier study, the research showed, as hoped and hypothesized, indirect majority attitude changes in response to an in-group minority's persuasive message. The message argued that students should volunteer 10 hours of their time, without recompense, to work on projects at the university (e.g., projects could involve general office work, campus clean-up, etc.).[2] Focal change was notably absent in Crano and Chen's experiment, also as predicted. These findings replicated the earlier research by Alvaro and Crano (1997). However, Crano and Chen found that those students who received the message attributed to a small minority of their fellow students (an in-group) were considerably more amenable to a tuition increase (the indirect attitude object) than were those who received the identical message that was attributed to the majority of their peers.

These findings replicated the original study. The new research extended Alvaro and Crano's (1997) study by *revisiting the same respondents two weeks later* and reassessing their attitudes. As predicted, Crano and Chen (1998) found that the participants whose indirect attitudes (toward a tuition increase) had changed the most showed significant delayed change on the focal issue (the "work for free" proposal), although the issue was not reinstated in the delayed measurement session.

Students who had been exposed to the majority showed no change on the focal (or the indirect) issue in the delayed measurement condition. This result suggests that the delayed focal change found in many earlier studies (Wood et al., 1994) might have been associated with the magnitude of immediate indirect attitude change, insofar as with large indirect attitude change, delayed focal change occurred. With minor immediate indirect change, no delayed focal change was found. These results suggest why some earlier studies that showed indirect minority-induced changes did not produce delayed change on the focal issue. Respondents in our study whose indirect change was not great did not show the delayed effect. Crano and Chen's results suggest some boundary conditions for the delayed focal change effect that often, but not always, is found in the research literature.

The Master Narrative

Our speakers' discussions of metaphor and narrative struck me as directly relevant to these results. Many of the speakers seemed to assume, implicitly or explicitly in Hanne's and Hammack's cases (this volume), that narrative is a means of, or foundation for, our self-identity, our demarcations of who we are and, importantly, of who we are not. One's self-identity is paramount in navigating the sometimes dangerous waters of inter- and intragroup relations. It allows us to know whom we are permitted to love, trust, and depend on and whom to fear, avoid, or fight. Those who do not belong to our in-group are viewed as somehow inferior, and clearly different from "normal people" like us. We tend to see these marginalized out-groups as more or less monolithic in thought and action: "If you've seen (heard) one, you seen (heard) them all," or "They all look (think) alike." In part, this monolithic myopia is a result of a lack of knowledge of, or experience with the out-group. The primacy of the notion of interchangeability is a fundamental feature of definitions of out-group members, and it facilitates the jump to the assumption that whatever *they* believe is in some way different from, antithetical to, and inconsistent with all we hold dear. Out-groups, assemblages of people with whom we do not share a common narrative, often are defined in terms of beliefs, customs, and behaviors that are, by definition, *assumed opposite* to ours (Cohen, 2012; Rokeach & Mezei, 1966). This kind of thinking paved the way for the pogroms, ethnic cleansing, and holocaust we have witnessed during our lifetimes. It is perhaps for this reason that propaganda in times of war often uses language suggesting that our enemies "don't even care about their own children." Such cold-coldheartedness is so extreme, so beyond the pale, so foreign to us all that we consider those it describes as non-legitimate members of the human race—and thus, fair game for extermination.

The discrimination directed toward members of the out-group need not be of the life-and-death variety to affect them. We learned that strongly held stories (or master narratives) may suppress other, perhaps equally valid ideas or narratives. In the early days of the civil rights movement, for example, many in the white majority viewed blacks, those "other" people, as different (and hence, inferior) in important ways. They were thought to hold values and beliefs different from, and at odds with, those held by the majority. "They" did not care about the family as much as "we" did, did not plan for the security of their future, were not as willing to work as hard as we, were always looking for a handout, and, thus, got what they deserved. This is the typical majority posture, and it justifies the subjugation of the minority (this is a general rule; it need not be played out only in terms of race or civil rights). Martin Luther King, Jr.'s beautiful rhetorical force was singularly directed toward defeating this specific narrative. In his celebrated "I have a dream" speech, he insisted that his love and hopes for his children (and, by extension, the love and hopes of those he represented) were no different from those of his white neighbors, that they would be judged not "by the color of their skin but by the content of their character" (King, 1963). Rhetorically, in making his appeal, he bolstered his claim for equality from the very beginning of his oration by appealing to a truth that must resonate with all who claim to be American, that "We hold these truths to be self-evident, that all men are created equal." If both in- and out-group agree on this fact, and they must accept this or deny the fundamental tenet the American identity, then maintaining group boundaries on the basis of incidental features like skin tone becomes indefensible, along with being patently absurd. King was able to persuade many in the recalcitrant majority of his time that their exclusionary beliefs were contrary to the central "equality" feature of the American identity. He did not do so by a one-shot speech, but by a life in which he relentlessly pushed this position. The inconsistency between segregationist practice and the American ideal could not hold: those who recognized the illegitimacy of the exclusionary logic were forced to change. Those who refused to recognize the inconsistency were forced to create a new narrative in which the central premise of the old identity was qualified beyond recognition.

In the jargon of social psychology, King's approach was an attempt to create a *superordinate group*. We are not black or white or brown or yellow, he argued, we are Americans or, later in his career, human beings. Barack Obama adopted a similar communicative approach when he observed that there were no red or blue states, only the United States. Obama at that time was appealing to Americans of all stripes to come together under the same flag, the same set of guiding principles, and the same master narrative to work for the betterment of the country. His intuitive grasp of the importance of the story, the simple parable that exposes the grand truth, distinguished him from many of his contemporaries, and he used this understanding to gain the country's highest office. It is my view that any group attempting to emerge from the burdens imposed by minority status, and all that involves, must abide by a set of rules, without deviation. If followed faithfully, these rules offer the minority the possibility of prevailing, of obtaining fair treatment. The rules the minority must follow are simple, but not easy to abide by, and the first and most critical of them is to become "in-group," to become part of the assemblage of actors that sets the rules and thus defines good and evil. It is only in this way that the minority may procure a fair hearing (see Crano, 2012, for an expansion of the rules of minority influence).

To facilitate the intermingling of disparate narratives, the minority's stories must in important ways overlap or coincide with those of the group in power. If we share nonoverlapping or conflicting narratives, communication becomes problematic and less likely to bring about resolution acceptable to both sides of the debate. To see the importance of conflicting narratives one need only read of the horrific bloodshed that was so much a part of life in Sri Lanka for decades. Here, unlike the Martin Luther King, Jr. story, we have an example of two groups whose own identities depended in part on master narratives that more or less denied the legitimacy of the other's. The Damelas, or Tamils as they have come to be called, established tenancy of the beautiful island more than two millennia ago. They were known for their industriousness and organizational skills. Because they were traders, these traits ensured their survival. Over the years, however, the position of the Tamils was undone by the more numerous Sinhalese, who ultimately controlled the state with 75% of the population.

The Tamils are a religious and linguistic minority in Sri Lanka, and their master narrative was quite different from that of the Sinhalese. More than merely being different, the incommensurability of the groups' narratives, starting with the creation myth and moving forward, is striking. Despite this, for centuries the Sinhala and Tamil people coexisted, notwithstanding differences in customs and the very languages they spoke. Communication between the groups was not unusual, and the groups lived in relative harmony. Their narratives differed, but the *possibility* of communication and development of shared narratives was maintained. All of this changed in 1956, however, when the majority in the Sri Lankan Parliament introduced and passed the Official Language Bill, which made Sinhala the sole official language of the land. All public employees were to use Sinhala in their work or lose their jobs. This was more than a symbolic slap in the face of the Tamil minority. It marked the beginning of their end. On an island they had inhabited for more than two millennia, the Tamils found themselves relegated to the lowest rung of society's ladder, and the Official Language Bill ensured that they likely would stay there. With Sinhalese power came prejudice and discrimination against a group that was readily identifiable by anyone who cared to do so. The Tamils found themselves in an increasingly untenable position, denied opportunities and facing ever-diminishing possibilities, unable to incorporate their narrative into that of the majority. Ultimately, after appeals to the UN, which ruled favorably on their behalf to no avail, the Tamils resorted to violence. Riots, pogroms, and counter-reactions were common from the late 1950s, culminating in a bloody civil war. It was fought until the decisive defeat of the Tamil Tigers in May 2009. For all practical purposes, the cause of the Tamil minority in Sri Lanka was lost. Failing to become a part of the master story, the master narrative, made the Tamils fair game for the more powerful Sinhalese majority, and many paid the ultimate price for this failure. Could it have been otherwise? Perhaps, but there must be at least some openness on the part of the majority before progress is even a possibility. For many Tamils, this condition was never met despite their willingness to compromise at every turn.

The general operative parameters of this story are so common as to be banal. The same general outline could have been used to tell the story of the Hutu massacre of the Tutsi in Rwanda—we need only search and replace the names of the combatants. The same might be said of the sad fate of Yugoslavia, and the rending of the Yugoslav master narrative that Tito had constructed, some say artificially, and on which the fate of the nation was precariously balanced. The clash of worldview in Yugoslavia was fully exposed with the death of the country's leader, and the ethnic cleansing that followed was as predictable as it was tragic.

The Exclusionary Narrative

There's another side to the master narrative idea that should be understood as well, and that is that weak minority groups that cling to a master narrative that is exclusionary, and thus incommensurate with that of the majority, rarely fare well. Whether or not you sided with the vision and worldview of the Black Panthers, it was easily predictable that the group did not have a long shelf life and that their ideas were not likely to prevail. Deciding that the majority is evil is one thing; deciding to fight the majority from the position of true weakness is another.

The "birther" controversy that surrounded the citizenship of the United States' first African-American commander-in-chief may be read as another example of an abortive attempt to derail the master narrative of the "leader of the free world." Despite undeniable evidence to the contrary, some in the US electorate maintain staunchly that President Barack Obama is not a "natural born citizen," and thus is ineligible to serve as CEO of the country. This claim had (and has) virtually no chance of succeeding, although many in the hierarchy of the opposing political party refuse to disavow the assertion. This absurdity can be read in many different ways, but from the vantage of this conference, it is perhaps best seen as an attempt to deny the master narrative of a master politician. If this futile exercise could succeed, then the Obama story would have no resonance with that of the rest of us. As such, his "rags to riches" narrative, a part of the master story of the great American experience, could be judged illegitimate. This being the case, all he had said and done would become null and void. The birthers implicitly understood the process of delegitimization, even if the facts in evidence never supported their case. What they did not understand is that attempting to undo the will of the majority with an obviously specious minority position was not likely to gain traction without a very large smoking gun. Persistence is necessary if the minority's position is to prevail, but it is no substitute for believability.

Innuendo Effects: Nudging the Master (Metaphor)

This is not to say that the master narrative cannot be moved about, or shifted, to foster one's goals. The lesson to be learned from our study of warring with words is that words can be used not just to persuade others to do one's bidding, but to alter their fundamental worldviews, to modify their master narratives. Orwell (1949) was right. Words can be used to redefine reality, but the attack on reality does not necessitate use of the broadsword. In an intriguing and somewhat frightening study, Dan Wegner and his associates (Wegner, Wenzlaff, Kerker, & Beattie, 1981) demonstrated the awesome power of simple innuendo on human judgments. In a series of carefully controlled experiments, Wegner asked his research participants to read simple headlines. In the first study of the series, each participant read four headlines, one of which contained an incriminating assertion (e.g., "Bob Talbert Linked With Mafia"); a second headline was posed as a question (e.g., "Is Karen Downing Associated With Fraudulent Charity?"); a third headline was in the form of a denial (e.g., "Andrew Winters Not Connected to Bank Embezzlement"); the fourth headline was a neutral (control) assertion (e.g., "George Armstrong Arrives in City"; Wegner et al., p. 824). The headlines were balanced across the entire sample and were systematically counterbalanced across subjects so that a given headline appeared in all four forms, with different names completely balanced across headlines. The methodological precision of this study was a joy to behold.

After reading the headlines, research participants rated each of the four persons listed on a series of evaluative scales, bounded by the endpoints: good–bad, kind–cruel, sociable–unsociable, honest–dishonest, and so on. Statistical analysis of ratings revealed that participants evaluated the individual described in the incriminating assertion headline significantly more negatively than the person mentioned in the control assertion. No surprise here. However, the individual named in the question headline, the innuendo, was judged as negatively as the person named in the incriminating assertion, and significantly more negatively than the individual appearing in the control assertion! Asking "Is Bob Talbert Associated With Mafia?" was as damning as stating "Bob Talbert Linked With Mafia."

Apparently, moving evaluative attitudes toward an unknown other is child's play—if the child is smart enough. But clearly there must be limits on the generality of this effect. Would not an innuendo leveled at one's best friend or lover be less credible, and less likely to matter to us than one implicating a mere acquaintance? Would not the credibility of the source of the innuendo make a difference? The results of the study confirmed only one of these sensible expectations.

In Wegner and colleagues' (1981) second study, participants were told the persons appearing in the headlines had been past candidates for the US House of Representatives, and thus, presumably, were persons of high repute and integrity. Operations similar to those of the first experiment followed, with one exception: some of the participants were told the headlines had been taken from the *New York Times* or the *Washington Post*, two of the country's most respected dailies; the others were told the headlines had been taken from the *National Enquirer* or the *Midnight Post*, which typically are not listed among the nation's most respected news sources.

The general pattern of results replicated those of the first study. Apparent reputation of the persons named in the headlines did not appear to make any difference. Did the source of the headline matter to the participants? Some-what. When the highly credible sources—the *New York Times* or *Washington Post*—directly implicated an individual, he or she was judged more negatively than when the source was of lesser repute. However, the impact of the question innuendo was not affected by its source. That's right—it did not matter to the participants whose name was muddied in the headliners—the innuendo was damning even if its source was judged as incredible by the very subjects who were influenced by it. Could one use a similar technique to massively alter the master narrative? It may be difficult to do so, but there seems little doubt that the narrative could be nudged in one direction or the other with the appropriate technique, and the use of innuendo might be one of these.

Misdirection

This result suggests some important features of the human response to attempted persuasion or social influence, namely, that although we tend in the war of words to remain independent in the face of pressure, we are susceptible to subtle persuasive tactics. Brehm built a theory around the idea of resistance to pressure, and his reactance theory has been used to advantage in many media campaigns designed to prevent behaviors that people like to perform but should not—unprotected sex, drug misuse, and overindulgence in the many other plea-sures of the flesh (J. Brehm, 1966, 2000; S. Brehm & Brehm, 1981). As in most wars, including the war of words, the attacking army must be aware of the strengths and weaknesses of the defenders. Years of research on resistance to persuasion has suggested ways in which people defend themselves against counter-beliefs, and this research has illustrated quite clearly, from the earli-est days of our discipline, that more central beliefs are more heavily defended (Knowles & Linn, 2004; Rokeach, 1960; Scott, Kline, Faguy-Coté, & Peter-son, 1980), as are beliefs that are held with greater certainty (Tormala, 2008; Tormala, Clarkson, & Petty, 2006; Tormala & Petty, 2002, 2004). Wegner and colleagues' (1981) study obviously did not involve well-established beliefs. In fact, the objects of judgment that were rated—"Bob Talbert," "George Arm-strong," and so on—were figments of Wegner's fertile imagination. They were unreal, created for the purpose of study.

Even so, his research suggests an important fact that comports well with consistent results established in a related area of social psychological research involving the forewarning of attempts at social influence. Quite simply, indi-viduals warned that they were about to receive a communication designed to change their attitude on an issue typically bolstered the belief by moving in a more extreme direction than their original position (Quinn & Wood, 2004; Wood & Quinn, 2003). Of course, there are ways of offsetting or even revers-ing this tendency, but the fundamental perverseness of the human psyche, or perhaps, the survival relevant trait of sticking to one's guns, seems relatively well established in the attitude change literature. Obviously it is important that the words get through if one is to win the war of words, and the use of narrative and metaphor are central weapons in this war.

How can we make the words stick? One of the best ways is to ensure that they are processed with as little resistance as possible. This has been a central tenet of the attitude change gang from the earliest days of persuasion research (Hovland, Janis, & Kelley, 1963) and carries into today's work on dual process models of persuasion (Petty & Cacioppo, 1986). Wegner's insights suggest that one way of persuading an individual is to convince him or her that you are not attempting to do so.

Research by Alvaro and Crano (1997), discussed earlier in this chapter, may be seen as an instance of this process, but an even more straightforward example of this far from straightforward technique is available in a recent investigation of drug prevention in young adolescents (Crano, Siegel, Alvaro, & Patel, 2007). This study was concerned with persuading young at-risk adolescents to avoid use of inhalant drugs, a class of substances that sometimes causes severe debilitation or even death. To do this, the researchers created two nearly identical persuasive communications. They took the form of 60-second antidrug commercials, which were aired during a break in a longer presentation of prevention of bullying that the researchers had produced. The bullying video was played in middle school classrooms and was interrupted, as many televised shows are, by two commercials at the midpoint of the presentation. Two different messages were prepared. They addressed the students directly, or were (apparently) pitched to the students' parents, even though only students watched the presentation. In the directly targeted condition, the message asked, "Are you in the sixth, seventh, or eighth grade?" Four times during the course of the commercial, the target of the ad was reinstated: "You may think . . . if you do . . ." Near the video's end, the participants were addressed directly: "Students . . ." The commercial used in the indirect condition began, "Parents, do you have a young teen at home?" Later statements boosted the focus of the ad: "Your child . . . they are . . ." Near the end of the message, the apparent target of the ad was reinstated: "Parents . . ." The content of both messages was otherwise identical.

The results of this experiment indicated that the students who received the indirect "parents" commercial evaluated it significantly more positively than did those who saw the identical ad aimed directly at the students themselves. This difference had serious implications, as intentions to use inhalants were significantly linked to their evaluations. Clearly, the analyses suggest that to affect the young targets of the persuasive communication, the message might be apparently aimed at their parents.

Beyond the practical application of the "misdirection" result, however, is the theoretical insight it offers. This finding seems to indicate that words meant to alter our perceptions and evaluations of people and ideas are most likely to succeed if they are not seen as consciously developed to create change. Put another way, disguised persuasive messages will prove more effective than will obvious ones. This may not be surprising, as subtlety often has proved a useful tool. However, the observation suggests that in the war of words, the frontal assault may prove the least effective of all the many possible strategies.

Metaphor

One of the (potentially) most subtle of the indirect strategies is metaphor, the nuclear weapon of persuasion. Use of metaphor in everyday communication is as common as sands in the Sahara, yet its formal empirical study in psychology is not as usual as might be expected (see Billow, 1977) given the interest it has ignited over the years. On a brief foray into its history, we find Aristotle (in Butcher, 1951, pp. 77–79) defining metaphor as "the application of an alien name by transference either from genus to species, or from species to genus, or from species to species, or by analogy, that is, proportion." This definition only brings us halfway: It tells us the *what*, but not the *why* of metaphor. Obviously, metaphor is a tool, but its common use suggests the tool is not cumbersome—in the hands of a skilled mechanic, the tool can produce superb visions, which on reflection may generate meaning. Metaphors are used because with few or no words (in the case of illustrations), they evoke strong associations, much like the smells of one's mother's cooking, and they carry these important meaning-heavy associations with utmost efficiency,

The metaphors we choose project our identities as surely as do our badges, insignia, uniforms, or other official marks of rank. Groups with names like the Black Panthers or the Tamil Tigers are not projecting the image of peaceful negotiation, and it is important to understand that the groups chose these names; they were not attached to them, and even if they were, the groups did nothing to disclaim the identification. Metaphors help control the tone and perhaps, even the possibility of interpersonal or intergroup interaction. Calling another nation a collection of imperialist pigs, for example, shapes the relationship in fundamental ways. It does not endear that nation to the source of the designation, nor does it signal the likelihood of successful negotiations between the parties. The metaphor conjures much more than the mere picture of the object described by the words used to form it. The terms of metaphorical speech are pregnant with meaning, providing shortcuts through the sometimes brambly thicket of logic. They are processed often without deep thought, and thus their assumptions may be accepted uncritically, always to the detriment of proper understanding. The danger of thoughtless acceptance of hidden premises should be obvious, given Wegner and colleagues' (1981) work on innuendo, which in spirit owes much to Grice's (1989) rules of conversation and their violation. Wegner and friends showed in their study of innuendo that the mechanics of metaphor, the manner in which metaphor can trick the cognitive system and confound the Gricean "rules" of conversation by reversing or misdirecting the standard implicature of the very words used, can result in powerful persuasion. The metaphor works because it is accepted, and those caught on the wrong side of the metaphor often labor long and hard to reverse it to no avail. John Kerry's famous explanation of his vacillation on funding the Iraq war—"I actually did vote for the $87 billion before I voted against it" was probably the most damaging words spoken during his run for the presidency against George Bush in 2004 (Roberts, 2004). The "flip-flopper" sobriquet that was pinned on him by his opposition was difficult to counter, not because it required much to explain why he changed but because such an explanation would have taken page after page of detailed exegesis, whereas Mr. Bush needed only to respond with a single compound noun. Can it be that metaphors can be defeated only by other metaphors? Probably not. Given sufficient time, space, resources, and a mindful audience, a soundly argued position probably can undo the more economical metaphorical quip. However, these conditions are rare, especially in political discourse. So how do we deal with this clear threat to truth and logic? That interesting question is addressed in all that came before in this book. You might want to consult the expert opinions that are so well represented in the earlier pages.

Notes

1 Petty and Cacioppo (1986) stressed the importance of strong communications in evoking persistent attitude change, a theme that has been brought into research on minority influence by Alvaro and Crano (1997) and others (e.g., Martin & Hewstone, 2008).
2 As might be expected, almost no student participants in a preliminary study had judged this proposal favorably.

References

Alvaro, E. M., & Crano, W. D. (1997). Indirect minority influence: Evidence for leniency in source evaluation and counterargumentation. *Journal of Personality and Social Psychology, 72,* 949–964. doi:10.1037/0022–3514.72.5.949

Aristotle (1951). Poetics. In S. Butcher, *Aristotle's theory of poetry and fine art*. New York: Dover.

Billow, R.M. (1977). Metaphor: A review of the psychological literature. *Psychological Bulletin, 84,* 81–92. doi:10.1037/0033–2909.84.1.81

Brehm, J. W. (1966). *A theory of psycholoical reactance*. Oxford, England: Academic Press.

Brehm, J. W. (2000). Reactance. In A. E. Kazdin (Ed.), *Encyclopedia of psychology* (Vol. 7, pp. 10–12). Washington, DC: American Psychological Association.

Brehm, S. S., & Brehm, J. W. (1981). *Psychological reactance: A theory of freedom and control*. New York, NY: Academic Press.

Cohen, G. L. (2012). Identity, belief, and bias. In J. Hanson (Ed.), *Ideology, psychology, and law* (pp. 385–403). New York, NY: Oxford University Press.

Crano, W. D. (2000). Milestones in the psychological analysis of social influence. *Group Dynamics: Theory, Research, and Practice, 4,* 68–80. doi:10.1037/1089–2699.4.1.68

Crano, W. D. (2010). Majority and minority influence in attitude formation and attitude change: Context/categorization—leniency contract theory. In R. Martin &

M. Hewstone (Eds.), *Minority influence and innovation: Antecedents, processes and consequences* (pp. 53–77). New York, NY: Psychology Press.

Crano, W. D. (2012). *The rules of influence: Winning when you're in the minority.* New York, NY: St. Martin's Press.

Crano, W. D., & Alvaro, E. M. (1998). The context/comparison model of social influence: Mechanisms, structure, and linkages that underlie indirect attitude change. In W. Stroebe & M. Hewstone (Eds.), *European review of social psychology, Vol. 8* (pp. 175–202). Hoboken, NJ: John Wiley & Sons Inc.

Crano, W. D., & Alvaro, E. M. (2014). Social factors that affect the processing and subsequent effect of persuasive communications. In J. P. Forgas, O. Vincze, & J. Laszlo (Eds.), *Social cognition and communication* (pp. 297–312). New York, NY: Psychology Press.

Crano, W. D., & Chen, X. (1998). The leniency contract and persistence of majority and minority influence. *Journal of Personality and Social Psychology*, *74*, 1437–1450. doi:10.1037/0022–3514.74.6.1437

Crano, W. D., & Hemovich, V. (2011). Intergroup relations and majority or minority group influence. In R. M. Kramer, G. J. Leonardelli, & R. W. Livingston (Eds.), *Social cognition, social identity, and intergroup relations: A Festschrift in honor of Marilynn B. Brewer.* (pp. 221–246). New York, NY: Psychology Press.

Crano, W. D., Siegel, J. T., Alvaro, E. M., & Patel, N. M. (2007). Overcoming adolescents' resistance to anti-inhalant appeals. *Psychology of Addictive Behaviors*, *21*, 516–524. doi:10.1037/0893–164x.21.4.516

Grice, H. P. (1989). *Studies in the way of words.* Cambridge, MA: Harvard University Press.

Hovland, C. I., Janis, I. L., & Kelley, H. H. (1963). *Communication and persuasion.* Oxford, England: Yale University Press.

King, M. L., Jr. (1963). "I have a dream" [Speech]. Retrieved January 4, 2014, from: www.americanrhetoric.com/speeches/mlkihaveadream.htm

Knowles, E. S., & Linn, J. A. (2004). *Resistance and persuasion.* Mahwah, NJ: Erlbaum.

Martin, R., & Hewstone, M. (2008). Majority versus minority influence, message processing and attitude change: The source-context-elaboration model. In M. P. Zanna (Ed.), *Advances in experimental social psychology* (Vol. 49, pp. 238–326). New York, NY: Academic.

Martin, R., Hewstone, M., & Martin, P. Y. (2008). Majority versus minority influence: The role of message processing in determining resistance to counter-persuasion. *European Journal of Social Psychology*, *38*, 16–34. doi:10.1002/ejsp.426

Moscovici, S. (1985). Social influence and conformity. In G. Lindzey & E. Aronson (Eds.), *Handbook of social psychology* (3 ed., Vol. 2, pp. 347–412). New York, NY: Random House.

Moscovici, S., Mucchi-Faina, A., & Maass, A. (1994). *Minority influence.* Chicago, IL: Nelson-Hall Publishers.

Moscovici, S., Mugny, G., & Van Avermaet, E. (Eds.). (1985). *Perspectives on minority influence.* Cambridge, England: Cambridge University Press.

Orwell, G. (1949). *Nineteen eighty-four; a novel.* New York, NY: Harcourt, Brace.

Pérez, J. A., & Mugny, G. (1987). Paradoxical effects of categorization in minority influence: When being an outgroup is an advantage. *European Journal of Social Psychology*, *17*, 157–169. doi:10.1002/ejsp.2420170204

Petty, R. E., & Cacioppo, J. T. (1986). *Communication and persuasion: Central and peripheral routes to attitude change*. New York, NY: Springer-Verlag.

Quinn, J. M., & Wood, W. (2004). Forewarnings of influence appeals: Inducing resistance and acceptance. In E. S. Knowles & J. A. Linn (Eds.), *Resistance and persuasion*. (pp. 193–213). Mahwah, NJ: Erlbaum.

Roberts, J (2004, September 29). Kerry's top ten flip-flops. CBS. Retrieved January 4, 2014, from www.cbsnews.com/news/kerrys-top-ten-flip-flops/

Rokeach, M. (1960). *The open and closed mind*. Oxford, England: Basic Books.

Rokeach, M., & Mezei, L. (1966). Race and shared belief as factors in social choice. *Science, 151*(3707), 167–172. doi:10.1126/science.151.3707.167

Scott, W. A., Kline, J. A., Faguy-Coté, E., & Peterson, C. (1980). Centrality of cognitive attributes. *Journal of Research in Personality, 14*(1), 12–26. doi:10.1016/0092–6566(80)90036–7

Seyranian, V., Atuel, H., & Crano, W. D. (2008). Dimensions of majority and minority groups. *Group Processes & Intergroup Relations, 11*, 21–37. doi:10.1177/136843 0207084843

Tormala, Z. L. (2008). A new framework for resistance to persuasion: The resistance appraisals hypothesis. In W. D. Crano & R. Prislin (Eds.), *Attitudes and attitude change* (pp. 213–234). New York, NY: Psychology Press.

Tormala, Z. L., Clarkson, J. J., & Petty, R. E. (2006). Resisting persuasion by the skin of one's teeth: The hidden success of resisted persuasive messages. *Journal of Personality and Social Psychology, 91*, 423–435.

Tormala, Z. L., & Petty, R. E. (2002). What doesn't kill me makes me stronger: The effects of resisting persuasion on attitude certainty. *Journal of Personality and Social Psychology, 83*, 1298–1313.

Tormala, Z. L., & Petty, R. E. (2004). Resistance to persuasion and attitude certainty: The moderating role of elaboration. *Personality and Social Psychology Bulletin, 30*, 1446–1457.

Wegner, D. M., Wenzlaff, R., Kerker, R. M., & Beattie, A. E. (1981). Incrimination through innuendo: Can media questions become public answers? *Journal of Personality and Social Psychology, 40*, 822–832. doi:10.1037/0022–3514.40.5.822

Wood, W., Lundgren, S., Ouellette, J. A., Busceme, S., & Blackstone, T. (1994). Minority influence: A meta-analytic review of social influence processes. *Psychological Bulletin, 115*, 323–345. doi:10.1037/0033–2909.115.3.323

Wood, W., & Quinn, J. M. (2003). Forewarned and forearmed? Two meta-analysis syntheses of forewarnings of influence appeals. *Psychological Bulletin, 129*, 119–138. doi:10.1037/0033–2909.129.1.119

Index

abortion, as subject of attitude study 274
Abu Ghraib 142, 183, 193
Advani, L.K. 232, 233
affect 55, 59, 61, 65, 261
Afghanistan, US invasion of 14, 183; war in 30, 39, 178, 179
agency 20, 24, 54, 252, 257, 259, 262
Ahmadinejad, Mahmoud (President of Iran) 28, 31
Albright, Madeleine 152
All-India Muslim League 217, 227
All-Indian Muslim Personal Law Board (AIMPLB) 230
Al-Qaeda 30, 112, 185, 195, 200
Alvaro 273, 274–5, 276, 283
al-Zarqawi, Abu Mussab 185
amalgamation, metaphor of 165–6
American Exceptionalism 13, 152, 186, 191–2
American Political Science Association 160
analogy 3, 26, 89, 150, 160, 161, 284
anarchy 156–8, 162, 167, 171, 172n4, 172n9
Anchor, Robert 19
Andrews, Molly 15
Annas, George 7
anthropology 58, 179, 203n4; cultural 17, 66
Aquino, Corazon 238
Arab Revolution/Arab Spring 29
Arafat, Yasser 29
Arbeit am Mythos (Blumenberg) 103
Archilochus 129
Arendt, Hannah 10
Areopagiticus (Isocrates) 84
Aristotle 5, 84
arms race 31–2
Ashcroft, John 181

Assad, Bashar al- 1, 8, 9, 24, 150–1
attitude change: and communication 285n1; exclusionary narrative 280; indirect 274–6; innuendo effects 280–2; master narrative 276–80; minority influence 272–6; misdirection 282–4; use of metaphor 284–5
Axis of Evil 32–33, 178
Ayodhya movement 231–3

Babri Mosque 231–3
Banks, Kathryn 9, 100n5
Barr, Robert L., Jr. 181
Barthes, R. 189
Bastille, as metaphor 91–3, 100n8
Battle of Kosovo 15, 252
Beer, F.A. 3, 4
Begin, Menachem 148
beliefs: as central to narrative 57–9; changes in 273, 282; cultural 17, 18, 256; fundamental 15, 152; of out-group 277–8; political 253, 258, 259, 261; shared 211; unspoken 191
Benjamin, Walter 201
Berlin, Isaiah 59
Berlin Wall, fall of 20
Bernstein, Carl 145
Bharatiya Jana Sangh (BJS) 230
Bharatiya Janata Party (BJP) 212, 230, 231–4
Bin Laden, Osama 195
"birther" controversy 280
Black, Lewis 197
Blair, Tony 24, 30, 253
Blumenberg, Hans 103
body politic metaphor 9–10, 226; use of by Burke and Paine 85, 88–90; conceptualization of 83–5; further

division 253, 261; of terrorists 185, 187, 200
ignorance 94, 139, 250, 256
Ilyin, Mikhail 34
Image, The (Boorstin) 144
image schemas 33, 81–3; 96–8, 99n2, 99n3
imagery, Biblical 188, 200
India: desire for Home Rule by 216; evocation of Golden Age of 228; group prototype in 213; identity in metaphorical 15–16; master narratives in 212; metaphor of India as a woman 10, 218–19; myths of origin in 212; national identity in 211–12, 219; Vedantic past of 212
Indian National Congress (INC) 211–12, 216, 227, 229, 231, 233
indigenous communities 14; in Guatemala 69; in New Zealand 14
Ingrao, Charles 36
in-group bias 56, 62
in-group identification 214, 226; *see also* in-group bias; out-group identification
innuendo effects 280–2
insurgency 18, 153, 185
Intelligence Advanced Research Projects Activity (IARPA) 17–18
intelligence agencies, US 17–18
interest: as motivating factor 55–6, 95; national 123; political 163, 262; public 38; reciprocal 94; self- 196; types of 18, 156
intergovernmentalism, metaphor of 167, 170
international conflicts 28–33
international cooperation, narrative of 156–7, 161
international regimes 157–64
International Regimes (Kramer) 158, 159, 160
International Relations (IR): alleged scientific nature of 118–20; feminist 23; theory 156, 170–1
intersectionality 131
Iran, and the "Axis of Evil" 32–3
Iraq: and the "Axis of Evil" 32–3; invasion of 14; *see also* Iraq War
Iraqi prisoner mistreatment 178, 183, 193
Iraq War 30, 39, 137–8, 153, 178, 183, 253; Bush's case for 188; timeline 207–10

Islam 28, 231–2; demonification of 112–13; in India 217, 225–6, 227, 228–9, 230; media representation of 17; conflict with the West 36, 109, 112–13
Isocrates 84
Israel and Israelis: construction of narrative by 67; and the Holocaust narrative 62; identity in, 15, 57; use of metaphor by 6, 29–30; narrative as performance in 60; peacemaking in 36–7; shared beliefs in 59; *see also* Israel-Palestine conflict
Israel-Palestine conflict 36–7, 138
Italy: use of Mohammed caricature in 111–12; myth of resistance against Nazi-Fascism in 13, 108

James I (England) 9
James, William 55, 64
Jinnah, Muhammad Ali 234n1
John of Salisbury 9
Johnson, Mark 5, 80
journalists, use of metaphor and narrative by 37–40; *see also* media
journey schemas 81–2
Jung, Carl 110–11

Kapuściński, Ryszard 144, 145
Karadžić, Radovan 145–6, 151
Keen, Steve 27
Kennan, George 3, 123
Kennedy, Edward 189
Kennedy, John F. 196
Keohane, Robert 158, 160–1
Kerry, John 178, 285
Khan, Sammyh S. 10, 15
Khomeini, Ayatolla 66
Khruschchev, Nikita 32
King, Martin Luther, Jr. 6, 24, 36, 100, 273, 278–9
Klamer, Arjo 21, 27
Kosovo crisis 15, 252
Krasner, S.D. 158
Krause, Keith 125
Krugman, Paul 27
Kukathas, C. 34
Kuwait 30

Lakoff, George 5, 24, 30, 80, 152
language: cognitive nature of 250; economic 161; English rhetoric 11, 62; figurative 139; framing 165; of